Brighton Ghosts, Hove Hauntings

Brighton Ghosts, Hove Hauntings

JOHN RACKHAM

LATIMER PUBLICATIONS

Published by
Latimer Publications
Brighton BN1 8FQ

ISBN 0-9539592-0-1

Design and typesetting by John Saunders Design and Production, Reading
Printed in Great Britain by Biddles Ltd   www.biddles.co.uk

Contents

Acknowledgements

Cover photograph: courtesy of the Royal Pavilion, Libraries and Museums, Brighton and Hove

Cover illustration (ghostly monk): Nicky Johnson

Martha Gunn etching: courtesy of Brighton Local Studies Library

Ghostly handprint: courtesy of The Ghost Research Foundation

"There are three steps in the revelation of any truth: in the first it is ridiculed, in the second, resisted; in the third, it is considered self-evident."

Arthur Schopenhauer (1788–1860)

Introduction

WHEN I FIRST had the idea of writing a book about the ghosts of Brighton and Hove, I was aware of three initial sources of information: a small selection of relevant newspaper cuttings which I had gathered over the years; a number of books which contained stories about local ghosts, and the fact that I had some friends and acquaintances who, at various times, had related their own odd experiences, or knew of others who had encountered the supernatural. I had also read somewhere that Brighton was the most haunted resort in Britain, though the writer presented no evidence to substantiate the claim.

On this basis, the potential for a book of any bulk seemed limited and I thought that, even with the inclusion of some historical content, I would find it difficult to reach 20,000 words, representing quite a slim book if I restricted myself to Brighton and Hove. Considering this, I decided to include stories from some of the surrounding villages, for I knew that several had ghostly tales to tell.

In retrospect, I have had misgivings about this decision. While some of the stories coming from the villages have been truly fascinating, I soon learned there was far more paranormal activity taking place in Brighton and Hove than ever I had envisaged, so much so that, given the time, I could have produced a book as thick as this one based on Brighton alone!

However, a good proportion of my early research was concerned w nearby Sussex villages and not wishing to see this work go to waste, I h included these stories. In any case, I believe that the people who so k related their experiences would feel that I had let them down if I garded their input.

By the time I had completed this book, an endeavour lasting n five years (acquiring stories about hauntings is not an insta when one is concentrating on a limited geographical area!), viewed more than 400 people. I am sure most, if not all, w what they had to say. The statements of those who seemed too vivid imagination, or who otherwise provided susp have been disregarded. This is not to say that these people were insincere, but the supernatural is a subject that is not only open to imagination and hallucination, but also to interpretation! Contrary to what I had anticipated, most of those interviewed were willing to have their names published, though a few, understandably, preferred to be mentioned instead by just their job title or under a pseudonym.

In an endeavour to be as comprehensive as possible, I have included most of the previously recorded ghost stories, such as those associated with the Royal Pavilion, Preston Manor, the Theatre Royal, Hangleton Manor and the several haunted pubs in the area, but in almost every instance I have been able to update these by including more recent events. My main aim, however, has been to chronicle newer hauntings.

For the sceptic, ghosts do not exist; cannot exist. As they are illogical, all reports of ghosts must be put down to human fallibility in one form or another. After all, it is easy to see shapes in the shadows, imagine the tail end of a dream to be reality, react to primitive memories when alone in the dark, and hallucinate under certain physical or mental conditions.

Brighton has grown considerably since this map was published in 1778. Perhaps unsurprisingly, this old part of the present town seems to be especially haunted.

As a natural cynic, and as someone who has never seen a ghost, the viewpoint of the sceptic is one I can appreciate. Yet, in my researches, I have interviewed countless erstwhile disbelievers who have had to wrestle with their convictions following personal collisions with the paranormal.

As already mentioned, almost all of the people interviewed during the compilation of this book seemed sincere when relating their experiences. I present these experiences as told to me, hopefully without distortion or bias. Readers are left to make up their own minds about the reality or otherwise of the evidence presented.

By the time they have reached the last pages of this book many readers will, understandably, be incredulous. How can there be so many ghost sightings within such a limited area? Remarkably, as I have already inferred, the answer must be that in addition to the haunted places mentioned, there will be many more which have escaped my attention. Certainly the evidence points to there being far more ghosts around than the average person realises.

On 2 February 1998, the *Daily Mail* published the results of a survey of the paranormal carried out in conjunction with ICM. In this, 11 per cent of men and 14 per cent of women claimed to have had a direct experience of a ghost.

Over the years, other surveys have shown similar findings. For example, a 1980 survey conducted by Audience Selection for the *News of the World* revealed that 14 per cent of respondents believed they had experienced a haunting. Little seems to have changed since 1890, when the Society for Psychical Research questioned 17,000 people to find out how many had seen a ghost. A total of 1,684 claimed that they had (just under 10 per cent, but the use of the word 'seen' in the question may account for the lower figure in this survey, for many hauntings are, of course, concerned instead with sound, touch, smells, or the movement of objects).

Even if we take the lower figure of 10 per cent, it indicates that some 24,000 people out of the total 240,000 population of Brighton and Hove may have experienced a haunting! Further evidence showing that ghosts are more widespread than most people suspect results from the first-hand researches of a small number of investigators into the paranormal who have concentrated their efforts within a limited area. One such is former police officer John Birch.

Mr Birch was based at the Farnham (Surrey) police station for m than 20 years until his retirement in 1978. While a police office Birch's duties sometimes brought him into contact with people w anxious or frightened as a consequence of some allegedly ghost ence. These cases sparked his interest in the supernatural, and to research the subject. He eventually recorded more than 50 separate hauntings in Farnham, a town with just 36,000 inhabitants.

The first chapter of this book attempts the impossible... to state what ghosts are. While the book is primarily about local ghosts, I felt it would be helpful to acquaint the reader with some of the viewpoints and theories surrounding the subject, thus enabling a fuller appreciation of the remarkable range of experiences catalogued on these pages (Chapter 1, incidentally, in its final paragraphs, presents evidence which, I believe, goes some way to proving the existence of ghosts).

John Rackham

1 *What are ghosts?*

FOR THOUSANDS OF YEARS and in every culture, ghosts have been reported. Research organisations have been formed, quite often by investigators having a scientific background, and paranormal phenomona have been recorded and analysed.

The Society for Psychical Research has been investigating ghosts (and other paranormal subjects) since its foundation in 1882. There are numerous other organisations worldwide carrying out similar research. Most would have long since closed down if their investigations had fallen, in the main, on stony ground.

These facts alone do not confirm that entities from a spirit world exist, or that alternatively, some ghostly manifestations may be a quirk of a known phenomenon, such as electromagnetism, but they do suggest that after imagination, hallucination, fraud and other factors have been discounted, we are still left with a considerable mass of phenomena that defies logical explanation. One indication that supernatural forces do exist is evidenced by the fact that cumulative research has shown that there are various types of ghost and that these have certain constants.

The traditional concept of a ghost is that of some misty, or semi-transparent, or slightly glowing entity, usually clothed in the apparel of another age, which walks or glides from one point to another before fading away or disappearing through a wall or some other solid structure. It is frequently suggested that such ghosts are the spirits of dead people trapped in a limbo world within a particular location, there to manifest at intervals, almost always at night.

In fact, ghosts sometimes appear to be as solid and as three-dimensional as you or I. Indeed, in many instances, ghosts have not been identified as such until, to the astonishment of the witnesses, they have gently faded away. Ghosts have frequently been observed during the daylight hours. There have been many reports of people seeing ghosts of the living, and some have even seen their own ghost!

Many ghosts demonstrate their presence in ways other than visual. The pre-eminence of the visual ghost in the popular mind is probably due to its prime place in legend and in fiction, while in the recounting of true supernatural experiences, the visual ghost is likely to be considered the most exciting and memorable phenomenon.

In addition, many researchers, because of their concentration on haunted locations having a rich history of visual sightings, tend to over-emphasise this sort of ghost in their subsequent reportage. There is certainly no rush of psychic researchers eager to ghost-watch in minor properties where there is only an occasional wall-rapping or the shuffling of ghostly feet!

The most frequently encountered spectre is almost certainly that which is popularly associated with the spirits of the dead (some researchers use the term 'interactive' to describe this type of ghost). It is alleged that many of these spirits remain to haunt us because of some disquiet. Often there is a link with a murder, suicide or some other form of traumatic death.

Perhaps the spirit is unhappy because its material body has been buried in unconsecrated ground? Possibly it might want to warn others of a perceived danger? Or death has been so sudden and unexpected that the actuality of death has not been recognised, with the spirit finding itself stranded in some form of limbo?

Ministers of religion present a wide range of views on the subject. Some believe ghosts – or at least, some ghosts – are the spirits of the dead, while others are dismissive. Adherents of fundamental beliefs often believe ghosts to be evil entities masquerading as the spirits of humans.

If ministers of religion carry out their duties over many years, it is fairly certain that during this time they will be approached by a number of people wanting their advice or help in dealing with a supernatural situation. Spiritualists, of course, believe that ghosts prove there is survival after death and that communication with these spirit forms is possible.

As already indicated, the way in which ghosts present themselves are numerous. They may appear as semi-transparent or shadowy figures or be seemingly quite solid. Sometimes, merely a part of the entity will show itself. Often, the manifestation is one of sound only; a disembodied voice, pacing footsteps, galloping hooves, and so on. Interestingly, and despite the writings of Shakespeare and Dickens, ghosts rarely talk during a visual appearance. Indeed, stories of ghosts which can be seen, and heard speaking at the same moment, are unusual enough to merit a degree of caution in the researcher.

Sometimes the movement of objects will indicate the presence of an entity. For example, minor items might be moved around, or even removed for a few hours or days before appearing again. But far stranger things can happen. Some ghosts appear able to move large objects that would test the strength of several men, while others are able to introduce objects (apports) to an environment where they were never present in the first place. Again, there may be mysterious smells, ghostly lights, or dramatic changes in temperature.

The duration of hauntings varies considerably. Some last hundreds of years; others but a few weeks or months. Sometimes there is, curiously, just a 'one-off' paranormal incident at a location – though, of course, there may have been others which have not been reported by witnesses, perhaps for fear of being ridiculed, or have otherwise been unrecorded. There have been countless instances of ghostly happenings taking place when no human has been around to report the event, this evidence being captured on remote tape recorders or security cameras.

There are several categories of ghost. The interactive ghost has already been mentioned. The evidence presented in this book indicates that it is the most common type of ghost. This is because the research for the book has trawled comprehensively over a variety of major and minor hauntings within a specific locality, rather than concentrating on sites scattered over a wide geographical area where there may be a history of haunting and where the phenomena tends to be on a grander scale.

The interactive ghost often seems aware of, and may even respond, to the presence of humans. Many people believe that this type of ghost proves the concept of life after death. These ghosts may react to human voices, call people by their name, move objects, play pranks (which is possibly a way of attracting attention to themselves) and much more.

Another type of ghost is known as a recording ghost (some researchers use alternative terminology to describe the various categories of ghost). This manifestation is usually silent, though sound and smell are sometimes reported, and it tends to perform identically at each appearance. It is as if a clip of film is being replayed at intervals, each time to a different viewer. A Victorian woman will always walk along the same path and through the same doorway; duelling men will meticulously repeat the same swordplay. Where there is a divergence of experience, it may be that one witness has seen a different segment of the total 'scenario' to another witness.

Many researchers believe that the recording ghost has little or nothing to do with spirits. The theory, and it is only a theory, is that an event of high emotion is recorded, given the right geological, atmospheric and climatic conditions, to be replayed at a future time when similar conditions exist. It is as if the surrounding environment acts as a hidden photographic negative with the 'moving picture' being revealed at future moments, but only when all the contributory circumstances are absolutely right. This is by no means a new theory, for in the late 1800s Sir Oliver Lodge was already proposing such a possibility.

Favouring the theory is the fact that some ghosts do seem to vanish forever from haunted buildings following structural changes though, conversely (and puzzlingly), some buildings with no known history of supernatural events 'produce' new ghosts as a consequence of structural alterations. This concept does not, however, explain the appearance of ghost ships and aircraft, where the environment is in constant flux. It is suggested that, as they are not true ghosts, recording ghosts cannot be exorcised.

Another type of ghostly experience is the 'time slip', though time slips may well have an affinity with the concept of recording ghosts inasmuch as their origins may be the same, with the transfer of strong emotion to an environment which can, years later, be picked up by a suitably receptive individual at a moment when all the conditions are right (though there are many instances of the time slip phenomenon which don't appear to have high emotion as a basis).

Time slips are experiences where the individual seems to step back into another age, or views a past event as if a spectator. One of the best known time slip stories is that of two English women, Charlotte Moberly and Eleanour Jourdain who, while visiting the Petite Trianon gardens at Versailles in 1901, found themselves strolling among people wearing 18th century dress. At the same time, they were conscious of a strangely depressing atmosphere. These were intelligent women who would not willingly have risked ridicule through the telling of an improbable story – Miss Moberly was Principal of St. Hugh's, Oxford, while Miss Jourdain later became Vice-Principal of the same college. Other people, while in the same gardens, have reported similar happenings.

Such time slips can often be experiences on the grand scale. Such a psychic adventure came the way of Dorothy Strong in 1960 while she was travelling by taxi through the countryside near Otterburn, in Cumbria. Inexplicably, the taxi jolted to a halt. Perplexed, Mrs Strong and the driver peered through the taxi's windows to find themselves witnessing the advance of a phantom army wearing the rough uniforms of another age.

Although Mrs Strong was not aware of the fact, there had been previous observers of this extraordinary phenomenon. Neither did she know that it was in this area, in 1388, that a Scottish army defeated the English. Had Mrs Strong and the taxi driver witnessed one of these ghostly armies? Later, talking about the eerie experience, which lasted only seconds, Mrs Strong said: "Suddenly the taxi engine died and the fare-meter went haywire. It felt as if the taxi was being forced against an invisible wall."

A modern version of the time slip took place in 1993 when a middle-aged couple, Mr and Mrs Roberts, while on holiday in the West Country, stopped briefly in the village of Bampton to ask for directions. Impressed by the attractiveness of the village, made more glorious by an abundance of flowers, they resolved to return the next day, but when they did, they were dismayed to find the village offered a quite different appearance. Where had all the beautiful flowers gone? they wondered. Even the floral display on the village green was no longer there.

There were other anomalies. While in the village on the day before, some coffee from a flask had been spilled on a road map and stained it, but now there was no sign of the stain. They also recalled discovering, at the time of leaving the village on the previous day, that the car's clock had not moved on for a period of about 15 minutes.

Another category of ghost is the poltergeist, though the majority of researchers don't now consider poltergeists to be ghosts. The word is a German one meaning 'noisy spirit' and most people have read or heard about the inexplicable noises, flying objects and other disturbing activities associated with this phenomenon.

Poltergeists are almost always associated with young people around the age of puberty, though more usually with girls than boys. A prominent theory is that poltergeist activity is the consequence of a build-up of suppressed sexual energy which is projected psychokinetically by the individual (the focus).

Poltergeist activity is, very occasionally, linked to an old person. This might be where the individual concerned has a very volatile personality that is prevented from fully expressing itself because of an enfeebled or handicapped physical body.

Some researchers believe that poltergeist activity may be associated with a broader spectrum of people than the above. They suggest that some of the rappings, unexplained movements of objects, and other poltergeist-like manifestations that are sometimes experienced by quite ordinary people, may result from the triggering of psychokinetic energy during times of stress.

An alternative theory, at least in some instances, is that poltergeists are discarnate spirits which latch on to the human body at a time when the latter is vulnerable. These spirits may not have a human origin.

Ghostly presences may continue to haunt for many years, even centuries, but poltergeist activity rarely lasts longer than weeks or months – although there have been a very few instances of long-term disturbances. Most ghosts confine their activities to a single location, but with poltergeists, if the focus individual moves, the disruptive activity may also move.

The crisis apparition, another category of ghost, is a vision that appears at, or shortly after, the death or near-death of the person seen. These visions seem only to present themselves to relations or close friends. Such apparitions are more common in wartime and there have been countless instances of wives and mothers seeing their husbands or sons at the time of death or severe injury, and well before they would otherwise have known of the event. Whether these apparitions are true ghosts, out-of-body experiences, or some form of telepathic contact – a telepathically induced hallucination, perhaps? – is not known.

While many people believe that ghosts exist, a more difficult concept to assimilate is that the living may also have their apparitions. There have been many reports of people seeing someone, only to find out later that the person observed was elsewhere at that moment. Sometimes the person is known to the witness; at other times the sighting is of a stranger. An example of this was when the vision of an elderly woman in modern dress appeared several times behind the bar of a public house.

Given a description of the woman, some old customers thought that the witnesses could have seen the ghost of a landlady who had worked there many years before. However, the landlady was later found to be very much alive. It seems that she had so enjoyed her life at the pub that she often thought about the place and dearly yearned to be back there. Could the former landlady's intense thoughts have created a vision of herself in the pub she had left behind?

In a very small number of cases, people have seen their own ghost. The explanation for this phenomenon is a matter for conjecture, though in some instances where this has happened it seems to have been a preliminary to that person's death. There are also ghosts which only appear at certain times – usually on the anniversary of some event. While some of these seem to take account of changes in the calendar, others do not.

There are also malevolent spirits and it is suggested that some of these evil entities have a demonic rather than a human origin (fortunately, while humans may understandably be subject to fright when faced with something unearthly, the majority of ghosts are benign. Indeed, some occupiers of haunted properties become quite fond of their resident spirits).

There have been numerous reports of animal hauntings, ranging from snoozing cats to the spectral devil-hounds of folklore. There are also haunted objects. These can range from small artefacts to something quite large, such as the ghostly bus which appeared at intervals 'with headlights blazing' in St Mark's Road, North Kensington, during the 1930s.

The phantom bus – possibly another example of the recording phenomenon – used to appear in the early hours after most buses had ceased running. It was said to have been responsible for several accidents, one fatal, which took place as other vehicles swerved to avoid the sudden and unexpected vision of a bus directly in their path. Following structural changes to the road and pavement, the ghostly bus was never seen again.

Do ghosts change in appearance over the years, eventually to fade away? The evidence appears to indicate that they do. At least, those of the interactive kind do. There is the story of a phantom woman seen first in the 18th century. Witnesses described her as having black hair and wearing a red dress and red shoes. Some 70 years later, those who saw her referred to the dress as being pink. By the middle of the 19th century, the phantom was being described as grey-haired and wearing a white gown. By the late 1930s, the only incidents being reported were ghostly footsteps and the swish of a dress. In 1971, when the house haunted by the woman was demolished, workmen reported only 'a strange atmosphere'.

My own researches have shown that where witnesses have been questioned about ghosts they have seen, virtually all of those describing ghosts wearing fairly modern clothing (back to about the 1920s), have referred to coloured garments, while those describing ghosts wearing clothing of earlier times have almost always referred to monochrome clothing – clothing observed as being black, white or (more usually) grey, or combinations of these.

Indeed, the above points to a possible explanation for the numerous reports of phantom 'Grey Ladies' and 'White Ladies' seen over the years. While these ghosts may have been observed originally as wearing coloured clothing, the passage of years has transformed these colours into various shades of grey; sometimes even bleaching into white.

If, in referring to the appearance of ghosts, a time could be ascribed for the metamorphosis from coloured to monochrome apparel, it would be about 70 or 80 years from the date of the sighting, though this assumption is based primarily on the research associated with this book. Greatly intrigued by this discovery, for I have come across no in-depth reference to this suggested time span in any of the many books I have read on the subject, I decided, on the completion of this book, to compile a more precise record concerning the colour of the clothing worn by the spectres featured.

Ignoring all those ghostly forms variously described in the book as being misty, shadowy, glowing, wearing either dark or light clothing without mention of an actual colour, etc, I found that a total of 85 were noted as wearing black, white or grey clothing, or a combination of these shades, while a further two were seen as having cream-coloured clothing. The associated details suggest that nearly all of these sightings were of people from Edwardian, Victorian or Regency times, though the apparition of a man wearing a white, short-sleeved shirt, and grey trousers (see Chapter 13), obviously belongs to more recent times.

There are 24 ghosts described as wearing at least one item of coloured apparel. From the evidence, almost all of these appear to be dressed in post-1920s clothing. Where the known facts suggest an earlier date, it should be noted that the date of the sighting has a relevance. For example, an already published report of a ghost wearing a coloured, Victorian-style dress, would still meet the time-span criterion of 70 to 80 years if the actual sighting took place in the 1960s.

While there are a few oddities which do not fall in line with the above proposition it does provide evidence, albeit modest, to suggest that ghosts really do exist, for the witnesses whose stories are told in already published books and reports would not, at the time of stating their evidence, have been aware of this time-span concept.

A detailed examination of ghost sightings already committed to record in published books and other documentation could prove enlightening. Indeed, readers themselves might wish to look through any books they possess featuring true accounts of hauntings to see if the above proposition is sustainable, although my own perusal of relevant books has revealed that while authors frequently mention dress style (medieval, Regency, Victorian, etc,) when writing about ghosts, they often fail to describe the colour of the clothing. However, many stories which mention both style and colour appear to confirm the time span theory.

Unfortunately, I did not realise until a fairly late stage in the writing of this book how important clothing, its colour, and its relationship to a particular period of time, might be when querying interviewees about the spectres they had seen. This additional information would have provided a more comprehensive overview of the 'time-colour' question.

The proposition that ghosts degrade in colour over a period of years seems only to be relevant to interactive ghosts, for those dressed in the multi-coloured fashions of more distant ages (as opposed to the monochrome entities which seem confined primarily to Edwardian and Victorian times) have been seen by many people.

For example, spectral Roman soldiers attired in coloured uniforms have been witnessed in York and Chichester, while visions clad in many-hued Elizabethan, or other period costumes, have been observed elsewhere, but these entities seem to be of the recording variety so are, possibly, as already indicated, not true ghosts at all (and, cumulative evidence suggests, are far less likely to be encountered, being associated in most instances only with buildings that are hundreds of years old). Of course, monochrome entities associated with times prior to the 1800s are reported, but many of these – monks and nuns especially – may actually have worn black, white, or grey clothing in life.

While recording ghosts may span several centuries with their appearances, it does seem that interactive ghosts have a more limited span of existence (on this earth?), though there is ample evidence to suggest that other phenomena, such as phantom footsteps and rappings, may continue for many years after the visual manifestations have ceased.

Whatever the truth of this, and of the many other aspects of the supernatural presented in this book, there is much that is yet to be discovered. Many researchers will confirm that the more the supernatural is investigated, the more complex the subject seems to become. Certainly, there appears often to be some overlap between the categories of ghost. And, evidently, nothing can be taken for granted, for the subject is riddled with both contradictions and surprises.

2 *Old Strike-a-Light*

BRIGHTON DEVELOPED from an early fishing and agricultural settlement known as Bristelmestune, which was mentioned in the Domesday Book of 1086 when it had to pay an annual tribute of 4,000 herrings. But a Neolithic encampment existed at Whitehawk Hill, to the east of Brighton, as early as 2,700 BC.

Brighthelmstone (often spelled without an 'e' at the end), was the most common of the many subsequent spellings given to the place until Brighton became the official name in 1810 at the time of the appointment of the Town Commissioners – though the word Brighton appears to have been in use as early as 1669, when it appeared in the parish register.

It is believed that some 400 people inhabited the place at the time of Domesday. Growth varied little over the following years until, in 1514, the settlement was burned to the ground by French raiders, with only St Nicholas's Church escaping the torch. The French attacked again in 1545, but this time the raiders were driven off (in the British Museum there is a drawing which, although dated 1545, is thought to depict the raid of 1514. It shows all the dwellings in flames).

The town was rebuilt and, benefiting from the growth of its fishing industry – by 1580 there were some 80 vessels and 400 fishermen – soon began to prosper. By 1640, the population had reached 4,000. But leaner times were to come.

Most of the boats headed for the herring fisheries off the east coast, but falling catches, attacks on the fishing fleet by French and Dutch naval vessels and the erosion of the coast at Brighton had their effect. By 1680, only 30 boats remained and by 1700 the population of the town had dwindled to 1,500.

At the time, East Street, North Street, West Street and South Street marked the periphery of the town (with a few, scattered buildings beyond this boundary). But South Street was soon to disappear. It was part of Brighton's lower town; that area of beach where the crude homes of (mainly) fisherfolk had been erected. In 1703 and 1705 violent storms struck the town and these buildings were destroyed when heavy seas forced hugh banks of shingle up the beach.

The town's population continued to fall until about 1720 when it began to attract interest as a health resort, but the major boost to the town's prosperity came with the publication of a book which advocated the use of sea water, internally and externally, for the relief and cure of glandular diseases.

Written by a Lewes doctor, Richard Russell, it appeared in 1752 and soon excited the interest of the wealthy. This led to a growing volume of rich and influential people making their way by coach to Brighton to take advantage of the various sea water treatments, which were by then being offered for the alleviation or cure of a wide range of illnesses.

In their wake came the young, pleasure-loving Prince of Wales (eventually to become George IV), who first visited the town in 1783. In Brighton he found a place where he could enjoy himself away from the stifling influences of his parents and the Court. His enthusiasm for the resort led to the building of the exotic Royal Pavilion.

In 1818, Mrs Fitzherbert wrote that 'fifty-two coaches ran daily to London and brought people down for six shillings', but this reliance on horse-drawn transport ended in 1841 when the railway reached Brighton. It led to the town becoming not only a popular holiday resort but a lure for the day-tripper. The genteel – if often frivolous – pursuits introduced during the Regency period gradually gave way to the activities of the masses. It was the birth of the brash, racy, extrovert image that is associated with the Brighton of today.

The coming of the railway heralded a significant growth in population, which expanded from 46,000 in 1841 to 65,000 in 1851. By 1871 the population had expanded to 90,000; by 1891 to 115,000. In 1927 Brighton's boundaries were extended to include the formerly separate villages of Patcham, Ovingdean, Stanmer, Rottingdean and parts of Falmer and Saltdean. The population of the town is now about 150,000.

Towns with a long and varied history tend to have a rich past when it comes to legends, strange tales and stories of the supernatural, and Brighton has a satisfying share of these. In the matter of ghosts, there are a number of early accounts which refer to local hauntings.

One of Brighton's earliest and most frightening ghosts was Old Strike-a-Light (also known as Jack Strike-a-Light), an apparition so terrible of countenance that its appearance one wild, stormy night led to the death of a local fisherman.

The story of this particular ghost dates back to around 1760 and an inn called the Rising Sun, which at the time stood at the southern end of East Street. In what year the Rising Sun first opened for business is not known, but it must have been one of the town's first inns. It was originally called the Naked Boy and the sign above its entrance showed a painting of a naked child carrying a roll of cloth under his left arm and a pair of shears in his right hand with the wording:

So fickle is our English nation,
I would be clothed if I knew the fashion.

The change of name from Naked Boy to Rising Sun took place in 1755 after the widow of the previous landlord, a Mr Mockford, had remarried. It seems that Mr Thomas, the widow's new spouse, possibly being somewhat prudish, was disdainful of the original name.

The newly named inn continued to be a popular rendezvous for local fishermen while its dark, dank cellar was almost certainly used by smugglers as a temporary haven for illicit cargoes shipped over from France, for smuggling was then one of the town's major activities.

A combination of high tides and stormy weather sometimes led to the cellar being swamped with sea water – without adequate breakwaters to limit its incursions, the sea sometimes washed into East Street (a contemporary etching shows water up to the wheel hubs of a stage coach). Dampness also oozed in from the soggy soil of The Steine (through which a muddy stream, the Wellsbourne, then flowed – it now runs underground). Fed by the constant dampness, stalactites of fungus hung from the cellar ceilings, some over a foot long.

Whether Old Strike-a-Light made an appearance during the tenancy of Mr and Mrs Thomas is not recorded, but it seems that the awful being's early activities were confined to this gloomy cellar. Here, the ghost would confront employees working in the flickering candlelight with an awesome presence. A barman might find himself alone with the creature – which took the form of a monstrous man, some 7ft tall, with grey, lifeless eyes set in a grotesque, ashen face.

For his cellar manifestations, Old Strike-a-Light would sometimes wear a miller's smock, at others a black cloak, but always there would be a white conical hat upon his head. He usually sat astride a beer barrel, all the while clinking a coin in a pewter dish (though it was claimed later that reports of the cellar appearances were just fanciful additions to the 'true' story of Old Strike-a-Light).

Another five years or so were to pass before the ghost's most spectacular visitation. By then the tenancy of the inn had changed hands, the new hosts being a character called 'Shaky' Bradford, and his wife – the latter, quaintly, being referred to as Nanny Shaky.

Many good ghost stories appear to have, as their backdrop, a night that is dark and tempestuous, and it seems that the final and most terrifying appearance of Old Strike-a-Light took place on just such a night. It led to the death of Swan Jervoise, a local fisherman of French descent.

The fishing vessel Jervoise owned was returning to Brighton with its catch of herring, and he and his crew were struggling to keep the boat on course as it rose and dipped uneasily on the swollen, wind-buffeted waves. As Jervoise peered anxiously through the blackness, his eyes finally picked out an orange glow. The glow came from the 'towne fyre basket', a large iron brazier filled with blazing fuel which acted as a guide for those at sea. The brazier was suspended from a yardarm which stood at the seaward end of The Steine.

As the boat moved closer to the shore, Jervoise and his crew became aware of another source of light, a series of bright, intermittent flashes which appeared to originate from some point slightly to the west of the beacon. By then, most people would have long since retired to bed and all should have been blackness except for the beacon's flames.

When the boat finally touched shore, Jervoise was able to establish that the dazzling shafts of light were coming from the Rising Sun, situated a little to the west of the beacon. Mystified, he called on his crew to winch the boat up the beach while he set off in the direction of the inn to discover the reason for the mysterious beams of brilliance.

As he hesitated in front of the inn's door he heard a noise from within. It sounded like the striking of flint against steel. Almost simultaneously, there was a blinding flash of light from the inn's windows. Jervoise hammered upon the door with his clenched fist. There was no response, so he banged on the door again. Once more he heard the scrape of flint on steel and again the inn's windows flooded with light.

Suddenly, the door swung open and the massive, dreadful form of a man appeared, his baleful eyes staring out from a face that was 'pallid as a sear cloth'. For a moment the towering figure stood where it was before sweeping past Jervoise and into the night, black cloak billowing. Jervoise had heard tales of Old Strike-a-Light. He knew it must be him, and screamed out in terror.

If the noise of Jervoise banging on the door hadn't woken the innkeeper, the latter was certainly alerted by the fisherman's cries. Quickly lighting a bedside lantern, the landlord made his way to the door. He knew Jervoise as a customer and, seeing the quivering fear of the man, he pulled him inside. When the fisherman started gabbling about the ghost he'd seen, the landlord led Jervoise into the bar and towards a seat by the still faintly glowing fire.

"Sit there for a moment," commanded the landlord, putting a rushlight on the table before stoking some life into the dormant embers of the fire.

"I'll get a drink to calm you down. Then you can tell me what happened." The landlord hurried through a door into the taproom bar, returning moments later with a tankard of ale.

Cold, and pathetic with fear, Jervoise leaned towards the fire, though finding little comfort in its flames. Suddenly, he had the feeling he was no longer alone. Looking over his shoulder he was horrified to find that the nightmarish creature he had seen only minutes before had returned and was now but a few feet behind him and staring intently towards the fireplace. He watched as the spectre slowly raised an arm and stabbed a crooked finger in the direction of the hearthstone in front of the fire. It was all too much for Jervoise. He slumped to the floor in a faint.

Finding the prone body of Jervoise, and failing to bring him back to consciousness, the landlord decided that the only thing to be done was to drag the fisherman to a makeshift bed to enable him to rest as peacefully as possible for the remainder of the night.

The next day, Father Anselm of the Order of St Bartholomew was called in to minister to the still distressed and enfeebled fisherman. Jervoise hesitatingly told his story to the priest. In the following minutes, consumed again by visions of the terrifying hours that had passed, Jervoise drifted into death.

Some days later, under the direction of Father Anselm, who had taken especial note of where the spectre's finger had been pointing, the inn's heavy hearthstone was prised up. Underneath was a substantial treasure of gold coins.

The bulk of this treasure appears to have been transferred to the Mother Priory at Lewes (though in another version of the story, the treasure was shipped to the principal of the Order in Normandy). There is no record of any part of the treasure going to the landlord of the Rising Sun, but it seems likely that he would have received some recompense for the fact that the treasure was found on his premises.

Certainly, Shaky and Nanny Bradford, who had always in the past struggled to pay their bills, now seemed to enjoy a more expansive and leisured lifestyle and it wasn't too long before they retired to a residential hotel in Brighton, where they lived in comfort until the end of their days.

Around this time, a heavy stone slab in the cellar of the Rising Sun was lifted to reveal a sword that could not be made to shine because of the blood which had caused it to rust. Some human bones were also found, and it is said that the Rev Henry Mitchell, the then Vicar of St Nicholas's Church, allowed these to be interred in the churchyard.

No more was seen of Old Strike-a-Light. His continued existence as a spectre was, perhaps, no longer necessary now that he had achieved his aim of bringing the hidden treasure to the attention of the living.

It has been suggested that Old Strike-a-Light never really existed; that, in fact, the story was put about by smugglers to deter inquisitive excise men from showing too much interest in the illicit activities centering on the Rising Sun.

Later, the Rising Sun, following renovations, became the Sun Hotel. It was demolished in 1869, along with the White Horse Inn and other properties, and an extension to Brill's Baths was built on the site. Brill's Baths were eventually demolished to make way for a small group of buildings, including the former Savoy cinema, which was completed in 1930.

3 *Betsy Bedlam and the Whitehawk Lady*

AS WITH OLD STRIKE-A-LIGHT, a number of the discarnate entities that struck terror into the hearts of Brighton people in the past have long since departed the spectral stage and faded into folklore. Among these was the fearsome Betsy Bedlam, so named because her staring eyes and contorted face were equated with those of the inmates of London's infamous Bedlam lunatic asylum (Bethlehem Hospital). Betsy Bedlam haunted Belle Vue Field in the 18th century, terrorising all who saw her.

This field, whose centrepiece was a ship's capstan, became the site for the visually impressive Regency Square – built in 1818-28. Belle Vue Field was frequently used for fairs, shows and military reviews.

In addition to Betsy Bedlam, the locals were fearful of a headless horseman who galloped along Brighton Racecourse. The racecourse, situated on the flat-topped hill formerly known as Whitehawk Down, dates back to 1783. The first race meeting took place in the August of that year. The attendance of the Prince of Wales in the following year helped ensure the success of the venture.

But one of the early races began disastrously. The crude starting line snapped up at the same time as one of the horses, excited and eager to move off, surged uncontrollably forward. The helpless jockey was propelled straight into the snaking line. It struck the unfortunate man across the throat, and he was decapitated. For decades after this gruesome event, there were reports of people seeing the spectre of a headless man, believed to be the luckless jockey, galloping across the downland on his ghostly mount.

The downland around Brighton Racecourse was also the scene of another tale of the supernatural. Towards the end of the 18th century and for some years after, a spectral entity known as the Whitehawk Lady haunted the area. The ghost was that of the lovely Editha Elmore, the only daughter of a rich squire of Woodingdean, who died in mysterious circumstances after she had consulted a gypsy fortune teller.

In 1791, eight years after the first race meeting had taken place, an associated fair was established. The Whitehawk Fair, as it was called, proved so popular that it became a regular event and it was to one of these early fairs that Editha Elmore went, along with her beau, Ralph Mascall of Ovingdean Grange.

At the fair, she briefly left Mascall to enter the tent of the Romany fortune teller, Meg Lade. After pocketing a silver coin, the gypsy told Editha she would shortly meet a handsome, young stranger. Describing him in some detail, Meg Lade hinted that the stranger would steal Editha's heart.

Later, and quite by chance, Editha met a young man who seemed to match exactly the gypsy's description. That night, avoiding her boyfriend, she met the young man and went dancing with him. For the following night, the pair arranged a midnight tryst on the Downs, but there was a sudden, fierce storm and, although there were witnesses who saw them begin their ascent up the hill, neither Editha nor the young man were ever seen again.

Mysteriously, some months after this, the charred body of the gypsy seer was found in the burial ground at Ovingdean, where her grave was marked later by an unhewn stone. Meanwhile, some terrified locals began reporting the appearance of Editha's ghostly form. A skeleton thought to be hers was dug up by a ploughman in 1807.

The re-burial of the skeleton in consecrated ground, it was thought, would end the Downland appearances of the ghost, but there were witnesses prepared to affirm that the phantom was still scaring people up to a century later, while in 1884 it was reported that Editha was now being seen in the company of a spectral male companion!

4 *Preston Manor: Spirits of another age*

IMMEDIATELY TO THE NORTH of Preston Park stands Preston Manor. This fine old house successfully captures the spirit of upper-class Edwardian life and times though, being tucked away from mainstream Brighton, most visitors (and many townsfolk!) miss out on its charms.

Preston Manor was originally built around 1250, rebuilt above the main floor of the medieval house with small, additional pavilions to flank the main block in 1738, and substantially altered and added to in 1905. In 1794 it was bought by the Stanford family and it remained in their possession until 1932. In that year, following the deaths of Sir Charles and Lady Thomas-Stanford, the manor and its contents were bequeathed to Brighton.

The manor, which is open to the general public, has been kept virtually as it was when the Stanford family lived there, and the visitor, moving through the elegant rooms with their 18th and 19th century furnishings, may well experience a feeling that time has stood still.

One of Preston Manor's intriguing aspects is its reputation as a haunted building. It is said to be home to at least two ghosts and there has been a considerable number of sightings over the past 100 years or so, including some of recent date.

The White Lady is the best known of the manor's spectres. She has appeared at intervals from the 16th century onwards, though the most descriptive accounts of her are those attested during the 19th century. During the latter part of the 1800s, it is said that she appeared on average, to one person or another, about once every six weeks. Before introducing some of the witnesses to the supernatural happenings of those times, let us first return to the history of the manor.

In 1794, William Stanford purchased Preston Manor and about 1,000 acres of surrounding land from Baron Western of Rivenhall for £17,600. When William Stanford died in 1841 his son, also called William Stanford, inherited the manor. A year later the second William Stanford married Eleanor Morris. Two children resulted from the marriage; a boy who died aged five months, and a girl, Ellen, who died in 1932 (as Lady Thomas-Stanford – see above).

In 1853, William died. The following year Eleanor married Captain George Macdonald of the Princess of Wales' Own Regiment. There were three children of the marriage – Flora, and twin sisters Diana and Christiana (more usually known as Lily). George Macdonald died of kidney failure in 1881. His widow and the girls continued to live at the manor following his death. Supernatural events taking place at the manor during the 1890s have been well documented.

On a bleak autumn day in 1896, Lily Macdonald was changing a lampshade in the drawing room when she sensed she was no longer alone. Turning, she was astonished to see a woman with long, fair hair and dressed completely in white come towards her as if to speak, but then walk past her. The woman's face, she thought, looked pale and strained.

Lily was familiar with the stories about the White Lady and felt sure that this suddenly appearing stranger must indeed be her. She nervously followed the apparition through the billiard room and to the foot of the stairs, vaguely comforted by the fact that no descriptions of the ghost had ever indicated it was harmful.

As the White Lady briefly hesitated on the stairs, Lily was bold enough to try and put a restraining arm on her, saying: "No... Don't go now". But Miss Macdonald's arm went straight through the spectre, which instantly vanished.

On another occasion, it was her sister Diana who encountered the White Lady. She had been playing tennis and, hot and weary, had returned to the house to wash and change. It was just after 6pm. As she climbed the stairs, she glanced up to see a woman standing on the staircase. At first, she thought it was the housemaid, but quickly realising it wasn't, was about to ask who she was, when the figure dissolved before her eyes.

This wasn't Diana's first contact with the supernatural, for shortly before her tenth birthday while running from the first floor nursery (before it was moved to the attic), she saw two men struggling on the staircase near the south-west room. One was dressed completely in white, except for a close-fitting red cap. The other man looked dark, but she couldn't see him clearly.

Terribly frightened, and worried that the men might see her, she turned and crept back to the nursery. When her nursemaid saw her, she thought the girl was ill and put her straight to bed. Diana, possibly because she thought no one would believe her, never told anyone about this experience until much later in her life.

An army colonel – a friend of the family – intrigued by the stories of ghostly happenings at the manor, but as an army man somewhat sceptical by nature, hoped that his visit would offer an opportunity to investigate the stories (another military man, Captain W W Sandeman, was among those claiming to have seen the ghost). The colonel didn't have long to wait.

One grey afternoon, while he was crossing the entrance hall, the White Lady appeared a few feet away from him. The colonel didn't know if ghosts had the power of speech, but he took a chance and asked the woman who she was and if he could help her. He was surprised to receive a response.

The White Lady replied that she was a nun who had wrongly been excommunicated from the Church. On her death, she had been buried outside of holy ground and without religious ceremony. As a consequence, she could find no rest until her remains were reburied in a churchyard. The White Lady then vanished without revealing anything further.

On 11 November 1896, prompted by the colonel's experience, a seance was held at the manor. It was attended by four people: Mrs Macdonald and one of her daughters, Douglas Murray (a local author and family friend), and Ada Goodrich Freer, a medium (years later, the medium was accused of being fraudulent).

The seance took place in the Cleves room (it is believed the name derives from the fact that a copy of a Holbein painting depicting Anne of Cleves used to hang there). Particulars of the seance were taken down in shorthand and transcribed later. A note on this manuscript states: 'Remarks spelled out by the Board are written in red ink.' This suggests that a Ouija board or planchette was used.

Initial attempts to contact the ghost were rebuffed. The spirits expressed annoyance at being disturbed and the sitters were told to go away. But the medium persisted. Her request to receive the woman who had been haunting the manor brought the response that there were two spirits.

Asked their names, the reply was "Agnes and Caroline" – the speaker appeared to be Caroline. She said she was a nun in about 1535 and her surname was Marchmont. She went on to say that Preston Manor was occupied by Marchant. Asked whether she meant Marchmont or Marchant, she replied by saying that nuns had no name. Asked what date Agnes had died, she snapped "Curse her!" Asked why she hated Agnes, Caroline indicated that the woman had been excommunicated by the Church for her serious misdeeds.

Interestingly – and it is virtually certain the medium would not have known this – by 1552 a William Marchant was the copyholder (tenant) of a quarter (some 62 acres) of the Common Laines (farmland) by Preston Manor. Might he have resided at the manor?

Following further exchanges between the medium and Caroline, Agnes spoke. She said that in her time the manor was used as a hostel for pilgrims journeying to Canterbury and to a shrine. Asked what shrine she meant, she said 'Winton-by-Sea'. She then referred to a harbour which she called 'Whitebay' (these place names are unknown in the south-east). Agnes also talked about an underground passage which ran from the manor to the sea – a large part of this had collapsed, she added. The tunnel was to be used as a refuge if enemies ever attacked (a tunnel is said to exist, but is bricked up). She also claimed there had been a monastery nearby with 42 monks (there is no historical evidence for this).

It seems that a Friar Martin then made his presence known to the medium. He said that he had been mainly responsible for the excommunication. Agnes had committed no crime, he now realised, but others had spread lies about her. Rest would come to her spirit sooner than she thought. Coincidence or not, material events were soon to confirm this prophecy.

Almost three months after the seance had taken place, the drains at Preston Manor became blocked and a foul smell filled the house. Workmen were called in to clear the blockage and on 29 January 1897, while digging a trench a few feet from the corner of the south terrace, which runs alongside the dining room (now the Macquoid Room), they came across a skeleton. The skeleton was in a twisted heap, as if hurriedly thrown upright into a hole in the ground. A doctor identified the skeleton as being that of a woman of about 47 to 55 years of age. The condition and orange colour of the bones, he affirmed, indicated that the skeleton was well over 300 years old.

The Vicar of St Peter's, the small church close by the manor, was asked if the skeleton could be buried in the churchyard. Those were less tolerant days, and as a Protestant minister he felt obliged to refuse, for he presumed the bones to be those of a Catholic. However, the skeleton was surreptitiously buried in the graveyard some 24 hours later during the hours of darkness, the Stanford family conniving with the gravedigger.

Writing on 29 January 1898, Douglas Murray, who was present at the original seance, referred to a later seance being held in the Cleves room during which Sister Agnes had expressed happiness at her body being reburied in the churchyard. Almost a year later, Mr Murray wrote that Mrs Macdonald had told him that in the two years following the skeleton's reburial there had been no further phenomena at the manor. "The ghost is laid and apparently at rest," he asserted. But this situation was not to last.

On a fine evening in July 1903, at about 8.30pm, some four months before Mrs Macdonald died (on 28 November), Diana noticed a woman dressed in black walking through the billiard room. She watched as the woman continued into the drawing room before walking through an open French window into the garden. Puzzled, Diana hurried after the woman, but when she reached the garden, there was no sign of her. A quick check revealed that the garden gate was still locked, which meant that no human could have left the garden.

In the autumn of 1903 Mrs Macdonald, who had been ill for a long time, was deteriorating still further in health and was confined to bed in the south-west room, which at the time was called the Blue Room (it is currently the library). A Nurse Glasspool was called in to take up residence at the manor and look after her.

Early in November, Mrs Macdonald needed some attention from the nurse. It was between two and three o'clock in the morning. Screens had been placed around the bed to provide some privacy for the patient, who now needed constant care. All of a sudden, Nurse Glasspool's activities were disturbed by the sight of a woman peering intently around the screens at the foot of the bed. In an instant she was gone, but the nurse had noticed the fair hair and presumed it was Lily, the only daughter resident in the house at the time.

Nurse Glasspool hadn't been told about the ghost, otherwise she might have refused her job at the manor. So at breakfast time she approached Lily and said: "Oh, excuse me miss, but would you mind speaking to me if you come to see Mrs Macdonald at night? I was rather frightened with your coming in and not saying a word."

Lily knew that she hadn't visited her mother's bedroom in the small hours, so was puzzled for a moment. Then it dawned on her that the nurse must have seen the ghost. Not wishing to alarm the woman, Lily quickly composed herself.

"Yes, certainly. I never thought you would be alarmed. I'll remember to say something to you next time I come in at night."

During the late 1800s, the south-west room had already been a focus for a variety of supernatural incidents. These included the sound of breaking crockery and strange tappings in one of the room's cupboards and once, a new silk dress which had been hung in the cupboard was later found to be riddled with small, diamond-shaped holes. On two further occasions, other dresses left in the cupboard met a similar fate.

Meanwhile, floating up from the basement came the occasional sound of wooden tubs or barrels being rolled around when it was known that no one was down there. Mr Murray, in a letter dated 10 December 1898, also referred to the 'opening and closing of heavy mahogany doors by an invisible agency'.

One spring, a few years after the turn of the century, Diana – now Mrs Claude Magniac, following her marriage – was to experience yet another frightening incident. She had retired to bed in the south-west room at about 10.30, but woke up some hours later to a sense of disquiet. As she lay awake, she heard the clock on the landing strike two. Just after that, there was a slight rustling noise which seemed to move towards the bed. The old nursery fender, which had been transferred to the room, then started to rattle.

Immediately, she had the impression of someone leaning over her and sighing; someone immensely evil. Too fearful to move, she closed her eyes and remained rigid in bed as the eerie sound continued. At the moment the unearthly sighing ceased, there was another rustling noise, this time moving towards the bedroom door. This was followed by a further rattling of the fender. Then there was complete silence. Diana eventually felt able to open her eyes. The ordeal seemed to have lasted for a long time, but in reality it had probably been just minutes.

A Mrs Studd was a visitor at the manor during Mrs Macdonald's lifetime and she was once given the south-west room to sleep in. She awoke to see a disembodied hand moving up and down one of the posts of the four-poster bed she occupied. Greatly alarmed, she fled to the south-east room, where Diana was sleeping, and woke her to ask if she could spend the rest of the night there, even if it meant sleeping on the floor.

Mr R Peregrine Birch, of Apple Tree Cottage, Hare Hatch, Twyford, Berkshire, was an occasional guest at the manor. In a letter to a friend dated 14 September 1930, but referring to some years before, he wrote that he had never seen the nun but that he had experienced frightful things while sleeping in the south-west room. He had heard uncanny noises coming from the dress cupboard, while one night there had been loud taps on the cupboard door, together with the sound of shuffling footsteps. Not daring to look inside the cupboard, he had barricaded it.

On another night, having a bad cold, he retired early to his room. There was a bright fire in the grate and the room was otherwise illuminated by four candles. Before going to bed, he sat down to read for awhile. His reading was interrupted by the sound of the brass curtain rings above his four-poster bed jangling against each other. He looked up and saw that the bed itself seemed to be shaking slightly. Without rising from his chair, he looked around the bed, but could see no reason for the disturbance.

In the following instant he had a similar experience to that of Mrs Studd, for he saw a ghostly hand, seemingly a man's, clutching one of the bedposts. The hand then moved slowly upwards before disappearing. He was so terrified he bolted from the room to a nearby bedroom, which he knew to be unoccupied, and spent the rest of the night there.

Stories of ghostly events at Preston Manor have continued. In 1976 a Mrs Phelan, visiting from Croydon, was on her way during daylight to Mass at St Mary's Church in nearby Surrenden Road. As she passed Preston Manor, she saw what she thought was the figure of a nun dressed in white, standing on the lawn in front of the manor. As she hesitated to take a longer look, the nun faded away.

In 1992 Anna Hinton, then aged 13, had been to a dance and was being driven home by her father. It was around 9.15pm when the car turned into Preston Drove. As it passed Preston Manor, Miss Hinton looked out of the car window and was surprised to see, close by the manor, a woman dressed wholly in white.

Although it was dark at the time, with only parts of the manor being picked out by the ambient street lighting, the figure in white had a luminosity which made it stand out from the shadows. Miss Hinton had the impression that the woman was seated on a bench or chair and that she was crying or praying, for she had her hands over her face. As the car moved on, Miss Hinton stared harder at the figure, but in that moment she found herself looking at blackness. The vision had gone.

A spectral Grey Lady has also been seen at Preston Manor. The first recorded report of her existence is probably that from the early 1900s, which tells of a housemaid frightened by the sight of a phantom woman in grey, whom she spied through the window of the boiler-room, then situated in the basement of the house.

During the Second World War, volunteer firewatchers were on duty each night in case incendiary bombs hit the building and several of these saw the ghostly figure of a woman in a grey dress. Among them was Doreen Rayner.

"I was only 16 when I was there," she said, "A first-aid post had been set up at the manor and I learnt first-aid so that I could help out. I lived nearby at the time and if I was at home when the air raid sirens sounded, I'd hurry to the manor.

"But I also used to help out with the firewatching, which meant that I often had to go onto the roof. One night I was going up to the roof and was nearing the top of the staircase when I saw a woman just ahead of me. She was wearing an old-fashioned grey dress and seemed a bit misty in appearance. Then she disappeared.

"I was a bit shocked, but I carried on to the roof, only to see her reappear by the parapet for a second or two before vanishing once more. Both times she was facing away from me, so I never saw her face. I knew who it might be, of course, for I'd heard the others tell of a ghost."

In the immediate post-war years, when night security officers were still called nightwatchmen, two watchmen on duty at the manor sat down to while away the time by playing cards. Between games, one went to visit the toilet. While he was there, the other aimlessly shuffled the cards.

This watchman was suddenly aware of someone standing behind him and turned, expecting to see his colleague. Instead, he found himself looking at a woman wearing a long, grey dress. As he rose in panic from his chair, the woman faded away. His colleague, returning from the toilet, had seen nothing unusual.

Early in 1993, security and information officer Rosina Potter arrived to begin her day's duties at Preston Manor. It was just before 8.30am, and one of her first tasks was to unlock the doors and open the window shutters in the manor's entrance hall and the adjoining rooms. As she went about her work, she was surprised to hear a man's voice calling out the name Ellie.

The voice had come from the direction of the doorway to the drawing room. Although her colleagues were due to arrive within the next few minutes, as a security measure she had re-locked the entrance door immediately after entering the building, so knew that at that particular moment she was the only person there. She at once searched the drawing room, and then the rest of the manor, but found no one.

If the voice had a supernatural origin, it could have been calling Eleanor Macdonald. Or the diminutive name could have been that of Ellen Stanford (who was to become Lady Ellen Thomas-Stanford), Mrs Macdonald's daughter by her first marriage, who outside of her marriage to Vere Fane Benett, spent much of her life at the manor.

A few months after the curious incident which had engaged the attention of Rosina Potter, it was the turn of Gerry Fleet, another security and information officer at the manor, to open all the doors and shutters at the start of the day. Soon after his arrival, while going up the first few steps of the main staircase, he noted a sudden fall in temperature. At the same time, his scalp began to prickle. Ascending a little further, he now found himself five or six stairs away from the first floor landing.

Looking up, he was astonished to see a woman wearing a long black dress with a bustle walk across the landing from the south-west room to disappear into the north-east room. Mr Fleet followed the woman into the room, but there was no one there. He then searched the rest of the building, but found nothing unusual.

Among the items on display at Preston Manor are photographs of Kylin, a Tibetan spaniel, which was a much-loved pet of the Stanford family. The dog died in the 1920s. In 1975, a visitor who was close to completing his tour of the manor was stunned to see 'Kylin' run past him. The visitor had already studied the photographs of the family pet and, as Tibetan spaniels are quite rare, had presumed he had seen a dog which was not of this earth!

However, this was no returning revenant, but a real flesh and blood animal. It was a Tibetan spaniel belonging to the manor's then custodian who had been so impressed by the look of the dog shown in the photographs that he had purchased one for himself. The custodian wasn't resident on the premises, but was walking through the grounds with the spaniel when it unexpectedly ran off and through the open door of the manor!

St Peter's Church, a stone's throw from the manor, is also haunted. This tiny church, which is often referred to as Preston Old Church (partly to prevent confusion with the much larger St Peter's Church situated in the centre of Brighton), was at one time the parish church of Preston village. It is believed the present building was begun by Ralph Neville, the Bishop of Chichester, who around 1226 sometimes resided at the manor.

The mural paintings inside the church were executed about the time of Henry III. Unfortunately, the combination of age, the fact that they were plastered over in Puritan times, and the disastrous fire of 1906, has resulted in the murals being less extensive and much less glorious than they once were.

In 1968 a small, sixpenny booklet was produced to provide visitors with a brief history of the church. The text of this booklet contains the words: 'Recently some members of the choir were emphatic that they witnessed a ghostly figure emerging from the south side of the church and disappearing in the churchyard'.

The text went went on to relate the separate experience of a couple of people unconnected with the church who, while walking past the church one Sunday evening, had encountered two women dressed in medieval costume. The women had initially appeared ahead of them. They then turned right before passing through a tombstone on the west side of the church, whereupon they vanished.

In the 1970s, a couple walking through the churchyard had a similar experience when they saw a woman coming towards them wearing medieval dress. They presumed she must have been taking part in some pageant and greeted her as she passed, although she failed to reply. Turning around to take another look at the woman, the couple were astonished to see no sign of her.

During the same decade, Jacquie Reynolds and a friend were strolling through the gardens near the church. As they walked, their interest in the flowers by the path caused them to separate slightly. As they did so, the apparition of a woman appeared between them. She was dark-haired, wore a long and fairly plain white dress and was only about 5ft tall. The mystery woman walked along with the friends for several paces before vanishing.

A curious spectre – or perhaps more correctly, a part of a spectre – has twice been seen by a woman who regularly visited the church to enjoy a few quiet, contemplative moments (because of its small size, the church has not been used for normal services for some years, though it remained open daily for the benefit of visitors until the growing potential for vandalism brought a need for more stringent security).

The first sighting was in 1992; the second, just over a year later. Had the apparition been complete, it probably would have been of a woman wearing an old-fashioned, cream-coloured dress, but all the visitor could see was just the voluminous rear part of the dress running down from the waist to an ample train at the bottom.

On the first occasion, the oddly incomplete ghost, which glided slowly along for a few feet before fading, was observed at the rear of the church. On the second occasion it was seen in that part of the church immediately beneath the tower, prior to disappearing through the base of the tower.

5 *The Royal Pavilion and Dome*

WITH ITS ONION-SHAPED domes and minarets, its Chinese-style furnishings, its flamboyant decor and its atmosphere of extravagance and make-believe, the Royal Pavilion has rightly been described as one of Europe's most extraordinary palaces.

The first building erected on the site for George IV, when still Prince of Wales, was a smaller and less ornate structure than that seen today. Constructed by Henry Holland in 1786-7, it was known as the Marine Pavilion. The name 'Pavilion' has survived all subsequent transformations of the building.

Between 1801 and 1803, this royal residence was enlarged and provided with its first Chinese interior. At about the same time, William Porden was commissioned to build the nearby Stables and Riding House, which are today known as the Dome and Corn Exchange. Between 1815 and 1820, the famous architect John Nash provided the Royal Pavilion with its present Indian-style exterior. The opportunity was taken to refurbish the interior of the building, once more in the Chinese style.

After the death of George IV in 1830, his brother William IV continued to use the Royal Pavilion as a seaside residence, as did Queen Victoria, but she is said to have hated the place. She paid her last visit in 1845. Five years later, the Pavilion was sold by the Crown to Brighton Corporation for £50,000.

Several ghosts have been witnessed in and around the Royal Pavilion and at least one of these is said to be that of George IV. An underground passage connects the Royal Pavilion with the Dome and it is here that the ghost of the royal personage is said to have been seen. Unfortunately, this alleged sighting took place many years ago and no details have survived.

A banquet held at the Royal Pavilion between the two World Wars seems to have attracted a different ghost, which at the time was claimed to be that of Martha Gunn, the famous 'dipper' or bathing lady, who went on to become a friend of George IV.

Shortly before the banquet began, the caterer in charge of the arrangements went into the banqueting room to check that all was well. He inspected the table settings, moved a plate here and a glass there, and rearranged some of the flowers. Then, looking up for a moment, he was surprised to see an elderly, rather rotund woman coming from the direction of the kitchen. He was even more surprised to observe that she was dressed in the style of another time.

The woman, paying no attention to the fact that the caterer was in the room with her, walked up and down the tables as if checking that everything was in its correct place. The caterer attempted to follow the woman, but was still about 20 or 30 feet away from her when she swept straight through a closed door. The caterer dashed to the door, but thrusting it open, he found just an empty corridor on the other side. He hurried along this until he came to an attendant and asked him if he had seen anyone leave. The attendant assured him that no one had passed that way.

The caterer, on being questioned, described the woman as wearing a long, bunched-up skirt, a triangular shawl and a large bonnet. Eventually, thinking he might be able to identify the mystery woman, he decided to look through some old prints featuring Brighton society events. Seeing Martha Gunn on one, he exclaimed: "That's her – bonnet and all!"

He may have been right, for etchings of her show that she was a very recognisable person, though it is commonplace for ghosts to be linked incorrectly to famous people. Taking into account the ghost's activity around the tables, she may instead have been a palace servant of some sort.

There is an amusing anecdote relating to the friendship of George IV and Martha Gunn. It seems that one day this lady was in the royal kitchen at the same time as the king. There was a great deal of activity going on, for a meal was being prepared. Glancing across the kitchen, the king happened to spot Martha surreptitiously pushing a slab of butter into the pocket of her voluminous skirt.

The wily king strolled over to the fireplace and called on Martha to join him. While saucepans of food bubbled away over the crackling logs, the king amiably held the woman in conversation. Soon, the heat of the blazing fire caused the butter to melt and trickle onto the floor. Her misdemeanour was revealed! But Martha was a friend, and the king demonstrated his tolerance by letting her off with just a mild admonishment.

Very few visitors to the Royal Pavilion are aware of the fact that, for many years, private residential rooms took up a part of the top floor of the building. These were occupied until 1968 by successive directors of the Royal Pavilion and their families. The area has since been refurbished, with part of the area now taken up by a restaurant and part converted back into the original Adelaide Suite.

The last resident of the rooms prior to their conversion was Clifford Musgrave, who was director of the Royal Pavilion for many years until retiring in 1968. During his tenure, he reported two supernatural experiences.

The initial incident took place early one evening, soon after Mr Musgrave had completed his duties for the day. Leaving his office, he walked through the Pavilion until he reached the door leading to his residential flat. Opening the door, he ascended a narrow stairway. At the top of the stairs, another door opened into a corridor and looking along this, the first thing that caught Mr Musgrave's attention was his wife's mother, who was temporarily staying at the flat. He observed that she was just about to enter the bathroom, which was at the far end of the corridor on the left.

As he walked along the corridor, he looked into the sitting room, which was also on the left, thinking that his wife might be there. Instead, he was surprised to see not his wife, who had not at that point returned home, but his wife's mother, who was seated in an armchair reading a newspaper! So who had he seen walking into the bathroom? Mr Musgrave hurried to the far end of the corridor... but found the bathroom empty!

On another occasion, a film company had obtained permission to shoot some period scenes in the King's Apartments. Over the years, the Royal Pavilion has been featured in a number of educational and promotional films as well as in films intended for general release to the public, the most famous of the latter being *On a Clear Day You Can See Forever,* which starred Barbra Streisand, Jack Nicholson and Yves Montand.

The film in question, however, was a more modest promotional production requiring just a day or two's filming. Mr Musgrave had to go out on business, but before doing so, he decided to take a look at what was taking place on the film set. He found the actors and actresses, dressed in period costume, enjoying a brief interval before a further session of filming.

Taking the producer to one side, Mr Musgrave indicated that he had to go out for a while and would not be back for several hours. He asked the producer to ensure that everyone working on the set kept strictly to the area in which filming had been authorised.

Mr Musgrave's business activities concluded much earlier than he had anticipated, so he soon found himself back at the Pavilion. Walking through the building, he heard the sound of screeches and laughter coming from one of the royal bedrooms. It was some distance from the area in which the filming was taking place.

Hurrying to the room, he was dismayed to find crumpled bedclothes strewn around and two of the actresses wrestling playfully upon the bed.

After ordering them out, and having an admonitory word with the producer, he returned to his flat, where he asked his wife if she would tidy the disarranged bedroom.

Going to the room, Mrs Musgrave set about re-making the bed. As she reached the end of her task, she ran her hand over the bedcover to smooth out the fabric's remaining ripples. At that moment she had the vivid impression that someone was standing behind her. In the same instant, a low, male voice murmured: "Thank you! Thank you!" She turned at once, but there was no one there.

In the mid-1970s a woman visitor approached Flo Joinson, a Royal Pavilion warder – as the attendants were then called – and told her that her brother and his bride had, a year before, spent their honeymoon in Brighton. During their stay the newly married couple had visited the Royal Pavilion and the husband had taken a number of photographs – interior photography was still permitted at the time. One photo was of the banqueting room, and this was handed to Mrs Joinson.

In the 1970s there were fewer visitors than there are now, so the banqueting room was cleared of historical furniture during the off-season so that dances and other social functions could take place. The honeymoon couple had strolled around the room during which time the husband had taken the photograph.

Mrs Joinson looked down at the snapshot in her hand. The banqueting room was empty of people except for one man, who was facing away from the camera. Only the top half of the man was visible. He was wearing what seemed to be a purple cloak with a white collar at the top. The man had white hair, or it might have been a wig.

The woman visitor explained to Mrs Joinson that her brother had taken a shot of what he thought was an empty room. So whose image was it on the photograph? The visitor told Mrs Joinson that she could keep the print as others had been taken from the negative. This print was shown to a number of people. Some felt it was genuine, while others considered it to be a fake. But assuming it was a fake, why would anyone go to such trouble for no apparent reward?

Unfortunately, Mrs Joinson – who retired in 1980 – lent the photograph to a young man she knew who lived near to the Royal Pavilion and who was interested in its history. He moved away from the area shortly afterwards without returning the photo.

Security officer Jacqui Chamberlain twice encountered a ghostly manifestation while on duty. The first occurred one autumn morning in 1991. It was around 8.30am, and she had just begun to ascend a spiral iron staircase in a storage area close to the Adelaide Suite when she saw, through the apertures separating each of the stairs, the frightened face of a man. He was cringing, as if hiding from someone. Moving closer, she saw that he was wearing very drab, brown-coloured clothing; the sort of clothing worn by a poor working man in Victorian times, perhaps? She was just about to challenge the intruder when he vanished without trace. According to another employee, the secretary of a former director of the Royal Pavilion once saw the ghost of a woman in period dress on the same staircase.

Jacqui Chamberlain's second supernatural experience took place one December evening in 1993. She was walking through the King's Apartments when she saw a man ascending a staircase in the vestibule area. She could see only the back of the man, but noted he was wearing a shirt or blouse of a silvery, satin-like material with cream-coloured pantaloons. She couldn't see his face, but she saw that his hair was dark and curly.

The oddest thing about the man was that he was climbing an apparently invisible staircase; a staircase which had once existed but which, she found out later, had been demolished in the early 1800s at the time that John Nash was transforming and expanding on the original neo-classical villa created by Henry Holland. The ghost mounted a few more 'steps' before fading. Might it have been the ghost of the Prince Regent? Without an indication of what the face was like, who can tell?

Some months after this incident, a male security officer was approached by a middle-aged couple. The woman, white-faced and trembling, claimed she had encountered something supernatural and very frightening while in a ground-floor corridor. She refused to describe what she had seen, saying she found it too distressing to talk about. Strangely, the man she was with had seen and felt nothing, though he did add that his wife was 'a bit psychic'.

The ghost of a monk has been seen in the Pavilion grounds, close by the South Gate. Details of this sighting are given in the next chapter.

During the First World War King George V directed that the Royal Pavilion, Dome and Corn Exchange be used as a hospital for Indian soldiers. Apparently, some of the 4,306 wounded men transported to these buildings woke up from their unconscious state to believe, on seeing their exotic surroundings for the first time, that they had already arrived in Heaven!

The Dome which, as mentioned, was initially established as the Royal Stables, has since served as a venue for many activities – political rallies, business conferences, church services, orchestral, pop and military band concerts, drama productions and much more. It, like the nearby Royal Pavilion, has a history of hauntings.

The most frequently reported ghost is that of a White Lady, so called because of the long, white dress she wears (some witnesses have described the ghost as wearing grey clothing, but of course, there may be a second ghost). It has been said that the apparition has a likeness to Mrs Maria Fitzherbert, the morganatic wife of George IV.

Over the years, the White Lady has been seen by a number of employees, while some visiting entertainers are said to have spotted her in the balcony area while they have been on stage during rehearsals. She has also been observed in the Stall Circle. One nightwatchman (in the days when that term was still in use) retired after many years' service to claim he had seen the ghost on several occasions, usually at the rear of the balcony.

Mick Badrocke, a night porter at the Dome for 20 years until retiring, saw the White Lady several times. Once, while on the sundial stairs – so called because of their association with the roof architecture – he also saw a spectral soldier wearing a red, brass-buttoned jacket with epaulettes and tight-fitting black trousers. On the soldier's head was a tall, black helmet which sloped slightly downwards from the front to the back. There was a silver regimental badge above the peak of the helmet.

There is the curious story of another night porter who worked at the Dome many years ago. He was walking around the periphery of the auditorium when he found himself in an area that was oddly cold. At the same moment, he spotted some coins on the floor and bent over to pick them up. Taking the coins in his hand, he was horrified to find that he was unable to properly straighten up again. The condition remained with him for the rest of his life. Logically, of course, there might have been a latent back problem which chose that particular moment to emerge, while a draught could have been responsible for the cold area. Who can tell?

Another witness of the White Lady was security officer Peter Bourne, who saw the ghost in 1984 (he was employed as a steward at the time). He described the apparition as being a dignified, pale-faced woman with a bouffant hairstyle and wearing a long, white, and seemingly semi-transparent dress. He observed her slowly walking, as if down a flight of stairs, at the rear of the balcony. However, he knew there were no stairs at that point, though a flight of stairs had once existed there.

Peter Bourne also witnessed the Dome's other occasionally-reported ghost (described in an old Dome information pamphlet as being that of the Royal Coachman, but whose appearance might suggest, instead, that the spectre was actually that of the Riding Master in charge of the Royal Stables).

Mr Bourne was standing in an aisle close to the centre of the auditorium seating when he saw what he at first thought was an intruder entering the front stalls area from what is known as the stage left door. That was until he was able to fully take in what he was seeing (this experience took place on a warm summer's day some six years after his White Lady sighting).

The Dome's central mercury lighting enabled him to clearly observe the amazing figure which had come into view. It was that of a portly man wearing a medium-brown coloured jacket with a tail at the rear, a cream and white shirt with a frilled front, cream pantaloons, a white waist sash, a cream and brown diamond patterned waistcoat across which stretched a gold watch-chain, a broad-fitting top hat with a dark feather in it, and leather riding boots which came up over the knees.

The man had red, puffed-looking cheeks and glaring eyes – Mr Bourne had the impression the man seemed angry about something. Especially noteworthy was the fact that the phantom man seemed to be approaching 7ft in height!

As the flamboyantly-dressed figure reached the second of the balcony support pillars it was also spotted by security officer Steve Mullings. The two men then saw the apparition continue walking until it reached the fourth support pillar, at which point it vanished.

It is interesting to note that a differently attired ghost, a man wearing an old-fashioned lounge suit, was seen standing in the same area by Duncan Morrison, a steward at the Dome. The incident took place at about 6.30 one evening during the late 1980s. At the time, a repertory company was rehearsing in preparation for a later performance. As he was off duty, Mr Morrison decided to watch the on-stage activities from a seat near the front of the auditorium. As the rehearsal progressed, he wasn't unduly surprised to see that someone else was taking an interest in the proceedings.

At first, Mr Morrison only became aware of the man in the lounge suit from out the corner of his eye. Wondering who it might be, for the auditorium was otherwise empty, he turned his head to look more closely at the figure. Not recognising the man, Mr Morrison presumed he was connected with the repertory company. A few seconds later, he was shocked to see the man in the lounge suit literally fade away.

Mr Morrison didn't query any of the actors. Concentrating on their roles and with dazzling spotlights trained on them, they were probably unaware of events taking place in the auditorium, but Mr Morrison was pleased to discover that his imagination hadn't got the better of him when a security officer who had been standing at the back of the building revealed that he, too, had observed the 'disappearing man'.

The late 1980s also provided a shock for theatre technician Peter Hartley. He had been given the task of installing a ring intercom and show relay system in the Dome, and much of this activity involved working in areas that were difficult to access, such as under the flooring and within wall cavities.

At one point during the installation, some cable had to be threaded along a small hole which ran through a $4^1/_2$-inch concrete support wall situated under the flooring in an area close by the orchestra pit. To help him in his task, Mr Hartley had the assistance of Curtis Strange, a young man gaining work experience within the then existing Youth Opportunities Programme.

For the purpose Mr Hartley had to stand on a ledge inside the cavity of a main wall, while Mr Strange had to lie full-length on the other side of the support so as to pull the cable through when it emerged from the hole. As they were working in the dark, both men had a trailing lamp for illumination.

All of a sudden, Mr Hartley felt a prickling of the skin and was conscious that some presence had joined him. A moment later he felt a tugging at his ankle, but when he looked down, there was no one there. Nor could there have been in such a confined space, while any approach along the cavity wall by a human would have been detected instantly.

Other unexplained activities reported by Dome staff include the sound of footsteps walking across the stage and mysterious rattlings of the chain on the inside of the fire exit at the back of the stage, in both instances when no one else was in the area.

Author's note: Douglas Reeve, resident organist at the Dome for many years and, for a time, its manager, is possibly another witness of the White Lady. According to a woman I interviewed, Mr Reeve claimed, while taking some visitors (which included the interviewee) around the building, that he had seen the apparition 'several times'. However, when I phoned Mr Reeve in 1996 (he died in July 1999), he refused to discuss the matter.

6 *Strange stories from The Lanes*

BRIGHTON'S OLD TOWN is bounded by East Street, North Street, West Street and, to the south, the sea. At its core is The Lanes, a fascinating mosaic of cramped and colourful shops, timeworn houses, narrow streets, and the animation associated with visitors from many places, for this compact area is one of Brighton's most popular tourist attractions. It is also the most haunted part of Brighton!

Despite the medieval ambience, few of the existing buildings in the Lanes were constructed prior to 1700, though the cellars (and possibly part of the walls) of some are much older than the buildings themselves. It is claimed that one of the oldest houses in this warren of slender streets is 43 Meeting House Lane, which is said to date back to around 1620. However, while its appearance might seem in accord with that time, it is thought that it may not have been built until the early part of the 18th century.

An even earlier construction date has been put forward for three cottages situated on the southern side of Black Lion Lane, which are identifiable by their projecting, slate-hung upper storeys. It is claimed that they date from about 1563, but research indicates a more probable date of 1642, which still leaves them as being among the oldest houses in Brighton.

Janet O'Riordan, an artist who lived in one of these houses until 1996, reported several paranormal incidents. Early in 1995 her friend Angie Main stayed overnight, occupying a rear bedroom on the top floor. During the night she awoke to the sensation that the room was rocking. At one point during this eerie experience, some unseen force snatched the bedclothes off and Miss Main had the distinct feeling that someone was blowing on her face.

Later in the same year Juliette Ouest, a visitor from France, stayed overnight. Shortly after she had climbed into bed in her room on the first floor, she heard a man and woman talking. The mumbled voices seemed to be infiltrating up from the room below – which was odd, for Miss

Ouest knew that the only other person in the house at that moment was Miss O'Riordan, who had already retired to her top-floor bedroom.

Then Miss Ouest heard the sound of footsteps ascending the narrow stairs leading to her bedroom. Seconds later she felt the bed on one side of her sag as if someone was getting into it and stretching out beside her. But the dim light filtering through her bedroom window failed to pick out any form, human or otherwise, to explain this sensation. In the next moment she felt spectral hands touch her waist. Greatly alarmed, but suppressing a scream, she leapt out of bed, but even as she switched on the light she had the impression that the entity, whatever it might be, had already departed.

Miss O'Riordan was, for some years, the co-director of an art gallery which occupied three floors of another of the old houses. Up until early 1996, when a medium was called in to move the ghost on, this building was haunted by a Victorian woman who had become pregnant out of wedlock. Although she went on to have the child, the continuing shame and the poverty associated with being an unmarried mother led, it is believed, to her committing suicide in an unusual fashion; by throwing herself down the steep, narrow staircase, an action that broke her neck.

In 1992 there was an exhibition of modern art at the gallery and the work of one sculptor, Dominique Rey, was displayed in three separate cases. These were individually titled Men, Love and Sex. Each of these exhibits incorporated organic matter and all three were hermetically sealed within their respective cases, an intentional aspect of the exhibits being that the organic part of each sculpture would gradually deteriorate within its sealed environment. The mainly glass construction of each case allowed this degeneration to be fully witnessed at its various stages.

Unfortunately, the exhibit entitled Sex began to smell rather badly. Its main organic component was a dead herring fitted with a glass eye (designed to create the impression that it was following the movements of the viewer). Apparently, the sealing of the case was defective and the malodorous consequence became daily more pervasive. Miss O'Riordan attempted to contact the sculptor, but without success.

Maggots were now beginning to emerge from the herring (eggs must have been deposited on it prior to its inclusion in the exhibit), and it was obvious that the case would have to come down... and quickly! But before human hands could unscrew the 2½-inch long screws which, together with the heavy duty steel brackets, were supporting the display case, it crashed to the floor.

While it was odd that the case should fall when it was so strongly secured, it was even stranger that the screws, which at the most might be expected to be slightly curved in the circumstances, were found to be bent into a tight U-shape. Had the resident spirit taken an objection to the expanding putrescence and decided to do something about it?

Early in 1995, Miss O'Riordan was preparing to go out with two friends for the evening. The friends had arrived early, and Miss O'Riordan had made some tea for them. Later, as she was clearing up the crockery, she felt something touch her on the back. She turned, but there was no one there – her friends, she saw, were still seated in their chairs. There was a further tap on her back by something unseen. She mentioned the matter to her friends, who had noticed nothing unusual

A few minutes later, all three were ready to leave and were about to go out into Black Lion Lane when Miss O'Riordan felt impelled to collect a book she had left in the gallery next door. Entering the gallery, she was dismayed to find a burglar ransacking the place. He escaped by pushing past her.

Miss O'Riordan wondered if the resident spirit of the house had been trying to warn her of the intruder's presence in the gallery, first with the taps on the back and then, when these failed to alert her, by generating a compulsion to collect the book.

"There was no particular urgency to collect the book at that moment, but I do feel there was a protective presence in the house," Miss O'Riordan said. "I'm a bit psychic and I had the strong impression that a sea captain once lived there. I had a chair in the living room which sometimes creaked, just as if someone was settling into it."

Browsing among the antiques shops in The Lanes has long been a pleasure for visitors and town residents alike. The 1960s were good years for this type of business and there were many more shops selling antiques in the area than there are today. One antiques dealer, a Mrs Funnell, had an odd tale to tell. Early in the 1960s, a lady who was one of Mrs Funnell's most valued customers was about to enter the shop when she hesitated, then walked on. The customer returned a few minutes later, but again she appeared to change her mind, immediately turning on her heels to walk away.

The dealer was puzzled, but thought little more about the incident until, later that afternoon, the woman returned for a third time. On this occasion she entered the shop without hesitation. Mrs Funnell queried why she hadn't entered the shop earlier.

"I didn't come in before because I saw you were engaged," the customer volunteered.

"But there was no one else in the shop," replied Mrs Funnell.

"Oh, yes there was," said the woman. She waved her hand in the direction of an ancient armchair standing in the shop. "There was an old man in that armchair. He was sitting there on both occasions."

Mrs Funnell reiterated that she had been alone in the shop at the time of the woman's calls. Had the customer seen a ghost? The shop was one of a number demolished later to make way for the building of Brighton Square, the modern addition to The Lanes which was completed in 1966.

Another antiques shop in The Lanes was the focus for a curious phenomenon which took place in the early 1950s. At intervals, the exotic scent of orchids filled the shop. But the story leading up to this phenomenon involved a murder.

The woman who owned the shop had a son who worked for a local florist. Having such a job, it was quite usual for him to visit the shop to present his mother with a bunch of flowers. One day, he told his mother that he had proposed to his girlfriend and she had accepted.

While his mother was delighted at the news, the announcement of his engagement enraged his wealthy employer, a homosexual, who had become very fond of the young man. From that time, the friction between the two men escalated. Finally, after a number of violent rows, the florist, consumed with jealousy and rage, strangled the young man.

Later, the ghost of the young man, fair-haired and wearing a sports jacket, was seen by a number of people in his mother's shop. After she had sold the shop, the lad's spectre continued for a time to demonstrate its presence, sometimes by being seen sitting in a favourite chair, at other times through the hiding of some ornament. The shop was later demolished.

About the same time as the above incident, an old lady living alone in a house in Meeting House Lane called the police several times because of the unexplained noises she was hearing at night. Eventually, she moved out, and soon after this the building was restored and altered, with the ground floor being converted into a shop (the former Robinson's Bookshop).

Shortly after the building work had begun, the sound of dripping water was heard on the ceiling of the middle floor. While the sound was continuous, there was never any sign of water. Indeed, there were no water pipes at all on the floor above. The builders took up the floorboards, but nothing was found to explain the persistent dripping sound, although an elderly workman said that he'd heard the building was supposed to be haunted. A few days later, the dripping noise stopped as suddenly as it had started. There was a suggestion that beetles were responsible, but there was no evidence of these.

The impressive Georgian house occupied by solicitors Woolley, Bevis and Diplock, in Prince Albert Street, dates back to about 1790. The house was originally built for a miller. At various times, a wine merchant and a baker also occupied the premises. A single-storey shop, added in the early 1900s, spoiled its appearance and this was removed in the 1960s during restoration work carried out by Mr E S Diplock.

During the hours of daylight, all seems well within the four walls of the building, but after dusk, some staff have noticed a palpable change in the atmosphere. Receptionists Lesley Hogbin and Vanessa Newman, when working late, found there was an uneasy sensation, accompanied by a feeling that some unseen presence was close at hand.

Maintenance man Stephen Ross, employed by the solicitors for more than 33 years, was glad when his duties no longer required him to work into the evening. While frequently conscious of a perceptible change of atmosphere in the building after dusk, he discovered that a top room was particularly spooky. When working there he often found the atmosphere so charged that the hairs at the back of his head stood on end. But what unnerved him most was the strange noises he sometimes heard, but only in that one room.

"It was a dull, slow, pattering sound, but nothing like a small animal, such as a mouse, might make," he said. "The sound was too constant and it would always come from behind me, whichever way I might be facing at the time. I never dared turn to investigate."

The Friends Meeting House in Prince Albert Street was built to serve the local Quaker community. Completed in 1805, it was altered in 1850. The north wing was added in 1876-7. The garden at the front of the building contains the graves of 54 adults and 30 children. The fig trees in the garden, it is believed, were grown from the seeds of the original fig tree that stood in the grounds of St Bartholomew's Priory. Today, while still used as a place of worship by the Religious Society of Friends, the building is also utilised as an adult education venue known as the Friends Centre.

On 30 April 1997, Joanna Hotton and her friend, Catherine Oehlers, arrived at the Friends Centre for the first evening lecture of the summer term course for which they had enrolled. Their particular class finished later than the others, and it was close to ten o'clock when the students finally dispersed.

Before leaving the building, the two friends visited the ground floor toilet (their classroom was on the same floor). When they emerged, they made their way to the main exit, but were dismayed to find it already locked. They then searched the ground floor for another exit by which to leave, but were unsuccessful. The only telephones in the building were behind locked doors, but both had mobile phones.

That evening they had taken down the phone number of their lecturer because she had suggested that students should phone her if they were unable to attend future classes. Miss Hotton attempted to use her phone, but found the battery dead, so Mrs Oehlers dialled the lecturer's number. The only response was from an answerphone, but the friends presumed that at that hour the lecturer would be going straight home, so might soon arrive to discover the recorded message stating their plight.

While they waited, the friends sat down at the bottom of the stairs leading to the first floor. They didn't immediately seek a light switch, for their surroundings were illuminated to some extent by the artificial light shining through the large glass panels of the rear entrance doors in Meeting House Lane. The minutes ticked slowly by. Filtering into the building was the comforting sound of chatter and laughter from the nearby Bath Arms.

As the friends conversed in low voices, another sound reached their ears. It was the clink of keys. This was followed by the scrape of a key turning in a lock. Then there was a ripple of human movement and again the grating of a key being turned. The immediate reaction of the two women was to believe that there must have been someone else in the building all the time.

As they rose to greet whoever it might be, they heard the shuffle of approaching feet. In the corridor by the stairway there was a slight fluttering of paper as some of the messages and small posters pinned to a noticeboard reacted to – could it be? – the proximity of someone walking past (while both women heard all of the sounds, this latter occurrence was only observed by Miss Hotton).

Miss Hotton called out: "Hello! Is anybody there?"

But there was no reply, not even when the friends nervously edged forward a few paces and repeated the call. Alarmed by the lack of response, they found a single chair and placed it close by the Meeting House Lane exit where, now distinctly uneasy, they sat precariously, almost back to back, on the edge of the chair.

The two women decided they could no longer rely on the hope that their lecturer would respond to the message left on her answering machine, so Miss Hotton, using her friend's mobile phone, called her brother-in-law, who in turn contacted the police. Even so, it took some time to locate the keyholder. By the time the women were released, they had spent nearly two anxious hours in the locked building.

It was the first time the two women had visited the Friends Centre and they had no prior knowledge of any paranormal events associated with the building. Later, they discovered that other people in the past had had similar experiences to their own.

At the corner of Union Street and Meeting House Lane is the former Elim Free Church. Meeting House Lane takes its name from the original concept of this building and not from the nearby Friends Meeting House, mentioned above. The Elim building began its life in 1688 as a meeting house for Presbyterians. It was originally surrounded by gardens in which hemp, used by the local ropemaking industry, was grown. The rather stark building was enlarged in 1810 and partially rebuilt in 1825.

After the Elim congregation moved to a new church in Albion Street in 1988, the vacated building stood empty for some years. In 1994 a brewery company took over the property and work began to convert the building into a public house, the Font and Firkin. This opened early in 1995.

Bizarre events accompanied the conversion of the former Elim Church into a pub. Building workers involved in the conversion were alarmed to find that tools and equipment left overnight were found to be in a different place the following morning. Might the discovery and removal of human bones during building work have triggered this and other inexplicable happenings?

Towards the end of the 19th century, a number of dead bodies were removed from burial chambers below the ground level of the church to be buried elsewhere. However, some bones appear to have remained, for when building workers, towards the end of 1994, excavated a part of the ground floor area as a prelude to slightly lowering it to accommodate brewery vats, a number of human bones were discovered.

Coincidental with this, an odd sequence of events took place on the premises of Selbys the Jewellers, a shop immediately facing the former church and separated only by a narrow lane. Nothing paranormal had previously taken place at the jewellers, so puzzled staff, aware of the reconstruction work taking place opposite, wondered if the peculiar and unnerving incidents which took place in the shop had a connection with the building work being carried out.

Towards the end of autumn 1994, two early Davenport porcelain plates, part of a set of six mounted on a wall of the jewellery shop, fell to the floor; one breaking, the other remaining intact. But they didn't just fall; they shot out from the wall at exactly the same moment to land a few feet away. They should have been quite secure in their holders.

With a bit of mental juggling, something approaching a logical explanation could be presented to explain the affair of the Davenport plates, but in the December, something even more remarkable was to occur. Indeed, four uncanny incidents took place within the space of two hours on a Saturday afternoon.

In some ways it was fortunate that the events occurred on a Saturday for, being the major shopping day of the week, there were several people in the shop to witness the two main happenings, including three shop assistants.

One of them, Judy Saunders, was close by when the sliding glass door of a display cabinet shattered. No one had been touching it at the time. Then it was noticed that the amber section of a necklace on display elsewhere in the shop had mysteriously disintegrated.

Later, a woman entered the shop with a pushchair. The child in the pushchair was clutching a plastic bottle of Coca-Cola in one hand. Within moments, the bottle exploded, fortunately without injuring anyone. The fourth peculiar incident of the afternoon came when the jeweller's wife, Julietta Selby, discovered that the glass on her wristwatch had shattered. She felt sure she had not hit the watch against anything.

At the beginning of 1995, shortly after the Font & Firkin opened for business, a barmaid alleged that she saw an ashtray shoot off a shelf of its own volition. However, the interesting aspect of this series of paranormal events is that, in the main, they were confined to the few weeks when building work was actually in progress. There was one further incident (the manifestation of a woman wearing a grey shawl – see below), but this was at a later date and seems unconnected with the events recorded above.

Towards the end of 1995, Sammi Davis, a barmaid at the Font and Firkin, joined her colleagues at a table for a late night drink and a chat before all left for home. The last customers had left some time before, the exit doors had been locked and the bar tidied up.

Miss Davis was the only one of the small group of bar staff facing an exit door. Just inside the exit door are double swing doors with glass panels. While briefly looking in the direction of the doors, Miss Davis was astonished to see the face of a woman peering through one of the glass panels. The woman had a grey shawl over her head and what could have been a grey dress (Miss Davis, who thought the woman looked about 30 years old, could only see that part of the garment immediately below the neck).

The shock of seeing the woman, whose appearance lasted but seconds, must have been evident on the face of Miss Davis, for one barman commented on her startled look. On relating what she had seen, her colleagues hurried over to the door, but found no one there. A check on the exit doors confirmed they were locked.

The ghost most associated with the Lanes is that of a young nun who is said to have suffered a gruesome death following her elopement with a soldier (though another version of the story has her running off with a monk). For the sad story of her love affair and its awful conclusion, we must go back many years.

The influential Cluniac Priory of St Pancras at Lewes was founded in 1076 by William de Warenne. Just under a century later, sometime between 1120 and 1147, a chapel (or chantry), dedicated to St Bartholomew the Apostle, was built in Brighton, with a small number of monks being transferred from Lewes to administer it. A prior's house was also built.

Not much is known of the history of the Chapel and Priory of St Bartholomews, but it may have been a monastic farm. Both buildings were situated at the southern edge of the Lanes, close to where the Town Hall now stands. The foundations of walls have been found, which indicates that the priory was enclosed. Almshouses, it is believed, were also built. In 1778, several skeletons, possibly of monks, were unearthed on the west side of the Town Hall.

When the French carried out their major raid on the town in 1514, St Bartholomew's Chapel was completely destroyed, but the prior's house was only partly demolished. It was later rebuilt and became the residence of successive Vicars of Brighton until its demolition around 1790.

Legend has it that the nun lived and carried out her duties at the priory. During her lifetime it was guarded by soldiers, for the times were notorious for the bands of ruffians who roamed the countryside, while pirates sometimes swept ashore to pillage.

The nun fell in love with one of the soldiers and the pair decided to elope. Unfortunately, their absence was quickly discovered and a party of soldiers was sent out to apprehend the couple and return them to the priory. The soldier was tried and executed as a deserter. The nun was walled up in a tiny space within the priory grounds and left to the slow agony of death by starvation. This was a traditional way of dealing with nuns who had seriously broken their vows, for it entailed no spilling of blood by senior ecclesiastics. Over the centuries since her terrible death, the nun is said to wander through the Lanes; a little, grey-clad wraith.

A woman on firewatch patrol in the Lanes during the Second World War claimed that she saw the spectre, dressed in a grey habit, walking along Meeting House Lane. It was unusual to see anyone in the Lanes at that late hour in wartime, so the woman called out, but to no effect. She then hurried after the nun, but before catching up with her she was astonished to see the grey-clad figure drift through the bricked-up doorway which still exists in Meeting House Lane (some people have mistakenly assumed that the nun was walled up behind this door, but in fact, the doorway is less than 200 years old).

It is an intriguing legend, but the story of the Grey Nun seems an unlikely one. St Bartholomew's Priory, in its early years, served a very small community and it is thought that only a few monks (the oldest account quotes two or three with their prior) were despatched there from the Mother Priory at Lewes. Even if nuns had later joined the monks at St Bartholomew's, the religious group would still have been tiny.

Assuming this, to maintain an adequate guard around the clock would possibly have required more soldiers than there were monks and nuns! And why would a spectral nun disappear through a doorway, bricked up or otherwise, which had not existed during her lifetime? In addition, where is the pre-war book or other documentation which records the nun's story? All accounts of the affair seem to have been published after 1950.

As for the ghost itself, little or nothing seems to have been recorded other than the sighting attributed to the unidentified wartime firewatcher (originally reported by bookseller Leslie Robinson in his book *The Lanes of Brighton* – the firewatcher was one of his customers. Significantly, Mr Robinson makes no mention of the legend itself).

Assuming the sighting of the wartime ghost to be fact, a more likely explanation would seem to be that the phantom is either that of a Quaker woman, or that of a fisherman's wife (or even, perhaps, the Quaker wife of a fisherman!).

While nuns have little or no historical connection with The Lanes, Quakers regularly frequented the area. When attending services at the Friends Meeting House, many used the doorway mentioned above, prior to it being bricked up (in conjunction with other building work), to gain access to the Meeting House.

The requirement for Quaker women was that they should wear clothing that was both simple and modest. Grey was a preferred colour and bonnets were popular for most of the 19th century. Many Quaker women wore peaked bonnets. At a distance, and especially in wartime blackout conditions, the firewatcher could easily have mistaken such a bonnet for a nun's wimple.

In the 1700s, and in the following century until about 1830, prior to the bonnet assuming popularity, some Quaker women wore shawls over their head. Again, at a distance and in poor light, such a headcovering might be mistaken for a wimple. At that time, of course, many fishing families occupied cottages in The Lanes, and it is certain that many fishermen's wives would also have covered their heads with shawls.

While the above observations may suggest that the grey wraith of the Lanes was mistakenly identified as a nun, there is a further consideration. Might the phantom woman in the grey dress and shawl seen by barmaid

Sammi Davis at the Font and Firkin and the woman in grey seen by the wartime firewatcher be one and the same? It is a tantalising thought.

On 21 December 1974, the *Brighton & Hove Gazette* did carry a story in which Hove-based author Elizabeth Ing stated that, while visiting The Lanes, she had felt the 'presence' of the spectral nun. Another curious experience came the way of Mike and Pearl Elsmore as they were walking along Meeting House Lane in the late 1970s.

It was a still, chilly autumn day with few pedestrians about. As they passed the bricked-up doorway associated with the spectre, the couple encountered a slight mist which almost instantly faded and an unnaturally cold pocket of air. At that precise moment a motor-bike, which had been propped up against the flint wall just a few feet to the left of the doorway, fell to the ground (the bike had probably been wheeled into The Lanes by its owner, for vehicles cannot be ridden there).

Mr Elsmore, concerned that petrol leaking from the motor-bike posed a fire risk, retraced his steps to lift up the bike and place it back against the wall. As he and his wife once more passed the bricked-up doorway to continue their stroll, they again encountered the small, oddly cold area.

Bears & Friends, a shop in Meeting House Lane, specialises in everything to do with teddy bears. The shop dates back to the 17th century and one of its first uses was as a butchery – structural alterations in 1993 revealed the original cellar cold room in which meat was stored. Cow horns were also found. There is evidence that in the 1700s it was used as a bank. The premises were also used at some time by a printer. The finding of a pair of boots bricked into a wall may indicate a former occupant's desire for good fortune – boots to kick out evil spirits – rather than an indication that a shoemaker once had a business there. In the 1970s, it was a greengrocer's.

Prior to 1993, the shop was for 12 years an antiques gallery made up of small, individual units. During this time, several people saw a spectral, middle-aged man, some on more than one occasion. One witness, Judy Saunders, saw the ghost walk across the gallery. She said the ghost was that of a middle-aged man with 'salt-and-pepper' coloured hair. He was wearing a dark, knee-length top-coat with trousers having a mixed grey and brown pattern. In one hand he carried a bag which she thought looked as if it was made of linen.

On another occasion the ghost was seen by Mrs Ray Hart. She only had a rear view of the entity, but her description of the clothing was similar. She said the man was wearing a dark, knee-length coat, though she observed that the trousers were grey. She described his hair as being darkish (the difference in colour could be accounted for by the fact that, with many middle-aged people, the hair at the back of the head retains its original colour for some time after the front hair has turned grey). Mrs Hart also noted the bag, which she thought looked similar in shape to a doctor's bag. She described the material as being 'like canvas'.

A different experience came the way of Marion Webb, who was also employed in the antiques gallery. One day, while talking to a colleague, some unseen force pushed her arm right back – it had been held akimbo.

Louise Wiles, who also worked there, recalled a time when the temperature dropped dramatically for no apparent reason. In the same moment, she felt a prickling down her spine. On another occasion, when in the toilet, she heard three loud, consecutive thumps on the wall. Her colleagues confirmed there was no one in the vicinity at the time.

Early in 1997, a customer visiting the Museum of Childhood, which formerly occupied a lower floor at Bears & Friends, was astonished to see a pale-faced, scruffily-dressed little girl, aged about two, sitting on the stairs. The customer was about to speak to her, when the girl just faded away.

Some years ago there was a jewellery shop in The Lanes (for business reasons it cannot be identified) where the day-to-day activities were disrupted by what at first were seen as minor irritations but which, as they escalated over the months, began to test the patience of those involved and, eventually, to have a detrimental effect on the business itself.

Initially, it was the shop's lighting which was affected. Electric light bulbs tend to have a limited life, but when they began to fail on a regular basis after only two or three weeks of use, there was some concern that faulty wiring might be the cause. The fact that the strip lighting at the rear of the shop was also starting to malfunction seemed to support this view, so an electrician was called in and some rewiring carried out. Although the electrical system was now claimed to be in fine working order, the incidence of bulb failures increased, while each new tube for the strip lighting began to flicker and fade after only a few days.

Then the limpet alarm attached to the shop's safe went off for no apparent reason. When this happened on two or three further occasions, the sensor was adjusted so that it was less sensitive to vibration, even though this was not desirable from a security aspect. But it made no difference, and as each alarm call involved a linked police response and also meant calling out, and paying for, a technician to reset the sensor, there was increasing concern.

Meanwhile, other disquieting events were taking place. A passer-by rushed into the shop one day to say there was smoke in the window. The cause was a revolving display unit which had begun to smoulder. On another occasion, a large sapphire and diamond ring vanished mysteriously from a window display. It seemed impossible that it could have been stolen from its quite inaccessible position in the window. It was never seen again.

Strangest of all, perhaps, was what happened to the shop's plate glass window. Manufactured to a high security standard, it was comprised of laminated sheets of toughened glass to provide a window able to resist very heavy blows. If savagely attacked, it was likely to craze in the same way as a car windscreen might, but without easily giving way. However, this window became the focal point for something quite baffling. A small crack, hardly noticeable at first, appeared on one side of the window. The next day, it was seen that the crack had grown an inch or two. Over the next three weeks, and at the rate of a few inches a day, it travelled right across the window in a peculiar serpentine pattern. Of course, the window had to be replaced. The workmen who replaced it, and who must have replaced many such windows in their time, said they had never seen anything like it before.

The point was now reached where the electric light bulbs were failing every three or four days. Eventually, the proprietor decided that enough was enough, and transferred his business. By then, the misfortunes had continued for about a year.

At the beginning of this twelve-month period, the sales assistant employed in the shop noticed nothing unusual beyond the escalating but still minor mishaps that intruded into her working week, but after two or three months had passed, she became aware of an occasional change of atmosphere at the rear of the shop. Later, this atmosphere seemed to bring with it an actual presence; some being she could not see, but knew was there.

As more weeks went by, the unseen presence at the rear of the shop began to take on a visible form, and the sales assistant found herself looking at a young man dressed in a black frock coat. He was only occasionally seen, and then but briefly. When he appeared, his face seemed to be laughing in a mocking fashion, although it was a soundless laugh. It was always a silent figure. By this time, the various mishaps affecting the shop had reached an alarming intensity.

Each appearance seemed to bring with it a slight increase in the strength of the apparition, together with a growing sense of evil. The sales assistant wondered if this frock-coated entity was responsible for the shop's continuing misfortunes, and was greatly relieved when her employer decided to vacate the premises.

A ghostly monk has been seen in The Lanes on several occasions, as well as in other parts of Brighton. Legend has it that the monk was expelled from St Bartholomew's Priory following a serious misdemeanour. He is one of three ghosts said to haunt Brighton Town Hall, which is situated at the southern edge of The Lanes. The present Town Hall was built in Bartholomews in 1830 on the site of a former market. The original Town Hall was erected close by in 1727. It included a garage for two fire engines and a workhouse which, after being enlarged around 1800, held some 150 inmates. South of the workhouse were the stocks, pillory and a pig market. The workhouse closed in 1822 after a new workhouse had been built in Church Hill.

As the Town Hall stands close to where the priory once stood, it is not surprising, perhaps, to find that the spectral monk haunts the basement, and that several people claim to have seen him. The basement was used for police purposes in Victorian times and the grim old cells used for locking up prisoners are still there, though they are currently utilised for storage. Animals are sensitive to the supernatural and security officer Danny Lawrence recalled that Fred, a former town hall cat, refused to venture into the basement.

On 13 March 1844 a murder took place in the basement, the victim being Henry Solomon, Brighton's Chief Constable. John Lawrence, a local man, had been brought to the Town Hall after being arrested for stealing a roll of carpet from a furniture shop in St James's Street. His accomplice had escaped. Mr Solomon had already interrogated Lawrence and was attending to other matters when the thief, who had been ordered to sit by the fireplace until again required, suddenly picked up a poker, rushed at the Chief Constable, and savagely brought the weapon down upon his head. Mr Solomon died from his injury early the next morning. Lawrence was subsequently found guilty of murder and hanged at Lewes.

Early in the 1980s, a former security officer, while in the basement, saw the apparition of a man in a top hat and a long black coat. It has been suggested that this could be the ghost of the murdered Chief Constable.

Another ghost said to haunt the Town Hall is that of a woman wearing a voluminous black dress with a white pinafore and a black, conical hat – apparel rather similar in style to that of the Welsh national costume. Several employees have seen this apparition descending the impressive, wide interior staircase that faces the front entrance to the Town Hall (currently, visitors have to enter the building through a more prosaic side entrance).

The last known sighting of the woman in black took place in 1978, the observer being a male employee on evening duty. On another occasion, the same employee, while walking through the Town Hall's reception area, noticed a sudden and quite dramatic drop in temperature. A moment later, something like a gown brushed against his arm and hand as some unseen entity swept past.

At the beginning of the 1970s, a female cleaner saw the woman in black materialise on the stairs, while in the same decade a male employee was so shocked by the sudden appearance of the eerie spectre that he was found cowering with fright beneath one of the tables that used to be positioned near the bottom of the staircase.

The particular attire of this ghost suggests that it could be that of the matron of the workhouse which formerly stood close by. When the present Town Hall became fully functional, in the early 1830s, a Mr Paine was appointed resident hallkeeper. His wife shared his quarters and a second possibility is that it is her ghost that has been seen.

The ghostly monk has been observed elsewhere in Brighton in addition to The Lanes (unless, of course, there is more than one phantom monk). After dark one evening in the 1960s, some boys playing in the graveyard in Queen's Road quivered with terror when faced with the cowled figure of the ghostly monk (the gravestones in this small cemetery were removed some years ago, and the plot is now laid out as a small public garden adjoining Brighthelm Church and Community Centre).

In the spring of 1993, two students temporarily resident in Brighton to learn English – a young man from Turkey and a Swiss girl he had befriended – danced away a few hours in a West Street club before leaving at around 1.30am. The way home to their student accommodation took them through the grounds of the Royal Pavilion. They had only walked a few paces through the south gate when they saw the cowled figure of a man. They knew at once they were witnessing something supernatural, for the spectre seemed to bring with it a strange, almost electric sensation.

Describing it to his teacher the following morning, the Turkish student said the figure was motionless and stood quite close to them. It was wearing a black cloak with a cowl, while the face and feet – which were bare – were a slightly glowing white. He said that he and his girlfriend were so frightened they were unable to move until the apparition had vanished.

This is a significant sighting, for while the phantom monk has been seen in The Lanes and the surrounding area several times, because of their brief residence in Brighton, their poor English and their limited contact with local people, these students almost certainly would not previously have known of the monk.

This chapter ends with another story from the Font & Firkin. Early in 1995, shortly after the pub had opened, Sharon Adams, the brewer, was working in the cellar. She was acquainted with the story of the ghostly Grey Nun, so when she felt a presence behind her and turned, she was shocked to be confronted by a pale-faced woman with staring eyes and wearing dishevelled clothing. Regaining her composure, Miss Adams quickly realised that the woman was flesh and blood, so challenged her.

The woman claimed that she had every right to be there, for she owned the pub. She was, Miss Adams found out later, a local eccentric who had wandered into the cellar from the street. As the woman refused to budge, Miss Adams hurried away to fetch help, but when she returned with a colleague, the woman had vanished as surely as any ghost!

There are a number of haunted pubs in and around The Lanes, in addition to the Font & Firkin. These are featured in Chapter 13.

7 *Churches and graveyards*

ST BARTHOLOMEW'S CHURCH, in Ann Street, must be one of the most interesting ecclesiastical buildings in Britain. It was built between 1872 and 1874 in the Italian Gothic style, supposedly to the dimensions of Noah's Ark. In fact, the measurements are markedly different. St Bartholomew's is 180ft long, 58ft wide and 135ft high, while, based on the Biblical cubit, an ancient measurement of about 18 inches, Noah's Ark was approximately 450ft long, 75ft wide and 45ft high. The church's association with Noah's Ark actually derives from the fact that its appearance resembled that of a Victorian toy model which was popular at the time of the church's construction. The austere exterior of St Bartholomew's – it was built to its great height using mainly bricks with a minimum of ornament – belies its magnificent interior.

The building of the church was financed by the Rev Arthur Wagner, who was closely associated with the controversial Tractarian Movement. The architect was Edmund Scott, a virtually unknown local man. The church cost only £18,000, which must make it, in terms of cubic space, one of the least expensive churches ever built in Britain. Today, it is widely known for its regular orchestral concerts. Visiting choirs are also welcomed. In the early 1980s, however, one choir made an unscheduled appearance before an audience of one!

Alec Archer was appointed verger of St Bartholomew's in 1980. One afternoon, three years after taking up this post, he was sitting to the left of the altar, alone and quietly reading a prayer book. Looking up, he was astonished to see a boys' choir, dressed in their cassocks and surplices and accompanied by three priests, emerge from the other side of the altar to wend its way through the church.

Though the choir gave every visual indication that it was bursting forth in song, no sound emerged from the choirboys' throats. The only sound to be heard was a slight shuffling noise. It was as if everyone in that procession was wearing slippers, with only the gentle scuff of these intruding upon the silence. Seconds later, the spectral choir faded from sight, leaving the church as quiet and empty as it had been a few moments before.

Was this a time slip experience? Who can tell? But about two months later, Mr Archer had a further paranormal experience. He was once more alone in the church when he observed three monks wearing black habits emerge from a door on the western side of the church. They were visible for only seconds.

A few days before Easter 1998, Jill Mayes and a friend walked into St Bartholomew's to enjoy the quietude. As they stood beyond the large, heavy plate glass doors situated just inside the church, two of the doors began to swing wildly to and fro of their own accord. This phenomenon continued for about ten seconds. There was nobody else nearby and the weather was calm.

Many years ago, a supernatural experience of quite a different kind came the way of a worshipper at All Saints Church, which dominates Church Hill, Patcham. The church has a long history, its nave dating from the 12th century, though much of the exterior was the result of 13th century rebuilding. The 19th century also saw considerable restoration work. An entry in the Domesday Book suggests that an earlier church existed on the site.

The ghostly experience involved the father of author Cecile Woodford, who recounted the eerie story in her book, *Portrait of Sussex*. The father, still a young man at the time, decided to attend the Christmas Eve service at All Saints. On arriving at the church and taking his seat, he looked around him and wasn't too surprised to note that the congregation was sparse, for it was a bitterly cold night.

As the service progressed, his eyes moved to a woman in a nearby pew. Tall, thin, and dressed in grey, he noticed the extreme pallor of her face and thought she must be ill. His concern was heightened by the fact that her clothing seemed totally inadequate for the chilly surroundings. He moved along his pew a few steps and reached over to put his overcoat around the woman's shoulders, whispering a few supportive words as he did so. She accepted the gesture in silence.

As the service continued, he looked at the woman several times. When the congregation rose to sing the final hymn, he turned his head once more, only to see that the woman had gone. His overcoat lay crumpled where she had sat. He swivelled his eyes around the church. The woman was nowhere to be seen. He was sitting close by the entrance door and would have noticed if she had left the church.

At a later date he was chatting to some locals in a nearby inn (probably the original Black Lion, which once stood in Old London Road). On relating his odd experience, he was informed that he must have seen a ghost, for others before him had witnessed the silent, pale-faced woman in All Saints Church. However, there have been no reports of this spectre for many years.

St George's Church, in St George's Road, was built in 1824-5 to serve the new estate of Kemp Town. It is one of Brighton's few surviving Georgian churches and was a favoured place of worship for Queen Adelaide.

There was a ripple of excitement at the beginning of 1997 when renovation work in the crypt uncovered the family vault of former prime minister Sir Robert Peel (Sir Robert is best remembered for founding the Peelers, which evolved into the Police Force we know today), although he was not himself buried there. The opening of the vault revealed wreaths which were still intact after more than a 100 years. The gates of the vault had been locked in 1888 after the funeral of Laurence Peel, Sir Robert's younger brother, and its location was forgotten after a fire destroyed family documents.

Early in 1997, a visitor called at the church to discuss a forthcoming concert. As she was being shown around the crypt, which runs the length of St George's, she heard footsteps walking across the floor above. These were accompanied by the sound of something heavy being dragged along. She commented on the matter, but as the door of the church had been locked from the inside, her companions suggested it must be a trick of the acoustics; that the sound must be coming from outside of the church.

Moments later, the same sounds returned, but this time there was no doubt that they were coming from the floor above. A member of the party immediately went upstairs, but found the church empty and silent. On another occasion, an opera singer who had arrived at the church in connection with a forthcoming concert heard the sound of footsteps walking along the gallery when no one was there.

Derek Froud was the organist at St George's for 12 years until 1996. He used to rehearse once or twice each week, an activity which meant that he was often alone in the church. He heard footsteps pacing around the church on several occasions during his years there, while at other times he had the eerie feeling that someone was standing by him and looking over his shoulder. He sometimes had this odd sensation during church services.

Geoffrey Miller, his predecessor, was also subjected to uncanny experiences. One dark evening while rehearsing, and when the only illumination was the lighting above the organ, a strange glow, quite unlike that made by artificial light, filled the whole of the church. It lasted for several seconds before disappearing as mysteriously as it had arrived.

The most remarkable experience was probably that of Helen Gearing. It took place at around 9.15 on a Sunday morning in 1996. Being responsible for the preparation of the table displaying religious literature and for the distribution of hymn and prayer books throughout the church in readiness for the morning service, Miss Gearing was the first to arrive.

As she went about her tasks, her eyes caught a movement in the gallery. Looking up, she was astonished to see the figure of a headless man. He wore a biscuit-coloured frock coat and was walking along the gallery. The apparition faded away after travelling almost the length of the gallery.

The church was closed throughout most of 1999 while major work took place to convert the crypt into a community centre. During this time two building workers reported encountering an unusually cold area by the Peel family vault.

The Church of St John the Baptist, in Bristol Road, was consecrated in 1835. In May 1993, the *Daily Telegraph* and the Brighton *Evening Argus* published a photograph of the interior of the Corinthian-style church which allegedly showed the ghost of a girl (or woman) in a bonnet.

The story of the photograph goes back to the 1930s, when the London-based Qualis Photo Company was commissioned to take a series of shots of the interior of the church. One photo, when developed, showed the pews empty except for the ghostly figure in a bonnet. The parish priest at the time elected to keep the photograph away from public scrutiny, but it was released to the Press at the time of the church's 150th anniversary celebrations.

The logical explanation is that the photograph is the result of a time exposure where someone has walked into the camera's field of view, stayed in one place for a part of the exposure time, then moved on with the result that the person pictured remains as an indistinct image in that part of the photograph. But Father Ian Doyle, who was the priest at the time of the celebrations, said: "Who is to say that it isn't a ghost?"

Unfortunately, the Qualis Photo Company no longer exists, so an examination of the negative by experts, which might have settled the issue, is not possible.

St Nicholas's Church stands on high ground at the southern end of Dyke Road. Parts of the present church date from the 14th century, though the Domesday Book of 1086 suggests that a church stood on the site well before this. Up until 1795, it was the only church serving Brighton, but over following years, with other more fashionable churches opening in the town, it suffered from neglect. Later, the Rev Henry Michell Wagner commissioned Richard Carpenter to oversee restorations.

Unfortunately, Carpenter proved over-enthusiastic with the rebuilding, so that today only the flint tower, the chancel arch and the nave arcades remain from the 14th century structure. Particularly interesting, however, is the Norman font which dates from the 12th century or earlier, and which may have come from the original church of the Domesday Book.

While St Nicholas's Church itself has not, apparently, been associated with tales of wraiths and revenants, the same cannot be said of its churchyard, for there have been several reports of hauntings, with one legendary story pre-dating the building of the present church.

The churchyard is the final resting place for a number of Brighton's most famous citizens. These include Captain Nicholas Tettersell, who helped Charles II escape to France; Sake Dene Mahomed, who introduced Turkish baths to Britain and who was later appointed 'Shampooing Surgeon' to George IV; Martha Gunn, the most famous of the Brighton bathing machine 'dippers' and a close friend of George IV, and Phoebe Hessel, who gained renown through disguising herself as a man so that she could join the army and thus remain close to the soldier she loved. The churchyard is also believed to be the site of a plague pit which contains either the victims of the Black Death of 1348-9 or those of the plague of 1664-5.

J A Erredge, in his *History of Brighthelmston*, relates the legend of a doomed galley which, after foundering off the Sussex coast, is said to return each year in ghostly form to re-enact the tragedy. The legend is associated with a large stone cross which once stood close by St Nicholas's Church.

It appears that a long and bloody feud between the Lords of Pevensey Castle and the Earls de Warenne, the Lords of Lewes, reached its climax one bright May morning with a major battle between the two sides on the slopes of Mount Caburn, near Lewes. The conflict was heralded with a warning blast from the horn of the warder of Lewes Castle who, from the castle's north turret, had observed Lord Pevensey, mounted on a white steed, advancing towards the castle with his men.

The wife of the Earl de Warenne, cradling her first-born infant son in her arms, hurried to the turret so that she could witness the battle. From there, she observed that Lord Pevensey had gained the advantage of reaching the top of the hill and was already launching an attack on the hastily mustered men commanded by her husband.

While the ferocity of the charge sent de Warenne's soldiers reeling, the brave Earl single-handedly fought on. In doing so, he was immediately singled out by Lord Pevensey, who urged his steed towards the beleaguered man. Lady de Warenne, watching anxiously from the turret, was horrified to see Lord Pevensey close upon her husband with battle-axe raised.

In that moment the noble lady raised her infant son above her head and vowed to St Nicholas, the protector of the faithful in danger, that if her husband's life was spared, their son would never wed until he had placed the belt worn by St Nicholas, which had been acquired by the family, on the Blessed Virgin's tomb at Byzantium.

The saint seemingly responded to her plea, for the good Earl dextrously avoided the blow and Lord Pevensey, caught off balance, almost fell from his horse. Taking advantage of this, the Earl de Warenne plunged his sword in behind the backplate of his adversary's armour and Lord Pevensey, mortally wounded, toppled from his horse. Seeing this, Lord Pevensey's followers fled in dismay, and the Earl de Warenne returned to his castle in triumph.

Twenty summers passed and the Earl's eldest son, Manfred, had neglected to honour his mother's vow. Each year the glorious victory over Lord Pevensey's men had been celebrated. Now the celebration was to take place once more in the castle. With all the guests assembled, the wassail bowl was passed round and the bards sang merrily. Manfred took the hand of the beautiful Lady Edona, the woman he had promised to marry, and led her to join in the dancing. When the festivities were at their height, an icy wind swept through the hall, blowing out every candle and every flaming torch.

The total blackness that followed lasted only moments, for vivid flashes of lightning spectacularly illuminated the hall, and the din and clamour of battle fell upon the ears of all those present. The revellers were then astounded to see the battle of 20 years before being played out again across the rich tapestries that draped the walls around them.

The hillside battleground could be seen distinctly. So could the combatants as they fought. It was as if it were daylight, but at the point where Lord Pevensey was seen to raise his battle-axe, the vision faded away and the hall was once more plunged into darkness. Lights were quickly brought by the servants, but most of the guests dispersed, being too terrified to remain.

The event was taken to be an omen, and the following morning the Earl de Warenne journeyed to Brighthelmstone where he sought the guidance of the Holy Fathers at St Bartholomew's Chapel. He was counselled to build a ship to transport his son to the Blessed Virgin's tomb. Only after honouring his mother's vow with the successful completion of this journey could the son marry the fair Edona.

The vessel duly left from Meecham (Newhaven) to arrive safely at Byzantium, where Manfred carried out his sacred task. It was a year before the vessel was again close to England. On 17 May, a vessel was observed off the coast at Wordinges (Worthing) and a Father of this Chantry noted that the ship carried the pennant of St Nicholas.

A messenger was sent at once to the Earl de Warenne. Within a short time the Earl, his wife, and their retinue, along with Lady Edona, the Lord of Bramber, the Abbot of the priory and all the brotherhood, had assembled under the Earl's banner on the hill by St Nicholas's Church. Hymns of thanksgiving were sung as the ship came nearer.

In the next moment their joy turned to horror as they saw the ship keel over. It had struck a hidden rock off Shoreham. The onlookers gasped in disbelief as the sea engulfed the vessel. Lady Edona was so distressed by the dreadful sight that she fell to the ground with shock, dying where she lay. Just one foreign sailor survived the tragedy to swim ashore.

The Earl de Warenne lived only a few more years, but this was long enough for him to build a new church of St Nicholas on the hill where he and his wife had watched the final, dreadful moments of the doomed ship. Lady Edona was buried on the spot where she had died, close by the entrance to the church.

On each anniversary of the sinking, it is said that a ghostly reenactment of the tragedy might be seen by onlookers standing on the clifftop. Others claimed that a sighting of the ghostly galley meant that a storm was in the offing.

It is an intriguing story, but unfortunately undermined by several discrepancies. Even if we disregard the fact that Lady de Warenne would have needed exceptional eyesight to observe details of the fighting on Mount Caburn, a distance of about two miles, the Earl de Warenne of the legend was the eighth and last of the line and his marriage was childless. Indeed, none of the Earls de Warenne had a son named Manfred, while the tomb of the Virgin Mary is located not in Byzantium (Istanbul) but, traditionally, in the Vale of Kidron, at the foot of the Mount of Olives (though some evidence exists to favour Ephesus, in Turkey, as being the location).

There is the base of what is believed to have been a large cross close by the entrance to St Nicholas's Church, and this is claimed to be where Lady Edona was buried. However, records suggest that the site is really the burial place of a Saxon warrior and his steed – it was then the custom on a warrior's death to slay his horse and bury it with him.

The cross is believed to have been considerably damaged or destroyed during the Reformation. The original plinth largely survives. An octagonal column, sculpted by D. Burns Brown, was erected on this base in 1934.

A phantom horse is said to charge around the graveyard, the suggestion being that this is the steed of the buried Saxon warrior. There is a little more substance – if that is the right word! – to the story of a ghostly white horse and rider seen gliding across the graveyard by a member of the Home Guard during the Second World War. This snippet of information formed part of a reader's letter published in the 3 May 1999 edition of the *Evening Argus*.

The letter gave no details of what the rider was wearing, so we do not know if it was the ghost of a Saxon warrior or an entirely different spectral horseman, for others have reported seeing a rider wearing Regency dress, including high boots and a long cloak. It has been claimed that this rider and horse have been seen trotting through the graveyard, even in recent years.

At dusk one evening in 1976, a local woman was walking into the graveyard from the Wykeham Terrace entrance when she saw an amazing figure emerge from behind one of the graves. It was of a man wearing clothes similar in appearance to those of the Sandman of legend. From his shoulders flowed a black cloak, while a wide-brimmed, flat-crowned hat, also black, partly hid his shadowed face. The woman's footsteps froze, and she stayed rigidly where she was to watch as the sinister-looking figure advanced two or three paces away from the tombstone. Then in a trice the spectre was gone, consumed by the creeping twilight.

Barry Bond, who lives close to the graveyard, regularly took his two dachshunds through it during their daily walk. On a summer day in 1984 he halted in the churchyard, sitting down by the main path for a few minutes while his dogs scampered around. A few paces away from him was the family tomb of James and Mary Skinner, which dates from the early 18th century.

While the dogs ran free, Mr Bond spotted a man on the other side of the rectangular tomb. The man seemed to be rising from a sitting position. The lower half of him was hidden by the tomb. The man was slightly built and wearing a grey jacket and trilby. As Mr Bond watched, the man took off his trilby and ran a hand across his forehead. He then replaced the trilby before, seemingly, sitting down to disappear from view behind the tomb.

Some seconds later Mr Bond became concerned about his dogs, which had run past the tomb and on towards a wall which drops some ten feet down to Dyke Road. As he hurried past the tomb to bring back his dogs, he was surprised to see no sign of the man.

Mr Bond pointed out: "There was no way he could have walked away from the tomb without being spotted by me. There is an expanse of grass around the tomb and a sheer drop to the road straight ahead, while I was only about ten feet away from where I had seen him. There was no one else in the vicinity at the time."

The Brighton and Preston Cemetery, Hartington Road, opened in 1885. One day in the cemetery's early history, a hearse pulled by four black-plumed horses travelled through the arched gate and along the path leading to the mortuary chapel. Once there, the hearse came to a halt and four bearers reverently carried the coffin into the chapel, leaving the coachman outside to look after the horses.

Probably the coachman was thinking of more pleasant things than death and funerals, but his reverie was suddenly shattered when the horses, possibly frightened by some small wild animal running across their path, reared up in panic. The coachman ran the short distance to the horses to calm them down, but in the next second the agitated horses charged forward. The empty hearse jerked along in their wake and the coachman fell to his death beneath its whirring wheels.

Whether this horrific event took place exactly as described is not known, for there were no nearby witnesses, but over the following years a visitor to the cemetery would be perplexed to see nothing, yet find the silence disturbed by the eerie whinnying of nervous horses followed by the screams of a man, the thunder of hooves and the clatter of steel-rimmed wheels.

In the early summer of 1988, at around 2am, Peter Newman was walking home after visiting a friend living in the Woodingdean area of Brighton. As he made his way along Warren Road, he was astounded to see what looked like a blue light hovering a few feet above the Lawn Memorial Cemetery, which is located on the south side of the road. The strange light was about 150 yards away and as Mr Newman watched, it performed a series of odd, slow motion gyrations, all within a range of about five or six feet.

At first Mr Newman presumed it was a lamp of some kind, but he had the tingling feeling that there was something uncanny about it. Blue is not the colour one would normally use to illuminate a very dark area and, anyway, what purpose would there be to waving a large, coloured lamp around at that time of the morning? – he estimated it to be somewhat larger than a football in size. Although Mr Newman remained to watch the antics of the light for about five minutes, he eventually went on his way.

While there may have been a logical explanation for this incident, ghost lights are a well documented phenomenon. Those of the Will-o'-the-Wisp type are thought by some to be caused by the spontaneous combustion of marsh gases, but variously coloured lights have been reported where there is no perceived basis for their presence. Author Elliott O'Donnell recorded a number of incidences of mysterious lights, sometimes coloured blue, green or red, which had been observed at burial grounds, while in 1969, America's *National Geographic* magazine reported that strange blue-white lights had been seen at intervals above a graveyard in Silver Cliff, Colorado, since 1880.

8 Unusual hospital visitors

IF GHOSTS ARE to be found anywhere, then hospitals, where the brittle balance of life and death is daily tested, would seem to be logical locations for their wanderings. Brighton doesn't disappoint, for paranormal activities have been reported in at least three of the town's existing hospitals and at another, the Bevendean, which was demolished in 1989.

The Royal Sussex County Hospital opened in June 1828, though it was originally described as the Sussex County Hospital and General Sea-Bathing Infirmary. At the time, sea-water was still considered to be of importance in treating the sick, and the initial name of the hospital acknowledged this. The water was pumped to the hospital by pipe from the sea, an activity which ceased in 1876. The hospital, which has grown substantially over the years, acquired the 'Royal' in its name after it had received the patronage of Edward VII in 1905.

Prior to its demolition in 1989, the hospital's York Ward had a reputation for being especially haunted. At one time it was used as an isolation ward for patients with diseases such as tuberculosis and diptheria, but in the years immediately preceding its demolition, it primarily accommodated patients who needed to be isolated from potential infection because of immune system deficiencies.

One ghost haunting the ward took the form of a tall, thin, bespectacled, middle-aged man who wore a dark, double-breasted suit and a brown trilby hat. Looking quite lifelike in the dim night lighting of the ward, he visited individual patients at around 11pm and talked to them in a friendly, comforting way.

While his appearances were very occasional, they took place over a period of more than five years. Patients would later mention these nocturnal visits to nursing staff, not because they thought the visitor was a ghostly entity, but because they were astonished to have someone calling on them so very late at night. Only one member of staff, a female nurse, is believed to have witnessed the apparition. More generally, hospital staff would be questioned by patients who had been visited by the man. Among them was Bartley Quinn, facilities manager at the Royal Sussex.

"I was night superintendent at York Ward over a period of three or four years prior to its closure," he said. "During that time I had at least six patients ask me who the visitor was. Apparently, he always stood at the end of the bed, rather than coming close to the patient. He would ask them how they felt, reassure them as to the excellence of their treatment and suggest that they were making fine progress. He seemed entirely concerned with making the patient feel in good shape.

"Because he was wearing a hat, most patients he called on presumed him to be some sort of hospital visitor. I used to do my rounds of the wards between 7 and 8 o'clock each morning and it was then that I was questioned by the patients who had seen him. Of course, I never suggested they had witnessed something supernatural. To prevent any alarm, I would usually go along with their own interpretation of the visitor's identity.

"Whenever a patient mentioned the visitor, I always asked for a description of the man, just to confirm that the patient was talking about the same apparition that others had seen. I used to query the nursing staff on duty, but they always assured me that no one had visited the ward at that time," added Mr Quinn.

The ghost in the brown trilby was not the only spectral caller at York Ward, for a story about this ghost, which appeared in the *Evening Argus* on 13 March 1989, was quickly followed by a published response from Mrs S H Norman, who claimed that a female ghost haunted the ward.

Mrs Norman, recalling her wartime nursing experiences, wrote about an incident which took place one night while she was on duty in York Ward. She and a senior nurse were in the sister's office on the first floor, going over the patient care routine for the following morning. At around 10.30 they both heard the outside door opening. The door was made of iron and it tended to make a noise when being opened or closed.

Leaving the senior nurse in the office, Mrs Norman made her way to the top of the steps leading up from the ground floor, ready to greet who she thought must be the night sister doing her rounds, even though 11pm was more usually the time she did so.

Mrs Norman heard the ground floor door scrape to a close and this was followed by the sound of footsteps quickly coming up the staircase, accompanied by the swish of a starched apron. She peered down the stairs, but no one was in sight. Returning to the office, she expressed her puzzlement to her colleague.

"That's odd," Mrs Norman said. "I'm sure I heard someone come in through the door and up the stairs."

The senior nurse replied: "That was Sister Geer. She died some years ago and was on this block for many years." She went on to say that several nurses had encountered her.

York Ward was on two floors and it seems possible that Sister Geer, or some other ghostly nurse, was active on both floors. Sister Marilyn Holding once worked on York Ward's upper floor and, while she never saw a ghost herself, she does recall that several patients told her that they had seen the apparition of a woman in a long, grey dress.

From time to time, patients in the downstairs ward would also tell of a ghost. The usual description was of a middle-aged, grey-haired nurse in a long grey dress and a white apron. She would arrive in the ward, then moments later they would see no sign of her. Nursing staff knew the patients must be referring to a ghost, for being an isolation ward, entrance doors were kept locked when not in use, while the nurse's uniform belonged to another age.

At other times, patients reported seeing disembodied eyes hovering in the ward. In this connection, one nurse was badly shocked after a particularly horrific experience. Going to the ward's combined cloakroom and toilets, she pressed the light switch, but the lights failed to come on. She peered into the blackness. In that instant, caught in the light coming from the corridor behind her, was a pair of eyes... but without a body! Panic-stricken, the nurse raced away from the scene. Later, the cloakroom lights were found to be in perfect working order.

A far less traumatic incident was experienced by Sister Karen Wootten at around 5 o'clock one morning in 1988, She was in the York Ward kitchen when an oddly incomplete spectre appeared. It comprised just the lower part of a patient, who appeared to be male. All Sister Wootten could see was the bottom of a dressing gown, the legs below the hem of the gown, and a pair of carpet slippers.

The sound of footsteps in the corridor when no one was there and bedside alarm buzzers which went off of their own accord were other happenings which took place from time to time in York Ward. The ward seemed to be such a magnet for paranormal activity that a church minister was eventually called in to perform an exorcism. As mentioned, York Ward was demolished in 1989.

When hospital staff spoke of the nurse in the old-fashioned uniform seen in York Ward, they tended to use the term 'Grey Lady', but this spectre (or a similar one) has been encountered in other parts of the hospital. In 1967, Sister Pippa Shaw was a second year student nurse at the hospital. While there, she never saw the Grey Lady or any other ghost, but she does recall hearing phantom footsteps while on duty in Grant Ward.

She was a few yards away from the entrance to the ward when she heard footsteps ascending the staircase. Wondering who it might be, she swivelled her head around to look, but saw no one. However, the footsteps continued into a small room close by the top of the stairs where there were just two or three child patients. Alarmed, Sister Shaw dashed into the room, but except for the sleeping children, found nobody.

In 1989, Sister Wootten was on night duty in Grant Ward. It was around 3am and she was sitting in the office at the end of the ward. Sensing a peculiar change in the atmosphere of the office, she looked up from what she was reading and was amazed to see, standing by the small desk just outside the office, the semi-opaque apparition of a nurse dressed in a long, outdated uniform. The phantom vanished after only a few moments. Another nurse, Sister Holding, stated that some patients in Grant Ward had told of seeing a nurse wearing an old-fashioned grey uniform.

In 1990 while on night duty in Grant Ward, Staff Nurse Lesley Driscoll went to get some fresh bed linen. As she returned along the corridor from the stairwell area where the linen was stored she had the impression that someone was behind her, but on turning, she saw no one. However, when she reached the ward office half-way along the corridor, which has a window looking onto the corridor, a doctor sitting in the office attracted her attention to enquire about the woman he had seen walking behind her. Staff Nurse Driscoll said that she had seen nobody. The doctor insisted that he had seen someone and, concerned about security at that late hour, he searched for an intruder, but without success.

Some time later, Staff Nurse Driscoll mentioned this incident to another nurse, who told her of an earlier occurrence which had taken place. On duty at the time were Staff Nurse Claire Brandwood, who was seated at the ward office desk, and Staff Nurse Susie Fenton, who was standing almost next to her and using the telephone to speak to the relation of a patient. At that moment, the apparition of a woman appeared in the office, both nurses seeing her. The spectral woman, who was described as having a lovely smile, was looking towards Staff Nurse Brandwood. The ghost was visible only for seconds.

Once, one of the patients in Grant Ward had a cardiac arrest. The young doctor dealing with the emergency was new to the hospital. He had two nursing sisters helping him, but as he worked frantically to keep the patient alive, he saw another sister some distance away.

"Can you get that sister over to help us?" demanded the doctor. The nursing sisters working with him turned, but there was no one in sight. Later, on being questioned, it was obvious that the doctor had seen no living person, for the sister's uniform he described had been phased out many years before.

Writing in the *Evening Argus* on 12 December 1993, columnist Tom Moore referred to the strange goings on in Stewart Ward, which he learned of while an in-patient in a different ward. Apparently, because of financial curbs, Stewart Ward had been closed for a while – it had been a nine-bed orthopaedic ward. Yet at 4am each morning the patient's 'help' button by the ward's Bed 3 was pressed by some unseen hand. Apprehensive nurses, it seems, always investigated in pairs. Staff Nurse Jackie Streefland recalled one such incident.

"We tried wedging chairs against the handles of the doors in the ward, thinking some intruder might be responsible for pressing the button, but it made no difference," she said.

The alarm calls eventually ceased, but the mystery was never adequately solved. While it was suggested that an electrical fault was to blame for the help-button phenomenon, such a fault would be expected to occur on a random basis rather than at a specific hour.

Stewart Ward eventually reopened, but from time to time over the years there have been reports from patients in the ward who claim to have seen a nurse dressed in an old-fashioned nurse's uniform consisting of a long, grey dress with starched white apron, cuffs and cap.

Elderly patients in Chichester Ward have told nursing staff of a ghostly boy and girl seen in the ward, while some nurses working in Egremont Ward claim to have felt an unseen presence there, most noticeably in the day room.

The distinctive aroma of cigar smoke sometimes hangs in the air in the hospital's Ear, Nose and Throat Out-Patients Department. Most of the staff employed in the area have noticed the smell at some time, including Jo Church, senior clerk/ENT medical records, and Staff Nurse Christine Long. The smell is especially puzzling to visitors, for it is a 'no smoking' zone. It is located where there were once operating theatres, and the smell is noticed mostly in an area where the staff changing room used to be. It is attributed to a deceased anaesthetist who, years ago, used to sit in the changing room and relax with a cigar between operations.

Ghosts have also intruded into the off-duty lives of some of the nurses at the hospital. In one instance, a nurse residing in the nurses' home was deeply troubled by an unseen presence and called upon the help of the Rev Geoffrey Holness. The Rev Holness, chaplain at the Royal Sussex from 1977 to 1994, conducted a prayer service to cast out the unquiet spirit.

On another occasion, a nurse who had moved into a flat close to the hospital reported being visited by the ghost of a woman wearing a Victorian-style dress. Because of prior commitments, the Rev Holness was not immediately able to visit the flat, but when he was available, the nurse phoned to say that the ghost no longer frightened her. There had been further encounters, and she now saw that the apparition was pleasant in appearance and not at all threatening. In the circumstances, she thought she would prefer the haunting to continue.

Erected in 1865-7, the buildings at the top of Elm Grove now occupied by Brighton General Hospital were used as a workhouse and infirmary until 1930 (though it was used as a military hospital during the 1914-18 War). In 1935, what was known as the Brighton Municipal Hospital was established in most of the buildings on the site. Other buildings were added in 1937 and by 1940 the whole site had been taken over by the hospital. The name was changed to Brighton General Hospital in 1948. In 1999, plans to close the hospital were revealed.

The Rev Holness, in addition to his duties at the Royal Sussex, was the chaplain for various periods of time at other local hospitals. The Brighton General was one of these. At this hospital, in 1979, a number of nurses on night duty in C Block complained that from time to time, while trying to sleep during their one-hour rest period, they had been frightened by some invisible force which had pressed down on them.

While the Rev Holness was aware of the condition known among hospital staff as 'night nurse paralysis' – a rather jokey term used to describe the physical and psychological weariness which can result from the stresses and changed sleep patterns brought about by night duty – the related experiences of the affected nurses indicated that the situation was more serious. As a consequence the minister held a Mass in the day-room of C Block – the room where the incidents had taken place. There were no further reports of this unnerving activity.

One of the best known of the several ghosts said to haunt Brighton General Hospital is the Grey Lady (yes, yet another one!), so called because she wears a long grey dress and a grey bonnet. Whether she was originally a visitor or a member of the nursing staff is not known, but she eventually became a patient and is said to have died in Ward C2.

Halina Seabrook was working at the hospital as an auxiliary nurse in 1968 when, at 8pm, just as she was coming on duty, she encountered the ghost in the corridor of H Block. Shocked, she reported the sighting to her ward sister. The sister said that several nurses and other hospital employees had seen the ghost at various times. The ward sister went on to say that if the Grey Lady was seen in a corridor, it indicated that a patient's death was imminent, but if a nurse heard the ghost tapping on a window, it meant that a patient in the ward was in need of help and she should immediately seek out that patient.

In the summer of 1975, nursing auxiliary Tony Canino was on night duty in the hospital's A4 Block (though later used for outpatient and other services, it still had in-patient wards in 1975). At about 3am he sat down in the ward office to complete his medical notes. Looking up briefly, he was astonished to see through the window beside him that all the lights were switched on in the ward on the top floor of the hospital block opposite. It was surprising because that particular ward had been closed for several days to allow major refurbishing work to be carried out. At night during this time, the ward was normally left padlocked and in darkness. Mr Canino decided to call the night superintendent.

When the superintendent had joined him, they both looked out of the window. The ward opposite was still ablaze with light. A moment or two later, they were surprised to see someone's silhouette passing by the windows. Believing that intruders must have gained access to the ward, the superintendent called night security.

A security officer immediately went to investigate. He found the entrance to the ward still securely locked. Using his pass-key, he cautiously entered the ward, where the lights still blazed. There was no one there, but in the thick builder's dust which covered the floor there was a line of footprints, which indicated that someone had been walking along that floor. The odd thing was that the footprints were only to be found in the central area of the ward. They neither began, nor ended, at a door, nor even a window!

Mr Canino encountered another oddity in October 1976 when he was once more on night duty, this time in F Block. Terminally ill patients tend to lie fairly quietly in their beds, but one particular patient, a powerfully built man, was still robust and active in spite of his grave circumstances, shouting at frequent intervals and thumping on the cot-sides of his bed. This was very disturbing for other patients in the ward, so he was moved to a single room close to the ward office. Despite his apparent vigour, he died at around midnight.

An hour or so later, as Mr Canino and a nursing colleague were in the room putting fresh linen on the bed and generally tidying up, there was an unusual noise at the entrance to the room. It was as if someone was standing in the doorway and briskly stamping their feet, except that no one was there. The nurse in charge was called. The logical conclusion was that the noise was caused by a defective water pipe under the floor, so the duty engineer was summoned, but his investigation failed to find any mechanical reason for the noise, which still continued.

By this time, Mr Canino, a Spiritualist, had already reached the conclusion that the phenomenon might have a supernatural origin, and mentioned this to his colleagues. He said he'd like to try a short invocation.

"If you are a spirit entity," he appealed, "please depart in peace and with the blessing of the angels." Despite his beliefs, Mr Canino was almost as surprised as his sceptical colleagues when the stamping noises ceased immediately.

Ron Marshall joined the nursing staff at Brighton General Hospital in 1946, shortly after being demobilised from the Royal Army Medical Corps. Later, as a staff nurse, he remained at the hospital until 1968. He recalled two inexplicable incidents.

"Sometime early in the 1950s," Mr Marshall said, "I was on night duty in F Block. It was getting along for 3am and I was in the ward office writing my report when I saw a man standing in the office doorway. There was something strange about him, and I felt my skin prickle. He was wearing a white gown, but it wasn't like a modern hospital gown. It was more voluminous.

"As I left my chair to speak to him, he turned and went down the ward. Naturally, as it was the early hours of the morning and something could have been wrong, I immediately hurried after him. I saw him turn into a small side ward where there were just six beds, all occupied by geriatric patients.

"I was close on his heels, but when I went into the side ward, there was no sign of him. All six beds were occupied, but he couldn't have been one of the geriatric patients, for three or four of these were unable to leave their beds without assistance, while the others would not have been capable of walking at the speed of the man in the gown. Anyway, I was so close behind, he wouldn't have had time to get into bed without me seeing some movement.

"Later on during my time at the hospital, I was again writing my report – in those days you always had to hand in a report to the night superintendent before going off duty – when I felt a tap on my shoulder. I mumbled: 'Hold on a moment!' I wanted to finish writing the last couple of lines to complete the report. But then there was a more insistent tap on my shoulder. This time, I swivelled around immediately. But there was no one in sight."

Mr Marshall also referred to a ghost, nicknamed 'Charlie', who was never seen, though sometimes heard by both staff and patients.

"There were some stone steps at the side of F Block where the building overlooks Pankhurst Avenue and you'd plainly hear footsteps coming up these, but no one would actually arrive!"

Mr Marshall went on to work at the Sussex Eye Hospital, the Intensive Care Unit at the Royal Sussex County Hospital and, finally, at Bevendean Hospital, before eventually retiring. Despite the resident ghosts said to haunt the latter two hospitals, his only other odd experience took place at the Sussex Eye Hospital, where he worked for two years in the late 1960s.

This hospital was initially known as the Sussex and Brighton Infirmary for Diseases of the Eye. The original building opened in 1832 and stood in Boyce's Street. In 1846 a new eye hospital opened in Queen's Road, but following the completion of the present building in Eastern Road, the Queen's Road building had a change of use before being demolished in 1961.

Mr Marshall, recalling his experiences at the eye hospital, said: "Nursing staff on night duty were entitled to an hour's break at some time after midnight and they would take advantage of the rest room at the end of what used to be called the Treatment Ward. Nurses would go along to the rest room for a snooze, but they'd sometimes be woken by someone moving around right next to them or by the noise of furniture being moved around in the room. But they'd wake up to find they were alone. It happened to me several times." The hospital has since been refurbished and this rest room no longer exists.

Brighton's most haunted hospital was undoubtedly that at Bevendean, which closed in 1989 prior to demolition and the building of new housing on the site. Bevendean Hospital began its life in 1881, during an outbreak of smallpox, as the Brighton Sanatorium. Initially, it consisted of just three temporary wooden buildings, but eventually work began on a permanent structure. A three-storey building and two separate isolation pavilions were completed in 1898, with two further pavilions being erected in 1903. More buildings were added later. The hospital, which continued to specialise in infectious diseases, became known as the Brighton Borough Hospital, but in 1948, when it moved from municipal control to that of the Ministry of Health, the name was changed to Bevendean Hospital.

The ghost of a woman wearing a long, grey dress appears to have been the hospital's most persistent spectral visitor. She was witnessed quite a number of times over the years, and in several wards, by both staff and patients. She is thought to have been the ghost of a kindly woman who, until her death, regularly visited the hospital carrying a basket filled with food, which she cheerily dispensed to the poorer patients.

Patients and staff in Bevendean Hospital's Ward 5 would sometimes hear what sounded like a woman's footsteps passing by the beds, but no ghost was actually seen. The sound of ghostly footsteps was also heard from time to time in Ward 4, but these seemed obviously male. These heavier footsteps became familiar enough for staff to give the ghost a name – Joey! But Ward 4 had other spectral residents. Indeed, it was believed to be the most haunted ward in the hospital.

Staff Nurse Harry Blacklock worked at the hospital for 34 years until retiring in 1984. He recalled a number of strange happenings during his time there. The first took place during the early 1970s, just after he had been assigned to Ward 4. It was a Sunday morning and he and ward orderly Sheila James were taking urine specimens to the specimen testing room.

"We were walking through an alcove when we both saw a man in a blue dressing gown. Sheila muttered to me that she didn't think the man belonged to the ward we were in, so I turned to speak to him, but as I did so he began to slowly fade away in a sort of downward-moving spiral.

"Sheila spontaneously reacted by reaching out towards the man with her free hand. In that moment it seemed to us that the dressing gown cord around the man's disappearing body had dropped to the ground. It remained on the floor for a second or two after the body had disappeared, then it too faded away."

Some months later, Mr Blacklock was making a cup of tea in the small office at the end of Ward 4. Turning, he saw that a youngish man wearing a hospital dressing gown was standing in the doorway. It was late at night, so Mr Blacklock thought the man must be wanting something and asked if he could help. At this the man smiled, but without replying, turned to re-enter the ward. Mr Blacklock, somewhat puzzled, immediately went after him, but looking along the dimly-lit ward he saw no one in sight other than the two rows of patients in their beds. All seemed to be asleep.

He said: "I was through the door so fast that no one could have reached even the nearest bed. Had a patient done so, it would have taken a few more moments for him to have taken off his dressing gown, anyway, before he could have got into bed."

A more sinister force made its presence felt later in the 1970s. Nursing staff on night duty were entitled to an hour's rest break. Often, they used this hour to catch up on sleep. While more senior staff might have disapproved of the practice, individual nurses and orderlies would frequently use an empty bed in a ward for the purpose, sleeping fully clothed on top of the blankets until woken at a pre-arranged time by a colleague.

Nursing orderly Frank Wilton was due for his rest break at midnight. Finding an unoccupied bed at the far end of Ward 4, he quietly pulled the curtain around the bed so as not to disturb nearby patients, took off his shoes and settled down to sleep. He was eventually awoken by someone, or something, pressing what felt like a pillow down on his face. He struggled frantically to fight off his unseen assailant. After only seconds, the assault on him stopped as abruptly as it had started. Jumping off the bed and pulling the curtain aside, Mr Wilton looked around the dimly lit ward. There was no one in sight but the sleeping patients in their beds.

It could all have been a bad dream, except that an hour or so later,

Harry Blacklock had a virtually identical experience. His break began at 1am. Stretching out on the same bed that his colleage had recently vacated, he was soon asleep. But once more the malign force arrived, with Mr Blacklock waking up to push away whoever, or whatever, was attempting to suffocate him. Again, there was nothing unusual to be seen in the ward.

Mr Blacklock and Mr Wilton were also involved in another curious incident. Mr Wilton was again on night duty in Ward 4, while Mr Blacklock had been assigned to another ward. As he was nearing the end of his duties, Mr Blacklock's ward telephone rang. It was Mr Wilton. He was writing his night report, but wanted some information about a couple of patients to enable him to complete it. Mr Blacklock hurried to Ward 4. After he had provided the information requested, he returned to his own ward. He had been back only a short while when the phone rang again. It was Mr Wilton.

"Do you remember the chair you sat in a few minutes ago when we were talking?" he queried.

"Yes," Mr Blacklock replied.

"Well, only moments after you left, something very strange happened. An old, white-haired man appeared to materialise out of thin air. He sat in the chair you were sitting in, but faded away again after three or four seconds."

Ward 6 also had its ghosts. Patients watching TV in a small room at the end of the ward would occasionally find themselves tapped on the shoulder by some unseen being. And on various occasions, other patients claimed they had seen nurses wearing old-fashioned uniforms moving around the ward. More unnerving was the weird experience of a female nurse on night duty.

A patient had died that night and after the body had been transferred from the ward to the hospital mortuary, the nurse stripped the bed. After she had removed the pillows from the pillowslips, she decided to air them on the balcony. A strict instruction applicable to all night nursing staff was that doors opening onto the balconies should be checked to ensure that they were properly locked and bolted – insomniac patients wandering onto a balcony in the dark would obviously be at risk.

This nurse knew she had checked the balcony doors; knew that they were locked. But as she approached the double doors, they suddenly crashed fully open. She dropped the pillows and screamed, waking most of the patients in the ward.

A strange occurrence took place one night in Ward 8. A nurse coming on duty wondered why two nuns were visiting one of the women patients at such a late hour and asked if the patient had taken a turn for the worse.

"Nuns?" queried the nurse going off duty. "There are no nuns in the ward."

"But I've just seen them," persisted the first nurse.

The two nurses dashed out of the office where they had been standing and looked down the ward, which was illuminated only by a pilot light. There were no nuns; only the sleeping patients. The patient visited by the phantom nuns died a short time afterwards.

Dr Rose Hunter was employed at Bevendean Hospital for about 20 years before retiring in 1977. Some two years prior to her retirement she was completing her rounds in a ward that was primarily occupied by patients with chest infections. As she approached the corridor by the entrance to the ward she spotted a nurse walking past. She thought it was a nurse she had been wanting to speak to concerning a particular patient, so hurried after her.

As Dr Hunter stepped into the corridor, she had a rear view of the nurse, who was only a few yards away. Then the nurse, as if she had had a sudden change of mind, turned and went into the nearby kitchen. Dr Hunter, still a short distance behind, immediately followed her into the kitchen, but looking around saw no sign of the nurse she wanted to speak to.

The doctor asked nearby staff where the nurse was who had just preceded her. The reply was that no one had entered the kitchen for several minutes. Baffled, Dr Hunter insisted that she had followed a nurse who had only, two or three seconds before, walked into the kitchen. The doctor was then asked to describe the nurse, which she did.

"Oh!" responded one of the staff present, "I know you might find this hard to believe, but I think you could have seen a ghost. Your description is the same as other staff who have seen it. It's the ghost of a nurse who died while looking after patients during the smallpox outbreak."

The outbreak referred to began in December 1950 after an infected RAF man, Flight Lieutenant Hunter, had briefly stayed in Brighton on returning from India. Bevendean Hospital, which admitted most of those infected, was placed in quarantine for more than a month. By the time of the all-clear in the following February, ten people had died, including three nurses.

In 1988 auxiliary nurse Nadia Hillier had an odd experience while on duty in a second floor ward at Bevendean. At the time, the hospital was being run down prior to its closure, and the ward Nurse Hillier was working in was, as part of the closure procedure, only partly occupied by patients. These were soon to be transferred to other hospitals, or discharged altogether.

A third of the ward was already filled with empty beds and stacked-up chairs and lockers. This area was curtained off from the patients. It was a bright, sunny day and at the entrance end of the ward, Nurse Hillier stopped for a moment to speak to a colleague, Nurse Avril Carter. As they talked, Nurse Hillier saw another nurse cross the far end of the ward, immediately in front of the curtain hiding the redundant beds and other furniture. The nurse, she observed, then seemed to go behind the curtain.

Which was odd, Nurse Hillier thought, for the exit at that end of the ward was locked. In addition, she hadn't spotted the nurse entering the ward in the first place. But much odder was the fact that the nurse she'd seen was wearing an old-fashioned nursing uniform with a hemline that finished at the ankles.

Nurse Carter was facing a different direction, so hadn't seen the strange nurse. She expressed surprise that another nurse could have entered the ward without being seen by either of them. Nevertheless, Nurse Hillier was so positive she'd seen someone that she hurried to the end of the ward and looked behind the curtain. There was no one there. Nor could anyone have moved through the tightly stacked furniture.

Nurse Hillier spent three months at Bevendean prior to the hospital's closure. She then transferred to Brighton General Hospital where, in the autumn of 1992, she had another strange experience while on night duty in C3 Ward. Taking her rest break at 3am, she strolled to the day-room, the TV-equipped room normally used as a lounge by patients, stretched out on the sofa that was there, covered herself with a blanket and settled down for a short sleep.

She hadn't been asleep for long before she was woken up by someone pulling the blanket up over her head and pressing down on it. She struggled to push the suffocating blanket away from her face. Sitting bolt upright, she looked around her. There was nobody else in the room. She found her body covered in a cold sweat.

Following the closure of the Bevendean Hospital in 1989 and its subsequent demolition, it would be logical to think that any ghostly activity would have been obliterated with it. Not so! It seems that despite the construction of a new residential estate on the site of the former hospital, one building of the old complex remains and it is here that a variety of bizarre events took place until as recently as the autumn of 1995, when a church minister was brought in to conduct a prayer service to rid the building of its unquiet spirits. This building is the Bevendean Sports & Social Club which, despite its present-day exterior, is actually a conversion of the building formerly used as the hospital's social club.

Early in 1995, Tony Button, the then manager of the club, was clearing up in the main club room following the end of a late-finishing social function. At about 4am, he was using the vacuum cleaner when he thought he heard his name being called. Switching the equipment off, he heard nothing, so presumed he must have been imagining things.

He was about to switch the machine on once more when he again heard a voice. This time, with the vacuum cleaner switched off, his ears were not mistaken. It was the voice of a woman and, quite clearly, it was calling his name. The manager knew that no one else was in the building, for he had personally ensured that everyone had vacated the building before locking up.

This wasn't the only incident at the club involving a strange voice. Barmaid Amanda Medwin (not her real name) was going down from the snooker room and had just passed through the door at the bottom of the stairs when she thought she heard someone say "Hello!" It sounded like a man's voice.

Turning, but seeing nobody, she walked on. Again, a voice called "Hello!" Puzzled as to who it could be, she retraced her steps to the door. There was still no one in sight, so thinking it might have been the door making a strange noise, she opened and closed it. It moved quite silently. As she walked away, the voice again called "Hello!" This time, without looking back, the unnerved Miss Medwin hurried away.

There is another snooker room on the premises. This is in the basement and some staff refused to go into this room alone because of its peculiarly unsettling atmosphere. This sense of discomfort also seemed to prevail in the adjoining cellar.

Working in the kitchen one day in 1995, Amanda Medwin was loading the electric glass-washing machine with used glasses. Naturally, the machine was switched off during this time, yet while her arm was still inside the glass-washer it suddenly switched on of its own accord, sending jets of scalding water over her arm. The burns necessitated hospital treatment. In addition to the machine being switched off, the door of the machine was open. Because of an in-built safety mechanism, this would normally have prevented the machine from working, even if the 'On' switch had been pressed.

On another occasion the glass-washer mysteriously switched on, even though the door was open, when Miss Medwin and Eli Sandoz, who was employed in an upstairs office, were in the kitchen making coffee. Miss Sandoz straight away switched it off. Later, the two women were walking through the bar, which was closed at the time, when they noted that the cash register, which had been switched off, was now illuminated. Once, when Miss Sandoz was alone in the kitchen, a saucepan standing on a rack above the sink flew through the air to land at her feet.

Over a period of months, other club employees reported being present when, without warning, the electric kettle in the kitchen switched itself on.

In addition, the lighting in the kitchen, as well as in the bar, frequently dimmed or flickered, a phenomenon witnessed by a number of people, both staff and club members. Sometimes, the lights went out completely for a few seconds before returning to normal. Other incidents included inexplicable rappings on walls and the noise of doors opening and closing when no one else was present, heard by administration employee Lisa Irvine and Miss Sandoz.

Miss Irvine and colleague John Gayfer sometimes had the feeling of a presence watching them while working on the first floor of the club, while Miss Sandoz once had the impression of of a man standing in the office doorway. He was wearing a blue dressing gown over pyjamas.

One of the oddest experiences at the club was that of cleaner Leanne Burton. She was working in the reception area when she saw a woman wearing brightly-coloured clothes emerge from the door at the bottom of the stairs leading down from the upstairs office. The woman then walked across the reception area and through the door leading to the toilets.

Because Mrs Burton was engaged in her cleaning duties at the time, she didn't look too closely at the woman until she had reached that door, but noted fleetingly that she had long dark hair. Seeing this, she presumed the woman to be Miss Sandoz, who also had long dark hair, so she was most surprised when, a moment or two later, Miss Sandoz came down the stairs, for she was wearing a completely different dress to that of the mystery woman.

As the club was closed at the time, it now seemed likely that the woman in the bright clothing was a stranger (questioned later, Mrs Burton described the dress as being of 1960s style). When the woman failed to reappear, Miss Sandoz went into the toilets to investigate. She found no sign of the mystery woman, and no door by which she could have left without being seen. A seemingly successful prayer service to terminate the haunting took place at the club in September 1995.

9 Studies in the supernatural

BRIGHTON COLLEGE, founded in 1845, appears to have more than one resident ghost. The college began its history in Portland Place with the establishment of a day and boarding school for boys. Encouraged by a positive response to this enterprise, a larger, more permanent building was soon being planned. The new college building, designed by Sir George Gilbert Scott in the Gothic style, was constructed on the north side of Eastern Road. The foundation stone was laid in June 1848 with the Earl of Chichester performing the official opening ceremony a year later. Over the years, other buildings have been added. Girls were initially admitted to the college in 1973, but only to the sixth form. The college has been completely co-educational since 1988.

Though not seen for many years, the ghost of a boy wearing khaki uniform once haunted the college chapel. The spectre, thought to be that of a cadet in the college's Officer Training Corps, used to be seen in the vicinity of the chapel organ. One witness was Jack Burnett James, the father of thriller author Peter James, who saw the spectre in the early 1920s.

Another ghost is said to be that of Canon William R Dawson, headmaster of the college from 1906 to 1933. Dorothy Fenwick, matron at the college between the 1920s and 1950s, saw the apparition several times, twice in the college library. She recognised the ghost as being that of the former headmaster.

A third college ghost, that of a woman attired in a grey, Victorian-style dress, has been seen in the school hall and in the armoury.

Roedean School, undoubtedly the best-known girls' school in the UK, was founded in 1885 at Lewes Crescent with an initial roll of just ten girls. It expanded into other premises before moving to Sussex Square as the Wimbledon House School. Further growth led to the building of a new school on an 18-acre site purchased from the Marquess of Abergavenny. Building commenced in March 1897, with Roedean School opening in

January 1899. Subsequently, more land was purchased and other buildings and facilities added.

A ghostly presence has been associated with the school chapel and a nearby gymnasium, which were linked by a cloistered area. Since the 1980s, when the gymnasium was converted to other uses (it is now a language laboratory), there have been no further reports of supernatural activities.

A woman in a grey dress haunts Moulsecoomb Place, Lewes Road. This former manor house, together with the 315-acre estate on which it stands, was bought by Brighton Corporation in 1925 and has been used at various times as a school annexe, a branch library and as the headquarters of the Parks Department. The building was acquired by the University of Brighton in 1993 and is currently in use as an administrative centre for student services and welfare.

While the facade of Moulsecoomb Place was built in 1790, some of the construction behind it is of earlier origin. A south wing was added in 1906. The timber-framed cottage situated at the rear of Moulsecoomb Place is the oldest secular building in Brighton. It dates back to about 1500, although some references quote 1350-1400. The cottage has been used by the Moulsecoomb Social Club since 1930. Both Moulsecoomb Place and the cottage are said to be haunted by the mistress of James II. Legend has it that she committed suicide by drowning herself in the well by the cottage. There have been several sightings of the ghost.

Fred Ellis, a lorry driver with the Parks Department, once occupied the residential flat at Moulsecoomb Place. He is said to have seen the ghost on several occasions during his stay. A secretary working in the building also saw her.

The most detailed account of the phantom comes from contract supervisor Vic Kemp who, with his family, occupied the flat from 1962 to 1972. Early one morning in 1970, he awoke to find a woman leaning over his bed. She was dressed in a long, grey gown and a bonnet-type hat. There was a slight haziness about her appearance. Mr Kemp looked on in astonishment as the woman then walked over to the casement windows, where she seemed to go through the motions of adjusting curtains before finally leaving the room. She did this by walking straight through the closed door!

Gwen Bashford, who was stewardess of the Moulsecoomb Social Club at the beginning of the 1980s, often felt there was some supernatural presence in the club's cottage premises which especially manifested itself on the first floor. She once had the experience of lights on this floor constantly switching on and off without cause.

In the late 1970s, Jack Poulton, who joined the club in 1960 and who has been a committee member for 29 years, was going up to the first floor to prepare the disco equipment in readiness for an evening social event, when he felt that someone was on the stairs behind him. He turned to look, but saw no one. After a few more steps, the impression that someone else was on the staircase grew stronger, so he looked around again, but there was still no one in sight.

On nearing the top of the stairs, Mr Poulton became aware of a quite electrifying atmosphere and felt the hair at the nape of his neck rising. The sense of someone ascending the stairs just behind him was now very strong. Apprehensively, he turned his head once more, but found the staircase empty.

In former years, some club members noticed a spine-tingling atmosphere when finding themselves alone in one of the first floor rooms – once a table tennis room, it was later used for playing pool. The sensation was of some indefinable entity standing close by. Mr Poulton was among those who experienced the phenomenon. By the end of the 1980s, whatever entity was responsible seems to have abandoned the room, for more recent years have passed without incident, but whatever spirit might have tarried there, it continued its activities elsewhere in the building.

In more recent years, Bert Batchelor, the entertainments secretary, heard footsteps pacing across the first floor when no one else was present, while Sharon Poulton, Mr Poulton's granddaughter, was once sitting in one of the club's ground floor bar areas with her boyfriend, Kevin Gulliver, when she noticed something almost imperceptible moving across the stage in the club's bar. She had the impression of a woman in her early twenties.

On a Sunday morning in 1996, two children playing in the vicinity of the club's cottage premises were startled to see a woman's face peering out of the window of the short linkway that connects the cottage to Moulsecoomb Place's converted tithe barn (now used for conferences), for they believed the building to be empty and locked.

When club officials arrived just before midday to unlock the premises in readiness for lunchtime trading, the children told them of the woman they believed was trapped in the building. The premises were searched, but no woman was found, and it was confirmed that the building had earlier been properly secured against intruders.

Halls of Residence for students existed in Percival Terrace and Eastern Terrace until recent times, though some of the houses were also used for educational purposes. The ten listed houses in Percival Terrace were built between 1845 and 1850. Numbers 1 and 2 were used for teacher training by the Brighton College of Education. Numbers 7 to 10, at least in later years, were primarily residential for the use of Brighton Polytechnic students. Brighton Polytechnic, established in 1970, merged the Colleges of Art and Technology. The College of Education was absorbed in 1976. Eventually, Brighton Polytechnic became part of the newly established University of Brighton.

In the mid-1960s, Collette Clark was a student residing at 10 Percival Terrace. While there, staff told her that the ghost of a woman wearing a long, grey dress had been seen on several occasions in the basement refectory. In addition, and without human aid, lights dimmed or switched on and off. On 13 November 1987, the front of number 10 collapsed completely when a large crater opened up in front of the house. Number 9 was also made unsafe, and both houses were demolished. They were eventually rebuilt.

Eastern Terrace consists of nine impressive four-storey houses, all built between 1822 and the mid-1840s. Sir Albert Sassoon occupied number 1 from 1876 to 1896. The oriental-looking Bombay Bar (part of the Hanbury Arms), to the rear of the house, was originally built in 1892 as a private mausoleum for Sir Albert. In 1914, the house was converted into the Court Royal Hotel, another conversion taking place in the 1950s when it became Court Royal Mansions.

While there are no reports of this building being haunted, the same is not true of some of the other grand houses in Eastern Terrace. A number of these have been divided into flats and Peter and Elisabeth Nicola, a married couple occupying one such property, had the first inkling that there was something unusual about their flat in 1991, shortly after moving in. In bed at the time but with the light still on, they were startled to feel the bed sag on one side as if someone had sat on it. Fully awake, they turned at once to look, and were startled to see a depression in the bed. It was as if some unseen form was sitting there.

Over the following months, lights, radiators and their TV set inexplicably switched on and off at various times. One electric switch left permanently in the 'on' position was situated behind a panel which had to be unscrewed to gain access, but this fact was no obstacle to whatever force had flicked it off.

Number 9 Eastern Terrace was for a time the seaside residence of the exiled King Manoel II of Portugal after his country had, in 1910, become a republic (his main residence-in-exile was in Twickenham). At one point in its history the property was converted to become the Royal Sussex Hotel, but it was a brief existence. In 1919 the building was taken over by the Municipal Training College, a teacher-training establishment, which remained there until moving to Falmer in 1965, by which time it was known as the Brighton College of Education.

In subsequent years number 9, along with the later acquired numbers 7 and 8, were used primarily as halls of residence by Polytechnic – and later, University of Brighton – students. These properties were vacated in 1995 prior to conversion for private residential use.

There are several strange stories associated with these three houses. Many years ago, a scullery maid who worked in one of them was found hanging from a meathook in the basement, having committed suicide. Whether the strangely cold spots sometimes encountered in various parts of the house have anything to do with this tragedy, or whether they have a more mundane cause, is not known.

In September 1995 Lyn Allard was in one of these houses, carrying out some preliminary cleaning prior to moving in. She had timed this task to coincide with a visit by a gas fitter, who was to connect the supply. As she worked on an upper floor, she became aware of a presence. Her sense of unease increased when, although the air was still, two doors opened and closed of their own volition.

Some time later the gas fitter arrived, brought upstairs by the cleaner from the adjoining house. Mrs Allard took the opportunity to mention the odd happening to the cleaner, who promptly informed her that the place was haunted by a young girl carrying a teddy bear under each arm.

Number 9, as already mentioned, was at one time the seaside residence of Portugal's King Manoel II. During his stay at the house, the servants' quarters were situated in the basement. In later years, after the property had been taken over for the use of students, this basement was where the students took their meals. And it was in this basement refectory that students sometimes heard a most unexpected sound.

Christmas is the time when most students head for home, but for various reasons, a sprinkling of students usually remained. On 25 December 1994, three University of Brighton students who had decided to spend their Christmas locally were passing the entrance door to the refectory when they were surprised to hear the sound of carol singing coming from within. Puzzled, they tried the door, but found it locked. The singing continued for a few moments more, and then stopped. From within, there was now complete silence.

When the new term started, one of the three students, Sophie Lombard, decided to make enquiries. Catering staff told her that she and her friends were not the first to have heard the unexplained sounds, for the carol singing had been heard in previous years. It was presumed that King Manoel's servants had once sang carols on Christmas Day, and that over the following years, some unearthly means had allowed these voices from the past to return and haunt the present... but only on Christmas Day!

On another occasion, it was the chef who had an unusual experience.

He always kept a box of matches on a shelf in the refectory's kitchen. The first to arrive one morning, he was surprised to find that the matches had been scattered over the floor; especially so because he had been the person responsible for locking up the kitchen at the end of the previous day. He was even more surprised to find the phenomenon repeated over the following two nights.

10 *Stage frights*

BRIGHTON HAS A FINE theatrical tradition, though the town's first theatre was a modest one. This opened in 1764 and was really just a barn on the north side of Castle Square which had been converted into a theatre large enough to serve the few thousand people then living in the town. Unfortunately, the season ended abruptly each year at harvest time when the barn reverted temporarily to its conventional use!

The final performance in these unpretentious surroundings took place in 1770, but four years later a small theatre was erected in North Street. This in turn closed its doors in 1789, following diminishing attendances and an acrimonious quarrel between the theatre's proprietor and its manager, but it wasn't long before the licence was transferred to a building in Duke Street. Here, performances continued until 1806, with the theatre being demolished the following year.

A year or so before the theatre closed, the Prince of Wales made an official visit and subsequently, the name Theatre Royal was adopted. When a new theatre was built in New Road in 1822, the name was continued (with the Prince of Wales, when resident in Brighton, regularly attending performances). While there has been considerable rebuilding of the Theatre Royal's interior at intervals over the 170 or so years since, it still retains its atmosphere of opulence.

Other theatres and music halls opened in the 1800s and early 1900s to provide for the town's expanding population. During the 1930s and immediately following the Second World War, local residents and visitors had a choice of at least six theatres. With the passage of time, however, the growth of television took its toll.

The resident ghost at the Theatre Royal has, over the years, been seen on more than a few occasions by actors, staff and theatregoers. Known as the Grey Lady because she usually appears in a grey dress, she is just one of several Grey Ladies haunting theatres in Britain – among them the Theatre Royal in Drury Lane, the Theatre Royal in Bath and the Connaught Theatre in Worthing.

Sightings of the Grey Lady at Brighton's Theatre Royal were being reported well before 1960, but in that year Melville Gilliam, the theatre's manager, encountered her backstage. Ten years later, manager Jack Keates spotted the Grey Lady outside Number 1 dressing room. He thought she looked like the actress Sarah Bernhardt, who had appeared in *La Dame Aux Camelias* at the theatre, but descriptions of the ghost indicate it is more likely to be that of Mrs Nye Chart, a former manageress and actress, who with her husband ran the theatre from 1867 until his death, and who continued to manage it until her own death in 1892.

In 1970 Jack Peach found himself alone for a few seconds with the Grey Lady after he had entered the Number 1 dressing room. Later in that decade, reported stage manager Roy Roe, the actor Martin Jarvis was twice tapped on the shoulder by some unseen entity as he was washing the make-up from his face in Number 2 dressing room.

Joy Merta, who for 12 years supervised the bar nearest to the theatre's entrance, in 1976 reported seeing the Grey Lady sitting in a corner of the bar. The bar was otherwise empty, for the theatre had only just opened. As Mrs Merta went about preparing the bar for the first rush of customers, she was a little surprised to see the woman, for she hadn't noticed her arrival.

"She was wearing a lovely grey chiffon dress," Mrs Merta said. "She seemed to be a very gentle lady and was in no way frightening, but before I could say anything, with a sweet smile she vanished. The odd thing about the apparition was that it didn't seem to have any feet or ankles."

In 1981 an usherette reported seeing the Grey Lady. In August the following year, actor Gerald Flood was appearing in Alan Ayckbourn's comedy *Relatively Speaking*. One morning during the run of the play, Anne Flood, his wife, was busy in the theatre's laundry room when she heard a door banging. As the noise was distracting her, she hurried along the corridor to close it.

As she tried to push against the door, she felt something resisting on the other side. Opening the door fully, she found herself facing a woman wearing a grey dress. The dress was tight about the waist and had a full skirt. On the woman's head was some grey veiling. She seemed to be aged between 50 and 60 and was about 5ft 6ins in height.

Aware of something unearthly about the woman, Mrs Flood felt unable to move or speak. In the next moment, the apparition walked briskly past her. Not long after, storeman Alan Harmsworth arrived at the theatre to comment spontaneously on the strange atmosphere pervading the building.

Mrs Flood said later: "I had the immediate feeling it was a dead person. She had silvery hair and a commanding presence. She was visible for about a minute."

Around the same time, electrican Steve Costello, who was employed part-time at the theatre, was required to work through the night to complete an installation job in the gallery area. He knew he was alone, so when a close-by male voice said "Good evening!", he jumped with shock. Apprehensively looking around him to confirm that he really was alone, he quickly descended from the gallery and, unnerved, left the completion of his task until the following day.

On 23 October 1984 the *Evening Argus* reported that Sylvia Randall was backstage during a rehearsal of *Carousel,* in which she had a leading part, when she saw a woman unknown to her in the No 1 dressing room. Thinking it might be an intruder, she returned within seconds, but found no sign of the woman.

She felt sure she would have noticed, had the woman left the dressing room. Mrs Randall described her as being aged about 35 and wearing a long white dress with puffed sleeves. If this was indeed a ghost, it was quite unlike the theatre's more usual apparition in grey.

In the mid-1980s, entertainer Danny La Rue was appearing at the theatre. Arriving in his dressing room prior to an evening performance, he was surprised to find that the wigs he used in his act had been moved away from where he had placed them. He knew he had left his dressing room locked, for in addition to the wigs, he was concerned about the safety of his stage costumes and other personal items.

Later in the same week, he again found that the wigs had been switched around during the time the dressing room had been locked. Nothing else had been moved. His subsequent enquiries revealed that only the cleaner had entered the room and she insisted she had not touched the wigs.

Danny La Rue said later: "The way the wigs had been left seemed to indicate that someone had been trying them on. I don't know if the theatre's Grey Lady was responsible. I like to be open-minded about these things, though I once had an odd experience when I was appearing at the Theatre Royal in Bath, which is also said to have a ghost. While there one evening, I felt a forcible tap on my shoulder, but on turning I found nobody there."

In the same week, Wayne King, Danny La Rue's pianist at the time, had a more unnerving experience. Ascending the stairs to the 'gods' prior to rehearsals to get an idea of what the stage looked like from that elevation, he paused for a moment by a door at the top of the stairs.

Resting his hand on the handle of the door, he appreciatively looked around at the theatre's ornate decor. In the next moment he felt a heavy pressure on his hand. It was as if someone or something unseen was pushing downwards and he was horrified to find that, however hard he tried, he was unable to wrench his hand away from the door. As a pianist, his hands represented his livelihood, so Mr King was especially concerned. Moments later, the pressure ceased as suddenly as it had been applied and he found he was able to remove his hand quite easily.

In the 1980s, sound and lighting technicians Ian Hardy and Steve Brown were brought in to install special lighting at the theatre in readiness for a presentation that was to begin the following day. The task meant they would have to work through the night. During the early hours of the morning, both became amazed witnesses of the spectral Grey Lady. At the time, neither knew the theatre was reputed to have a ghost.

"It was around 4am when we saw her," said Mr Hardy. "I'm not quite sure of the year, but I think it was 1986. She had an old-fashioned grey dress on and we saw her up in the gods. She walked towards the bar area before disappearing behind some curtains.

"I didn't immediately tell Steve I'd seen what I thought was a ghost. I assumed he'd think I was imagining things. It wasn't until later, when we were having a chat, that he admitted that he'd seen the woman as well, but like me he hadn't wanted to appear foolish."

The Grey Lady was also seen in the 1980s by barmaid Liz Sullivan, who was alone in the stalls bar at the time. Towards the end of the 1980s, a male cleaner who had been working in the theatre during the morning and who was required for further duties after the Thursday matinee, decided to remain in the theatre and watch the afternoon performance. He occupied an empty seat at the back of the stalls.

Looking around the theatre, he was astonished to see a woman sitting behind a small family group in one of the boxes. He felt there was something strange about the woman and he noted that the group seemed to be unaware of her presence. In the next second or two, he noted, the woman had vanished.

In 1996 Michael Cashman was appearing in a play called *Love*. One night, after the audience had left the theatre, he sat alone in the darkened auditorium, enjoying the peace. After a few moments, he heard footsteps coming towards him and turned to peer through the gloom, but could see on one. He called out, but there was no response, so he quickly left.

The following night he again sat on his own and once more he heard the tread of phantom footsteps. This time he was definite that he also felt a ghostly presence. When he returned to the theatre in 1997 to star in *The Tempest,* he was hoping to experience further evidence of some spirit entity, but it was not to be.

Impresario David Land, owner and chairman of the Theatre Royal from 1984 until his death in 1995, spoke to a number of actors and members of staff who claimed to have seen the Grey Lady.

"They were quite adamant about what they'd seen," he said, adding:

"Personally, I've never experienced anything paranormal while in the theatre, but I must admit that it can be an eerie experience to walk alone through the place after dark."

The ghost of Vesta Tilley haunts the Hippodrome, the one-time variety theatre in Middle Street, which is currently a bingo hall. Of course, no one is absolutely sure the ghost is that of the famous old-time music hall entertainer, but descriptions of the apparition do tally with her likeness as depicted in old photographs.

The Hippodrome was one of Miss Tilley's favourite theatres. She enjoyed a drink or two, and spent many talkative hours in the theatre's Tudor bar. This bar has long been closed and the manager's office now stands where much of the bar was situated. It is in this area that Vesta Tilley's ghost has been seen.

Prior to his retirement, maintenance man Alfie Brett spent almost all his 50 years of working life at the Hippodrome and saw the ghost on several occasions. Though initially frightened by the spectre's appearances, he eventually came to accept that the spirit was a benevolent one.

Another maintenance man, Ray Cathcart, was interviewed on local radio in the mid-1970s. He confirmed that the 'kind, friendly-looking' apparition was supposed to be that of Vesta Tilley and claimed that several people had witnessed her, some seeing her in a black dress, while others had referred to a grey dress.

The last person known to have witnessed the ghost was Ivor Novell (no, not Novello!), who was at one time responsible for the sale of bingo books at the Hippodrome. He later took up a managerial post elsewhere. Box office cashier Peggy Murthwaite recalled the night Mr Novell saw the apparition.

"It was back in about 1977," she said. "Ivor came racing down the stairs and blurted out that he'd seen the ghost. He was as white as a sheet."

While the spectral Vesta Tilley hasn't been seen for several years, some Hippodrome staff have noticed that the temperature in the area once occupied by the Tudor Bar appears on occasions to be unnaturally chilly compared with other parts of the building.

The Hippodrome initially opened in 1897 as Brighton Ice Rink, but in 1901 it was enlarged and converted into a circus and theatre. As the Hippodrome, it went on to become the town's leading variety venue. Its days as a theatre ended in 1965, after which it briefly found a use as a television film studio. Its transformation into a bingo club took place in 1967.

The Grand Theatre, which once stood in North Road, also had its ghost – or ghosts. It opened in 1891 as Ginnett's Circus. In 1894, it was converted into the Eden Theatre. The policy of offering the public a wide variety of entertainments continued after the name had been changed, in 1904, to the Grand Theatre of Varieties.

In 1931 a new owner, taking advantage of the 'talkies' boom, converted the theatre into a cinema. It continued in this role until October 1940. In 1941 it reopened as a variety theatre. The Grand Theatre finally closed in 1955, after which it was converted into a factory for the manufacture of reproduction furniture. The premises were destroyed by fire in 1961.

The Grand probably had more than one ghost. The faint, eerie strains of a band playing *Take Me Back To Dear Old Blighty* were sometimes heard in the theatre. This ethereal music could be linked to a tragedy of many years ago when a First World War soldier was found to have hanged himself backstage.

Theatre staff became familiar with the unearthly events which took place from time to time. A recurring incident was the slamming down of 15 seats in the second row of the 'gods'. They would thump down in succession. It was a phenomenon which usually took place when the theatre was empty but for the cleaners. Two cleaners once found themselves looking at a young bride, beautiful in her wedding dress and carrying a bouquet. Although she looked real enough, it was a ghostly vision that dissolved as they watched.

During and after the Second World War, the Grand featured shows that were just within the censorship restrictions imposed by the Lord Chamberlain. One popular artiste was Phyllis Dixey, who appeared in nude tableaux (performers were prohibited from moving while unclothed). Presentations had such titillating titles as *Red Hot and Tasty* and *Peaches and Screams*. The downmarket trend was the theatre's desperate response to the combined threat posed by cinema and television. Gresham House now occupies the site.

The *Evening Argus* of 26 September 1979 reported some bizarre goings-on at the Gardner Arts Theatre, on the University of Sussex campus, which was completed in 1969. Cleaners told of hearing clanking noises above the stage of the theatre which were a prelude to the appearance of a spiral of grey, wispy smoke which swirled from one side of the stage to the other.

"It's pencil slim and curly," said cleaner Phyllis Mann, "and when it appears, everything goes cold. A couple of us have seen it more than once, It's quite scary when you're on your own in the place."

Supernatural or not, it seems to have been a short-term phenomenon, for there were no repeat performances in subsequent years!

11 *Media mysteries*

UNDERSTANDABLY, given the nature of their work, journalists and press photographers tend to be a cynical lot, but while newspaper staff might be expected, among themselves, to gently ridicule any ghost stories that come their way, what is the position when the haunting is on their own doorstep?

In the 1970s, when the head office of the local *Evening Argus* was situated in North Road (it is now in Crowhurst Road), three of the newspaper's photographers had experiences they found hard to explain. Each baffling event took place in the area of the photography office and darkroom, situated on the top floor of the building.

On one occasion, photographer Dave Bennett needed to change the film in his camera. To avoid spoilage, for he was handling partly-used film, it was necessary for him to use the darkroom. Closing the door of the darkroom behind him, he flicked off the light. As he began to remove the film, he sensed he was not alone and turned his head. There, standing some three feet away from him and slightly luminous in the dark, was a woman with a child in her arms.

Mr Bennett was unable to describe what clothing the woman and child wore, but he had the impression that the woman was aged about 30 and the boy about eight or nine. Immediately on seeing the ghostly mother and child, he shot out of the room as fast as his legs would take him. He insisted that he hadn't imagined things, and added that the paucity of remembered detail was due to his not remaining long enough to look fully at the spectral pair.

A quite different experience, reported in the 9 June 1977 issue of the *Evening Argus,* came the way of chief photographer Dennis Wixey. He had gone into the darkroom late one evening at a time when structural alterations were in progress.

"I was up there on my own when something climbed on my back," Mr Wixey said. "My clothes stuck to me as if there was a high wind, and whatever it was didn't get off until I had gone back through the door into the office."

Another photographer, Jerry Casswell, was drying off pictures in the darkroom office one night at about 11pm when he felt a presence behind him. Turning, he was astonished to see, some 20 feet away at the far end of the office, the figure of a man dressed in a long highwayman-style topcoat. The coat reached down to his ankles and had four short capes hanging across the shoulders. On the man's head was a tricorn hat. This unexpected visitor from the past appeared to have lost his left arm below the elbow.

"I don't believe in ghosts," affirmed Mr Casswell, "but what I saw I just can't explain. The face of the man was a greyish-green colour and to some extent in shadow, but he looked a most evil character. His clothing was also greyish-green in colour. It may seem an odd thing to have done, but I shouted at him to go away.

"In fact, I swore at him. Then I turned back and carried on, somewhat fearfully, with what I was doing. I hardly dared look again to see if he'd gone, but after a minute or two I did turn around and was relieved to see he'd disappeared."

In addition to the experiences of the photographers, other employees working in the photography area reported hearing ghostly footsteps.

Major rebuilding work took place at the North Road premises in the late 1970s. This included the addition of a 'penthouse' floor close to the photography department. As has already been mentioned in this book, refurbishment work often results in a cessation of ghostly activity, and this seems to have been the case in this instance. In December 1999 the whole of the former *Evening Argus* building, including what had been the printing works in Robert Street, was devastated by fire.

Jerry Casswell once had a peculiar experience while on duty away from the office. During the mid-1970s, he and a journalist colleague were despatched to the house of a medium who was due to visit an allegedly haunted council house after she had been invited to rid the building of its troublesome spirit.

Once at the medium's house, Mr Casswell and his colleague sat down in the living room to enable the medium to outline what she would be doing and the journalist to ask questions. The men observed two paintings standing on the mantelpiece above the fireplace; one at either end. The medium explained that these were 'spirit paintings' depicting her Red Indian guide.

Mr Casswell was sitting in an armchair about three feet away from the mantelpiece, listening to what was being said, when the painting nearest to him shot off the mantelpiece and hit him on the back of the head, fortunately with only the lightest of blows.

"While I was shocked," he said, "I think the medium was even more shocked. She seemed rather embarrassed and didn't appear to know quite what had happened."

Elsewhere in Brighton another building involved in the business of disseminating local news became the focus for a series of strange events over several years. These took place at the BBC broadcasting station situated at 1 Marlborough Place.

When local radio began to take off in the 1960s, BBC Radio Brighton was one of the first to commence broadcasting. The station officially opened in February 1968, though the station had broadcast emergency blizzard warnings in the previous December.

In 1983 an extension of coverage led to the station changing its name to BBC Radio Sussex. In 1993, after a period when non-peak output was shared with BBC Radio Surrey, both stations adopted an umbrella name, BBC Radio Sussex and Surrey. Some months later saw the broadcasting of identical programmes from Guildford.

The station was renamed BBC Southern Counties Radio in 1994, the new name resulting from a poll of listeners. With Guildford now confirmed as the radio station's headquarters, the Brighton operation was substantially reduced. A language school now occupies a substantial part of the premises, though a residual BBC presence has expanded in recent times.

These premises were once part of a hotel, the Blenheim, whose main frontage was in Church Street. An upper part of the hotel extending to the corner of Marlborough Place was primarily used as an accommodation wing for staff. Here, a young chambermaid committed suicide by leaping out of a window. Her action is believed to have been the consequence of sexual harassment by a senior member of staff. The girl's tragic death appears to have initiated a series of supernatural events, but the unfortunate chambermaid may not have been alone in haunting the building, for there have also been reports of at least one male ghost.

Geoffrey Draper worked for the BBC at Marlborough Place as a freelance producer and presenter for more than ten years until 1994. He regularly worked in the preparation/production studio situated on the top floor where, on occasions, he noticed an inexplicable drop in temperature.

"I often worked in the studio," he said, "and when this fall in temperature took place it was quite odd, for you would find that the sensation of cold wasn't present in every part of the studio. You could stand in one place and the temperature would appear normal, then you'd move two or three paces into another part of the studio and you'd find the temperature noticeably lower."

A similar experience befell Ian Collington, a producer at the radio station between 1978 and 1993. At around 2am one morning in 1979, he was working alone in the top floor studio when he became aware of a dramatic drop in temperature, seemingly of several degrees.

"I was intrigued, and searched for a cause," he said. "It obviously wasn't the air conditioning or anything else like that, yet I knew I wasn't imagining things."

Mr Collington was to share an even more baffling experience during the afternoon of 26 November 1993. The day was a very busy one, being devoted primarily to programmes supporting the BBC Children in Need charity. He was working in the top floor studio with his assistant, Ann Nehammer. Because of the extra workload and the charity aspect, Mrs Nehammer's daughter, Annaliese, had joined them to lend a hand.

Annaliese had just placed a sheet of A4 paper into the typewriter she was using when the paper inexplicably began to flip rapidly backwards and forwards. This activity stopped for a moment, then recommenced once more before again coming to a halt. Then for a third time the paper began to flip backwards and forwards. Annaliese was baffled by this, for there was no indication of a draught. The phenomenon was but a prelude to something yet more bizarre.

There were two steel storage cabinets standing against one of the walls in the studio and on top of one of these was a large cardboard box. To the astonishment of Mr Collington and the two women, the box suddenly shot off the top of one cabinet, flew over the top of the second cabinet, then landed on the floor with a mighty crash. It sounded as if the box had been filled with glassware of some kind, but when the box was opened it was found to be empty!

Once, while working alone on the top floor, producer Chris Warbis heard the sound of a girl crying. Mystified, he searched the top floor area, but found nobody there.

The radio station's record library was situated on the third floor. Ghostly footsteps were sometimes heard in the corridor outside of the library, while the smell of perfume would curiously hang in the air. Though the smell of perfume might be associated with the spirit of the chambermaid, the ghost of a young man is also said to have haunted this floor.

Stewart Macintosh was a presenter at the station from 1974 to 1979. Late one night in 1976 he was in the library, preparing records and material for the next day's *Coastwise* programme. As he was the last person in the building, on completing his task he switched off all the lights, returned to the ground floor and went out into the street. He then made his way to where he had parked his motorcycle.

He had just set off for his home in Shoreham when he realised he had omitted to lay out some listeners' letters with their music requests – everything had to be absolutely ready because of the morning's early start – so he turned around to make his way back to Marlborough Place. On re-entering the building he was still wearing his motor-cycle gear; a black nylon overall suit and a red crash helmet.

BBC staff were able to use a lift shared with the insurance company occupying the adjoining offices in Church Street and Mr Macintosh used this to take him back to the record library. As he stepped out of the lift into the darkness of the third floor vestibule, he found himself facing a remarkable apparition which was moving rapidly towards him. There was no time to move out of the way and the entity walked right through him.

Mr Macintosh said: "It was a misty white form coming out of the dark. The shape was that of a human, but the outline was vague. The figure was slightly built, so I suspect it was that of a woman. There was a sense of sadness about the figure and when it passed through me it felt like ice."

Production assistant Jill Donald was employed at the radio station from 1978 until the operation moved to Guildford. On several occasions during this time she came across what she believed was the smell of a perfume, which she thought was that of Parma violets, an inexpensive scent very popular in pre-war Britain. No cause could be found for this smell. She recalled particularly a day in the mid-1980s when her duties required her to dash up and down the main staircase several times, for she kept encountering pockets of the perfume. On another occasion she was working in the basement when she was grabbed by the shoulder. She turned to find nobody there.

Liz Budai, a record librarian at the station from 1979 until 1994, was one of several BBC people who heard phantom footsteps walking along the corridor by the record library. She also came across the smell of a perfume 'like Parma violets' during her time at the station.

"Interestingly," she said, referring to the variety of odd happenings associated with the building, "the incidence of these events seemed often to coincide with the construction work taking place. To meet changing broadcasting needs, there were fairly frequent alterations to the studios."

There were yet other paranormal events associated with the two top floors of the building. Drinks of all kinds were, understandably, kept well away from records and recording equipment, but on one occasion a presenter was astonished to see an almost full mug of coffee shoot some distance from the table on which it stood to splatter some records with the hot liquid. On another occasion, without warning, a plastic toy dinosaur shot off a desk to land several feet away!

On the upper floors, lights sometimes switched on and off of their own accord. The last employee to leave the building might switch off all the lights, lock the doors, then step into the street and look up, only to see that the lights were on again on one floor or another.

Pat Jameson, a newsroom copytaker and secretary at the radio station from 1973 to 1994, was one employee who had a startling experience involving the lights. It was around 3pm one Saturday afternoon early in 1994, and she had gone up to the top floor to use the photocopier. On completing her task, she went down the staircase leading to the ground floor.

The staircase lights had been left on at each floor so, as sunshine was streaming through the windows, Mrs Jameson switched off the lights at each floor as she descended. On reaching the foot of the stairs she paused. In that moment she was shocked to see the top floor lights come on again, rapidly followed by the lights on the other floors.

"It was like a chain reaction," Mrs Jameson said. "The lights just flicked on one by one of their own accord from the top floor downwards. It was quite weird!"

But this wasn't Mrs Jameson's first experience of the radio station's supernatural aspect, for two years after joining the BBC she was making her way down to the second floor and had reached a small flight of stairs leading from a mezzanine floor situated between the second and third floors, when she became aware of someone just behind her. It wasn't that she heard any sound, but she felt a distinct movement of air, together with that sixth sense that tells you someone is close.

There was a door immediately in front of her. Presuming that whoever was behind her must be in a hurry, she quickly pushed the door open and moved sideways so that they could pass. In that brief moment she felt a chill breeze, and in the early evening light that trickled through the small window nearby, she perceived something grey, wispy and ill-defined sweep past her. At the time, Mrs Jameson was unaware that the building was supposed to be haunted and she insisted that her experience was not due to any trick of the light or her imagination.

Beverley Thompson, a BBC reporter working from Marlborough Place, had several brushes with the inexplicable. Once, at around 8.30pm, she was working in the ground floor newsroom. Against the wall on one side of the room was a long desk and on this rested about 200 recording tapes. These were bulky tapes, and they were stacked in groups of ten with each group being securely bound by vinyl tape. Suddenly, despite the fact that the tapes were attached in this way, a single tape shot onto the floor. A moment or two later, two piles of tapes tumbled to the floor. Ms Thompson observed that these tapes had been too far back on the table and too carefully stacked to have fallen of their own accord.

In January 1995, at around 7pm, Beverley Thompson was working in one of the two basement studios. A monitor screen there was linked to a video camera in the reception area. This enabled BBC staff to see who might be waiting in the reception area, for some of these visitors would have arrived to take part in a programme due for imminent transmission.

There was a sudden cry of surprise from one of the people working in the studio. Alerted by the exclamation, Ms Thompson and her colleagues turned to look at the monitor. What they saw appeared quite mystifying. They could see the body of someone walking backwards and forwards, but whoever it was must have been so close to the camera that only a part of the body could be seen.

However, what Ms Thompson and her colleagues were looking at was physically impossible, for the reception area camera was positioned close to the ceiling and looked downwards. This meant that anyone picked up by its lens was reproduced on the monitor as a full length, foreshortened figure with the head, being nearest to the camera, appearing disproportionately large (which was an aid to identification). No reason could be found for this puzzling incident.

The most disturbing paranormal event affecting Ms Thompson took place in May 1996. She was on duty in the newsroom with two of her colleagues. Some time later she left the room to go to the ground floor toilet. On opening the door, and before she had time to reach for the light switch, she saw someone standing in the corner of the toilet.

Caught in the shaft of light coming through the door from the corridor behind her, Ms Thompson thought at first that she was, somehow, staring at her own reflection, but in the next instant realised that this could not be so, for the figure she was looking at was much shorter than herself; perhaps less than 5ft tall, compared to her own height of 5ft 9ins. In addition, the figure was wearing a long, old-fashioned grey dress. At this point, Ms Thompson realised that she must be facing something supernatural. Shocked, she immediately returned to the security of the newsroom.

The basement of the building, where Studio 2 was situated, wasn't immune from the unusual. Here, broadcasting equipment sometimes malfunctioned for no apparent reason. Tape recorders unexpectedly turned off, for example, while on one occasion the hands of the studio clock whizzed around alarmingly. There was also the occasional but unexplained smell of burnt toast. This basement was rumoured to be haunted by the ghost of a former janitor.

Betty Shine, the internationally-known medium and author of several books dealing with psychic powers and the supernatural, was interviewed at the radio station on a number of occasions. Following upon one of the last of the broadcasts she made, she stayed on to carry out an exorcism. This appears to have been successful, for there were no further reports of paranormal happenings in the building.

12 *Unregistered guests*

THE OLDEST HOTEL in Brighton is the Old Ship. The earliest mention of its existence dates back to 1665 when it was an inn, but the original building could have been erected at least a century earlier, for there are records of an unnamed building on the site in 1559.

The hotel didn't initially overlook the sea. It was tucked away in a side street, Ship Street, from which it expanded over the years (Ship Street was once known as Ye Hempshares, for hemp, used by local ropemakers, was grown in the vicinity).

The hotel's most renowned proprietor was Nicholas Tettersell, captain of the coal brig *Surprise* who, in October 1651, helped Charles II escape to France after the king's army had been defeated by Oliver Cromwell's Roundheads at the Battle of Worcester.

Following the Restoration, the wily Tettersell set out to remind Charles II of the life-saving service he had rendered. Repainting his coal brig and renaming it *The Royal Escape,* he sailed up the Thames to anchor where his boat was sure to be seen by the reinstated monarch. The ruse paid off. Tettersell was appointed captain of his own ship on naval pay and with an additional pension of £100 a year. In 1671, he acquired the Olde Shippe, as it then known. Later, he was elected the town's High Constable.

In 1751 a Dr John Burton stayed at a local inn, believed to be the Old Ship. He subsequently wrote in a letter: 'The streets were thronged with people and most appeared to be needy and wretched.' But a new, more prosperous era for the town was just beginning.

First Brighton was, following the eulogistic writings of the eminent Dr Richard Russell, gaining renown for its sea-water 'cures'. Second, it was to benefit from its continuing association with the Prince Regent. During this time, the Old Ship enhanced its reputation as a rendezvous for high society with the Prince Regent himself gracing some of the dances held in the hotel's ballroom. With such a long history behind the hotel, some supernatural consequences to that history might be anticipated. Certainly, there have been baffling incidents.

Many years ago a chambermaid entered a bedroom in the hotel's older west wing and discovered a man and woman sitting on the bed. The chambermaid was just beginning to apologise for her intrusion, for she had believed the room to be unoccupied, when the couple faded away before her eyes.

In 1986, a night porter clearing up the stage area of the hotel's ballroom was shocked to see a ghostly figure gliding alongside the wall to his left. The form was ill-defined and slightly misty, so he could not tell whether it was male or female.

Late one night the following year, two night porters were in the hotel's otherwise deserted main foyer. One was sitting in a leather winged-back armchair, while the other was standing next to him. Their conversation stopped abruptly when they saw a mist begin to form close to the bottom of the nearby stairs. Astounded, they watched as it expanded until it was about 3ft high, when it materialised into a small, silently crying child. A few moments later, the child faded away as inexplicably as it had arrived.

A few months after this, head night porter Cyril Fox was patrolling the hotel, carrying out a security check. It was around 5am. After walking through the Gresham Room, he reached the swing doors of the ballroom. Despite the emerging light of dawn outside, the ballroom was still very gloomy due to an absence of natural light in the area.

As he made his way through the ballroom towards its kitchen area, he felt a hefty blow on his left shoulder. He looked around him, but in the dim light could see nothing that might have caused the blow. Switching on the lights confirmed this observation.

Another haunted hotel is the Royal Albion, situated opposite Brighton Pier (otherwise known as the Palace Pier). The hotel, which opened in 1826, though the western wing is of later construction, stands on the site of Russell House, built by Dr Richard Russell in 1754 and demolished in 1823.

The 'Royal' prefix was added to the Albion's name in 1847, but late in the 19th century the hotel was allowed to run down before closing in 1900. Its saviour was Harry Preston (later to be knighted), the charismatic owner of the nearby Royal York Hotel, who bought the Royal Albion in 1913, refurbished it, and turned it into a meeting place for the famous (the Royal York Hotel, sold to Brighton Corporation in 1929 following Harry Preston's retirement, was converted into offices, and is now known as Royal York Buildings).

It is said that the ghost of Sir Harry Preston still haunts the Royal Albion, especially in the area of the function room which bears his name. Here, the visitor may become aware of a sudden and inexplicable chill in the air or see doors open and close of their own volition, in some instances even when they have been wedged or had a chair placed against the handle. The hotel's lift has also moved up and down without apparent cause. Night porter Justin Brown observed that these incidents nearly always took place on a Sunday evening.

In 1985 an engineer was working in one of the hotel's larger bedrooms when he received a severe blow on the ear. He was alone at the time. It was no imagined blow, for his ear remained swollen for several days. Peculiarly, even on the most sweltering of summer days, this particular room was noted for being unusually cool when compared to other rooms in the hotel. For commercial reasons, the room was divided later into two with a separating wall. From that time, the room's temperature remained normal.

A remarkable incident took place in 1989. Hotel maintenance man Adrian Grant and four work colleagues were enjoying a tea break in the office attached to the basement workshop, situated under the Harry Preston Room, when they heard the noise of a heavy stone or pebble hit the floor of the workshop before bouncing two or three times.

The window of the office looked out over the workshop and the office door was open, but none of the five hotel employees saw anyone enter the workshop, nor did they hear anyone coming down the staff staircase, which then had loose, metal nosings on each step which rattled when anyone used the stairs. When two of the men left the office to investigate, no stone was found.

In November 1998, a large part of the Royal Albion was destroyed by fire. Time will tell whether the fire has brought the hotel's haunted history to a conclusion. The hotel reopened for business in September 2000.

The Metropole Hotel (now the Hilton Metropole), in King's Road, opened in 1890 to become the largest hotel in the country outside London. Just prior to its opening, some 1,500 visitors travelled by train from London to enjoy a private viewing.

A number of curious and inexplicable incidents have taken place at the hotel. In 1981 a waitress was preparing a table in the Cameo Room (later renamed the Windsor & Arundel Room), when the tablecloth and its contents suddenly shot about 10 feet into the air before crashing down again. The waitress screamed and held up her arms protectively as crockery, cutlery and glassware tumbled back onto the table and the floor around her.

A year or so later, night cleaner Patrick Kenny was working in one of the hotel's upstairs corridors. Wall lights along this corridor are decorated with hanging glass beads. Though the air was quite still, the beads hanging from one of the light fittings were observed to be swinging so violently that they clinked against each other. Yet all the other lamps in the corridor seemed unaffected.

Intrigued, Mr Kenny walked along to the light. Lifting his arms, he held the beads still for a moment, but immediately he released them they again began to gyrate. There was no evident reason why the beads should have moved so strangely.

Mr Kenny decided to call the night manager and both men witnessed the phenomenon. The beads were again held still, yet once more they swung around on being released. However, a few moments later, the beads abruptly ceased their gyrations and remained as still as those hanging from the wall lights along the rest of the corridor.

There have been reports of unusual drops in temperature in the vestibule area of the Metropole's sixth floor where, many years ago, a night porter died while on duty. A baby has also been heard to cry in the front, eastward part of this floor on a number of occasions and similar crying has been heard in one of the hotel's lifts, though no baby was present on these occasions.

The Belgrave Hotel, at the corner of King's Road and West Street, was built in 1882 as the Orleans Residential Club, but in 1898 it was refurbished before re-opening as the Victoria Hotel. It was known as the Sheridan Hotel until mid-1998.

In 1987, the hotel's night porter found, shortly before he had completed his duties, that six fire extinguishers had been laid out in a line at the bottom of the hotel's main staircase. It was early in the morning and he knew they had not been in that position two hours before when he had patrolled the area.

He found that three of these extinguishers had come from the kitchen. Another was from a store, one was from a staircase and one came from a goods lift. It could have been a practical joke perpetrated by another member of staff, or even by a customer, except that the kitchen and store had been locked all night and the porter had control of the keys. There have been no reports of supernatural activities at the hotel since that single incident.

In his book *Haunted Britain,* author Elliott O'Donnell mentioned two haunted buildings in Brighton, though he failed to identify their precise location. One was a boarding house described as being near the Royal Pavilion, where Albert Glovert, a resident of Kensington, stayed during the summer of 1922.

On his third day in Brighton, Mr Glovert went for a long walk prior to returning for tea. As he went upstairs to his room to freshen up before the meal, a woman wearing a green dress and holding a handkerchief to her face came down the stairs towards him. He thought this might be because she had neuralgia or some other complaint. It was a very hot day and he was surprised to note that the woman, taking into account the high temperature, had chosen to wear a dress of quite heavy material. After she had passed by him, he thought little more about her.

At about noon the next day he was walking along the first floor corridor towards the main staircase when he saw the same woman, still holding a handkerchief to her face, come out of a bedroom ahead of him and make her way to the landing, where she entered another room. Sensing something peculiar about her, he questioned a maid, who replied that she hadn't seen anyone answering the description given. Mr Glovert was on the verge of speaking to the landlady about the matter, but then decided she might not take kindly to his enquiries.

Two days later, as he was returning to his room, he again saw the woman in the green dress. She was walking ahead of him along the corridor, and he was surprised to see her stop by the door of his bedroom. She then turned around and slowly took the handkerchief away from her face.

The sunlight flooding into the corridor threw every feature of the face into strong relief. She was fairly good-looking, except for her mouth, which Mr Glovert thought quite ugly. It was agape and showed long, yellow teeth protruding like great tusks, particularly the eye-teeth, which had gold fillings which glinted in the sunlight. At the same time, there was a bleak look in the woman's eyes. In the next moment, the woman reached out her hand and opened the door of his room before going in. Bewildered, Mr Glovert rushed in after her, but on swivelling his eyes around, he was astonished to see no sign of the woman.

He tackled the landlady about the affair as soon as he could, but she indignantly denied that the boarding house was haunted and suggested that he must have had an hallucination. During the remainder of his stay, Mr Glovert saw no more of the apparition.

Two years later, and quite by chance, he met the landlady at a friend's house in Kensington. In the ensuing conversation, she told him that she had given up the house in Brighton and confirmed that it was indeed haunted. Though she had not seen the apparition herself, others had, but not wishing to scare visitors or maids, she had preferred to play the matter down.

The other haunting referred to by Elliott O'Donnell was that concerning a restaurant near Brighton seafront. In the spring of 1937, Robert Claydon was having lunch in the restaurant. As the waitress approached his table while bringing him his second course, she stumbled and fell, the food she was carrying being scattered across the floor. Mr Claydon hurried to help her to her feet, while another waitress came over to clear up the floor. The waitress who had fallen assured him that she was unhurt, but when he left he felt obliged to give her a generous tip though, he was later prepared to admit, he also found her very pretty.

A year later he was again in Brighton and resolved once more to have lunch at the restaurant, where he hoped to be served by the same attractive waitress. He was disappointed to see no sign of her, but remained to be served by another waitress. As she returned to his table a few minutes later, a similar accident happened to the one he had witnessed previously. As she passed the same spot in the restaurant, she stumbled, and the tray of crockery she was carrying crashed to the floor.

This time the waitress seemed badly shaken and frightened, and Mr Claydon heard her tell the supervisor that she had been tripped. The supervisor refuted this suggestion, and went on to tell the waitress that she had been told always to avoid this part of the floor.

Noting that the floor was quite smooth, Mr Claydon was a little amused, but also intrigued by what he had heard. When a different waitress brought his sweet, he questioned her. She said that several waitresses had fallen at the spot for no apparent reason, usually at about the same time of year. She added that they had been instructed to avoid walking past that particular spot.

Mr Claydon resolved to talk to the manager about the matter. At first the manager was hostile, almost rude, but when he had been assured several times that his questioner had nothing to do with the Press, he admitted that there was something strange about the small area of floor where the waitresses had stumbled.

He said he had managed the restaurant for about 20 years, but shortly before he started work there, one of the customers had died at that spot in peculiar circumstances. The manager said that from that time on, and at that precise spot and at a similar time of year, though not in every year, waitresses had mysteriously been tripped by something unseen. He went on to say that it was feared that the waitresses might spread a story that the restaurant was haunted, so to prevent this, and also so as not to frighten them, they were told that something was wrong with the floor and that they should avoid walking past there.

In 1970, Nadia Hillier was employed as a waitress at the Wimpy Bar in Old Steine (Shakies Grill now occupies the premises). While she was there, the first floor restaurant was closed briefly for refurbishment.

Working with Miss Hillier was another waitress, a Sri Lankan girl. This waitress, needing to visit the toilet, and aware that the one on the first floor was now out of use, asked if there was another toilet in the building. She was told that there was one in the basement.

After a minute or two, the waitress was back up from the basement, shaking with fright and barely able to speak. It seems that she had opened the toilet door to see, standing before her, the legs and feet of a little girl... but nothing else of her body! There were white stockings on the legs, while on the feet were black, patent leather shoes with silver buckles.

About a fortnight later, Miss Hillier went into the Queen's Head pub, in Steine Street, which backs onto the premises then occupied by the Wimpy Bar. As she sipped her drink, she mentioned the 'ghostly legs' incident to one of the barmaids. On referring to the white stockings and silver-buckled shoes, the barmaid cried out in surprise.

"That must be our ghost," she exclaimed, and went on to say that the ghost of a little girl had appeared one night after closing time when the female staff, including herself, were waiting for a taxi to take them home. The girl, with her hair in ringlets and wearing a white dress with an apron, had materialised for a short while on the bar counter. She had sat there with her legs dangling over the side, and seemed to be crying bitterly, though no sound was audible. There were white stockings on her legs and black, patent leather shoes with silver buckles on her feet!

The barmaid understood that the ghostly girl had been seen by other bar staff in past times, and that there was a connection with a fire at the pub long ago which caused some deaths.

On 13 June 1974 the *Evening Argus* reported that the Brunswick Restaurant, 67 Ditchling Road, was haunted by a plate-smashing ghost. Mike Wilde, the restaurant's owner, told reporter Wendy Taylor that the poltergeist-type activities had begun the previous December, just after he had taken over the restaurant.

From that date until being interviewed by the reporter, Mr Wilde said that at least one plate or saucer was found smashed every week, although on one occasion 26 saucers crashed to the floor in a single incident. Initially, being sceptical about psychic phenomena, he was reluctant to put any paranormal label on the breakages, which seemed to take place when no one was in the kitchen. Then early one evening while busy frying potatoes, he actually saw a plate leap from a wall rack and speed through the air to smash on the kitchen floor a few feet away. Some weeks later, a pan holding peppered steaks glided off a burner and landed under a table some four feet away.

Mr Wilde was especially puzzled because the saucers were made of green, heat-resistant glass and in normal circumstances were virtually unbreakable. One day, he decided to experiment by forcefully throwing a couple down onto the kitchen floor. They shattered into tiny pieces. However, Mr Wilde pointed out, when they were found broken as a consequence of paranormal activity, the broken pieces were always large.

Interestingly, all the paranormal activities took place in an area of the restaurant which was once, prior to structural changes, just a small room. As the incidents continued, Mr Wilde decided to contact Ian Barclay, a church minister, who carried out an exorcism. This, apparently, proved ineffective, for soon after the exorcism, two ashtrays and a glass containing spoons were seen to slide from a table and float to the floor.

After reading the *Evening Argus* story, Charles Page of Sandgate Road contacted the newspaper to say that the ghost could be that of his mother, Maud Wares, who had died aged 44 after prolonged ill-treatment at the hands of her second husband. She and Mr Wares ran a general store on the site which was later to be occupied by the Brunswick Restaurant.

Mr Page said that his stepfather frequently hit his mother and often threw plates at her. Although her medical certificate stated that she had died in childbirth, a few days earlier she had been hit with a trowel and the child she had been expecting was born dead.

Just before she died, Mrs Wares called out: "The will, the will!" Which was puzzling, for no one knew anything about a will. However, Mr Page suggested that where the plate-smashings had taken place was where the small living room used to be and where his mother kept her papers.

However, the nature of the paranormal activity and the fact that it lasted only weeks indicates that a poltergeist-type phenomenon was at work rather than a conventional ghost. This is probably confirmed by the fact that nothing of a paranormal nature has taken place at the Indian take-away which has now occupied the premises over several years.

The *Brighton & Hove Gazette* of 26 October 1979 reported a haunting at Leadbelly's Restaurant, in New Road, next to the Theatre Royal – the Il Teatro Restaurant now occupies the site.

Patrick Sullivan, the manager of Leadbelly's, claimed that the ghostly activities had started on the night he arrived at the restaurant, when a knife flew through the air past his eldest daughter, Vanessa. Where it had come from was a mystery.

On another occasion the till key went missing. The staff gave up after spending the best part of an hour searching for it. They had even taken up the carpet to look. Later, they were flabbergasted to see the key lying on the carpet.

Staff at the Theatre Royal next door reported hearing strange knocking sounds coming from the restaurant in the afternoons during the time Leadbelly's was closed with no staff present. One waiter claimed he had seen an old man sitting in the basement. The apparition had quickly faded. Staff at the Il Teatro, which has occupied the premises since 1986, have noted nothing unusual.

Former proprietors of the Brighton Belle Restaurant, in Middle Street, had to contend with unaccountable knockings and other phenomena, while the nine-year-old son of one owner was shocked to find himself facing a male apparition. At some time in the past, a man living on the premises is said to have committed suicide by hanging, and this dreadful termination of a life could account for the restaurant's supernatural intrusions.

Mr Jun Jun, an Indonesian, and his business partner Brian Ferguson, had several baffling experiences after taking charge of the restaurant. One day in 1997, when there was no one else in the building, they were busy preparing for opening time. All of a sudden, the handle of the door leading from the restaurant to the first floor started to rattle noisily, after which the door swung open. Puzzled, Mr Jun Jun went over and closed it, making sure that the latch had clicked into place. Just moments later, the door shot open again.

On another occasion, they were both upstairs watching TV when a plastic replica of a birth-stone that was standing on the nearby mantelpiece suddenly shot upwards to hit the ceiling before ricocheting off at an angle to strike the TV screen.

Once, a painter and decorator engaged to carry out some work in the restaurant stopped to take a short break from his task. Sitting at a table with a cup of coffee, he turned his eyes to look out of the front window of the restaurant.

Presently, he was surprised to see three photographs, which had been standing close to each other in the window, fall to the floor, but not all at once. They fell consecutively, with a fractional interval in between, as if someone had flicked each one off the ledge in turn. The workman put them back where they were.

When Mr Jun Jun came downstairs, the man related what had happened. A few minutes later, when both were present, the phenomenon repeated itself, the photographs falling down in exactly the same order. There were no draughts to account for the incident.

13 *Old Town pubs*

In this and subsequent chapters, the term 'landlord' is used in its broadest and most popular sense to include owners, tenants, managers and others in charge of the day-to-day, on-the-spot activities at a pub.

IN 1800, BRIGHTON – or Brighthelmstone as it then was – had a population of 7,300 and a total of 41 inns and public houses, but as the population grew, so did the number of licensed premises. By the 1890s there were 572 public houses and beerhouses (pubs without a spirits licence) in the town, and the average family spent 15 per cent of its income on alcohol. There were 26 pubs in Edward Street alone; a dangerous district where policemen patrolled in pairs. The town's population at the time totalled 115,400. Today, with a population of about 150,000, Brighton has some 300 pubs.

Many Brighton pubs are well over 100 years old. Some are more than 200 years old and a few even have a history extending to 400 years. A surprisingly high number of these are reputed to be haunted. Indeed, at least 30 local pubs are, or have been, haunted in one way or another. That is roughly one local pub in every ten, a statistic likely to bring the broadest of cynical smiles to the face of the unbeliever. But read on!

About a third of these haunted pubs are situated in the Old Town – that part of Brighton bounded by East Street, North Street, West Street and the seafront, while the majority of pubs in the tight maze of narrow streets in and around The Lanes seem especially to have been a focus for one ghostly incident or another.

The Black Lion pub, in Black Lion Street, stands on ground once occupied by the Black Lion Brewery, which was established about 1546 by Deryk Carver, a Flemish immigrant. The brewery in those times was often used for clandestine Christian meetings.

It may seem odd that a brewery should be used in this way, but Carver lived in turbulent times when religious divisions were sharp and religious tolerance minimal. If your beliefs didn't accord with those in authority, you joined congregations who met in secret. Deryk Carver eventually paid the penalty for his beliefs and activities, becoming the first Protestant martyr. Apprehended towards the end of 1554, he was burnt in a barrel 'at the signe of the Starre', in Lewes, on 22 July 1555.

There were two previous Black Lion inns in the street. The first stood at the south end, close to the former marketplace and overlooking the then existing cliff top. About 1789, its name was changed to the Thatched House. Another Black Lion was built almost opposite the Black Lion Brewery, but this was demolished early in the 19th century.

The Black Lion Brewery closed in 1968 and the building was demolished a few years later. The present Black Lion pub was built in 1974, substantially to the specifications of the former brewery and using many of the original flint cobbles and slates. The 16th century cellars remain. The newly built pub was initially called the Deryk Carver to commemorate the brewery's founder, but the traditional Black Lion name soon replaced it.

In the late 1980s a barman working in the cellar was stunned to see several crates of beer move around as if being pushed by someone unseen. On another occasion a former manager went into the cellar to find that the reserve gas cylinders (used in the beer-supply process), which had been left strapped to a wall, were now scattered across the floor, though the straps holding them were still buckled up.

In 1995 several building workers were brought in to carry out renovations at the pub. While the project was under way, they were accommodated in the first floor function room. One night, one of the workers was lying in bed awake when he saw a silent, shadowy figure materialise and then move around the room before vanishing. The room was only illuminated by the light of the street lamps from outside, so he was unable to see any detail. The light was sufficient for him to check that his colleagues were still in bed and asleep. None of the building workers had been aware of the pub's ghostly reputation.

Only Black Lion Lane, a narrow twitten, separates the Black Lion from the Cricketers Hotel. The Cricketers is probably the oldest pub in Brighton – it is said to have been built in 1545. It was orginally called the Last and Fish Cart (a last equalled 10,000 fish), though at the time the locals referred to it simply as The Last. Inscribed above the door was the verse:

Long time I've looked for good beer,
And at 'The Last' have found it here.

The name was changed in 1790 when it was taken over by a Mr Jutten, a keen cricketer who played for Brighton when the town fielded its own cricket team. The architecturally interesting 'Green Yard' at the side of the pub was the last site of the town pound – as late as 1887 a flock of sheep was impounded there after the drunken drover had been arrested.

Graham Greene, the author of *Brighton Rock* and *The Third Man,* is among many celebrities who have frequented the Cricketers. Even Jack the Ripper may have stayed there briefly prior to his dreadful murder of five London prostitutes. This claim was made by Melvin Harris in his book, *The True Face of Jack the Ripper.* He suggested that Jack the Ripper was really Roslyn D'Onston, a journalist, black magic practitioner and former army surgeon, whose stay at the Cricketers during the time it was residential fitted in with the overall facts of the case.

Author Ivor Edwards, in a later book, *Jack the Ripper's Black Magic Rituals,* also reaches the conclusion that the infamous murderer was Roslyn D'Onston and that he had, in 1888, stayed at the Cricketers immediately prior to carrying out his grisly deeds in London's East End (bizarrely, Edwards also suggests that D'Onston murdered Edmund Gurney, the well-known psychic investigator. Mysterious circumstances surround the death of the latter, who at the time was staying at the Royal Albion Hotel).

The Cricketers has long been associated with ghostly events. Jan Jackson was its manager from 1993 to 1996. One night, soon after moving in, she was woken from her sleep by the sound of barrels being rolled across the cellar floor.

"There was no mistaking the sound," she said, "but when I went down to investigate, not a barrel was out of place."

Other unexplained incidents were to follow. Bottles and glasses unaccountably fell off shelves, doors slammed shut of their own volition and the serving of beer would stop in mid-session as a consequence of the gas cylinders in the cellar inexplicably turning off. In addition, Mrs Jackson sometimes felt a nearby presence when she was alone in the bar.

Once, when Mrs Jackson was about to go downstairs from the residential part of the pub to the ground floor, her French poodle, Remy, refused absolutely to budge from the top floor landing. The dog must have sensed something unusual, for when Mrs Jackson went downstairs without the dog, every light she had switched on while descending flicked off of its own accord.

A live-in barman at the pub, on a number of occasions when lying awake in bed, heard the sound of footsteps ascending the staircase when he knew no one was there.

He said: "An intruder would have been attacked by the poodle, but when these particular footsteps were heard on the stairs, she just growled anxiously and kept her distance."

Graham Matless, who was in charge of the Cricketers' small first floor restaurant for nearly two years from 1995, had some quite odd experiences. On two occasions while he was there, some brandy glasses shot off a shelf to land right way up on the floor. The strangest event, however, took place one night soon after the restaurant had closed.

One of his duties was to 'cash up' the till situated in the small bar adjoining the restaurant, but before doing so he went around the restaurant to blow out the candles on each table. On completing the cashing up, he returned to the restaurant, only to be confronted by the sight of every candle being once more alight.

Edward and Sue Griffiths managed the Cricketers from March 1996 to January 1997. On three occasions during this time Mrs Griffiths observed the spectral figure of a man. He wore a long black cloak and a wide-brimmed black hat. The face of the man was pale and ill-defined.

Once, Mrs Griffiths saw the man in the bar. On the two other occasions, he was ascending the stairs to the first floor – once immediately behind a barman who was also going upstairs. The barmen on these occasions saw nothing unusual, but while she was behind the bar one day, a customer who had not visited the pub for some years came in and referred to the pub's ghost. Unaware that Mrs Griffiths had seen the spectre, he went on to describe its appearance. His description tallied with that observed by her.

Paul Nash, who became manager of the Cricketers in August 1997, had only been at the pub for four months when an agitated woman went up to him one night to report that she had just had an eerie experience. Closing time at the pub had already been called and the last customers were leaving. At this point she went to the ladies' toilet, where she found the lights already off. Undeterred, she made her way inside. While there, she felt two hands stroke her forehead. She insisted there was no one else in the toilet at the time. At least, no human!

Mr Nash observed that locked internal doors at the pub were sometimes found open again for no identifiable reason while, similarly, a rope that was each night placed across the bottom of the stairway leading to the first floor was, from time to time, found to be unhooked the following morning. In addition, some pierrot dolls displayed on shelves in the bar appeared to have a life of their own, shooting to the floor when no one was around.

Author's note: While cask conditioned beer (real ale) is drawn up from public house cellars by hand pump, keg beers (sparkling bitter, lager, and some stouts), plus most ciders, reach the bar through being propelled along the beer lines (tubing) by a mixture of (in most instances) oxygen and carbon gases released from gas cylinders. If these cylinders are turned off – it takes three or four full turns of a cylinder's rotational valve to do this – the service to customers is immediately halted.

For some unaccountable reason these gas cylinders appear to have a fascination for whatever paranormal forces tend to be at work in haunted hostelries. While the toppling of glasses and bottles, the opening and closing of doors and the switching on and off of lights, all without human aid, might be thought of as fairly predictable activities in ghost-afflicted pubs, none of these phenomena compare in frequency with those involving gas cylinders. The Black Lion and the Cricketers have already been mentioned in this respect, but in fact, about half of the haunted public houses featured in this book have had problems with gas cylinders.

Publicans and bar staff can't be accused of imagining things when the supply of beer stops right in the middle of a busy lunch-hour session, so I checked if there might be a mechanical reason for the cylinder failures (this problem is very rare in non-haunted pubs). The technical manager of a leading supplier of gas cylinders to the licensed trade told me that he already knew of the problem and had himself been called out on two occasions to allegedly haunted premises – a pub and a night club – where the cylinders were spontaneously turning off. He failed to find any technical reason for the malfunctions. In one instance he found the valve mechanism so stiff that it took quite an effort for a human to turn it!

The Bath Arms, in Meeting House Lane, was built in 1864 as the True Briton Inn. Only three years were to elapse before its current name was adopted, influenced no doubt by the number of fashionable health baths being opened in Brighton. One of the pub's early landlords is said to have committed suicide by walking into the sea and swimming towards the horizon.

The spectre of a man wearing a tricorn hat was witnessed in the bar in the 1980s. This is not the only apparition to be seen in the pub. Towards the end of 1993, Marie Dooley was clearing up in the bar after midnight when she briefly saw the ghost of a middle-aged man leaning against a ceiling support pillar. He was wearing a black, Victorian-style overcoat and a black, brimmed hat.

In the early part of the same year, assistant manager David French saw an empty pint glass shoot several feet off a shelf and smash onto the floor. Other bar staff (and even a few customers) have, at various times, seen bottles, glasses and other items move of their own volition.

The Druid's Head, in Brighton Place, is so named because a ring of stones, believed to be associated with Druidic rites, was located nearby. The building is said to date back to 1510, when it was probably a private residence. A beer licence was granted in 1830.

Refurbishment work carried out in the early part of the 1960s indicated that the building originally stood alone in its own gardens. Two tunnels, now blocked up, run from its cellar. One leads directly to the sea and was once used by smugglers. The other, running in the direction of the Royal Pavilion, was said to have been used by the Prince Regent who, frequently in debt, may not have been averse to purchasing free-of-duty contraband. It has also been suggested that he used the tunnel for secret assignations with women.

Lurking somewhere in the Druid's Head is the spectre of a man who is believed to have died in one of the tunnels. There is a rumour that two children also haunt the pub. Whether these ghosts have been responsible for the strange happenings taking place over the years is a matter for conjecture, but glasses and bottles have been known to move around on the shelves and slide along the bar counter without human aid.

Les Walker, tenant of the pub for 28 years, claimed that each of his three daughters had seen the ghost of a man, while Katey McElroy, who worked as a barmaid during the 1970s, recalled several spooky incidents.

"We used to sit in the bar after closing time and suddenly the lights would go down and then come on again. The dimmer switches were checked and new circuits put in, but it made no difference. And there was a mirror on the stairs which misted over for no apparent reason."

Simon Woodhall, who became manager of the Druid's Head in October 1993, recalled an incident which took place a few months before he formally took over the pub.

"I was relief manager at the pub for a couple of weeks during the previous May. It was outside of opening hours and I was alone in the lounge when I heard someone knocking loudly on the wall that separates the kitchen from the lounge. I immediately rushed to the kitchen, but found nobody there."

There was an especially odd incident in August 1994. It was a Sunday lunchtime and barmaid Cindy Wilkie was busy in the bar when she noticed a woman in a red dress standing close behind the customer she was serving. As the barman next to her was standing idly by, Miss Wilkie asked him if he would serve her. But in that moment, the woman in red just faded away. The barman, apparently, had been unaware of any woman.

Close by the Druid's Head is another haunted pub, the Pump House. The building dates back to at least 1776, though when it became a pub is not known. Its name comes from the timber-built pump house nearby that once conveyed sea-water to William's Baths. The shape of the pub's cellar suggests that at one time it formed part of a tunnel – possibly the same tunnel as that which served the Druid's Head. The facade of black mathematical tiles and bow windows was added to the pub in the early 1800s.

In the 1980s, some bar staff reported that when they were making their way downstairs, they heard low, mumbling voices coming from the cellar, but when they got there, the sound of voices stopped instantly.

Early in 1993, Fiona Cullen had a peculiar experience while living at the pub, which her parents were then managing (the family left to live in Somerset in September of the same year). At around 11.45 one night, the last customer had left and Miss Cullen was clearing up the bar counter.

Looking up for a moment, she saw a woman in a white dress standing by the glass-washing machine. Although the woman was facing away from her, Miss Cullen presumed it was her mother, Beryl Cullen, for the woman was of similar build. However, when Miss Cullen spoke to the woman, she faded away. Her mother, she discovered afterwards, had been upstairs at this time.

Early in 1994, a barmaid was preparing sandwiches in the food bar in readiness for lunchtime. It was soon after the pub had opened and there was only a sprinkling of customers, all being seated near to the front entrance. The barmaid had the feeling that someone was standing behind her. Turning, she was surprised to see a middle-aged woman in a black dress. As she didn't recognise the woman, the barmaid opened her mouth to question her, but before any words came, the woman in black vanished.

A few weeks later, close on midnight, assistant manageress Jackie Miller sat down at the desk in the pub's small basement office, which is adjacent to the cellar. The last customers had left, the glasses had been washed and the bar area tidied, but there was still some paperwork to be done.

As Miss Miller settled down to her task she heard footsteps crossing the floor of the bar above, accompanied by the mumble of voices. Her immediate thought was that some customers had hidden in the toilets at closing time and had only now emerged.

Feeling vulnerable and alone, she armed herself with a mallet of the type used for tapping beer barrels and, with her heart pounding, tiptoed up the stairs. The voices came closer as she reached the door of the bar, but at the instant she opened it, the voices stopped. She searched the bar and toilets, but found no one. A check on the doors to the street confirmed they were still locked.

The Royal Pavilion Tavern (formerly the Royal Pavilion Hotel), in Castle Square, opened in 1816, its first landlord being Edmund Savage, a coal merchant. At the time, Maria Fitzherbert, the morganatic wife of the

Prince Regent – they were married on 15 December 1785 – resided at Steine House, opposite the east-facing side of the pub. Though two shops now separate Steine House from the pub, in the early 1800s the two buildings were only separated by a lane.

Mrs Fitzherbert objected to the pub sign, then easily visible from Steine House, which referred to spirits (gin, ubiquitous and cheap, was considered at the time to be a 'common' drink). Ingeniously, the landlord substituted 'shades' – a word more often used in the past as an alternative to 'spirits' when the meaning of both words might refer to departed souls. Mrs Fitzherbert must have appreciated the subterfuge, for she gave her approval. The rear bar is still referred to as the Shades Bar. Afterwards, because it was thought fashionable, a number of Brighton pubs incorporated the word 'shades' in their names, or used the name to describe one of their bars, though the term has fallen by the wayside over the years.

The Royal Pavilion Tavern has a labyrinth of passages in its basement, and there is at least one tunnel, now blocked up, running towards the Royal Pavilion. The pub has a long-standing reputation for being haunted, though paranormal activities have been few in recent years.

One incident took place towards the end of the 1970s. At the time, assistant manager Anthony Scarrott and barman Steve Piper were on duty in the wine bar, situated at the rear of the pub. There were few customers at the time, so when a man started to walk up the staircase leading to the private residential part of the pub, he was quickly spotted by both Mr Scarrott and Mr Piper.

Mr Scarrott called for the man to stop, but as this request was ignored, he hurried after him. Mr Piper, sensing possible trouble, left his position behind the bar and also moved towards the staircase. On running up a few stairs, Mr Scarrott was surprised to see no sign of the man. Carrying on up the staircase, he reached the locked door at the top. There was no one there. Later, when he and Mr Piper discussed what they had seen, both found they were unable to describe what the man was wearing. His clothing had seemed grey and indistinct, and the man had quickly been swallowed up in the gloom at the top of the staircase.

In June 1997 at around 2.30pm, assistant manager Anne Rodgers went upstairs to the first floor club. By day, when this area is not in use, it is in almost total darkness, with the windows blacked out. As Miss Rodgers reached the top of the stairs she saw a bright, white light about 18 inches across. It was moving from left to right across the wall in front of her, undulating up and down as it progressed before finally fading.

Nothing could account for the light. The blacked-out windows prevented any external light coming in, while the only light left on in this club area was a red lamp positioned well away from the wall.

The Sussex Tavern, in East Street, was once a meeting place for smugglers. Until 1816 it was called the Spread Eagle. It is said that a ghost referred to as the White Lady once haunted the place, but if so, this apparition hasn't been seen for many years.

Another East Street pub, the Greyhound, had a mischievous spirit that enjoyed meddling with the video recorder in the sitting room of the residential part of the pub, as well as playing tricks in the cellar. In 1998, the pub was completely refurbished prior to re-opening under a new name, the Fish Bowl. Possibly, the considerable alterations will have chased away any spirits of the non-liquid kind! The pub dates back to at least 1687, when it was known as the Blue Anchor. It was renamed the Greyhound in 1783. The building itself was erected in 1658 as a private residence.

Brian and Jackie Denning became managers of the Greyhound on New Year's Day 1992. They quickly found that watching a video recording was not necessarily a relaxing way to spend a couple of hours when off duty. They would be watching a film when, without warning, the video recorder would stop, then slip into fast-forward mode. In addition, cassettes inexplicably ejected themselves before retreating back into the recorder. On one occasion, Jackie Denning and her stepdaughter, Carla, were watching a video film when the film clicked to a stop and the cassette repeatedly moved in and out of the recorder. After a few moments of this, the shocked women fled from the room.

On several occasions when going down into the cellar, the Dennings found that the cheeky ghost had exchanged full gas cylinders attached to the beer lines for empty ones.

Tradition has it that the ghost of a small girl haunts the pub. While no spectre of a child was seen by the Dennings, a relation, Karina Garvey, once felt something brush past her when working in the cellar. She looked up from her task and saw the faint, shadowy figure of a tall woman in her twenties. Barman Jason Dutton also reported instances of encountering a disquieting presence in the cellar.

A few doors further along East Street is the Prodigal public house (formerly known as O'Donovan's). Although opened as recently as 1995, it occupies part of the former Restoration public buildings. While that part occupied by the Prodigal was rebuilt in the 1880s, the cellar and basement bar area is much older and it here that staff have sometimes felt an oppressive presence.

Basement doors have opened and closed without obvious cause, while the cellar has been the source of a ghostly sound similar to that of beer crates being kicked. The shape of the cellar suggests that it once formed part of a tunnel leading to the sea. In 1998 the basement area became a separate establishment known as Ali-Cats, with an entrance in Brill's Lane. During the refurbishment work, building workers heard unaccounted-for human groans and there were sudden drops of temperature.

Dr Brighton's, previously known as the Star and Garter Hotel, stands on the corner of King's Road and Little East Street. It dates back to about 1750. Twin Irish giants, almost 8ft tall, were exhibited there in 1785.

Dr Brighton's acquired its name in the 1920s after its then landlord, the flamboyant Mr H C Taylor, took a cue from William Makepeace Thackeray's book, *The Newcomes,* in which the author wrote: 'One of the best physicians is kind, cheerful, merry Doctor Brighton'. Mr Taylor placed signs outside the premises which referred to the hotel's 'consulting hours' and which proclaimed: 'Dr Brighton prescribes for your enjoyment...' followed by a list of the drinks obtainable. But Dr Brighton's remained a secondary name for the hotel until the early 1980s, when the lease changed hands. The Star and Garter designation was phased out and the premises ceased to be residential in 1982.

A tunnel, now bricked up, runs from the cellar. In former times this was supposedly used by smugglers. Some years ago, one landlord, curious as to what secrets lay behind the cellar wall, knocked part of it down. He was greatly surprised to find, in addition to the anticipated tunnel, a room built into one side of the tunnel which contained several magnificent Regency-style lavatory pedestals! There must be an interesting story to account for these abandoned pieces of sanitary ware, which presumably are still there.

Barry Jones was the landlord of Dr Brighton's for five years until 1982. During its final years as a residential hotel it had ten bedrooms to let. Mr Jones recalled that customers staying there quite often commented that they felt a presence in their rooms or that they had the uncanny feeling that they were being watched. At the time, the hotel had a contract with the Theatre Royal to provide accommodation for visiting actors and other entertainers and quite a number of these referred to the peculiar atmosphere.

A succession of weird events have taken place over the years since Dr Brighton's stopped taking guests. In the late 1980s, live-in barmaid Miriam Crendell (not her real name) occupied a bedroom on the second floor. Sometimes, when off duty, she surreptitiously took her boyfriend up to her room. On one of these occasions, while she was washing her hair, her boyfriend sat on the bed with a magazine.

Afterwards, while she was sitting at her dressing table, the couple chatted. Suddenly, the floor beneath Miss Crendall's feet began to vibrate slightly. In the next moment, all of the ornaments and cosmetics on the table shot sideways onto the floor. With this came a sharp, cracking noise as a wall mirror in the room fractured.

Shocked, Miss Crendell let out a cry and jumped to her feet. Her boyfriend also leapt up from the bed. At that moment, they became aware that someone was occupying the old armchair in the corner of the room. It was a man, but the figure was grey and misty, so that little in the way of detail could be seen. As they watched, the apparition dissolved.

It would have been understandable if Miss Crendall and her boyfriend had chosen that moment to escape from the room, but as the boyfriend was a clandestine visitor, the couple had to compose themselves and wait until it was prudent to leave. Miss Crendell did eventually relate her experience to the landlord's wife.

Michael and Christa McCafferty were managers at Dr Brighton's for three years until January 1993. Mrs McCafferty said that keys sometimes disappeared, mysteriously to reappear hours later in some other part of the pub. Then there was the barman who returned, white-faced and shaken, after a visit to the gents' toilet in the basement, where he had been tapped on the shoulder by someone unseen. Every Friday, a window cleaner called at Dr Brighton's. His duties included cleaning the glass-panelled secondary door just inside the pub's sea-front entrance.

"Do some of your customers go out on their hands and knees after drinking here?" he jokingly enquired of Mrs McCafferty. She wondered what the window cleaner was getting at.

He elaborated: "Well, I often find fingerprints on the bottom panes of glass near the floor, and have wondered how they've got there."

Mrs McCafferty had never noticed the fingerprints, but now she looked out for them. When the fingerprints once more showed themselves, a close look indicated that they were those of a child. No children lived on the premises, nor were children normally permitted in the bar. The fingerprints appeared quite regularly for a while, and always on the lowest panels of glass, then the phenomenon ceased.

Were the fingerprints a creepy consequence of a tragic death that took place in the pub's cellar more than a century ago? It appears that the landlord at that time was a secret abortionist who carried out his illicit activities in a room at the top of the building, but at other times in the cellar.

There was no one to look after the children of one poor woman who had been left to recover on a crude bed in the cellar, so they were allowed to stay with her. Unfortunately one child, a young boy, stumbled and fell as he raced around in the gloom. When his forehead smashed into the edge of a barrel, death was almost instantaneous.

In December 1995 the child's fingerprints, which hadn't been seen for a year or so, reappeared several times over a couple of weeks. In addition to being on the glass panels of the door, similar fingerprints were spotted on a wall mirror in the bar.

From time to time, customers using the basement gents' toilet – formerly a part of the cellar – returned to the bar to report that they had seen the shadowy figure of a man reflected in the mirror above the washbowl, but on turning, had found they were alone.

Alison Reid was working behind the bar in 1994 when a male customer came up from the toilet to claim that he had seen the strange image in the mirror. It was mid-afternoon with few customers so, as there was a barman on duty to deal with these, she suggested to the customer that they go down together to investigate.

Entering the gents' toilet, they saw nothing in the mirror at first, but in moments the image of the man appeared. He seemed to be standing just behind them, but on turning they found no one there. When they looked back at the mirror, all was normal. Soon afterwards, the mirror was removed, and for some months the toilet was without a mirror. Early in 1995, during a general refurbishment, a new, smaller mirror was fitted.

In the same month as the mirror incident, manager Alan Moore was talking to a customer while both were seated in the bar. Suddenly, the lampshade from a wall fitting close to where they were seated shot from its holder, which was odd, because not only was it retained by three screw fittings, but its trajectory was at an angle which took it directly towards the head of Mr Moore. Fortunately, he saw the lampshade in time to deflect it with his hand. There were a small number of brass and copper ornaments on a high shelf in the bar, and several times one or more of these shot off the shelf to land a few feet away.

Norman Shankley, a relief manager at Dr Brighton's for a brief period during the late summer of 1994, found some strange force at work after a bulb had fallen from a wall lamp. The bulb hadn't broken, but when he tried to push it back into its fitting, he found he couldn't. Something was preventing him from doing so. After a few minutes, he gave up, but about 30 minutes later, he decided to have another try. This time, the bulb went into its fitting at the first attempt.

In the autumn of 1994, whatever supernatural agency was at work turned its attention to the area of the pool table. Each night after closing time the table was brushed and the plastic triangle, used to position the balls at the start of each game, was placed in a recess beneath the table, but frequently, on the following morning, the triangle was found to be back on the top of the table.

The cues were also targeted. These were always left in a wall-mounted rack overnight, but some mornings one or two, or sometimes all of them, would be found scattered on the floor. Given the strength of each individual clip, it was difficult to see how even one cue might fall over, let alone several. After three or four weeks, the pool table phenomena finally fizzled out.

Malcolm Gilbert took over as tenant in November 1996. He soon observed that the pet cat he had brought with him was behaving strangely for, from time to time, its fur hackled and it would spit at something which it seemed to see, but which Mr Gilbert could not himself see. He also had problems with light bulbs and shades which should have been secure, but which fell from their fittings for no definable reason.

The King's Road Arches, on the lower esplanade, were built in the 1860s so that fishermen would have somewhere to store their tackle and repair their nets. As the local fishing community contracted, almost all of the arches were converted for other uses. One of these arches eventually took on a new identity as the Fortune of War, a public house which still retains a sense of things nautical. There is also some evidence that the place is haunted!

In 1996, assistant manager Neil Hayward reported that some staff were uneasy when working alone in the cellar because, at times, they had the impression that some unseen presence was there. The strip lighting in the passage leading to the cellar was left on when anyone was on the premises, but the passage was plunging into darkness three or four times a week when the lights spontaneously turned off, only to come on again a few minutes later. No electrical fault was found.

Again, objects left in one place would sometimes be found later in quite a different place. These disconcerting movements of keys and other items affected both the bar and the cellar areas, though Mr Hayward admitted that with a mixture of full and part time staff who are kept very busy, it was difficult to establish whether these activities were really due to anything of a ghostly nature.

About a 100 years ago the landlord of the Fortune of War was a local character called 'Captain' Fred Collins (he was also a leading light in the fishing community). He was once involved in an argument with a drunken and aggressive customer. The argument degenerated into a fracas, with Collins, assisted by his son, dealing so severely with the customer that he died. Might the uncanny events taking place at the pub have a connection with this long ago event?

The Shark Bar, in West Street, was built early in the 19th century. Originally called the Carpenters Arms, it was renamed Christie's Hotel in 1901 and the Bosun in the 1970s. For a short while after that it reverted to its original name, the Carpenters Arms. In 1986 it was renamed the Nellie Peck, after a Mississippi riverboat of that name (which itself had been named after the captain's wife). Later, it became the Southern Spirit. In 1997, under new ownership, it was renamed Sweet Fanny Adams. The change to its current name came in 1999.

The pub's resident ghosts – there appears to be more than one – have demonstrated their presence in a variety of ways. One story of some years ago concerns a landlord who held a birthday party for his daughter in one of the basement rooms. During the celebrations, a vase on the mantelpiece shot several feet into the centre of the room, but this was but a minor incident among many which have taken place.

Trevor and Lynne Bennett became relief managers at the pub in the summer of 1993, remaining for seven months. At the time there was a pool table at the far end of the bar which was illuminated by wall-mounted spotlights. The Bennetts noticed that these spotlights sometimes dimmed for a few seconds or minutes before returning to their original power. Eventually, a tradesman was called in to check the electrics, but no fault was found.

Mr Bennett said: "Later on we noticed that the spotlights only dimmed in that way when we, or perhaps some of the staff, were working in that part of the pub and, becoming a bit bad tempered, had raised our voices. It was most odd."

He added: "That wasn't all. When you went down to the cellar to carry out some task, you'd often find that something unusual would happen. An electric bulb would blow, a door would slam of its own accord, or something would fall over. Steve Hart, my bar cellarman, said that he frequently felt as if he was being watched by someone when down there.

"I used to say: 'It's only me!' when I went into the cellar, just in case there was a spirit presence of some kind. I know it sounds ludicrous, but Max, our alsatian, absolutely refused to go into the cellar with me unless these words were said."

Some months later, aware of the apprehensiveness of Max, one barman decided to 'test' the cellar for himself by bringing his own alsatian to work. Despite encouraging tugs on its lead, the dog couldn't even be coaxed through the cellar door. Another bar worker, Steve Norsworthy, once had the experience of lights spontaneously switching on and off while he was busy in the cellar.

Working alone in the club bar on the first floor one evening prior to opening time, Mrs Bennett saw an electric light bulb fall to the floor from its wall fitting. It hadn't broken, so she immediately went to place it back in its socket. As the bulb had been alight, she presumed it would still be hot, but on picking it up she found it ice cold.

Plus 8, a pop group playing a gig at the pub, was using a projector and screen to add visuals to its performance. While positioning their equipment in readiness for their evening performance, the musicians were astonished to see the image of a girl's face materialise briefly on the screen. The projector was not switched on at the time.

An intriguing visitor called at the pub towards the end of 1993. He was a tall, distinguished, elderly man with a thin face and a grey handlebar moustache. He wore a long winter coat and carried a cane. After ordering his drink, he began a conversation with the Bennetts. He indicated that he had once been a regular customer at the pub.

He said that one morning in the 1970s he had called in at the first floor bar in its pre-club days for a drink – he liked the fact that it had a quieter atmosphere than the busier ground floor bar. As he entered the bar from the stairway, he noticed that the only people present were two old men who were seated at a table in a far corner of the bar. They were talking in subdued voices. As the bar was so quiet – it was shortly after opening time – the barman had disappeared for a few moments to get additional stock.

As he waited for the barman's return, the man with the handlebar moustache turned away from the bar to look around him. He immediately noticed that the two old men were no longer present. He had heard nothing and felt sure they couldn't have vanished in so short a time. Perplexed, he questioned the barman on his return. The barman assured him that the bar had been empty and that he had not served any old men with drinks.

The man with the handlebar moustache also told the Bennetts that there were once several framed black and white photographs hanging on one of the bar walls. These showed small groups of people who were apparently enjoying social occasions organised by the pub. He added that sometimes the landlord or his staff would come into the bar in the mornings, prior to opening time, to discover that these photographs had been inexplicably turned around overnight so that they faced the wall.

Neither the Bennetts nor any of the bar staff could recall seeing the man with the handlebar moustache before. Nor did they ever see him again. A few days later, Mr Bennett related the old man's story to a customer who had used the pub for many years.

"Do you remember him?" queried Mr Bennett, after describing the man's appearance.

"No!" responded the customer, "But, now you ask, I do recall the photos you mentioned. I seem to remember that some of them included a man with a handlebar moustache!"

Steve and Jane Jones took over as managers in January 1994, remaining for almost two years. They, like their predecessors, experienced the occasional alternate dimming and glowing of the pool table spotlights. Unaware that the Bennetts had already had the system checked, Mr Jones called in an electrician. Again, no reason for the dimming effect could be found.

A large stained glass window dominates the far end of the bar and staff and customers sometimes observed the shadow of a man moving across it. However, the base of the window is more than ten feet above ground level (at the time of writing, this window is hidden behind screening).

In the 12 months up to February 1995, the ghost of a man was witnessed by at least four people: doorman Paul Latham (who saw the spectre standing by a pillar in the bar), managers Mr and Mrs Jones, and customer Jerry Sheer. Another customer, in the pub at a quiet time of day, was jolted by the sight of a pair of bare legs, which appeared to be male, taking a few steps across the bar floor before dissolving. No other part of the body was visible.

Mrs Jones' sighting of the male apparition took place while she was clearing up in the bar outside of business hours. She had the impression that someone was standing close behind her and turned to see who it was. In that first brief moment, she thought it was her husband. The stature and dark, wavy hair were similar, and the white, short-sleeved shirt and grey trousers seemed normal enough, but in almost the same moment she realised it wasn't him. Shocked, she felt unable to move for a few seconds, by which time the vision had faded.

Could this phantom be that of a former landlord? Ghosts are frequently associated with sudden death and many years ago one of the pub's landlords was brutally killed after an argument with some customers. Biding their time, they chose their moment when the landlord went down to the cellar to change a barrel. Slipping down the cellar steps after him, they beat him up so severely that he died.

In 1994, two lantern-style electric lamps stood on the bar counter (following extensive alterations, the bar counter is today situated on the opposite side of the bar). Several feet apart, the lamps were mounted on brass columns. Between these hung a line of small flags advertising Budweiser beer. Towards the end of the year, Mrs Jones and two of the bar staff were close by the lamps when they were astonished to see them begin to vibrate. Then, consecutively from right to left, each flag was flicked upwards as if by an unseen hand.

On an afternoon in December 1994, Mrs Jones went up to the club bar. In her hands was a wire basket containing about 30 glasses. When she was halfway up the stairs, some strange force snatched the basket from her hands and threw it down, breaking most of the glasses. Earlier that year, Mr Jones experienced something similar. He took a tray of clean glasses upstairs to the club area and left it on the bar counter while he attended to other tasks. Suddenly and inexplicably, the tray and glasses shot off the counter. All the glasses were smashed.

Towards the end of 1994, a bottle spun off a bar shelf of its own accord and whizzed past Mrs Jones' head. At other times she felt something unseen touching her ears. In January 1995, two glasses unaccountably leaped off a shelf and sped past the head of barmaid Zoe Latham, missing her face by only an inch or two.

On another occasion Miss Latham had the terrifying experience of reaching out to pick up an empty glass that had been left on a table when, just before her fingers touched it, it shattered. She wasn't injured, but she observed that the broken glass was made up of some largish glass slivers of similar size and a lot of very tiny pieces, similar in appearance to those encountered when a car's laminated windscreen is smashed. She thought the profusion of very tiny pieces of glass didn't accord with what normally happens when a glass breaks.

The experience of barmaid Lisa Cole was even odder, for not long after the above incident she went to pick up an empty pint glass and was shocked when the top half came away in her hand. It was just as if a glass cutter had been used to cut an exact circle around the glass. Soon afterwards, her brother, doorman Sean Cole, was tapped on the shoulder by an invisible presence.

Even more disconcerting was the experience of barman Mark Barnes. One evening, he was walking towards the pool table, which he was about to tidy up. Because it was closing time, a game had been left unfinished, and some of the balls were still on the table. Just before he reached the table, Mr Barnes was astonished to see the balls start moving around of their own accord, some bouncing off the cush. One of the balls, he observed, stopped abruptly near the centre of the table as if gripped by an unseen hand. This eerie activity continued for several seconds. There was no one else in the vicinity.

Early in 1995, Graham Sweetman, the then proprietor, was walking through one of the unused and unfurnished basement rooms when the electric light came on, stayed on for a few moments, then went out. Which was very odd, for the power to that room had been disconnected.

Later in the year the pub came under new ownership and was completely gutted prior to a total refurbishment. Since then the incidence of paranormal events seems to have diminished, but in 1996 a cleaner working alone in the bar heard heavy footsteps walking across the floor above. Believing an intruder to be on the premises she called the police, but no one was found.

Towards the end of 1997, manager Nik Downes was attending to some paperwork in the pub's basement office when he heard the noise of someone stamping loudly on the floorboards of the bar area above him. He was alone in the pub at the time, so he at once rushed up to investigate. He found the bar empty and the entrance doors still securely locked.

On the same side of West Street is an Australian bar called the Walkabout, which opened in April 1999. Prior to this, and for a number of years, an amusement arcade occupied the premises, but at one time it was the site of a public house known as the New Regent. The building itself dates back to 1899, and for much of its history it was a residential hotel known as Chatfield's.

The New Regent's proprietor, Denys O'Loughlin, had previously been the manager of the Regent Cinema and Ballroom. His son and daughter-in-law, Danny and Jean O'Loughlin, were responsible for the day-to-day management of the New Regent. The family was resident there from 1975 to 1983.

Possibly more than one ghost haunted the pub. The apparition of a man dressed in chef's clothing was said to be that of a Mr Webster, who hanged himself in the staff quarters in 1903. On one occasion the ghostly chef, nicknamed 'Claude' by the staff, drifted through a bathroom door while Mrs O'Loughlin was having a bath. Shocked, she shouted for the apparition to go away. It dissolved almost instantly, but the majority of ghosts are only fleetingly visible anyway, so whether Mrs O'Loughlin's cries were responsible for its departure is a matter for conjecture.

On another occasion, Jean O'Loughlin was walking along a second-floor corridor on her way to the laundry room when she thought she saw her husband at the far end of the corridor. She hurried after him and called for him to stop, as she wanted to speak to him, but he disappeared around a corner. Quickening her footsteps, she saw him turn into a side passage.

She knew that she would now be able to speak to him, for the passage led to an exit door which she knew was locked. But she found no sign of her husband. Questioned later, he said he hadn't been in that part of the building at the time. Once, Danny O'Loughlin briefly saw a misty apparition standing on a staircase.

Could the ghost have been responsible for the sudden exit of an intruder in 1982? Early that year the O'Loughlins woke at around 2am to the sound of crashing glass. A front window of the pub had been smashed outwards by someone making a very hasty exit. Whoever was responsible could have left by undoing the locks and bolts on the inside of the front door. Instead, they chose to risk being cut badly by crashing through the window.

On investigation, a trail of spent matches and pieces of burnt paper were found on the floor of the bar, but nothing had been taken, which seemed to suggest that whoever had left in such a panic-stricken hurry could have been a customer who had fallen asleep somewhere in the cavernous pub, possibly in the toilet.

During the time the O'Loughlins ran the pub, lights crazily switched on and off, glasses were pushed off shelves and there were frequent unexplained thumps and bangs. On one occasion, milk left in the refrigerator was found outside it. On another, an ice bucket levitated from the bar and upturned to rain ice cubes onto a shocked customer. A cat belonging to the family used to howl continuously when it wandered into the rear part of the pub – the most haunted part of the building – and if someone approached to comfort it, it would react in a confused fashion.

In the pub's residential area, items of clothing vanished, only to reappear anything from a day to several days later and usually in a different place. It was a phenomenon that involved most of the O'Loughlin family. The playful spirit seemed aware of the family's favourite garments and tended to choose these for its tricks.

Sheila Weavill, at one time bar manageress at the New Regent, occupied a small flat in the building. There, the lights often switched on and off of their own accord, but more dangerously, the gas taps sometimes turned on. But the ghost appeared to indulge in this activity only when there was someone close by to notice the hissing gas and the smell.

Barman Kevin Telfer recalled the diversity of weird events which took place in the cellar and the adjacent wines and spirits store. He said: "All the lights in the cellar would go off together, even though there were four separate switches. At various times and for no reason at all, the taps on the beer barrels would turn off, the ice buckets would fall over and the ice machine would switch off. It was all quite extraordinary."

One night, Patricia O'Loughlin (Denys O'Loughlin's wife) heard a loud knocking on her bedroom door, but on opening it she found no one there. It was a phenomenon which was to be repeated many times. At first, Mrs O'Loughlin responded to the knockings by opening the door, but after this had happened on three or four occasions without there being anyone outside, increasingly frightened, she left the door firmly closed to subsequent knockings.

However, as the weeks went by, she became so used to the phantom knocks, for nothing disturbing seemed to follow them, that she began to lose her fear. In due course, she even began to joke about the matter. Sometimes the knocking escalated into a barrage of thumpings, as if someone was desperate to gain entrance.

One of the more upsetting incidents took place when some of the upstair rooms were being renovated. In one room the workmen discovered an old, cast-iron fireplace that had been plastered over. At around 11.30pm one night, after the pub had closed for business, Patricia O'Loughlin took Mr Telfer upstairs so that he could see the fireplace prior to its removal.

While they were in the room, they were startled to hear the agitated voice of a baby calling 'Mummy! Mummy!' This call was repeated and followed by loud screams. It seemed to come from only a few feet away, yet no child was visible.

On the next floor down, Jean O'Loughlin's sister Julie, then aged 16, and Shirley Fry, Julie's friend, who was staying at the pub, also heard the cries and screams. Knowing there wasn't a baby present in the building and frightened by the intensity of the screams, they ran into a nearby bathroom and locked the door, not daring to venture out again until they heard familiar family voices in the corridor outside.

This was Julie's second unnerving experience. The first had taken place one evening, a year or so earlier. At the time, she was sharing a bedroom with her friend Shirley. Julie still had some of the dolls of her childhood and two of these were kept in a large toy pram, a scale replica of an old-fashioned Silver Cross baby carriage, which was in the bedroom.

Shirley had gone to the bathroom, but Julie was already in bed. Although the bedroom light had been switched off, the door was ajar, so the bedroom was illuminated to some extent by the light coming from the corridor. As Julie waited for her friend to return from the bathroom, she became aware of another person in the room. Raising her head from her pillow, she saw a man standing by her pram.

The man was bending over the pram as if looking at the dolls. The next moment he appeared to push down the hood of the pram. Julie knew it wasn't her father. Her father was fairly slender, while she perceived that this man was quite stout. She noted he was wearing a check shirt and trousers of an indeterminate colour, but the odd thing was that his face and clothing seemed to be covered in tiny, moving silver dots.

She said: "It was rather like the snowstorm effect you get on a television screen when weather conditions are interfering with the reception. A few moments later Shirley came back from the bathroom. As she pushed the door fully open, the man just vanished. Shirley didn't seem to be aware of anything unusual, but I was so scared that I just pulled the blankets over my head. I found it impossible to talk to her about what I'd seen until the following morning."

On another occasion, Mike and Chris O'Loughlin, Julia's brothers (who were still in their teens at the time and sharing a bedroom), were startled, soon after they had gone to bed, to find the blankets on their beds pulled up around their necks. It was as if some invisible being was trying to tuck them in for the night.

Some nights, after the pub had closed, one or two of the staff would join the O'Loughlins in a first floor sitting room to watch a rented video. Among those taking advantage of this facility was Steve Dias, who was employed as a barman/bouncer. He was quite a fearless individual, but he finally refused to go down to the basement gents' toilet after being forcibly grabbed by an invisible entity. He had already been unnerved on earlier occasions when the basement lights had repeatedly clicked on and off when no one else was present.

One year, David and Jill Fox – relations of the O'Loughlins – arrived at the New Regent for a week's holiday. With them was their baby daughter Gemma. Soon after their arrival, a pair of Gemma's shoes was placed on the dressing table in the bedroom occupied by Mr and Mrs Fox, but a little later, when Mrs Fox came to put the shoes on the baby's feet, one of them had mysteriously vanished. As no one else had entered the room, this seemed impossible, but a thorough search of the room confirmed that the missing shoe was nowhere to be found.

By the time Mr and Mrs Fox were due to return home, they had come to accept that the shoe had totally disappeared. However, on the final day of their holiday when, suitcases in hand, they were actually leaving the pub, they were flabbergasted to see Gemma's missing shoe standing, perplexingly, in the middle of the hallway!

The New Regent was completely gutted in the mid-1980s prior to its conversion into an amusement arcade. From this time, all has seemed normal.

14 *More haunted hostelries*

Readers may wonder at the large number of haunted public houses featured in this book. The explanation is simple. Because of its nature, the licensed trade is primarily staffed by people who remain at any one pub for only a short period of time before moving on. A particular person may well have worked at several pubs, so will have some knowledge of events at each of these. Including, of course, any hauntings! The trend towards pubs having managers, rather than tenants or individual owners, has contributed to this fluidity of movement. In addition, pub landlords are more easily approachable than people in most fields of activity and, in almost every instance during my researches, they have given generously of their time. Finally, it may be that ghosts are particularly attracted to licensed premises, for haunted pubs are numerous throughout Britain. Many, of course, are far older than the properties surrounding them. Which probably helps!

THE MARLBOROUGH TAVERN, in Princes Street, was built in 1787. In 1885, following upon the death of his publican father, Tom Packham took over as landlord. He and his wife, Lucy, were entirely unsuitable to the task of running a pub, for both were drunkards. In addition, Tom Packham had a vile temper and often assaulted his wife and thrashed their three children, while she was lazy and dirty in her habits.

The climax of their ill-fated partnership came in 1900 when police hurried to the pub to arrest Mr Packham. He had become involved in a drunken argument with his wife, and the acrimony between the two became so heated that the landlord had lashed out at his wife's head with a bottle. The blow killed her.

Mr Packham was initially charged with murder, but at his trial this was reduced to manslaughter. Over the years since, the ghost of the wife is said to haunt the pub, although Eddie Scannell, the Marlborough's landlord for 28 years, reported only one odd incident.

"It was around 1976 and soon after evening closing time," he recalled. "The bar staff had gone home and I'd locked all the doors and was clearing up in the bar. Suddenly the temperature dropped and there was a cold draught. The next moment I felt something invisible brush past me. I was shocked enough to leave the rest of the bar work until the following morning!"

An upstairs room in the Marlborough has been converted into a small theatre holding about 50 people. A comedy, *Murder at the Marlborough,* based upon the 1900 incident and written by local writer John Montgomery, was first performed at the pub's theatre in 1979. For a part of the play, so as to lend greater authenticity, the players and audience descended from the theatre so that the 'killing' of the landlord's wife could actually take place in the bar.

Unfortunately, a woman customer already sitting in the bar was unaware of this arrangement. On seeing the 'victim' crash to the floor after being 'hit' with a bottle, she burst into hysterical screams. Hardly had she been pacified with a hissed revelation of the truth when a new customer arrived at the pub. Surprised to see such a crush of people in the bar, he failed to notice the 'victim' still laid out on the floor and promptly tumbled over her, to appreciative applause from those watching!

The play continues to be performed from time to time at the Marlborough, more usually during the annual Brighton Festival. Regrettably, though, without the unscripted drama associated with its initial performance.

The resident ghost has become more active in recent years. This activity tends to coincide with the arrival of new staff. Manager Sue Kerslake found that her own arrival in the spring of 1997 was the prelude to several odd events. Gas cylinders in the cellar turned off without cause, bottles tumbled off shelves, as many as 20 at a time, and keys refused to operate tills, although a few minutes later and using the same key, an affected till would usually open without trouble. In 1998, she twice encountered a misty white form. It was too insubstantial to show any detail, but it was of roughly human size and shape.

Assistant manager 'Compton' started work at the Marlborough in June 1998. During the evening of her first day of duties she was busy with some paperwork in the basement office when she heard the sound of chains rattling violently just outside the office door. Curious, she investigated.

The chains, hanging on a nearby wall, had been used in the past for the lifting of barrels. Now, the new assistant manager observed, they were silent and unmoving. Aware that she was alone in the basement, she wondered what might have caused the rattling. No one had yet mentioned to her that the pub was supposed to be haunted. Her experience was yet another example of a supernatural incident being triggered by the presence of a new employee.

The Regency Tavern, in Russell Square, has long had the reputation of being haunted. The pub dates from around 1870, when it occupied the site where there had previously been two lodging houses (33 and 34 Russell Square). But these were no common lodging houses. Instead, they catered for upper class visitors who wanted to remain in Brighton for a few weeks or months. In the mid-1930s the Regency was extended to include number 32, which had been a boot and shoemaker's shop.

The boot and shoemaker's business was founded by William Moore in 1893 and one of the pub's ghosts is that of a young, disabled girl, thought to be his daughter who, panicking after smelling what she thought was gas, chose to jump from a first-floor window (possibly she had been locked in her room because of a misdemeanour). She later died from her injuries. After number 32 became part of the Regency, the ghost of the girl sometimes appeared on the first floor, though she has not been seen in recent years.

Another ghost at the pub is that of a former landlady who so enjoyed her long tenancy at the Regency that, following her death, she elected to stay on in spirit. This is possibly a Mrs Edlin, who was the pub's only woman licensee during its early years. She arrived at the pub with her husband in 1890, but he died three or four years later and from then on she presided alone over the pub's fortunes until 1902.

This phantom is still seen from time to time. Many years ago, journalist R C Millar, writing in the *Evening Argus*, recalled that the son of a newly arrived landlord had seen her on the first floor. The son, unaware that he had witnessed a ghost, expressed surprise that his father should take in a paying guest so soon after his arrival at the pub. But there was no flesh-and-blood resident at that moment!

In the past, ornaments and items of furniture in the pub have moved around of their own volition. Stuart Bowers, employed as a live-in barman in 1990, reported that a kettle and crockery in his second floor bedroom were sometimes moved around when the room was left locked and unoccupied. The atmosphere on the second floor was sometimes quite disturbing, he said, and he felt apprehensive when going up the staircase.

Other staff also reported a sense of unease about ascending to the second floor. In the 1980s, it was the bar area that became the target for spooky activity. Chairs which had been placed on the tables after closing time in readiness for the following morning's floor cleaning were found to have been placed back on the floor at dawn.

In 1990 the Regency became front page news when the landlady, Jackie Penfold, died of a heart attack as a result of the pub being attacked by missile-throwing, window-breaking football hooligans who had become frustrated by the fact that England had lost to Germany in the semi-finals of that year's World Cup Tournament. While Mrs Penfold was at the pub, her alsatian dog steadfastly refused to venture into the cellar.

That the cellar might dispense its terrors was confirmed by the frightening ordeal suffered by John Smiles. Towards the end of the 1980s, Mr Smiles was employed as a breakfast chef at the nearby Metropole Hotel. His working hours at the hotel allowed him to work additionally as a part-time barman at the Regency.

One day he was in the Regency's cellar and in the middle of transferring a beer line from an empty to a full barrel when he had the feeling that he was not alone. On looking up he saw, just a few feet away from him, the figure of a woman. But what was terrifying about the woman was not just the fact that the whole of her form seemed to exhude a greenish luminosity, but that she was moving towards him . . . indeed, was almost upon him.

In that second or two, Mr Smiles was unable to take in every detail of the woman, though he did observe that she was wearing a long, old-fashioned dress. He was still crouched down by the barrel when the woman's form passed through him. It was as if slivers of ice had passed through his body, he said later. In another second, the electric tension that seemed to be hanging in the air had gone, and he knew that the awesome apparition had departed.

White-faced and shaking, Mr Smiles fled from the cellar and headed for the bar. Mrs Penfold was the landlady at the time – the actions of the football hooligans and her subsequent death were still two or three years in the future. Seeing the ashen, flustered face of Mr Smiles, she expressed her concern. As he gasped out the reason for his distress, she quickly offered him a comforting whisky.

The Windmill public house, in Upper North Street, dates back to 1828, which marks it as being one of the oldest buildings in the area. It was originally a farmhouse surrounded by fields. Nearby was Vine's Mill, so when the farmhouse was converted into an inn, the Windmill was an obvious choice of name.

The Windmill's 'cellar' is an outhouse at the rear of the building, but at one time it was sited where the rear bar now is. The change of use followed upon a fire which devastated a part of the building. In the late 1800s the original cellar, being the coolest place around, was periodically used as a morgue. Possibly this has a relevance to the fact that the pub is haunted.

One former landlord, Ivor Potter, reported that glasses shot off shelves to smash on the floor, while his normally fearless Jack Russell terrier reacted to eerie changes in the atmosphere by running around in circles and hiding; a bizarre activity the dog had never previously demonstrated.

At another point in the pub's history, shortly after a busy lunchtime session, a newly arrived landlord went upstairs to change. Locking his bedroom door before going out on business, he returned a few hours later to find the room in chaos, with items of furniture moved around and ornaments tossed onto his bed. No reason was found for the disorder.

In 1997, Red Nose Day, in aid of the Comic Relief charity, took place on 14 March. William Booth, who had become manager of the pub three months before, decided to organise an evening of entertainment to benefit the charity. Joined by two helpers, he spent the morning decorating the rear bar in readiness.

One of the decorative items was a life-sized painting, on cloth, of a recumbent Egyptian mummy. While the preparations for the evening were taking place, the bar's jukebox was switched to automatic so as to provide continuous music. While the painting of the mummy was being attached to the rear wall of the bar, the music suddenly stopped, and there was a slight pause. Then a completely different tune began to play. Mr Booth described it as being very weird music indeed.

Thinking something had gone wrong with the jukebox, he walked over to it and was surprised to see that the music being played had no relationship to the illuminated reference number, which should have coincided with the track being played, nor to any of the titles shown on the selection panel. The eerie music continued for another two or three minutes before stopping, whereupon the track which it had interrupted began once more to play.

Mr Booth hadn't recognised the unearthly music from the wide selection offered by the jukebox, though he thought it might have come from a CD recorded by Enigma, a group known for its unusual sound. However, having played all of the Enigma music without coming across the mystery track, he carried on over the next two days to run right through every other track on the jukebox. It was to no avail. The recording of the strange music could not be found.

With its impressive exterior, the King and Queen in Marlborough Place is sometimes thought to be much older than it is, but the its mock-Tudor facade dates back only to the mid-1930s, when the pub was rebuilt. Nevertheless, this capacious hostelry has a long pedigree and a small part of the original structure, mainly the cellar area, has been retained.

The original King and Queen began its life as a farmhouse, built in 1723. A licence was granted in 1779. The original inn sign showed George III and Queen Charlotte, but when the pub was rebuilt, a new sign depicting Henry VIII and Anne Boleyn was displayed. For some years, as a gesture to the pub's origins, there was a return to favour of George III and Queen Charlotte as the preferred Royals on the inn sign, but in 1995 a replacement once more featured a corpulent Henry VIII and his second wife.

A useful additional income for the landlord of the original King & Queen was provided by the soldiers who occupied the barracks to the rear of the inn. The barracks were completed in 1796 to house around 400 infantrymen, though later it also became a base for artillery volunteers. A 10-inch square hole in the back wall of the inn enabled the soldiers to buy liquor illicitly, though in practice, the officers turned a blind eye to this trade. A replica of the serving hatch can be seen at the south end of the present bar.

On a wet and windy evening in 1986, a female trainee manager at the pub heard the sound of windows rattling and banging. It came from the first-floor Tudor Room, a room used for special functions. She at once went upstairs to close them. Although she was sure they had been properly secured, within moments of her leaving the room, they were again banging in the wind.

Puzzled, she returned to close the windows, but again, hardly had she left the room, when the windows once more started to bang. This time, understandably, she was reluctant to return, and another member of staff had to go upstairs to close the windows. This time they remained closed.

Early in 1994, shortly before morning opening time, a barman at the King & Queen was tidying up the area behind the bar when he heard shouting coming from the area of the large fireplace. He couldn't make out what the voice or voices were saying. There was no one else in the bar at the time and he felt sure the voices weren't originating from outside the pub.

When, in October 1992, Martin and Liz Bennett moved into the Mash Tun public house, on the corner of Church Street and New Road, they didn't realise they were to be managing premises haunted by a former landlady, Martha Boxell, who ran the pub during the First World War. At the time the Bennetts took over, it was still known by its original name, the Volunteer, which associated it with the barracks which had once stood across the road. Even on their first day at the pub, Mrs Bennett felt there was something odd about the place.

She was sitting at a dressing table in an attic bedroom, when she had the feeling that she was being watched. A few days later, though no one else was present in the attic, she again had the same sense of someone being there; of watching eyes.

Then there were the footsteps sometimes heard at around 1.45am. Mr Bennett suggested that although the footsteps sounded as if they were from within the pub, they could have been those of security staff at the Corn Exchange, which backs onto the pub, making their early morning rounds (a check with the security staff indicated that this was unlikely).

A little harder to explain, however, were the electric light bulb incidents, which took place some months after the Bennetts had moved in. Mr Bennett was relaxing in a sitting room on the third floor when a candle-style electric bulb in a wall-lamp suddenly shot several inches into the air from its fitting and smashed onto the floor (experiment will show that, normally, a suddenly released bulb will only be propelled a small fraction of an inch by the spring contacts of the holder).

Not long afterwards, Mr and Mrs Bennett were working in the office, also on the third floor, when a wall-lamp bulb shot out of its socket. Both incidents took place during daylight when the lights were switched off.

Some 15 years before the Bennetts arrived at the Volunteer, John Farnham was the manager. Although he didn't himself have a paranormal experience during his years at the pub, this wasn't the case with Reg Quinlan, a family friend. Mr Quinlan occupied a top floor bedroom at the pub throughout most of 1977, and on several occasions he reported that, without apparent cause, his clothing was scattered around the room. Once, after a brief absence, he returned to find that several items of his clothing had been cast down the staircase by the mysterious entity.

Staff at the Aquarium public house, in Steine Street, have to contend with a discarnate voice which calls them by their first names. Landlady Patricia Cook heard her name called on several occasions. She also reported an odd, charged atmosphere at the rear of the pub, but this was only evident early in the morning and dissipated after an hour or two.

Referring to the voice, barman Malcolm Gilbert said: "It's not very loud, so you only notice it when the bar is quiet. You are able to hear other people's names called as well as your own. It's uncanny, but we've got so used to the voice we don't worry about it."

Another barman, who worked at the pub in the early 1980s, recalled several incidents of objects moving around of their own volition.

The Golden Lion Tavern (formerly the Star), in Manchester Street, dates back to 1838. It is believed to be haunted by a former landlady. Certainly there has been a continuing story of unusual happenings.

The resident ghost might have an objection to artificial flowers, for early in the 1980s a cleaner was alone in one of the basement storerooms when she witnessed some plastic plants jump out of their pots and fall to the floor (the storerooms have since been converted into toilets). This phenomenon was accompanied by a garbled female voice. In another incident during the early 1980s, a former manager found himself being propelled down the cellar steps by invisible hands; fortunately without injury.

In 1989, Clive and Sue Thomas became the pub's managers, remaining until leaving the licensed trade 18 months later. On several occasions they found that crates, bottles and other items in the cellar had mysteriously moved well away from their usual positions.

The most bizarre occurrence took place a few months after the couple had moved into the pub. Barry Bray, a technical representative from the brewery company, called to service the pub's beer-pumping equipment. Mr Thomas took Mr Bray down into the cellar and for a few moments the two men stood talking at the bottom of the cellar steps.

As they chatted, Mr Bray, who had the cellar steps behind him, felt something hit him, quite painfully, on the back of the head. Shocked, he immediately turned to look up the stairs, thinking for a moment that someone might have thrown something at him as a prank, but the door at the top of the cellar stairs was closed. Mr Bray then turned his eyes to the floor to see what had hit him.

The object that Mr Bray picked up, and which both men now studied in amazement, was a small metal head. It was about three-quarters of an inch long and seemed to be composed of some amalgam of grey metal which was heavy for its size, but not as heavy as lead. The object appeared to be the head of a small statuette which had been wrenched from its body. But the really weird thing about it was the fact that it depicted the head of the Devil!

Mr Thomas was totally baffled, for he knew there was no such statuette in the building. He later passed the Devil's head to his wife and she, unhappy about it, threw it away. A few months later, Mr Thomas heard three loud, unexplained bangs coming from the cellar when no one was there.

Doris Williams began working at the pub in 1987. Twice during her time there, while alone and carrying out her duties, she heard her name being called. Once, she happened to be leaving the pub at the same time as the manager when both were hit at the identical moment with a wet tea-bag! There was no one else in the pub at the time.

Her most traumatic experience came when the apparition of a former landlady, whom she knew and who had died quite young and not long before, appeared in the basement bar (which is now a kitchen and storage area).

Rosemarie Richardson became the manager of the Golden Lion in 1997. She sometimes found, when reaching up to take a clean glass from the shelf above the bar counter, and before she had even touched it, that the glass would shoot away from her and onto the floor.

The King's Arms, in George Street, was at one time a centre for cock-fighting. The *Brighton Herald* of 17 January 1811 referred to such an event where five guineas was the winner's prize for each cock battle, with 20 guineas for the main battle victor.

In July 1816, a Captain Wombwell of the 1st Life Guards wagered 500 guineas that he could ride a tandem (a two-seat carriage drawn by two horses harnessed one in front of the other) from Westminster Bridge to the King's Arms, a distance of almost 60 miles, without changing horses. Despite the poor road surfaces of the time and torrential rain falling throughout his ride, the officer won his bet. Setting out at 4am from Westminster, he reached the King's Arms at 8.45am.

Dulcie Barker, landlady of the King's Arms for 15 years until leaving in 1994, was coming up the stairs from the cellar one morning when she stumbled. She had her arms full of foodstuffs from the freezer, which was situated in the cellar, and would certainly have tumbled backwards down the steps, with at least serious injury, had not a strong arm reached out and steadied her. Perhaps it wasn't an arm, but whatever it was, for no visible being was actually there, Mrs Barker was immensely thankful for its supernatural help.

It was not the first time that some unseen entity had stopped her from falling, because there had been a similar incident some three years before when she had lost her footing while climbing a staircase in the residential part of the pub.

Bar/cellarman Fred Marsh, employed at the pub for many years, saw a shadowy form move across the cellar on several occasions. Colin Millham, who took over the pub from Mrs Barker, said he hadn't seen any ghostly forms, but once, while working in the cellar, he had heard footsteps walking across the bar floor above him. As he was alone, with the pub closed at the time, he thought it must be an intruder, but on dashing upstairs to the bar, he found it empty.

The Golden Cannon, in St George's Road, is said to be haunted by the spirit of a landlord who ran the pub in the late 1800s, and who is said to have hanged himself in the pub's cellar. His ghost may not be very active nowadays, but from time to time it still lets its presence be known.

Eva Mavis, the Golden Cannon's landlady for 25 years until 1995 said: "We nicknamed him 'Frank'. You feel someone tap you on the shoulder and turn, but there's no one there. He's quite a friendly spirit, and both I and my staff are used to it happening."

There is a side story... Mrs Mavis's husband, Bren, died in 1983. He used to say to his wife that when he died he would keep an eye on her and would tip her glass over if he felt she was drinking more than she ought.

"Although I've sometimes accidentally knocked over a glass, my glass has overturned quite a few times of its own accord over the years!" averred Mrs Mavis.

In more recent times, the 'touching' incidents have ceased, though staff still report the occasional charged atmosphere in the cellar.

The Lion, in St James's Street, was built towards the end of the 18th century. Prior to the flint walls of the beer garden being rendered, the indentations made by hay racks and the large iron rings to which horses were tethered testified to the pub's original status as a coaching inn.

In the summer of 1936 licensee Henry Metcalfe murdered his wife by firing three shots at her. He then turned the revolver on himself. This double tragedy may have a connection with the paranormal events which have taken place since, though a story persists that during the pub's early years, when it was still residential, a maid was found dead in mysterious circumstances. She had apparently died from shock while alone in the basement staff quarters, for her face in death carried a look of abject terror.

Corinne Bailly was landlady of the Lion from 1982 to 1990. When she moved in she was unaware of the pub's disturbing past, but it wasn't long before she discovered that all was not as it should be. Internal doors sometimes swung wide open without cause, while one night she awoke to the sound of what seemed to be bracelets jangling against each other. With this came the smell of a sickly perfume. It was an experience that was to be repeated several times over the eight years she was at the pub.

Once, outside business hours, a friend who had called on her was looking towards the glass pane of an internal door when she was surprised to see, in addition to her own reflection, that of an old man. He was looking over her shoulder, but when she turned, she found no one there.

One chilly winter's day, Mrs Bailly was relaxing by the fire in the bar (the fireplace has since been removed). The pub was soon to open for the evening session and she was quite alone, but expecting her bar staff to arrive at any moment. As she gazed at the flickering coals, she felt the atmosphere change. With this came a slight creaking sound. Turning her head, she was astonished to see a few of the bar stools moving slightly. It was as if some unseen customers were taking their seats around the bar. She also had the impression that more people were present in other parts of the bar. Then, in moment or two, everything reverted to normal.

In 1990, John and Karen Topham took charge of the Lion. About a year later there were major alterations to the pub and, possibly as a consequence, the incidence of ghostly activities lessened. But they certainly didn't cease.

From time to time, Mr and Mrs Topham and some of their staff noticed sudden drops of temperature when working in the cellar, while barmaid Jo Hillman felt an actual presence on a number of occasions. A puzzled Mr Topham several times reported very noisy surges from the gas cylinders in the cellar, as well as spells of insistent rattling of the flap on the hand-dryer in the basement gents' toilet when no one was there and when there were no draughts to account for it.

The most intriguing incident took place in the lounge of the upstairs flat. Mrs Topham was lying on the settee when she felt something grip her shoulder. Turning, she saw an apparition standing behind her. It was only visible for seconds. Because of the shock it induced, Mrs Topham was unable to establish whether the form was male or female, though she did observe that it was wearing grey clothing of an indistinct shape.

The Battle of Waterloo, in Rock Place, possibly has two ghosts, though sightings of them are rare. One is that of a tall man dressed as a coachman; the other is of an old lady dressed in grey. Whether the skeletons of a woman and a cat found in a plastered-over fireplace, opened up some years ago during major alterations, have anything to do with the hauntings is not known.

The coachman is said to have been the Mayor of Brighton's driver at some time towards the end of the 1800s. When Tom and Peggy Butler were the pub's tenants, in the 1970s, one customer reported that he'd seen the ghostly coachman walking towards the gent's toilet.

Jim Smith, the landlord from 1990 to 1995, said that on two occasions customers had told him they had seen the apparition of a woman in a long, grey dress. Though he had not personally seen anything ghostly, when he first arrived at the pub he found that his two alsatians weren't too happy in their new environment.

"Sometimes, when they were in the residential part of the pub, they'd suddenly bolt downstairs with their fur hackling," he said. "It was as if something was chasing them, but they stopped doing this after about two months. If the pub does have a ghost, perhaps by then they had become used to it. Or it had got used to them!"

The Rock public house, in Rock Street, is notable for having a 50ft deep well in the rear bar. The well played a significant part in the building's early history. Prior to 1750 there was a barn on the site. This was later rebuilt to become a coach house when, with horses to be watered, the well was an obvious asset. Smuggling was virtually an industry in Brighton at the time, and the well's great depth was almost certainly used to advantage as a hiding place for contraband. The building was converted into a public house in 1787. For some years after this, it continued to be a meeting place for smugglers.

Some of the smugglers entering the Rock were dead ones! This came about because the pub's cellar was used as a morgue in its early days, the pub then being one of the few buildings in the area – it was mostly surrounded by fields and farmland. So the bodies of smugglers killed during clashes with the excise men joined those of others in the makeshift morgue.

In 1912 the Rock closed as a pub for a year or so to become a temporary booking and parcels office for the London, Brighton and South Coast Railway Company during the time a new office was being built at the former Kemp Town Railway Station. This had opened in 1869 and was a short walk away.

Added to the Rock's colourful history is a reputation for being haunted, with successive landlords reporting a diversity of unsettling events. These have ranged from objects moving of their own volition, to sightings of a spectral woman dressed in grey.

David and Sylvia Burrows took over as managers of the Rock in November 1995. They knew nothing of the pub's haunted past, so when they discovered, a few weeks later, that a water pipe running along the cellar ceiling had been, it seemed, pulled down several feet, with water gently spraying out from a small fracture, they put it down to some weakness in the pipe. Again, when the gas cylinders used to propel beer up from the cellar inexplicably turned off from time to time, they didn't go further than thinking it odd.

Early on a Sunday morning during the following January, they heard a crash in the first floor bathroom. Hurrying there, they found that a wall mirror had fallen to the floor. Curiously, it had landed face uppermost. By then they had heard rumours of the pub's haunted past from customers, but they still opted for a rational explanation for the various incidents.

Some weeks later, when a print and its protective glass fell from its wall-mounted frame in one bar, and a large Victorian advertisement board crashed to the ground in another, Mr and Mrs Burrows began to consider the possibility that something other than natural causes really was at work. The fall of the advertisement board, which took place late at night after all the customers had left, was especially puzzling, for it had been secured by long screws. It appeared to have been wrenched off the wall. But the most disturbing events were still to take place.

On the first Sunday of June 1996, the fire brigade was called out to quell a blaze at the pub. It originated on the first floor in an area where a clothes-washing machine was standing. Mounted on top of it was a tumble-dryer. The fire completely engulfed the first floor corridor. The fire brigade indicated that an electrical fault was to blame, but there were baffling aspects to the incident.

Mrs Burrows had used the tumble-dryer in the afternoon and had switched it off. An hour or so later, Mr and Mrs Burrows went out to dinner, returning in time for the Sunday evening opening. Later, while Mrs Burrows was in the bar, Mr Burrows went upstairs to attend to some paperwork. While there, he heard the tumble-dryer start up and presumed that his wife had put some more clothing in to be dried. But she had remained in the bar. No one had touched the machine. Eventually, as the bar became busier, Mr Burrows went downstairs to help his wife.

At about 11.30, when the Burrows were clearing up in the bar following the departure of the last customers, they heard cries coming from upstairs. Helen, their 16-year-old daughter, had woken up to find smoke coming into her room. Earlier, she had spent the evening with a friend, returned at about 10.30, and had gone to bed shortly after that. Fortunately, she came to no harm. Though the fire brigade was quick to arrive, the corridor was already well ablaze.

The fire was hot enough to melt some of the metal fixtures in the corridor yet, mystifyingly, very important documents in a leather briefcase that Mr Burrows had left close to the source of the fire were totally undamaged; not even warped – this despite the briefcase itself being by then just disintegrating carbon onto which gallons of water had been pumped.

One evening, about two weeks after the fire, some customers were practising on the pool table prior to a competition that was to be held. One of the customers was about to play, when he felt some invisible force restraining his hand. Bewildered, he struggled to pull his hand away from the table, but was unable to do so until, several seconds later, his hand was released.

Only days after this incident, Mrs Burrows went to take a red shirt from the wardrobe. Only recently purchased, it had been folded up, so she was astonished to find black streaks across the waist. Presuming that someone in the family had got their hands dirty from the fire-blackened corridor and handled the shirt, although no one admitted they had done so, she washed and dried it and put it back in the wardrobe. The next day when she took it out once more, she was astonished to see that the black streaks had returned.

This time, she looked more carefully at the streaks and noted that they had the shape of fingers. It was as if someone had pressed blackened fingers on the shirt, but not the palm of the hand. She washed the shirt out once more, but for a third time the black marks reappeared. This time, following another wash, the streaks remained as light brown marks.

A local medium, learning of the disturbing events, offered to help. She claimed the pub was haunted by a woman from Regency times and by an excise man who had died at the end of a rope after smugglers had overwhelmed him and put a noose around his neck before tossing him down the well. Following an exorcism, there were no further ghostly incidents at the pub.

The 300-year-old Stag Inn, in Upper Bedford Street, has a ghost which customers have nicknamed 'Albert'. Bill Harman, landlord of the Stag for six years until leaving in 1985, reported a number of strange happenings while there, including a sighting of the ghost by his son-in-law, John Protheroe, who rushed upstairs from the kitchen after a scary meeting with a tall, thin, spectral man wearing black trousers, a white shirt with black armbands around the sleeves and a white apron. Some months later, while in a corridor, Mr Harman also saw the man. At another time, the landlord arrived in the bar to prepare for opening time and found fruit machine tokens scattered across the floor.

In 1991, when Taff Hill was landlord, he reported that the ghost sometimes turned off beer taps, disconnected the beer lines, and touched members of staff. Once, within the sight of customers in the bar, the entity caused a fire door, normally kept closed by a strong spring, to fly wide open, then slam shut again (subsequent refurbishment has dispensed with the door).

On other occasions the ghost threw a barrel of beer down the cellar steps, dumped a case of bottled mineral waters into the freezer, causing the bottles to crack when the liquid inside them turned to ice, and made the contents of a full barrel of beer disappear.

Following a story about the haunting in the *Brighton & Hove Leader,* a Portslade reader contacted the newspaper to say that his grandfather had been landlord of the Stag back in 1896 and had told him of similar ghostly incidents.

A Lewes-based medium offered his services after reading about the ghost. He maintained that the ghost was that of a landlord who had choked to death after becoming entangled in the beer lines while in the pub's darkened cellar. However, though the medium's intercession may have brought about a quiet period of five years during which nothing particularly singular took place, 1999 saw a resurgence of the paranormal.

Bob Watkins had taken over as landlord in the preceding year. His initial months at the Stag passed by without anything odd taking place until a day came when the supply of beer to the bar dried up. Investigation showed that the gas cylinders in the cellar had been turned off. But by whom? At the time, Mr Watkins didn't equate the incident with anything ghostly, but when this cessation of the beer supply escalated to a point where it was taking place about once a fortnight, something other than ordinary malfunction seemed to be at work. But yet other uncanny events were to follow.

Towards the end of 1999, Mr Watkins' collection of glassware, kept on a shelf behind the bar, attracted the attention of the resident ghost. A glass boot in the collection suddenly shot off the shelf to smash on the floor, about twelve feet away. Several customers witnessed this incident.

During one of the Thursday evening quiz nights, a loudspeaker being used in the quiz shot away from its position to land some eight feet away. Although, at the time, not everyone in the bar was looking in the direction of the loudspeaker, about a dozen customers did see this happen.

Author's note: The suggested cause of the landlord's death must be questioned, for it seems almost impossible that someone could become mortally entangled in the rubber tubing formerly used for the pumping of beer. Furthermore, if the ghost was around in late Victorian times, as indicated by the Portslade reader, it is virtually certain there would have been no beer lines existing to cause such a death. While the beer engine – the pump which draws the beer through the lines – was invented towards the end of the 1800s, it wasn't in general use until years later, with most pubs continuing to have their barrels mounted on stillions at the rear of the serving area, the beer being taken directly from the barrel taps.

The Pedestrian's Arms, in Foundry Street, acquired its name in 1869 after it was taken over by John Stepney, a champion long distance roadwalker and a regular entrant in the London to Brighton walks. Opened as an ale-house in 1856, it was at first called the White Horse. Later it was named the Labour in Vain, and then the Lamb, prior to acquiring its current title.

Bill and Beryl Dye, who ran the pub for several years until 1984, soon sensed there was something not quite right about the pub's cellar. Interviewed by the *Brighton and Hove Gazette*, Mr Dye said: "I've never believed in the supernatural, but there is something here. I have felt it looking over my shoulder."

Gary Lewis, who took over as landlord after the Dye family had left, reported that on a number of occasions while working in the cellar, he had heard the sound of footsteps crossing the floor of the bar above when no one else was in the building.

The phantom of a woman jailer, complete with clinking keys, once haunted the George Beard pub in Gloucester Road, though it hasn't been sighted for more than 25 years. The ghost used to appear on the stairs leading to the cellar. In the early 1800s, a police station stood where the pub is now, with the basement having a number of cells for the detention of miscreants.

The present building dates from about 1850. It was initially called the Eagle Hotel, the inspiration for the name coming from the Eagle Iron Foundry, which stood two doors away (the Victoria Fountain, in Old Steine, was cast at the foundry in 1846). The foundry was eventually demolished to make way for the current castellated building, built around 1870 as an HQ for the Royal Artillery Volunteers. The building is now used for residential purposes.

Soldiers from this depot provided much of the Eagle Hotel's trade during the late 1800s and early 1900s, though the nearby Canteen pub (which at one time stood at the north end of the Robert Street building where the *Evening Argus* was at one time printed) provided strong competition, despite its rowdy reputation.

After the Eagle had been taken over by Beards, the Sussex brewers, the pub was renamed the George Beard to commemorate George Ravenhill Beard, who was at one time the sole proprietor of the company.

The Prestonville Arms, in Hamilton Road, was said to be haunted by the ghost of a former cellarman whose other-world expertise included being able to move bottles and beer crates around. However, there have been no reported paranormal events at the pub since the original incidents, which took place many years ago. The nature and limited time span of the events suggests that a poltergeist-type influence was at work, rather than the spirit of a deceased cellarman.

Towards the end of 1995 William Booth started work as a barman at the Nightingale public house (renamed Finnegan's Wake in 1997), in Surrey Street. He soon discovered that the working day was sometimes interrupted by little oddities. There were problems with the lighting, for example. The last person to leave the cellar each night might find that however many times the switch was flicked, the cellar lighting would, perversely, remain on. On such occasions, there would be nothing left to do but leave the lights blazing. Yet the following morning, the first person to enter the cellar would find it in darkness. No fault could be found to account for these freakish happenings.

One day, when Mr Booth was serving a customer, he heard a door open and looked up to see a grey-haired woman in a black skirt walk into the kitchen. He only had a back view of the woman, but he believed her to be Liz Bennett, the manageress. As he wanted to query something, Mr Booth finished serving the customer and hurried after her.

On entering the kitchen, he was surprised to find it empty. No one could have left, he said, without being seen by him. He later found out that Mrs Bennett had been upstairs at the time and was wearing clothing entirely different to that worn by the mystery woman.

When Mrs and Mrs Bennett left the Nightingale in the summer of 1996 to work elsewhere, Mr Booth became the pub's manager. By then he had already become used to the gas cylinders in the cellar being turned off by some unknown force, a circumstance which brought about an immediate and embarrassing halt to the supply of draught lager and some beers, with tetchy customers wondering why they couldn't be served. This might happen as often as two, or even three times, in a single week. Sometimes Mr Booth found that the gas cylinders had been turned off so forcibly that it was a struggle to turn them on again.

From time to time, pub staff heard the sound of phantom footsteps in the cellar. On one occasion Mr Booth was standing by the cellar door, talking to some visiting friends, when all picked up the sound of footsteps coming from below. His friends laughed when he told them of the pub's ghost, so he took them to the cellar where their eyes were able to confirm that there was no one there.

The ghost haunting the pub is said to be that of a woman who, many years ago, fell onto the line at Brighton Railway Station. Seriously injured, for some reason she was carried across the road into the Nightingale, where she died, though a doctor had reached her by this time. The story is told that, many years ago, when manifestations were more usually of the visual kind, the woman looked all the more frightening because she appeared to be covered in dressings and bandages.

The Prince George, in Trafalgar Street, was built early in the 19th century (in recent times there has been a change of name to, simply, the George, and it is now a vegetarian restaurant and bar). It was orginally a dairy, but it became licensed in 1820 and for some years cheerily supplied both milk and beer to its customers. As late as 1846 it was still being called the Prince George & Cowkeeper, so presumably sold both milk and beer until that time.

A section of the pub's cellar was at one time part of the basement area of the funeral director's business close by, and it was here that the bodies of the deceased were laid out, a fact that may have a relevance to the spooky happenings which have since taken place.

Kate Sharp managed the Prince George from 1994 until 1997. On several occasions she had to go down to the cellar because the resident ghost had turned off the gas cylinders, leaving staff unable to pull pints for the customers. The capricious spirit had other pranks up its sleeve. Twice in a single month during 1995 it pushed down the 'breather' spirals on eight or nine barrels. These spirals are normally positioned on the top of each barrel so that they protrude by about an inch, but all were found to be flush with the barrels (it would normally take a sharp blow with a mallet to achieve this).

Puzzlingly, objects in the cellar would sometimes be switched around from their usual places by some mysterious force, while Miss Sharp's Doberman pinscher refused to venture downstairs. If any attempt was made to lead the dog into the cellar, it would pull back with its fur hackling.

John and Sue Gravenor were previously in charge of the pub, having taken it over in 1988. During their time there, the gas cylinders in the cellar sometimes turned off for no reason and often so tightly that a spanner was needed to turn them on again. It may have been coincidental, but the Gravenors found later that this phenomenon occurred mostly when a publican or retired publican was laid out in the nearby undertaker's Chapel of Rest.

As with Miss Sharp's dog, they also found that their German shepherd refused to venture into the cellar. Instead, the dog would stand at the top of the steps barking furiously, just as if an intruder was down there. Some staff claimed they had seen shadowy figures in the cellar, while two or three barmaids were sufficiently frightened to avoid the place altogether. Cellar electric light bulbs sometimes disappeared from their sockets, never to be seen again, while others were found smashed on the floor.

Mrs Gravenor prepared each day's lunchtime meals in the kitchen at the rear of the bars. One day in 1990, after she had left the kitchen for a few moments, a regular customer looked through the serving hatch to see a middle-aged woman, who he had not seen before, standing by the deep chip fryer. When Mrs Gravenor passed through the bar on her way back to the kitchen, he asked her who the new assistant was. Mrs Gravenor, puzzled, walked into the kitchen. There was no one there. Nor was there any way someone could have left the kitchen without being seen.

In 1999 barmaid Lisa Bisset found that gas cylinders in the cellar were still turning off of their own accord, while once, quite mysteriously, all the spirals that had been inserted into the tops of the barrels were found scattered across the floor.

The Prince Albert, in Trafalgar Street, was built in 1841, initially as a residential hotel. Some of its trade came from the coach house which once stood next door. Reports of ghosts at the pub have continued for many years. It is said that there was originally a well on the premises and one of the pub's spectres is thought to be that of a man who accidentally fell into the well and drowned. It is uncertain who this man was; he has variously been described as the landlord, a cellarman and a smuggler!

What is certain is that inexplicable incidents have taken place at the pub and that some staff have felt an oppressive presence while in the cellar. George and Lilian Scholey ran the Prince Albert for 25 years until retiring in 1984. They were aware of the pub's ghostly reputation, but remained sceptical during their time there.

Mrs Scholey said: "It's true there were peculiar noises coming up from the cellar; odd thumps, creaking sounds, and so on. But it is a very old pub and you'd expect that sort of thing, though when my uncle Charlie Bore was looking after the cellar, he claimed that when he had taken the brass taps out of the empty barrels in readiness for collection by the brewery, he'd sometimes find the taps back in the barrels again. We used to reckon it was because he'd become forgetful in his old age.

"Mind you, our son Kevin believed there was something eerie down there and he felt it might help matters to draw a picture of Jesus on the wall. It was quite well done. I've a photograph of it. I don't know if the drawing is still there".

Following the departure of the Scholeys in 1984, John Maslen took over the running of the Prince Albert. He was there for ten years and during that time he had, at various times, two male lodgers living on the first floor. Both mentioned that they had been disturbed by the noise of children running up and down the stairway, close to their first floor bedroom. Which Mr Maslen thought odd, for there were no children on the premises.

One lodger, Ray Finch, who worked for British Rail, was on early shifts. Shortly after getting up at 4am one morning, he was surprised to hear the sound of someone running up the stairs and then on into the nearby function room. The footsteps sounded like those of children and they were accompanied by the excited laughter of a girl. Mr Finch quickly opened the door of his bedroom and looked around him. Seeing no one, he went into the nearby function room. It was empty.

Following the departure of Mr Maslen in 1994, Paul Brookes became the manager. On several occasions he heard furniture being moved around in the first floor function room when no one was present. One afternoon, after a pop group had left their instruments in the room in readiness for an evening gig, he rushed upstairs on hearing things being dragged across the floor. Opening the door of the room, he found no intruder, but he did note that chairs and musical instruments had been moved around and that the cymbals attached to the drum kit were still rocking.

Barman Chris Davies was working in the bar one day when he heard a loud crash in the function room. He described it as being like a heavy item of furniture being dropped, but when he dashed upstairs, he found nothing to indicate what had caused the noise.

John and Noria Summers, who owned the pub at the time, were in the bar late in 1994 when they heard the crash of breaking glassware up on the first floor. A search revealed that it was once again just a sound without a rational cause. Bob Thompson became manager of the Prince Albert early in 1995. Once, when alone in the pub, he heard someone pacing the floor of the function room above him, but on investigating, found nobody.

Some of the oddest events took place in the summer of 1995. Handyman/cleaner Peter Kingsley had arrived early in the day to start work when he found he could not get the vacuum cleaner to function. As the lights were not working either, he went down to the cellar to check the mains power switches. As he reached the top of the cellar steps, a packet of firelighters on some shelving shot out, missing his head by inches before smashing against the opposite wall. Shocked, Mr Kingsley called Mr Thomson, who was still in his residential quarters.

Earlier that day at about 1.30am, Mr Thomson, while in bed, had observed that the indicator light on a security monitor situated in his bedroom was no longer flashing. Had there been a power cut, or a malfunction in the equipment? Otherwise, for there were no unusual sounds coming from within the pub, all seemed well. Now, alerted by Mr Kingsley, he made his way to the cellar. There, he found that the power had inexplicably been switched off at the mains. Even odder was his discovery that the cooling equipment situated near the cellar entrance was coated on the outside by ice about an inch thick!

There was also the strange affair of the intercom system, which connected the bar to the kitchen. From time to time the bar would be buzzed, apparently by someone in the kitchen, but on listening, only a distant woman's voice could be heard. No words were decipherable. In fact, the sound was described as being almost like the sound of someone gargling. Whenever this voice was heard on the intercom, which was fairly often, the battery went dead, even if quite new. At £3 to £4 a time for batteries it became an expensive matter, so the intercom was dismantled.

One day, a woman psychic called at the pub. After using the staircase to the first floor she made the odd claim that two children, a boy and a girl, were 'trapped' in the glass of the small landing half-way up the stairs. This landing is partly comprised of thick rectangles of glass and dates from Victorian times when gaslight provided the pub's sole illumination. A gas lamp beneath the landing helped to light the cellar, with some of its light shining through the glass rectangles to illuminate the stairway above.

In 1997, tradesman Shane Watson was engaged to redecorate the pub. So as not to disrupt pub business, he carried out his task overnight, finishing after dawn each day. One morning, just after sunrise, he was coming out of the first floor toilet, which he had been painting, when he was astonished to see an extraordinary figure coming up the stairs. It had the shape of a human, but was composed entirely of what he described as being a luminous white mist. The apparition seemed to be sprinting up the stairs and in a moment was before Mr Watson. In the next instant, the glowing figure passed right through his body. He later described the experience.

"There wasn't a coldness, as you might expect, but afterwards I was unable to work for about an hour-and-a-half. My whole body was shaking. I suppose it was shock, but it didn't seem quite like that. It was as if something had been drained out of me by the thing. Up until then I had never believed in ghosts."

Pippa Terry became licensee of the Prince Albert in the early summer of 1998. Over the previous year she had been a barmaid at the pub. She said that one band, due to play at the pub, refused to do so after something invisible brushed past them with clattering footsteps while they were going upstairs to the function room. On another occasion, just prior to a performance by a group, the man standing just outside of the function room to collect entrance monies heard footsteps rapidly coming up the staircase, but when he looked, there was no one there.

Ben Jordan, a friend of the bar staff, helped out one day at a busy time by bringing some crates of bottled beer up from the cellar. He felt what he said was 'a nasty atmosphere' while there. In the next moment, a stack of beer crates tumbled over.

Cleaner Heather Morphee was carrying out her duties early one morning towards the end of 1998 when her 11-year-old daughter Leanne, whom she had taken to work with her, called out to say that there was a black cat on the stairs. Had a stray cat got into the pub? Mrs Morphee went to investigate, but no cat was found. Leanne had not been told of the pub's spooky reputation.

Early in 1999 Leanne again accompanied her mother to the pub. While Mrs Morphee was cleaning an upstairs room, there was the sound of a crash from the bar. Leanne was close by the bar at the time. They discovered that a brass trumpet, which had been hanging on the wall above the bar, had shot across the bar to land on the floor some five feet away.

In May 1998 Mrs Morphee went to Canada for a month's holiday. During this time a friend, Julie Maguire, agreed to carry out the cleaning duties at the Prince Albert. Not wanting to cause her friend any apprehension, Mrs Morphee said nothing about the haunting so when, on her very first morning at the pub, Mrs Maguire heard footsteps running up the stairs and walking across the floor above, she presumed it was someone living in the upstairs residential flat. It wasn't until the next day that she discovered there was no one occupying the flat; that she had been the only person on the premises at the time.

A few days later on arriving for work, she had hardly stepped inside the front doors of the pub when she heard running footsteps and the sound of children giggling. Thinking some youngsters had somehow got into the pub, she searched the place, but found no one. On another day, while mopping the floor of the ground floor pool room, she had the impression that she was being watched. In the next moment, she felt as if some ice cold, invisible entity had walked right through her. It happened so quickly that it wasn't until afterwards that she felt an element of shock.

There was yet another weird experience to come; one which Mrs Maguire found much more frightening than that which had taken place in the pool room. Usually, because of her early start, she completed her work some time before the bar staff arrived to prepare for opening time. On this particular day, shortly before she was due to leave, and while in the bar, she heard footsteps and the jingling of keys.

Disturbed by this, she decided to leave as soon possible, but when she attempted to go through the pub's double front doors, she found she was unable to do so. Though she locked and unlocked the doors several times and pushed and pulled on them, they refused to open. She peered through the thin slit of light between the doors to see if the latches were responding to the door handles and keys. She saw that they were, but still the doors would not open.

By now, almost in tears, she banged on the window to attract the attention of a woman passer-by. When the woman came close to the window, Mrs Maguire called for her assistance, but even with both women applying themselves to opening the doors, they refused to budge. Mrs Maguire, in desperation, was thinking of phoning the police for help, but in the next moments she heard the sound of ghostly keys jingling and of a lock turning. Uncertainly, she edged towards the doors. She was relieved to find that they now opened easily!

On her return from Canada, Mrs Morphee expressed a wish to have each weekend off, so Mrs Maguire was asked if she would like to take on the Saturday and Sunday cleaning duties. Though she agreed to this, it was with misgivings, for the alarming experiences of the previous weeks were still vivid in her mind. However, although she continued in this job on a regular basis over the months that followed, the only unusual activity she encountered was the very occasional sound of ghostly footsteps. Her more disturbing experiences, it seems, were confined to the four weeks of Mrs Morphee's absence.

In June 1999 the Royal Albert came under new ownership. In the days immediately preceding the change of ownership, and for no tangible reason, the pub's lights frequently switched off and, more bizarrely, some beer pipes froze up.

As an early reopening of the pub was required, some of the refurbishment activities following the change of ownership took place after dark. So it was that painter and decorator Darren Irving found himself working on the second floor at about 11.30 one night. He knew he was the only person in the building at the time, so he was surprised to hear the footsteps of someone on the floor below. At the same time, he heard what sounded like a female voice. On going downstairs, he found nothing to account for the sounds. A few days later, and again when he was alone in the building, he heard unusual noises coming from the bar. It sounded, he said, as if someone was walking on tin cans.

Of some interest is the fact that building workers, during the 1999 refurbishment of the pub, and while excavating a part of the yard at the rear of the building prior to erecting a new toilet, were astonished to come across the well presumed to have been the site of the drowning that had taken place many years before. No investigation was made of its contents.

Author's note: Because it was an especially interesting and ongoing haunting, I visited the Prince Albert on several occasions. During an early visit, I enquired if the drawing of Jesus still remained in the cellar. It did, and I was invited to see it. It is a slightly disturbing black and white crayon drawing dated 1964 and signed by Kevin Scholey. In later years there were attempts to obliterate it, but each time the drawing refused to succumb, its thick, dark lines continuing to push through the paint.

As Mrs Scholey, in an earlier conversation, had wondered if her son's drawing still existed, I decided to phone her to say that it did. She then said something quite interesting. When I originally spoke to her, I had mentioned the 'children running up the stairs' story, as told by Mr Finch. But Mrs Scholey knew nothing about the psychic's claim that a boy and a girl were trapped in glass on the stairway landing – at that time, the psychic was still to call at the pub.

However, Mrs Scholey said that after she had put the phone down on the first occasion I had spoken to her, she had recalled an odd happening concerning her mother, which she thought had some relevance to the 'children on the stairs' incident. It took place in 1970, when her mother was 80 years old. The mother used to enjoy a quiet drink in the small snug bar – the pub was then divided into three bars. Suddenly the mother, who was alone in the bar, called her daughter.

"Get these children out," she thundered. "They're a damned nuisance."

Mrs Scholey left what she was doing and peered into the snug bar, but could see no one. But her mother insisted there were two children there. One, she said, was a boy who was sitting quietly on one of the seats, but the other child was a girl who, the mother complained, 'keeps running around the bar and hovering around my handbag'. Although her mother had been in full possession of her faculties until then, Mrs Scholey now wondered if the old lady was beginning to become senile. In retrospect, there may be something deeper to this incident!

On being told about the garbled voice on the pub's intercom system, Mrs Scholey recalled similar, and frequent, experiences with their intercom. At the time, however, she put the voice down to kitchen staff 'larking about' – though she said they always denied this. As this system was connected to the mains, there were no problems associated with drained batteries.

The Bat & Ball pub, at the bottom of Ditchling Road, faces The Level, a park situated at the point where streams from Patcham and Lewes once joined. As a consequence, the area was sometimes flooded. When conditions were exceptionally severe, the flood waters spread to nearby London Road, resulting in its closure.

Later, the park was used for county cricket matches until, in 1823, these were transferred to Ireland's Royal Gardens, which were once located immediately to the north of The Level. But a look at the pub sign outside of the Bat & Ball reveals that the sport illustrated is not cricket, but instead the ancient game of bat and trap, which for hundreds of years was a popular sport in south-east England. Until the 1930s, pub bat and trap teams, including one from the Bat & Ball, played regularly on The Level.

The pub has a ghost which may be that of a former landlady. One witness was Norma Abbott, the stepmother of John Farnham, the pub's tenant at the time of her sighting. Mrs Abbott was alone in the bar, cashing up the till, at about 11.30 one night in 1991. The last customers had left and the doors were locked, so when she saw a movement out of the corner of her eye, she thought there must be an intruder, but on looking up, she had the surprise of her life.

At the far end of the bar by the dartboard was a barefooted woman wearing a white nightdress which came down to just below her knees. As Mrs Abbott watched in astonishment, the woman started to dance. She then twirled and jigged right through the bar and into a corner by the street exit where she just faded away.

Some days later, when Mrs Abbott related her experience to a customer who had used the pub for many years, the customer told her that there had once been a very extrovert landlady who used sometimes to dance through the bar. At a later date, curiously, a Jack Russell dog that was in the bar went berserk by that part of the wall where the phantom had initially manifested. It could not be quieted until it had been pulled away from the area.

At about 11.30 one night in 1992, manager Colin James, having locked all the doors, decided to play a few games on the fruit machine prior to clearing up the bar. He'd only just started to play when he sensed there was someone else in the bar. Turning, he saw a middle-aged woman with greying hair walking across the bar. She was wearing a grey blouse and a black, belted skirt. Thinking the woman had been accidently locked in – perhaps she had been loitering in the ladies' toilet? – he called out to her.

"Excuse me, love, but we're closed now."

The woman appeared to ignore him. Then, two or three steps later, she just vanished into thin air. The only other ghostly incident witnessed by Mr James – though a barmaid was also present at the time – was when a wine glass, which was well away from the edge of the shelf on which it stood, shot across the bar to smash onto the floor several feet away. Whatever spirit is present at the Bat & Ball, it appears to have been quiescent in recent years.

A few doors away from the Bat and Ball is another haunted pub, the Leek. It was previously known as the Leek and Winkle, and before that, the Brunswick (it stands in that section of Ditchling Road formerly known as Brunswick Place).

While stories of the supernatural have been associated with the pub for many years, several changes of management during this time have prevented meaningful investigation. However, some minor incidents of note did take place during the period 1977 to 1992, when Alan and Lynda Parkinson were managers.

On three or four occasions the couple discovered that the gas cylinders in the cellar had unaccountably been turned off while once, after the front door had been locked at the end of the day, some discarnate force seemingly interfered with the locks.

Mr Parkinson said: "At the time, the front door was secured by two Chubb locks, a Yale lock and two bolts. I'm sure that all of these were in place at closing time, yet when I went to open the door in the morning I found that the two Chubb locks had been unlocked and the two bolts pulled. Oddly, the Yale lock remained locked."

Nicci Mullen, who managed the pub for two years until the beginning of 1996, said that she and other members of staff had had their first names called out by an unseen entity on several occasions. This phenomenon always took place outside of normal opening hours and when the bar was quiet. Sometimes, while working in the cellar, Miss Mullen had the impression that she was being watched by some indefinable presence and once she observed a shadowy form gliding across the floor.

Ben Thompson, assistant manager of the Leek and Winkle for a year until March 1996, was one person working at the pub who, several times, had his name called by the disembodied voice. But he remembered other incidents.

"The lights used to flicker and dim before returning to full power, though no electrical fault was found," he said. "On one occasion, a bottle of tonic water exploded. The odd thing was that only a small bit of the bottom of the bottle remained. We searched everywhere for the cap and the broken glass from the top of the bottle, but they were never found."

A monk and a young girl haunt the Harlequin, a bar-restaurant in Providence Place, although a priest from the nearby church of St Bartholomew's was called in during 1996 to despatch the ghosts with prayers and a blessing. The nature of the haunting seems likely to be connected with the fact that the premises were once associated with St Bartholomew's.

Opened in 1893 as a church hall, the building was used over the years for a variety of church activities and, eventually, as a classroom for children. Following the provision of a new hall in New England Street as part of a school redevelopment project, the building was used as a car showroom and, later, as a restaurant. It was converted into a public house in the 1980s.

The ghost of the girl has only been seen in the area of the stairs and passage leading to the first floor toilets. The spectral monk also seems to confine his appearances to the first floor.

Gary and Maria Buckland became managers of the pub, then known as Marilyn's Bar, in 1995. They had only been there a few weeks when a woman customer, visibly distressed, rushed down from the first floor to say that she had just encountered the apparition of a blonde girl, who she thought was aged about eight.

Mrs Buckland, though never herself seeing the ghost of the girl, several times experienced a sense of foreboding when at the top of the stairs; a feeling she described as being 'like a panic attack'.

Both Mr and Mrs Buckland said they had seen the ghostly monk. He appeared as a 'gliding shadow' moving across the floor of the upstairs balcony area. Mr Buckland saw the apparition after the last customers had left on a Sunday evening in February 1996. It was shortly after 11.30, and he had just sat down with a hot meal at a table in the ground floor bar.

From where he was sitting, with his back to the north wall of the pub, he had a good view of the balcony. As he ate, he caught a movement out of the corner of his eye and, on looking up, saw a shadowy figure drift along the length of the balcony before disappearing. On another occasion Mrs Buckland witnessed the same phenomenon. In neither instance was the apparition sufficiently solid to identify it as being that of a monk, but such a ghost has been seen in a more tangible form in earlier years.

Following the prayer service at the pub, Mrs Buckland claimed that the atmosphere associated with the ghostly girl definitely lightened, though the Bucklands still had the feeling that the pub was not entirely free of some presence.

One of the more intriguing ghosts is that haunting the Horse and Groom, in Islingword Road, for this particular spectre is a former customer who seems reluctant to say farewell to his favourite 'watering hole'. He had his preferred seat next to one of the bar windows and after his death, as long as the seat was vacant, he was known to turn up on occasions to occupy it. The ghost is referred to as 'Fred', said to be his real name in life.

He hasn't been seen since the 1960s, though in more recent times he has made his presence known in other ways. The last person to have seen him is believed to be Vi Hammond, a former cleaner at the pub. Possibly Fred's failure to make any further visual appearances is due to being admonished by Mrs Hammond.

One day, on seeing Fred's spectre suddenly appear in his favourite chair by the window, and fortified by the fact that she had known the former customer while he was still alive, she bravely scolded: "Be on your way, Fred. There's no place for you here!"

In 1992, landlord Phil Murray and three male customers were present when Fred performed one of his occasional 'tricks'. It was just after Saturday lunchtime and there was an empty pint glass on the window shelf immediately behind Fred's seat. All four men witnessed the glass slowly move some two or three feet along the shelf before shooting onto the floor. Mr Murray was so intrigued by this phenomenon that he brought out a spirit level to see if the shelf was uneven in any way. He found it to be exactly level!

Every night before going to bed, Mr Murray gave the run of the pub to his two dogs. On being released into the bars, they usually bounded around a little before settling down. Shortly before midnight on Christmas Day 1993, as he was about to retire for the night, Mr Murray released the dogs as usual. They rushed into the bar, but when they came near to Fred's seat, both stopped abruptly. Their exuberance faded and their fur hackled. Mr Murray gripped the dogs by their collars and tried to pull them past the seat, but they wouldn't budge.

He thought it strange that this incident had taken place on Christmas Day, so the following Christmas he took the dogs into the bar at around the same time, wondering if there would be a repeat of the occurrence. There wasn't.

Gas cylinders in the cellar sometimes turned off when nobody was there and one night, after closing time, Mrs Murray was clearing up in the bar when the glasses in the glass-washing machine, which was switched off at the time, inexplicably began rattling violently and continued to do so for two or three minutes.

The Park View Hotel, in Preston Drove, was built over 100 years ago. It opened in 1898 as a gentlemen's sporting and dining club, though it is believed that this respectable identity hid another facet of its business which involved women of a very old profession. The early conversion of the building into a hotel may have been hastened when this illicit activity came to the notice of the authorities.

The Park View appears to have more than one ghost. Gossip has it that one spectre was that of a maid who worked there many years ago. The story was that she was seduced and made pregnant by the landlord. Later, during a fierce argument, the landlord knocked the girl down the stairs linking the lounge and public bars. Shortly afterwards, she died of her injuries.

However, an American woman who visited the Park View in 1997 told managers Jim and Sue Liddle that her grandfather had once been the pub's landlord, and he had told her that the haunting followed a tragedy which had taken place in the 1920s when a five-year-old girl had tumbled down the stairs to her death.

When Mr and Mrs Liddle arrived at the Park View in November 1994, they had no knowledge of its ghostly reputation, so the first incidents, though puzzling, were put down to natural causes. From time to time, the beer pressures faded. When this happened, it was found that the gas cylinders in the cellar had been partly turned off. The Liddles presumed some fault in the cylinders.

One morning, Mrs Liddle was clearing the breakfast table in the private residential part of the pub. Taking the crockery to the kitchen, she was surprised to find a small, unsmoked cigar in the sink. No one living at the pub smoked cigars, so she wondered how it had got there and why anyone would put such an item in the sink. Could it have been an apport?

It was the next incident which made the Liddles realise that the place must be haunted. One day, early in 1995, Mr Liddle's mother, Olive, was cleaning the staircase connecting the lounge and public bars. As she reached the bottom, she felt a peculiar warmth on the back of her head. On turning, she saw a circle of light hovering above the stairs, in the middle of which was a young girl's face. With a scream, Olive Liddle dropped her mop and bucket and raced into the bar.

The two years that followed saw little or no activity which could be classified as paranormal, but 1997 saw a resurgence of the unfathomable. Early in the year, Mrs Liddle was upstairs when she heard the pub's front door banging. The pub had closed for the night some time earlier, so using the internal phone system she called her husband in the bar where, assisted by a barman, he was clearing up. Neither had heard the banging. On checking the front door, it was found to be locked.

Later that year, Mr and Mrs Liddle were already in bed when they both heard the front door banging loudly. Again, a check revealed the door to be securely locked. In the same year, barmaid Viv Hill had just used the glass-washing machine and was placing the clean glasses on a shelf when she noticed a glass which she thought unusual.

The pub had a quantity of glasses which displayed the Carling logo, but this one glass had a different Carling design; one she had not seen before in her several years at the pub. She asked the manager, who had also not noticed this particular glass before, if she might keep it. He agreed, so she placed the glass on a shelf at the back of the bar with the intention of taking it home once her duties were completed. However, when she went to get the glass, which had been placed where it was inaccessible to customers, it was no longer there. It was never seen again.

Three years prior to the glass incident, Viv Hill's sister Helena became the focus for a most disturbing experience. It was a Sunday, and Helena had decided to call at the pub shortly after evening opening time so that she could speak to Viv, who was on duty in the public bar. There were only two customers present at the time.

After a while, Helena broke off the conversation with her sister to go to the ladies' toilet. When she hadn't returned after several minutes, Viv, by now somewhat concerned, left the bar to investigate. She found her sister still in the toilet, shaking with distress, and too frightened to come out.

Apparently, at the time Helena went into the toilet, a woman in a black dress was just coming out. The woman had looked at her with such malevolence and hatred that she had feared to see her again. Indeed, the stark impression had come into her mind that the woman in black was intent on stabbing her. Viv assured her sister that it was quite safe to return to the bar, adding that she had seen no such woman. At a later date, after Viv had mentioned the incident to others, she was told that in the past a woman customer had been very frightened on seeing a similar apparition.

Prior to the arrival of Mr and Mrs Liddle in 1994, there had been a variety of other strange events. In the late 1980s, a barman going down to the public bar was surprised to note that the handle of the door at the bottom of the stairs was rattling violently. It was outside of business hours and on opening the door, the barman found the bar beyond it quite empty.

Earlier in the same decade, the wife of one landlord, while taking a drink from one of the optics, felt a strange force pressing down on the hand holding the glass. Several seconds passed before she was able to move it. There was an even more frightening experience in store for her mother, who fainted after seeing the ghost of a man on the staircase. Wearing fairly modern dress, this apparition is thought to have been that of a previous landlord.

In 1989, bar staff were shocked when a box of onions which had been delivered for the kitchen flew off the bar shelf where it had temporarily been placed. A moment later, the bar till and a number of full beer bottles shot onto the floor.

On another occasion all the money which had been placed in a separate cash box in the pub's night safe was found scattered on the floor of the room in which it was located. The room and the safe had both been locked. An immediate check revealed that the safe was still locked, while a count of the money showed that none was missing.

In the same year, live-in barman Jamie Quinn returned to his bedroom to discover that, bafflingly, all his carefully folded up clothing had been taken out of a chest of drawers and from the top his desk and scattered about the room, and that the furniture had been moved around, most of it being pushed up against the window.

The Dyke Tavern, at the corner of Dyke Road and Highcroft Villas, was originally called the Windmill Inn. This name came from the former Preston Mill, which was sited nearby. The mill had once stood in Belle Vue Field (now Regency Square) as West Mill, but following complaints from local residents, it was moved in 1797 to the Dyke Road site on a sledge pulled by 36 yoke of oxen. It was demolished in 1881.

Throughout the years, staff at the Dyke Tavern reported the inexplicable movement of objects from one place to another. One item, an ice scoop used in conjunction with an ice-making machine situated in the cellar, found particular favour with the resident spirit, for there was a series of reports that it had moved without cause, sometimes to another part of the pub. Again, one or another of the gas cylinders in the cellar would spontaneously turn off from time to time, halting the supply to the bar of a particular beer.

Steve McIndoe, the pub's landlord from 1981 to 1987 – though he was non-resident for some of this time – became used to his staff reporting strange happenings. Lyn McIndoe, his wife, said that their normally courageous dog, a cross between an Airdale and an Irish wolfhound, could not be coaxed into the cellar; indeed, would shake with terror if any attempt was made to take it there.

Jon and Sue Chatterly, a married couple who worked and lived at the Dyke Tavern and who later became assistant managers, had a number of uncanny experiences there between 1992 and 1996. One involved their cat, which took an instant dislike to the hall outside the entrance door to the Chatterlys' first floor residential rooms. Usually a placid creature, it reacted abnormally if carried to this area. Its fur would stand on end, and it would growl and arch its back. When the Chatterlys eventually moved to a new address, the cat returned to its normal, serene behaviour. Strange footsteps were sometimes heard walking past the bathroom door. Mr Chatterly heard these footsteps on four separate occasions while he was having a bath; his wife hearing them on one occasion.

Rumours of the pub having a ghostly Grey Lady persisted for many years. For Mrs Chatterly, rumour became reality early in 1996. She was on her own in the bar one morning, cleaning the brasswork on the beer pumps in readiness for opening time, when she had the feeling of being watched. Turning, she was astounded to see, some 15 feet away from her and standing by the fireplace, a woman wearing a long, high-necked grey dress which had a pleated pattern above the waist. While the woman looked quite solid, Mrs Chatterly noted that her face was also greyish. The spectre soon faded.

In 1965 the landlord of the Bugle Inn, St Martin's Street, was troubled by lights switching on and off without reason, and by frequent and unexplained thumps and bangs from various parts of the building. As these activities were of a temporary nature, it is presumed that it was a poltergeist-type phenomenon.

A Second World War bombing incident forms the background to reports of a shadowy spirit haunting the Franklin Tavern, in Lewes Road. At one time known as the Lewes Road Inn, the pub was almost completely destroyed on 20 September 1940 when a Junkers 88 unloaded its bombs over Brighton.

The ghost is believed to be that of someone killed in the pub during the raid. Among those who died were landlord Ernest Sully and his wife, Rosina. Another victim was John Watson, who was cleaning the windows at the time. The pub was eventually rebuilt.

Over the years there have been several unexplained incidents. Jim Dobbin, who became the licensee in 1990, said: "I've never experienced anything unusual, but old customers have told me that the pub is supposed to be haunted."

Barmaid Tina Dolding, however, claimed she had seen a dark, shadowy figure on three occasions. The figure was so indistinct and ephemeral that she was unable to say whether it was male or female, but she said it always appeared in the same place; behind the bar by the door leading to the residential part of the pub.

15 *Shops and stores*

A SHOP BUILT during the early part of the 19th century and located close to the junction of Edward Street and Upper Rock Gardens harboured a ghost that brought fear and revulsion to all those who had the misfortune to behold it. During the years following the Second World War, the shop was used for the sale of second-hand goods, with the ground floor being given over to old furniture and bric-a-brac, while the cellar was used mainly for the storage of secondhand books.

An occasional visitor to the shop was Richard McColl, a local dealer in antiquarian books. Mr McColl was what is known in the bookselling trade as a 'runner' – that is, an individual who doesn't have his own shop but who acquires quality books by various means to sell on to both collectors and bookshops.

A collection of books would frequently come into the hands of the shop owner when he bought the complete contents of a house, and Mr McColl popped into the shop when he was in the area so that he could browse through such acquisitions. Calling late one afternoon, the book dealer found the shop owner busy with a customer.

"Sorry to bother you," interrupted Mr McColl, "but I was just passing and wondered if you had anything worth looking at?"

"If you're free this evening you could call in," responded the shop owner. "I've just got hold of another lot of books. I won't be here myself, but it will give you a chance to look through them at your leisure."

He knew Mr McColl well enough to trust him. "You can let yourself in. I'll give you a spare key and you can put the books you want to one side. We can sort out the cost later".

The book dealer agreed and that evening, at around eight o'clock, he let himself in and quickly descended the stairs to the cellar. He loved books and was looking forward to his task. To help make the time pass more pleasantly he took with him some sandwiches and a flask of coffee. There was no electric light in the cellar, so he also took a couple of candles.

The room had once been a large kitchen. Now it was a musty, gloomy place of flaking paint and cobwebs. At one end of the cellar was an alcove and within this was a large stone sink. Above the alcove was an archway of small, dark red bricks set in a peculiar zig-zag pattern. The whole place had an eerie, timeless atmosphere.

Mr McColl edged through the piles of books, placed the two candles at strategic points, and began his search. He didn't particularly relish working in the murky, muffled atmosphere of the cellar, but he quickly forgot his surroundings as he enthusiastically sorted through the books.

After a while he noticed that the air around him had become icy. At the same time, he had the disquieting feeling that he was being watched. The hairs on his body bristled, and he felt chilled and afraid. Raising one of the candles above his head, he swivelled his eyes around the room. In a moment, his eyes had reached the alcove, and in another instant they had discerned the shadowy entity that quivered obscenely by the chipped stone sink.

The body was that of a fat, grotesque, and almost naked woman with blotched skin and swollen joints, but it was the face that inspired the most horror, for it seemed to be that of someone already in a state of putrification. The face was grime-grey and collapsing into decaying ridges of flesh. Baleful eyes bulged out of sagging sockets.

The terrified book dealer cried out: "Who are you? What do you want?"

The sinister spectre hovered where it was and stayed silent. Quaking with fear, the book dealer picked up a heavy tome and threw it at the apparition. The book passed right through it and thudded against the wall behind. Almost immediately, the monstrous creature vanished. Grabbing the two candles and his belongings, the book dealer fled upstairs.

He had been told to leave the keys, when departing, with a woman who lived in the upper part of the building. He arrived at her door with a thumping heart. The woman quickly answered his knock. When Mr McColl told her that he had just come up from the shop's basement, she became quite agitated, saying that the owner should not have let him go down to the cellar after dark.

As she seemed so alarmed, and because she had to continue living in the building, he decided it would not be helpful to frighten her with his story of the awful discarnate being that he had found lurking in the cellar below but, curious, he did venture a question.

"What's so bad about the cellar?" he enquired.

The woman responded by telling him that the cellar had been haunted for more than 50 years and added that she had once had the misfortune to meet the spectre herself. She had been on the steps leading to the cellar when it had, apparently, passed right through her just after it had made its appearance. It was icy cold, she said, and she had had shivering spells for weeks afterwards. She had straight away rushed up to her room and locked the door, but she maintained that 'the thing' had kept flopping against it for an hour afterwards."

Later, Mr McColl resolved to look into the history of the building. He found out that some 60 years earlier, the cellar had been the scene of a particularly gruesome crime. A man had murdered his wife and had bundled the dead body into the cellar sink, where he proceeded to dismember it. His intention was to bury the various parts of the mutilated body beneath the stone floor, but before he could carry out this task, suspicious neighbours had alerted the police. He was arrested and charged with murder.

Author's note: The actual location of this haunting is the subject of some conjecture. It has been suggested that the building in question is that which is now an off-licence and which stands at the junction of Edward Street and Upper Rock Gardens. However, author Robert Thurston Hopkins, who first interviewed Mr McColl, uses the words 'not far from the juncture of...' – which suggests a different location.

More importantly perhaps, number 114, the site of the present off-licence, was never a second-hand shop during the relevant period. Mr McColl was a student at Brighton College until 1909, so his book dealings must have commenced after this date, while the book recording the story was published in 1956. Between these dates, 114 Edward Street was continuously occupied by a family newsagency. Until the early 1990s, prior to alterations, there was a stone sink within an alcove in the cellar of number 114, but nearby properties, some now demolished, contained similar structures in their cellars.

Lawleys, a china and glassware shop in North Street, stands on the former site of the Countess of Huntingdon's Church, which was demolished in 1972. Whether this fact has a relevance to the supernatural events associated with the shop's basement stockroom is not known.

About 1980, Richard Taylor, the then manager, is said to have seen three phantom nuns walk across the room before vanishing. On a subsequent occasion, a sales assistant had a shock when a ballpoint pen shot up from a table to hit her face. A few employees have commented on the slightly disturbing atmosphere sometimes evident in the stockroom.

Also in North Street stands Hanningtons, a leading Brighton department store, where a phantom Grey Lady is said to roam. Hanningtons dates back to 1808 when the founder, Samuel Hannington, acquired a small shop from Constable Brothers, who had established the business six years earlier.

The store's expansion over the years created a need for good, reliable staff. To assist in this requirement, a part of the top floor of the building was converted to provide residential quarters for a number of unmarried employees. It was a facility which continued from late Victorian times until shortly after the First World War. It is rumoured that the Grey Lady is the ghost of a female employee resident in the staff quarters who committed suicide following a failed love affair.

One of the most interesting confrontations took place in 1990 when a female employee was ascending a staircase in the upper floor administration offices. As she came to a bend in the stairs, she passed a thin-faced woman wearing a Victorian-style grey dress with a white apron.

Thinking the woman, who appeared to be in her mid-twenties, might be involved in some in-store promotional activity, the employee turned to comment, but in that moment the apparition faded. A few months later this employee (now retired), again saw the Grey Lady descending the same flight of stairs.

Might the ghost have been employed in the ladies' fashions area? Certainly this part of Hanningtons has been the focus for a number of inexplicable incidents. Gerald Rubython, a former deputy director of Hanningtons, said that in his early days at the store the then fashion floor manager had told him that he had seen the Grey Lady.

In more recent years, the spirit has continued to make its presence felt in the same part of the store. Fashion buyer Linda Nunan sometimes heard clothes hangers rattling of their own accord and once, during stock-taking, an electric blue jacket with pink piping, which stood out from the garments around it because of its bright colours, mysteriously vanished, with its hanger, to reappear in another part of the fashions' area several hours later. Then there was the occasion when Mrs Nunan was in the corridor near the stockroom. Someone tapped on her shoulder, but when she turned, there was nobody there.

Sales assistant Susie Pavlides had a baffling experience with an item of clothing after a browsing customer had expressed an interest in a red dress that was on display. However, the dress had been hung up with a matching red jacket and this had unaccountably disappeared from the hanger. A thorough search failed to locate the jacket. It reappeared eventually three days later in a crumpled state, on the floor, and close by the dress!

On one occasion, concession manager Margaret Hales was in a passage that leads to the ladies fashions' area when she felt an invisible entity passing her. There was a movement of air and an odd, electric sensation. At another time, she heard clothes hangers rattling noisily against each other when no one was in the vicinity.

Sales assistant Ann Michener twice experienced a pressure on her shoulder as if a hand had been placed on it. The first time was at the beginning of the 1980s. She was sitting alone in the small buyer's office – since converted into a fire escape area – when she felt a quite distinct pressing down on her shoulder. The second time the phenomenon took place was in 1993 while she was talking to a colleague.

Early in 1995, sales assistant June Botham was in a corridor close by the ladies' fashion floor when she noticed a dramatic drop in temperature. At the same time, all the hairs on her body began to prickle. Unknown to her was the fact that many years before a female employee had seen the Grey Lady in this corridor. One of the corridor's walls is a more recent addition to the original structure, and it is through this newer wall that the ghost drifted.

"It was just like windows being opened on a winter's day," June Botham said. "With the coldness came a sensation of something being there that I couldn't see. It was a scary feeling and I rushed into the nearby staff toilet and locked myself in. I hadn't heard about the Grey Lady. It was only later, when I related my experience to other staff, that I was told about her."

Hanningtons basement is another part of the store where odd things happen from time to time. During the immediate post-war years, the store still employed a nightwatchman, and he found that his Alsatian dog refused to venture into one part of the basement, however much it was coaxed.

In the mid-1970s, one long serving employee had to go down there to get some stock. Looking around, she saw that she was the only person present at that moment. However, standing by the nearby wall was a mannequin attired in a long, silver-grey dress. At least, the employee thought it was a mannequin, but when she looked up seconds later, the grey-dressed figure was no longer there.

In more recent times, a sales assistant requiring additional carrier bags from the basement had a shock after descending in the goods lift to collect a bundle of these. On leaving the lift after its descent, she left both the steel trellis doors on the basement floor and those on the lift itself wide open. This should have ensured that the lift remained immobile, so enabling her to return quickly to her counter without having to wait should someone else decide to use the lift. As she pulled out a bundle of carrier bags, she became aware of someone behind her. Turning, she was surprised to see a colleague.

"How did you get here?" she queried.

"I came down in the lift, of course," the colleague replied.

"But I left the lift gates open."

"Well, it was certainly at ground floor level when I reached it," replied the colleague. Other Hanningtons' employees have also found that the lift to the basement tends to behave erratically on occasions, though of course, this could be due to a mechanical fault.

In September 2000, it was announced that Hanningtons had been sold, but that trading was expected to continue until well into 2001.

The ghost of a nun used to haunt another Brighton department store. This spectre was seen by staff at the former Debenhams site in Western Road, and by some employees of Plummer Roddis, the retailers previously occupying the building, but the last known sighting is believed to have been in the mid-1970s.

This witness was Eileen Bond, an assistant linen buyer. She was in the area of the staff canteen (later converted into a restaurant for shoppers), when she saw the nun gliding up a nearby stairway. The apparition, dressed in a white habit and wimple with a long black cloak, was visible for only seconds before drifting through a wall. A convent was at one time situated at the eastern end of the building.

In 1979, the *Evening Argus* reported that a ghostly presence was causing a nuisance in the basement stockroom at Plumbs, the soft furnishings store which was for several years situated at 55 Western Road. In 1982, the business was transferred. The premises are now occupied by Sussex Stationers.

Over a period of about a year, the invisible entity regularly scared staff by moving boxes around and switching lights on and off. A senior female employee claimed that some staff were too scared to go down to the basement.

She added that, in addition to the incidents with the lights and the boxes, there were times when the radio in the basement turned on when she knew she had turned it off, while at other times the volume used to rise and fall as though some invisible hand was adjusting it. There was often a rotten, musty smell about, while the temperature used to suddenly go cold.

Eventually, John Junor, a medium living in Southwick, was invited to carry out an exorcism. He claimed there were, in fact, two ghosts, but said there was nothing evil about them. They were just two lost souls who once lived at that address.

Mr Junor claimed that one ghost, a man, seemed to be from the Edwardian era. This apparition manifested itself in a black and white striped shirt, with braces and dirty-looking trousers. The medium described the other ghost as being a rather bossy, housewifely type of person. There were no further reports of paranormal activities at the store following the exorcism.

A small chain of menswear shops trading as Flix formerly had a shop at 72 Western Road (today occupied by opticians). In the early 1990s the business was transferred to another shop in Western Road. This eventually closed. It is in the original shop that the ghost of Biri Poonia, the former owner of the Southampton-based chain of Flix shops, used to appear.

Mr Poonia, a Sikh, looked forward to visiting this Western Road branch, for it was his favourite shop in the group. After he died in a car crash in the 1980s, his spirit continued to 'call' at the shop. Employees who saw the ghost, described as 'misty-looking', included manager Ranie Sirah and assistant Crispen Dillistone. The ghost of Mr Poonia always appeared in the evening after the last customers had left and when staff had remained on duty to carry out merchandising tasks. It made its appearances on the first floor or on the staircase. There was usually a drop in temperature at the time. The current occupants of the premises have noticed nothing unusual.

A monk-like apparition has been seen on a number of occasions at 55/56 East Street, a shop now occupied by Sussex Stationers, although the last reported sighting was in 1979. One incident, investigated by author Joan Forman, took place in 1950 when the stationery shop was known as John Beal & Son. It was about a fortnight before Christmas and Miss Goodbody, the manageress, and Miss Fermor, a sales assistant, were working late into the evening to price a large quantity of diaries which had been delivered.

This activity was carried out in one of the two stockrooms situated above the shop. Some time into their task, Miss Goodbody found that she had left a list down in the shop and went to fetch it. Miss Fermor heard her go downstairs. Shortly afterwards, she heard footsteps coming up again. They ascended at a slower rate than Miss Goodbody's usual speed. Miss Fermor presumed that this was because the manageress was reading the document she had collected while climbing the stairs. The footsteps continued into the outer stockroom and up the two steps into the room where she was working.

Miss Fermor turned, expecting to see Miss Goodbody, but instead found herself facing a tall, dark figure dressed in a cowled robe. The frightening thing was that there was no face beneath the cowl. Horrified, she fled downstairs, where she found Miss Goodbody sorting through some papers. Miss Forman learned later that there had been earlier sightings of the cowled figure.

In 1979, a sales assistant saw a spectre clad in a hooded robe on three occasions within a period of weeks, although these experiences took place not in the stockroom, but in an area at the rear of the shop's basement. This witness described the entity, which each time passed within two or three feet of her, as being greyish in colour, slightly misty in its overall appearance and around 5ft 6ins in height. Because of this lack of solidity and the fact that the ghost's hood covered much of its face, she was unable to state its gender. Its appearances were accompanied by a sensation of coldness.

The sales assistant stated that she had not felt threatened by the ghost because it seemed to be totally unaware of her presence. During each of the three sightings it performed the same, silent ritual of appearing, walking past her without turning its head, and then dissolving when it reached a corner of the passage.

"Even so, I was still too frightened to move until the ghost had faded away," she commented.

The rear of the shop stands on land which, many years ago, formed part of the site occupied by a chapel, while underground passages, a feature of this old part of Brighton, are believed to fan out beneath the premises.

Around 1980, children living above a shop in Duke Street looked across the road at the empty shop opposite. As they pressed their noses against the window there was a ripple of excitement as they spotted two children staring back at them from the window of the flat above the empty shop. They saw the children on a further occasion and this time mentioned the fact to their parents, who expressed surprise, for they knew the premises opposite were locked up and unoccupied.

Later, the shop was taken over by Ruby Jones, a clothing and costume jewellery company. Later still, Pee-Wees, a Sussex-based group of hairdressing salons, opened a salon on the first floor of the building. Lee and Karen Gold, the directors of Pee-Wees, moved into the flat above the salon in 1986, staying for three years. After they had moved in, the Golds learned that two building workers who had earlier been involved in carrying out alterations to the premises were so unnerved by the unusual noises they had heard in the building, which was otherwise empty at the time, that they had refused to return. Other workers had to complete the alterations.

The Golds had two dogs; a Doberman pinscher and a German shepherd. It wasn't long before the dogs began to behave in an odd fashion. From time to time they would become very agitated, looking past Mr or Mrs Gold and growling, as if aware of someone the Golds couldn't see. On such occasions, the fur around the neck of the German shepherd dog bristled.

It wasn't long before the clothing shop manager complained to Pee-Wees' staff about the noise of people running up and down the stairs to the first floor. The complaints continued, which puzzled Pee-Wees' employees, for they had no knowledge of noisy activity on the stairs.

On being questioned, the shop manager said that he thought the footsteps sounded like those of children, but children rarely visited the salon and the salon staff felt sure they would themselves have heard if children had been racing up and down the stairs.

Some time later, Mrs Gold was standing in the ground floor passage, talking to Bridget Missenden, an assistant, when there was the sound of thumping footsteps and something invisible brushed past them. The noise of the footsteps was sufficient to bring out two assistants from the Ruby Jones' shop.

Once, when approaching the door of the first-floor toilet, Miss Missenden was astonished to see the door-handle swivelling noisily, as if someone was trying to get out. Mystified, she called out to ask who was there, but received no reply. As the handle again began to rattle, she opened the door, but found no one inside.

In 1993 Pee-Wees closed the salon, transferring the business to new premises in Kensington Gardens. Just prior to leaving the Duke Street salon, manager James Bishop was busy on the top floor, packing stock and small furnishings into boxes, prior to carrying them downstairs to await transportation.

Having taken several boxes downstairs, he returned once more to the top room to collect another box. As he went up the final flight of stairs, he had the feeling that someone was in the room. On reaching the doorway, he was alarmed to see the misty figure of a man standing by the window. The man, who wore a long raincoat, was stooping to look out of the window. When the misty apparition stood up and began to walk across the room, the unnerved Mr Bishop decided it was time to flee downstairs!

The shop, together with the residential part of the building, remained unoccupied for several years, after which there was a complete refurbishment of the premises prior to the arrival of new occupants. Since then, there have been no further reports of unusual phenomena.

16 *Eerie office encounters*

IN 1940, SHORTLY AFTER the Second World War had begun, Joyce Morrell went to work at the Fuel Overseer's Department, in King's Road. The building in which she worked had been empty for a long time and was due for demolition, but because of wartime exigencies it again came into use as a local fuel rationing office.

Although she had completed her training as a secretary, as the youngest person in the office, being aged 16 at the time, she was expected to make the tea for the six people employed there. All these employees worked on the ground floor, but the room where the tea was made was on the first floor.

"The offices were where the Thistle Hotel is now", said Mrs Morrell. "There were stories of a smuggler's tunnel under the building. Being wartime, the offices had no carpeting, so your footsteps echoed as you walked around. The first floor seemed very spooky, and I felt a distinct presence there. The other rooms on the first floor were kept permanently locked, as was the staircase to the floors above. I used to wonder what was behind all those closed doors.

"One day, I went up to the first floor room as usual to make the tea. When I had done so, I put all the cups and saucers on a tray and went to descend the stairs. All of a sudden, though I didn't see anything, something grabbed hold of my ankles and I tumbled down the flight of stairs. That would be about 12 or 14 uncarpeted stairs, yet I wasn't injured in any way. I don't even remember being bruised. It was most odd.

"All of the cups and saucers had tumbled down with me, yet none were even chipped, though I must admit that they were made of quite robust china!"

Royal York Buildings, in the Old Steine, stands on what was part of the site of Steine House, which was built early in the 18th century and which was considered to be Brighton's manor house. After 1801, three houses were built onto the adjoining stables. In 1819 the total structure was converted to become the Royal York Hotel.

Taking its name from the Duke of York, the Prince Regent's brother, the hotel became a fashionable venue, attracting the rich and famous. In 1827, success led to an enlargement of the hotel through the addition of the two houses to the west and the house to the east, forming the building as it is today. The manor house was demolished at about the same time.

By the end of the century the Royal York's popularity had waned to the point where it became almost derelict. In 1901, local personality Harry Preston bought the hotel and went on to substantially revive its fortunes. When he retired in 1929, Brighton Corporation bought the building and converted it into offices. These are today utilised by the local authority for a variety of purposes.

Early in the 1980s, Mollie Knowles called at Royal York Buildings to deliver a document. As she ascended the stairway to the upper floors, she heard the footsteps of someone coming up the stairs behind her, but when she turned to see who it was, there was nobody in sight. Her business at the offices took but a minute or two. As she returned down the stairs, she was taken aback to find that the part of the stairway where she had heard the sound of footsteps now felt icy cold.

After dark one night in the mid-1980s, there was a break-in. Alerted by an alarm, the police immediately contacted the facilities officer, who was the keyholder at the time. He was joined by a policeman and a policewoman, together with their two Alsatian dogs. Though a thorough search of the building was made, no intruder was found.

During this search, the policeman commented on the spookiness of the place. Interestingly, the two dogs also reacted to the building's atmosphere, for the hair around their necks hackled and they whimpered and whined in a cowed fashion.

Jim Newings was employed as a cleaner at Royal York Buildings for 14 years until retiring in 1993. On a number of occasions during that time while working on the second floor, he felt a nearby presence and heard the sound of footsteps when no one was there. Almost always, these footsteps were accompanied by the all-pervading smell of an exotic perfume. He attempted to identify this perfume by speaking to a relation who worked on a cosmetics counter, and by personally smelling a variety of scents, but found nothing to match the mystery perfume, which he described as being 'absolutely beautiful'.

A down-to-earth type of person, Mr Newings soon became used to the ghost's arrival and sometimes greeted it with a friendly comment, though a colleague recalled that on one occasion Mr Newings had jocularly suggested that, instead of following him around, the ghost should 'get hold of a bucket and mop and lend a hand with the bloody cleaning!'

One night in 1989 was especially memorable for Mr Newings for all, or it may just have been several – he's not sure which – of the telephones in the individual offices on the second floor began ringing. They all seemed to start ringing at the same time, then all abruptly stopped a few minutes later. He picked up one of the phones while it was ringing and listened, but all was silence at the other end. When he placed the phone back on its cradle, it immediately started ringing again.

On one occasion he was working in one of the rooms on the second floor. The door of this room was kept permanently open at the time, a wooden wedge being used to secure it in this position. Suddenly and mysteriously, the wedge shot away from the door, which then swung to and automatically locked itself, leaving a perplexed Mr Newings trapped within. It was outside of normal business hours, so his predicament wasn't discovered for some time. He was eventually released by a colleague who had set out to search for him.

Iris Crook was a supervisor cleaner at the offices for 13 years until retiring at the end of 1994. She also encountered the exotic perfume which sometimes drifted through the second floor, but it was on the third floor that she had her most memorable experience of the supernatural.

It was around 7.30 one evening in 1989. At this hour, most of the office staff working in the building would have left some two hours before, but there would be the occasional straggler who needed to catch up on a bigger than usual workload.

Mrs Crook had already cleaned the individual offices and had returned to the cupboard in which the cleaning materials were stored. This was situated in a small cubicle at the bottom of four stairs leading from the third floor corridor. As she turned away from the cleaning cupboard, she saw a woman briskly walking along the corridor. Under her arm were several document files.

Surprised to see someone working so late, Mrs Crook called out to her: "Excuse me! Can you please switch out the lights when you come back?"

The woman, who appeared to be in her mid-thirties, took no notice, but kept walking. In the next moment she had walked straight through a closed fire door! Mrs Crook said the woman was wearing what seemed to be clothes of the 1930s or earlier. These consisted of a woollen twin-set with a brown and yellow diagonally-striped skirt and lace-up boots. The woman's hair was dark and rather fuzzy, as if permed.

On several occasions during her time working at Royal York Buildings, Mrs Crook had a strong feeling that there was a presence in the third floor ladies' toilet. "It made my hair prickle at the back when I encountered it," she said.

On one occasion, a secretary working on the third floor heard a woman singing and then humming. As she believed she was alone in that part of the building, she went to investigate, but ran from the building in shock when she found nothing to account for the sound.

Once, a couple of electricians were engaged to carry out some maintenance work. This was to take place on a Saturday so as to avoid disrupting the normal weekday business. One electrician arrived early and immediately went into the building to begin his task, but when his colleague arrived some minutes later, he found the first electrician standing outside. The man had had a frightening experience. What had happened was kept quiet, but whatever it was, after a conversation outside of the building, the two electricians left and never returned.

While the evidence indicates the presence of a female ghost in the offices, the apparition of a man wearing a starched white shirt with a black tailcoat and trousers has also been seen. The story is that many years ago there was a love affair between a head butler and a maid prior to the building being converted into a hotel. When their employer learned of the liaison, he sacked the maid, who left the town soon after to work elsewhere. Devastated, the butler hanged himself in the staff quarters, which were then situated on the top floor of the building. It is here, in a back room which remains cool on the hottest of days, that the tragedy is supposed to have taken place, and it is here that the phantom has been seen.

Dominating Prince's Street is a large, red-brick building with a highly decorated facade which once served as the Parochial Offices for the Board of Guardians. The site had earlier been occupied by the County Court. The Parochial Offices opened in 1894, one activity being the registration of births, marriages and deaths. Following the dissolution of the Board of Guardians in 1930, the offices were taken over by the council's Public Assistance Committee.

From 1974, the premises were occupied by the Social Services Department. In the period 1986-9, the building had a temporary role as a Magistrate's Court prior to the completion of a new court building in Edward Street. From that time on, except for a brief occupation by squatters, it remained empty for several years. In 1998 the building was converted for residential use, though the facade and main staircase have been retained.

While the offices were still in use, a number of employees became aware of the disquieting atmosphere to be found at the top of the building. John Crook (the husband of Iris Crook, mentioned in the Royal York Buildings' story), whose duties as deputy to the senior caretaker took him to several public buildings in Brighton, was one of these.

He was responsible at the end of each day for checking all the individual offices in the Prince's Street building prior to locking them up. On many evenings at about seven o'clock, a ghostly bell used to ring on the top floor when, usually, he was the only person in the building. At other times he heard ghostly footsteps on the top floor, an experience also reported by other people. He also found that the upper part of the main staircase often had a creepy atmosphere. Mr Crook retired in 1990 after 20 years' service.

One employee actually saw an apparition. This was Helen Brown, a cleaner, who in the mid-1980s was alone in the building. It was about 7pm and she had just completed her duties. Because she wore high-heeled shoes in the street, she always put on comfortable slippers to carry out her cleaning tasks. She was just changing back into her high-heeled shoes when she heard a bell ringing within the building. The sound seemed to come from the top of the staircase.

Hobbling on one shoe to the staircase, she was flabbergasted to see, standing at the top of the stairs, a woman wearing a grey dress with a white pinafore and a white mop cap. She was ringing a handbell! Consumed with fright, Mrs Brown rushed into the street, leaving behind her handbag, overcoat, and her other shoe. Fearful of re-entering the building alone, she stopped a passer-by and asked him to accompany her back into the building so that she could collect her belongings. In her distress, on leaving, she omitted to switch off the lights and was admonished the next day for having left them on overnight!.

It is believed that the bell-ringing was, in past times, associated with the distribution of coal to the destitute. There was then a caretaker's flat at the top of the building, and the caretaker's wife used to ring a handbell to announce to the destitute people who had gathered on the ground floor that they could now collect their bags of coal, kept at the back of the building. As such bags were fairly heavy, they would be carried home by men. As some would have been working during the day, 7pm was a suitable time for collection.

Frank Healey was, for a number of years in the 1970s, employed by East Sussex County Council as a part-time supervisor cleaner at the former Careers Office in Queen Square. His work required him to be in the building after everyone else had departed. Frequently aware of the uneasy atmosphere he found there, he was glad to complete his work so that he could leave for home.

Sometimes, he heard footsteps descending the stairs when no one else was in the building. At other times, he heard someone humming a tune, but any attempt to locate the source met with failure. In addition, doors slammed shut of their own volition. Once, when going home, he looked back at the locked and empty building and saw a face peering out of an upper floor window.

Several years later, David Simmons, another cleaner, found that a top floor room had such an eerie atmosphere that, so as to feel more secure while on duty, he would sometimes jam a chair under the door-handle. Whatever spirits once disturbed the peace of the building, all has been tranquil in recent years. The offices are now used by the Probation Service.

The ghost of a woman wearing a blue dress is reputed to haunt The Old House (formerly Acacia House) in Preston Road. This fine old building, faced in knapped flint, dates from the 17th century. A family dairy business occupied the premises for many years until 1912. During the 1960s, a restaurant occupied the site. Following the restaurant's closure, the building was extensively refurbished prior to its occupancy by solicitors Aldrich, Crowther and Wood.

Whether the phantom woman was seen prior to the building's 1971 refurbishment is not known, but her unexpected appearance before some building workers involved in the renovations caused more than a little alarm. The ghost materialised on the ground floor in what had been the kitchen area of the restaurant. At a later date a woman cleaner, who had no knowledge of the earlier incident, reported that she had seen, in the same area, the apparition of a woman dressed in blue. Her description of the ghost tallied with that of the building workers.

17 *Fallen women . . . and a factory*

THE RAMBLING, sombre-looking Victorian building in Finsbury Road had initially been a workhouse. Later it was taken over by the Church Army to become a Home for Female Penitents – for women who had fallen by the wayside! However, it had been empty for years, so when the proprietors of Bevan Funnell Limited, a firm of traditional furniture manufacturers, learned that the premises were available at a reasonable rent, they were quick to indicate their interest.

Barry Bevan Funnell and his wife Pamela had established the company in a small garage in Hove in 1945. In 1947, at the age of 22, Mr Funnell was elected to Hove Council. In 1960 he went on to become, aged 36, the town's youngest ever Mayor.

Working diligently from modest beginnings, the Funnells later moved to larger premises in Margaret Street, Brighton. Further expansion led to the firm acquiring the Finsbury Road building. Seemingly ideal for their purpose, it was rapidly refurbished and equipped. The 40 or so employees moved in during the early months of 1952.

It soon became evident that something was amiss. Initially, a caretaker and his wife occupied living quarters in the upper part of the building. Each night, after everyone else had left the building, the caretaker did his rounds, locking and bolting every door, but later in the evening these would frequently be found open again. Even padlocks were found open. Sometimes, patrolling policemen would find the street doors undone and would call out Mr Funnell.

One night when Mr Funnell was alerted after a constable on the beat had found the entrance doors open, CID officers turned up to investigate. On entering the building, Mr Funnell and the CID officers could hear people talking on an upper floor. This was accompanied by the sound of running footsteps. The police raced upstairs, confident that at last they had caught some intruders. Arriving at the room where the sounds were coming from, the police flung open the door.

As the door swung open, the noises ceased instantly. Baffled, the police searched the adjoining rooms and then the rest of the building, but nothing was found to account for the babble of conversation and the sound of footsteps.

Sometimes staff heard footsteps on the upper floor during the hours of daylight when it was known that no one was there. If anyone went to investigate, they were left perplexed, for there would be no evident reason for the sounds they had heard. Other odd things began to happen. Staff coming into work would find that chairs had been moved overnight. Some might be overturned. On one occasion a dresser was found damaged after it had been inexplicably tipped over.

While they were waiting for their vans to be loaded, drivers were required to wrap some of the smaller items of furniture in corrugated packaging. This activity was carried out in a room on the first floor. Early one evening, just as it was beginning to get dark, one driver was working in this room when he saw a woman standing in the doorway. She was dressed in a black suit.

He presumed it was a customer, for these often called at the premises. Politely, he asked the woman if could help her. He was astonished when she not only failed to reply, but vanished instantly on the spot. He rushed through the door and sped down the passage, but found no sign of the silent visitor.

A few days afterwards, Mrs Funnell was working well into the evening, catching up on the invoicing and other tasks. Her pet dog, a mongrel called Blarney, liked to sit in the office with her, but on this occasion it wandered away. Some minutes later, Mrs Funnell was surprised to hear, from the floor above, the sound of the dog whining and whimpering.

It was very dark by then and Mrs Funnell wasn't too keen on venturing up to the next floor on her own, but nevertheless she climbed the stairs to arrive at a large room used for storage purposes. The room was divided into two by a heavy, sliding partition which had long since rusted on its bearings. It had rusted so thoroughly that it had resisted the combined efforts of strong men to move it. But now, Mrs Funnell was astonished to find, the heavy partition had been moved so that it completely isolated one half of the room. Imprisoned behind this partition, the trapped dog yelped in panic.

Racing downstairs, Mrs Funnell called for help from her husband and two male employees, who were at that time loading a van. Although the partition had been freed by some mysterious force from its original, rust-constrained position, it still took considerable effort by the three men to move it just a few inches. Fortunately, this was sufficient to release the dog.

Mrs Funnell did virtually all the office work connected with the business and the only typewriter in the building was kept in her office. On some occasions, the typewriter was heard rattling away when no one was in the office. If anyone opened the door, the sound of typing ceased immediately.

Some weeks later, Mrs Funnell went into a small washroom by her office. Used as a ladies' cloakroom, it contained a toilet, a small sink, a gas ring where tea and coffee were made and a row of coat hangars. As she entered the washroom, the row of hangers started swinging violently and clattering against each other. Then a box of matches on the side of the sink shot into the bowl.

Mrs Funnell noticed that a black, woollen cardigan was on one of the hangers. She was sure it hadn't been there earlier in the day. She then became aware that the cardigan was exuding the smell of perfume. No member of staff claimed the cardigan as theirs. Two days later, it disappeared as mysteriously as it had arrived. It was never seen again.

Mrs Funnell described the perfume as being 'heavy, musky and quite glorious'. It was a smell which was to become well-known to Bevan Funnell staff for they would, from time-to-time, come across it in various parts of the building. Sometimes the powerful scent would waft through the whole building in waves.

Understandably, all this paranormal activity had its effect upon staff. Learning of the hauntings, potential employees were frightened off. Some of the existing staff were shaken, some totally scared, but almost all stayed on out of loyalty to the company. However, most were reluctant to work on the premises after dusk. One female employee was so adversely affected she became a changed person. From being a plump, jolly woman who seemed full of life, she became thin and anxious-looking.

Something had to be done about all this. The Funnells weren't too happy about allowing Spiritualists to hold a seance on the premises, but with a sense of desperation they felt they had nothing to lose in doing so. The seance took place about a year after the company had moved into the building. The medium, a man, was apparently able to contact the ghost. He asked why it was troubled. The reply came through the medium, who spoke in a girl's voice.

"Matron is cruel to me. I am terribly unhappy. I've tried to be good, but I can't." She spoke in an uneducated Sussex accent and sounded a miserable, weeping thing, said Mrs Funnell, who was present at the seance.

Both Mrs Funnell and her husband were sceptical about the seance. It was well known that the building had once housed young, unmarried mothers and wasn't the reputation of many such places in Victorian times based upon wretched conditions and, quite often, pitiless punishment for those unfortunate girls who failed to meet the harsh standards laid down?

It would have been easy for a medium to take advantage of such knowledge. Nevertheless, a strange thing took place almost immediately after the medium had left. There was a surge of noise; doors banging, unseen people shouting and footsteps running. Then, abruptly, silence!

For several months, nothing of a supernatural nature took place. It seemed as if the spirits were at peace at last. But on the last Sunday before Christmas, Mr Funnell went into the building on his own. He often went in on a Sunday morning to catch up on paperwork, for on weekdays he was more usually involved in other management tasks. Letting himself into the little office more usually used by his wife, he was unprepared for the horrific phenomenon which was about to take place.

It was a bright, sunny morning and the rays of the sun lit up the office so that there was a minimum of shadow. On entering the room, Mr Funnell heard a soft thud. It came from the corner of the office and sounded like a book falling to the floor. He turned to look in that direction and what he saw haunts him to this day.

Appearing above a bench in the office was a human figure. It was greyish and incomplete and Mr Funnell could see the bench through the apparition. The figure slowly turned its head and Mr Funnell became aware of what he later described as 'a face shape with eyes'. He felt that the eyes were looking at him with incredible hatred and loathing. Terrified, Mr Funnell ran from the room and down the stairs. He was so shaken by this experience that he decided to call upon a priest to exorcise the building. Following the exorcism, there were no further paranormal incidents until Bevan Funnell vacated the premises in 1957.

Shortly afterwards, the building was demolished and a block of flats was erected on the site. The Funnells later learned that the occupants of one of the flats had contacted Brighton Council's Housing Department to complain that the windows and doors of the flat unaccountably swung open from time to time and that strange noises were frequently heard within the flat. Additionally, and inexplicably, books were sometimes scattered around the rooms.

After vacating the Finsbury Road premises, Bevan Funnell moved into what had formerly been the Grand Theatre, in North Road. As reported in a previous chapter, ghostly incidents once took place at the Grand. However, the Funnells experienced nothing supernatural during their years there, though they did find the building alive with fleas when they first moved in! Perhaps the building work required to convert the premises into a furniture factory drove out its spectral occupants? The building was almost destroyed by fire in 1961. The company is now located at Newhaven.

18 *Here and there – a miscellany*

IN THE EARLY PART of the 1800s, firefighting in Brighton was almost entirely in the hands of fire insurance companies which paid firemen to deal only with fires on the premises they had insured, though the Parish of Brighton did itself have one fire engine. By 1831, this had increased to three, with fire crews being paid only for attendances at blazes.

In 1867 the situation was formalised to a great extent with the establishment of a local Volunteer Fire Brigade. A Police Fire Brigade was formed in 1881, and there was friendly rivalry between the two organisations until 1921, when a fully-trained, full-time corporation fire brigade took over all firefighting responsibilities.

The headquarters for the new fire brigade was at Preston Circus, using an original building established in 1901 as the headquarters of the Police Fire Brigade. The present building, erected on the same site, was completed in 1938. Since 1974 the fire brigade has been the responsibility of East Sussex County Council.

The training tower at the rear of Preston Circus fire station is all that remains of the original fire station (although it was built sometime after 1901). This tower was the scene of a tragic accident in August 1957 when a fireman fell to his death from a top window of the structure during a training exercise. Could there be a connection between this man's death and some weird events which have since taken place?

One night, early in the 1970s, there was a heavy thunderstorm over Brighton and five of the firemen on duty at the time went out onto a covered balcony at the rear of the fire station to witness the spectacle. Vivid flashes of lightning lit up the rain that was sheeting down. As yet another craze of lightning sparked across the sky, it illuminated a human figure in the yard below. The five watchers on the balcony were stunned to see that it was that of a fireman. He was close by the training tower and seemed to be sitting on his upturned helmet – then a common practice among firemen taking a short break during training exercises. He appeared to be oblivious to the rain.

There were expressions of astonishment such as "Who the hell is that?" from some of the men on the balcony as they waited for the next flash of lightning to see if they could identify the man, but when it lit up the yard, there was no one there. It occurred to the men that it might be a colleague playing a prank, but when they hurried back into the fire station to look for a culprit, they found that everyone was accounted for and, furthermore, had dry clothes.

A small room in the fire station is today used for the repair of salvage sheets and ropes, but at one time it was a toilet. Late one evening in the mid-1970s during 'stand down' time, Sub-Officer Brian Purvis, who had been in the recreation room talking to some colleagues, left them to go to this toilet. Although it had an interior light, firemen rarely bothered to switch it on, for the entrance door was usually left open, with the light from the corridor being quite adequate if only the urinal was being used.

As Brian Purvis went through the door, he saw another fireman standing in the room. This man was dressed in a fire service jacket with a peaked cap and black waterproof leggings (yellow leggings weren't introduced into the fire service until a few years later). In the light coming from the corridor, the face of the man seemed slightly misty, though his uniform was in sharp focus. He stood quite still except for a slight movement of the head.

Sub-Officer Purvis nodded a brief 'Hello!' and carried on towards the urinal. It occurred to him in that second or two that there was something odd about the firefighter he had just passed. He hadn't immediately recognised the man and, as it was 'stand down' time, he wondered why he was wearing his uniform cap and leggings.

Turning his head to take a closer look, Brian Purvis was astonished to see no sign of the mystery firefighter. The man couldn't possibly have got out of the door so quickly, while even if he had, the sub-officer knew that he would have heard the scrape of the man's waterproof leggings as he left, and also heard his footsteps going up the stairs, for it is a quiet part of the fire station. It wasn't until that moment that Brian Purvis noticed that the temperature seemed abnormally cold.

Did Sub-Officer Mike Elsmore see the same spectral fireman some ten years before this? His encounter came when he was in a different toilet; one situated on the mezzanine floor. He had just washed his hands and was drying them while standing in front of a long wall mirror, when he noticed the reflection of another fireman standing just behind him. The face of the man was indistinct, but the sub-officer noted that he had grey hair and that he was wearing braces over a collarless shirt of the type once issued by the fire service. Turning to see who it was, the sub-officer was astonished to find he was alone.

At the rear of the fire station is a staircase which some personnel maintain has a rather creepy atmosphere. The stairs once led to firemen's living quarters, but these were converted into office space, so the staircase is now rarely used. Helen Jerram, a cleaner at the station for about ten years, sometimes heard a voice calling when she used the staircase. No one else was in that part of the building on these occasions, though the calls could have been a trick of the acoustics.

Fred Marchant and Gwen Bolingbroke, employed as cleaners on an occasional basis, both reported the feeling of being watched while on the staircase. In 1977, Mrs Bolingbroke was going downstairs when she passed a man coming up. He was wearing a white shirt and black trousers. She didn't recognise him, but presumed he was an officer because of his white shirt (other firefighters wear light blue shirts). A few moments later her duties took her to the fire officers' mess where she noticed that the man she had just passed was featured in one of the framed photographs hanging on the wall.

"Oh, I've just passed him on the back stairs," she said to an officer standing nearby. He responded with a laugh and said that this was impossible, for the man she had pointed out had been dead for years. Of course, she might have been mistaken in her identification, for the station does have officers from other stations who visit for training purposes. But then again...?

On an evening in 1996, a small number of firefighters were conversing in the fire station's recreation room when the handle of the concertina-type door leading to the adjoining gymnasium began to rattle. Then the door itself started shaking violently, after which the handle once more began to rattle. The firefighters were puzzled both by the intensity of the rattling and by the fact that nobody had come through the door, so Firefighter Peter Rumble went over to open it. At the instant he touched the handle, the rattling stopped. On opening the door, he found the gymnasium empty, but no one could have left the gym without being observed in the second it took to open the door.

Author's note: Following the introduction of women to the fire service, the term 'firefighter' replaced that of 'fireman'. In the fire service stories featured on these pages, the words 'fireman' and 'leading fireman' have been retained where they are appropriate to the time. The fire service ranks stated are not necessarily those extant at the time of the experiences.

Incredibly, Brighton's other fire station, the secondary one in Roedean, which was completed in 1956, has also been a focus for the supernatural, though all of the unexplained happenings at this station appear to have taken place prior to 1974. The events that did take place could be related to the fact that the station was built alongside a burial ground established in 1855 for the Quaker community. This burial ground became a victim of the construction work that was carried out to provide an access road to the Brighton Marina, formally opened in 1979. In 1972, the Quaker burial ground's interments were reburied at the Lawn Memorial Cemetery, Woodingdean.

At various times over the years up to 1974 there were reports of doors opening and closing of their own volition, curtains fluttering without cause, unexplained shadows drifting past the TV room, and the recreation room window opening spontaneously. Indeed, the recreation room seems to have been particularly prone to spooky events.

On one occasion, the firemen on duty were surprised to hear a loud clatter in this room. Fireman Lewis Laws (who eventually rose to become a station commander), went to investigate. He found that six or seven snooker cues had fallen from their racks, even though each cue had been held by its own retaining clip. He also recalled being present, with two other firemen, when there was the sound of breaking glass in the kitchen. A bottle of milk, left on the serving hatch ledge, had shot into the centre of the kitchen floor and smashed. Nobody had been near the kitchen at the time.

Late one night during the 1960s, Leading Fireman Jim Hickman, on looking along a corridor in the building, was surprised to see a slit of light at the bottom of the door of an office occupied during the day by the transport officer, Dennis Allen. Although Mr Allen sometimes worked after his usual 5.30pm finishing time, it seemed unlikely that he would be there at that late hour. Perhaps he had omitted to switch off the light when leaving the office?

Jim Hickman went along the corridor and knocked on the door. There being no response, he tried the handle. Finding the door locked, he decided to go outside the station so that he could look through the window into the office. Once there, he was puzzled to see that the office was now in darkness. On returning, he was even more perplexed to find the door of the office unlocked. The following morning, Dennis Allen confirmed that he had left his office at about 5.30pm.

On another night, the firemen on duty wondered who it could be when they heard someone walk across the fire appliance bay and then back again. The footsteps were heard for a second time, and then a third. Fireman Ken Bowler left his colleagues and went into the bay to investigate. He was confounded when the footsteps crossed the bay for a fourth time, and right past him, for there was no one to be seen.

Roedean fire station, being small, normally has a complement of five

A White Lady is Preston Manor's most renowned ghost, but other spirits also haunt this fine old building.

Ghostly figures have been seen emerging from Preston Old Church (St Peter's), which stands close by Preston Manor, while a partly materialised form has appeared inside the church.

George IV is one of at least three spectres said to have been seen in Brighton's Royal Pavilion.

Did the shade of local character Martha Gunn once appear in the Royal Pavilion's banqueting room? A caterer, after perusing old etchings showing the famous bathing 'dipper', insisted that this was the woman he had seen.

(*Right*) A spectral woman in grey is said to drift through this bricked up doorway, situated in Meeting House Lane. She is probably Brighton's best known ghost, but who was she in her lifetime?

(*Left*) A ghostly choir and spectral monks have been seen in the Church of St Bartholomew.

(*Above*) The cottage at Moulsecoomb Place is one of Brighton's oldest buildings. The mistress of James II is said to haunt the cottage, currently used by a social club. Children once saw a phantom face at the window of the linkway (on right of the photograph).

(*Right*) A phantom man attired in a black cloak and hat has been seen in the Cricketers, an ancient pub with an interesting past.

The Druid's Head, one of Brighton's oldest pubs, has a history of supernatural happenings.

The Stag Inn, Brighton, where strange events take place and where the apparition of a former landlord has been seen.

Hanningtons department store, where a Grey Lady is said to be the ghost of a former sales assistant who was thwarted in love.

This sombre building in Finsbury Road, Brighton, was at one time a home for 'fallen women'. In later years it was occupied by furniture manufacturers Bevan Funnell, when the legacy of its earlier history surfaced with a series of eerie happenings.

(*Top left*) Two friends were close to collapsing with terror when, after a night out, they encountered a 'beastly' entity at Moulsecoomb Railway Station.

(*Bottom left*) Strange tales of 'the other side' are associated with two of the architecturally interesting houses in Brighton's Wykeham Terrace.

(*Right*) Harvey's Cross, by a bridleway to the north of Saltdean, marks the spot where, in 1819, Colonel John Harvey met his death while out riding. A ghostly grey horse and rider still haunt the vicinity.

(*Below*) The Church of St Lawrence in the isolated village of Telscombe, where a ghostly bell has pealed and where, close by, a spectral man and his dog have appeared.

The north barn of Blatchington Windmill was the scene of a very disturbing experience for a shepherd during lambing time.

Foredown Tower, where phantom footsteps are thought to have triggered an intruder alarm.

(*Top right*) Wykehurst Park house, Bolney, where three people in a car were glad to make their escape from a darkly-cowled apparition.

(*Right*) A White Lady and a groaning man are said to haunt the cottage situated above the entrance to Clayton Tunnel. Do these ghosts have an association with the accidents which have taken place in the tunnel?

Prior to its conversion into flats, the King's Head Hotel, in Cuckfield, was said to be haunted by two ghosts; a young lad, and a servant girl quaintly referred to as Geranium Jane.

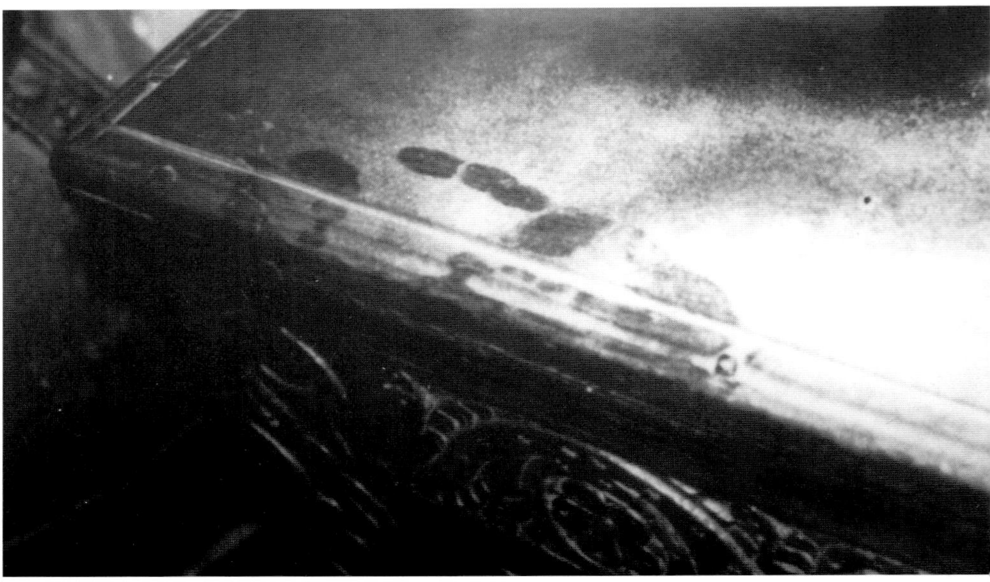

Although the undercroft at Michelham Priory was locked and alarmed overnight, in the morning this ten-inch long spectral handprint was found on the edge of a table that had previously been sprinkled with flour by members of the Ghost Research Foundation, who had been engaged in a ghost-watch.

firefighters on duty at any one time (although this number was slightly exceeded during its early years). Prior to the introduction of new communication procedures, one fireman was always present in the watchroom. This was necessary because Roedean then relied primarily on a phone link with the Preston Circus station.

Station Officer Fred Bishop was in the watchroom one night when, through the small window that looks out onto the fire station's entrance, he saw the door swing open. Expecting to see someone walk through the door, he was surprised when no one appeared. He then heard (though could not see), the internal swing doors open and close with their distinctive series of diminishing clunks.

His surprise turned to consternation when the door of the watchroom then opened, though still there was nobody in sight. In the next couple of seconds, the door leading from the watchroom to the fire appliance bay swung open, then closed again. Whoever, or whatever, had entered the fire station and passed through the watchroom, had been entirely invisible.

On another occasion, Fireman Ray Collins had a similar experience. He was sitting in the watchroom when, through the hatch window, he saw the front door open, though nobody passed through. He couldn't see the swing doors beyond that open, but he heard the sound of them. He was able to establish that nobody had actually entered the station.

Although on this occasion the doors to the watchroom and to the fire appliance bay didn't open, Ray Collins did, on other occasions, see the door to the appliance bay open of its own accord, while he once heard (though didn't see) the fire station's big, heavy, spring-loaded overhead door go up without human agency, while an up-and-over door operated by chains situated at the rear of the station opened in a similar fashion.

A third fireman, Maurice Glanville, while on duty in the watchroom, also had the unnerving experience of seeing all of the doors from the entrance door to the one leading to the watchroom open in turn, as if manipulated by some discarnate force.

Fireman Glanville had another brush with the paranormal one day in 1970 while cleaning the floor of the ablutions. As he went about his work, he felt a sharp prod on his shoulder. On turning and seeing nobody, he presumed it was another fireman larking around, so he went in search of the culprit, but his colleagues denied responsibility. On his arrival back at the ablutions, Maurice Glanville realised that they must have been telling the truth, for only one pair of wet footprints, his own, could be seen coming away from the ablutions. The tiled floor was glistening with soapy water and no one could have got close enough to have prodded him, even with a broom handle, without having trodden on the wet floor to leave a trail of tell-tale footprints.

It is the custom, during their 15-hour long spells of duty, for firefighters to spend some of this time in sleep (though they remain clothed, except for their boots, to facilitate a quick response to fire calls). One night in the early 1970s, Leading Firefighter Alec Anscombe switched out the lights in the recreation room and climbed into the portable bed which had been placed there. He believed he was alone in the room, but soon had the feeling that someone else was present. In the next moment he felt the foot of the bed depress, as if someone had just sat down on it. Springing from the bed, he switched on the lights, but found nobody there.

Leading Firefighter Tom Smith had a similar experience. One night he was in bed in the same room. As he lay there in the dark, he felt something like a cat jump onto the bed and run over his body. He leapt up straight away and flicked on the lights. The door had been closed and a search revealed nothing unusual.

Sub-Officer Mike Elsmore moved to Roedean fire station after several years' service at the Preston Circus station. Late one night in 1970 he was sitting in the recreation room, drinking a cup of tea, when he was startled to see the apparition of a man wearing a black cloak and a black, wide-brimmed hat of the kind typically worn by Quaker men in past times. The entity materialised in the south-east corner of the room and remained there, without any noticeable movement, for some five seconds before fading away.

On another occasion, in the early hours of the morning, Mike Elsmore was alone in the recreation room when he heard the faint sound of children singing. The sound seemed to be coming from within the room.

A particularly uncanny event took place at about 2am one morning in the early 1970s. Roedean Road runs past the fire station and even at this early hour vehicles constantly pass by, but on this occasion it was as if all the traffic had stopped. There was an unearthly silence; a curious sense of timelessness that descended on the station and which was felt by each of the six men on duty. Then, bizarrely, the silence was broken by the trill of a bird singing.

It was an unlikely sound to hear at a time when dawn was still three or four hours away. Some of the men thought the bird-song was coming from outside of the station, though others felt sure that the sound was coming from within the building. The eerie episode lasted for about two minutes, after which all reverted to normal, with the usual sounds of the outside world returning.

Two ghosts haunt the Royal Mail delivery centre in North Road. One is said to be that of a postal worker who was found hanged in the basement of the building. During the Second World War, to help ensure continuing communications should a bomb hit the building, the telephonists were moved to the basement, where additional concrete buffer protection was provided.

Soon after the war the telephonists moved out of the basement and it became a mailbag cleaning and storage area. The postal worker who took his life during this time was a man who divided his activities between telegraphy work at North Road and counter clerk duties at the Ship Street Post Office.

His ghostly form was seen on a number of occasions over the years following his death. However, there have been no known reports of this ghost being sighted since a major refurbishment in 1988, when the area was converted into a delivery section, but a number of employees still report a charged atmosphere in some parts of the basement and say that they would be reluctant to be alone there at night.

There is a second ghost which manifests itself in the annexe. Prior to the construction of the annexe, the area was a yard where post office delivery vans were parked. There have been suggestions that the ghost is that of an engineer who was working down a manhole in the yard. He emerged from the manhole at an unfortunate moment, being fatally injured when a moving van struck his head. However, the clothing of the ghost doesn't conform to what an engineer would normally wear (of course, there could be a third ghost on the premises!). Postman/driver Alan Smith is one Royal Mail employee who saw the phantom.

"The ghost I saw was wearing dark blue serge trousers with a red stripe down each leg and a short, beige dust-coat of the type once worn by indoor postal staff," Mr Smith said. "It was in 1980 or 1981, and I was on nights at the time. It was around 2.30am and I was working alone, stamping packets, when I looked up to see this man walking towards me.

"I said 'Hello, mate! How are you?' or something like that, but he didn't reply. I wondered why, but he just walked past without looking in my direction. After stamping another couple of packets, I looked up and was surprised to see that he had vanished. I couldn't think where he might have gone, for I was working in a well-lit area close by the doors.

"Just then, three colleagues came through the doors. I asked if anyone had just passed them, but no one had. I explained the situation. I hadn't recognised the man and I felt there was something odd about him, so all four of us searched the annexe, but we found nobody. There was no way the man could have left the annexe without being seen by me".

Withdean Grange, in London Road, was built in the 1860s. It was originally named Stanford Villa, and then Terrick Cottage. Early in the 1950s, it was bought by the General Post Office for development as a telephone exchange. Later, in four stages, new buildings were erected on the site with the old building being demolished in 1971.

Lesley Afzali was a night duty telephone operator in the new main building from 1990 to 1993, when the telephone exchange became automated. One night, during her employment there, she had a most distressing experience. Employees on night duty were entitled to a meal break on a rotational basis, and on the night in question, her break was due at 2am.

Feeling like a snooze, instead of spending the following hour in the rest/TV room where she was likely to be disturbed, she searched for somewhere quiet where she could close her eyes in reasonable comfort. In one office, lit only by the light from the corridor, she spotted a large padded chair with armrests. She thought it would be ideal for her purpose. It happened to be the then office of the telephone exchange manager!

Sitting in the semi-darkness, Mrs Afzali made herself comfortable and began to drift into sleep. The next thing she knew was that she was being shaken roughly by someone who was fiercely gripping her shoulders, but when she opened her eyes, she saw no one there. The grip then relaxed and a moment later she heard the footsteps of the invisible entity. They were out into the corridor and already becoming distant. The footsteps were quick and precise, as if made by someone wearing high heels. Shaking and fearful, it was several minutes before she dared to go into the corridor.

Had she had a frightful dream? Mrs Afzali is absolutely sure that what she endured that night did actually happen. Later, on telling others of her ordeal, she learned that another employee had had a similar encounter in the past. A security officer at the exchange confirmed that there had been reports of ghostly footsteps in the building.

Standing on its own on the west side of London Road is Patcham Place. This grade II listed mansion was originally built in 1558 for Sir William West. In 1764 it was rebuilt for John Paine with a facade of black mathematical tiles, pediment and Tuscan doorway. One of Patcham Place's later owners, Anthony Shapley, who was a signatory to King Charles I's death warrant, is said to have haunted the house for many years.

Patcham Place was so dilapidated by 1931 that its demolition was proposed. Later, it was purchased by Brighton Corporation. Canadian soldiers were billeted there during the Second World War. For most of the years since, the building has been used as a youth hostel.

While the ghost of Anthony Shapley no longer wanders around Patcham Place, there is a tail-end to the story, for hostel staff claim that a feeling of malevolence can sometimes be felt in the ground floor restaurant, especially after dark.

The TA Centre in Dyke Road, built on the Highcroft Estate, was completed early in 1940 to become the headquarters of the 70th (Sussex) Searchlight Regiment, Royal Artillery (TA). Two batteries of the regiment were situated there, with a third in Worthing. Over the years since the Second World War, the centre has been headquarters to a number of Territorial Army units.

While other buildings on the site were demolished to make way for the TA Centre, Highcroft House itself, a red-bricked villa built in 1876, still stands. There is an Officers' Mess on the first floor of this building, and it is here that the phantom of an officer has been seen. The officer, a lieutenant, is said to have committed suicide in the toilet.

The Royal Air Forces Association Club, in Castle Street, was until the mid-1980s situated in nearby Stone Street. There, in 1984, club chairman Peter Rogers had a memorable experience. It was a Sunday and the last lingering members in the club bar, on the first floor, had finished their lunchtime drinks and had tramped downstairs into the street, leaving Mr Rogers to clear up. As he set about this task, he heard someone coming up the 34 steps leading to the bar. The footsteps on the uncarpeted staircase were distinct.

For a moment, Mr Rogers was slightly irritated. An important football match was about to be screened on TV. To enable him to tidy up the bar as quickly as possible so that he could watch the game, he had asked the last person leaving to engage the Yale lock when closing the street exit door.

The footsteps stopped at the sliding door leading into the bar. When no one actually entered the bar, a puzzled Mr Rogers walked over to the door and slid it open. Seeing nobody there, he rushed down the stairs, opened the door – the Yale lock was engaged, he noted – and went out into the street. There wasn't a soul in sight.

This wasn't the only inexplicable incident to take place at the club. During Mr Rogers' several years there, he found that the gas cylinders attached to the beer lines turned off, for no apparent reason, on at least five occasions each year.

The club backed onto a retail shop in Western Road. This is now occupied by a photographic company who use the former club premises for storage purposes. Staff claim there is an eerie atmosphere in this area.

The Community Mental Health Centre, in Buckingham Road, opened in 1899 as a school. It has also been a maternity hospital and a social services centre. It has additionally been a focus for some curious happenings.

Beryl Long, a secretary at the centre from 1991, found that doors she had personally locked were later discovered to be unlocked, while lights that had been switched off overnight were found on again the next morning. To assist handicapped people, all doors in the corridors are of the swing-type. From time to time, even when the air was still, these were observed to swing open as if some uncanny force was at work. Mrs Long also heard footsteps on the first floor when no one was there, and she twice had her first name called when nobody else was in the vicinity.

Janet Cork joined the centre in the early 1990s, combining her work as a receptionist with other duties of a domestic nature. She occasionally heard ghostly footsteps on the first floor and sometimes switched off lights in the building, only to find them on again later, this at times when nobody else was present. Once she was confronted by a shadowy figure, which appeared briefly in a link corridor. The ghost of a nun wearing a grey habit was seen during the time the building was used as a maternity hospital. Might this have been the same spectre?

The Montague House Resource Centre, in Montague Place, is a day centre for the handicapped. In the mid-1980s there were several witnesses to the transitory appearance on the ground floor of an elderly, spectral man. He materialised in an empty armchair before the astonished eyes of a number of people who were seated in the same room.

Prior to this event, brooms, mops, and other cleaning items were once found to have been tossed into a lavatory pedestal situated in the ground floor toilet after they had been left overnight in a locked cupboard. About this time, Brian Thomas, a visitor who had brought his normally fearless lurcher dog with him, found that the animal backed away, cowering, when taken towards the toilet.

Moulsecoomb Railway Station is located at the rear of a complex of buildings occupied by the University of Brighton. It is a small station which is unmanned for most of the time. On the files of Sussex Paranormal Investigations, a research group based at Burgess Hill, is an extraordinary story involving two friends who found themselves at the station in 1986.

The friends, young women who had been enjoying a night out in Brighton, were reluctant to go home even though it was by then about 3am, so they went into the station waiting room to chat for a while and to rest their feet, for they had walked the two or three miles from town. After a few minutes, the attention of the women was diverted by the sight of an elderly man on the opposite platform. He was close to the footbridge running over the track, and was beginning to climb the footbridge steps.

Though comforted by the subdued glow of the station lamps, the two women were apprehensive, for the platform was darkly shadowed and they felt very alone. When the man failed to come down the footbridge steps onto their side of the station, they were puzzled. After waiting for a few minutes, they felt that they ought to find out what had happened to him so, despite a feeling of some unease, they moved towards the footbridge and crept up the steps. Surprised to find no sign of the man, they returned to their seats in the waiting room.

They had only just resumed their conversation when they heard a distant clamour. At first, it sounded as if it were people larking around, but then the sound changed and came closer. Moving nearer still, it seemed now to be like the squeal of an animal, a sound close to that made by a pig, but with a bleak, unearthly intensity. The friends were petrified.

The monstrous sound was now nearly upon them, but they felt almost too paralysed to move. One of the women, her feet aching after the walk from town, had taken her shoes off when they had arrived at the station. She had taken them off again after they had returned to the waiting room following their search of the footbridge. With shaking hands she now struggled to put them back on. While she was doing so, her friend edged a little out of the waiting room. Turning her head, she was about to whisper that all seemed clear when something unseen screeched in her ear. Terrified, she fled out of the station and down the steps leading towards Lewes Road.

The other woman, now with her shoes on, ran out to the top of the steps, but her terror was so great that she was on the verge of collapsing and felt unable to go down them. As she screamed for her friend to wait for her, she became aware of a presence close by. Although she could see nothing, it was breathing on her face. With it came faint grunting noises.

This proved to be the last act of whatever it was that had been oppressing the two women, for the frightening atmosphere seemed to lift in a moment, and they knew that the dreadful creature had gone. In tears, and still quaking with fear, they made their way home.

Stanmer Park, with its long history and old buildings, would seem a likely place for a ghost or two. It is claimed that the phantom of a priest once wandered through the wooded area of the park. Apparently, he was shot dead by an excise officer some 200 years ago when caught helping smugglers who used the wood as cover, but as far as is known there have been no new accounts of this haunting for many years.

Contained within the park is Stanmer village, a street of attractive old cottages, several of which date back to the 18th century (although the village, which was listed in the Domesday Book, existed long before this, with traces of it still visible in the ground today). At one end of the village is Stanmer Church. Built in 1838, it occupies the site of a 14th century church destroyed by fire. It has been reported that a phantom Grey Lady has been spied in the pews, but the present incumbent has no knowledge of such a spectre.

Stanmer House, close by the church, was erected in 1722, replacing a former manor house. From 1721 to 1947 the Stanmer estate was owned by the Pelham family, and it is rumoured that the shade of Thomas Pelham, who was to become the first Earl of Chichester, once haunted Stanmer House.

It is a story backed by little in the way of evidence, but an odd incident which took place in 1946 is worthy of mention. For much of the Second World War the mansion was occupied by the military, but after it was vacated, Alfred Mason, from nearby Falmer, was given the responsibility of keeping an eye on the place.

One day he handed the key of Stanmer House to his 26-year-old daughter, Doris, and 17-year-old son, also named Alfred, and asked them to check over the building. Taking the family bull mastiff with them, the pair set off. Their inspection of the house eventually led them to the top floor, where they made their way along the corridor of what, in former years, had been the servants' quarters.

They had only taken a few paces when the dog stopped, its fur standing on end. Obviously terrified, it then flew back along the corridor and down the staircase to cower by the front door. Doris and Alfred had noticed nothing unusual. Later, the top floor was converted into flats, one of which was for a time occupied by an employee of the Parks and Gardens Department. He and his wife reported being conscious of some unseen presence in their flat.

Late one night in 1992, Alison Reynolds was driving along Lewes Road. With her in the car were three friends. They had no particular destination in mind. In fact, they were just out for a pleasant spin, when it occurred to Miss Reynolds that, as it wasn't far away, they could visit Stanmer Park. She had heard that Stanmer House was haunted so, she suggested, as something to do, they could go and investigate. Her friends agreed.

On reaching Stanmer House, Miss Reynolds decided to drive the car onto the grass so as to face the front of the building. With the headlights on, she reasoned, they would all be able to keep watch on the building. No one really expected to see anything unusual. Indeed, somewhat bored after a few minutes, they decided to move off.

At that point, to Miss Reynolds' dismay, the engine refused to start. Turning the ignition key again and again, she failed to detect even a glimmer of response from the engine, though the fact that the lights were capable of maximum intensity showed there was no fault with the battery. After a few more abortive attempts to start the car, a further turn of the ignition key brought an instant response. Greatly relieved, Miss Reynolds drove off. There were no further problems with starting the engine over the following days. Perhaps there had been a temporary fault with the ignition system? But then again...?

Numbers 1 and 2, Edward Street, was the location of the Child Guidance Clinic (later to become the Family Consultation Centre) until the late 1980s, when the building was demolished. It was claimed that the centre was haunted. Senior educational psychologist John Foster, in charge of the centre, used to joke about its ghostly reputation, which included incidents such as roller blinds shooting up and down without reason.

Prior to demolition, the building was for a time boarded up and unused. During this period, facilities officer Doug Stanley had occasion to go to the building to check on its security. Arriving there, even though the rest of the building was freezing, it being winter, he found that a room which had once been the waiting room felt quite warm. On placing his hand on the surround of the gas fire, he noted it was as hot as if it had only just been switched off. Checking the gas mains, he discovered that the switch was off.

His next visit to the building came weeks later as a result of a call from the police. Water had been observed gushing into the street from the windows, which were positioned low down on each floor. This time Mr Stanley, who was normally based in the nearby Magistrates Court, took a colleague with him. They found that some taps had been turned on in the building, even though it had been left with all utilities switched off, while there was no sign of a forced entry. In addition, the former waiting room was again found to be warm, with the derelict gas fire especially warm to the touch.

19 *Houses of the haunted kind*

IN 1926, WRITER GEORGE AITCHISON recorded the macabre story of a house in Egremont Place which was haunted by a corpse-like woman dressed in black and, quite possibly, by another entity which indicated its presence with various noises. Mr Aitchison interviewed four witnesses, the main one being a Miss Louise.

The haunting lasted from the late 1800s until the early 1900s. Miss Louise, a teenage girl at the time, moved into the house with her aunt, who had a three-year lease on the property. On the first Sunday after they had moved in, the aunt, a devout Christian, began to read aloud from the New Testament. As she came to the words 'Judas went and hanged himself,' there was a loud crash in the bedroom above. This was followed by the sound of footsteps.

Thinking the disturbance might have been caused by a cat or dog which had somehow got into the room and knocked over a vase, Louise grabbed a poker and ascended the stairs. She found no animal in the room, nor was anything knocked over or broken.

Some weeks later, the aunt became ill and was confined to bed. On the Sunday, Louise sat down to play hymns on the piano in the sitting room. Eventually tiring of playing hymns, she went over to the music cabinet and selected some sheet music. On turning to go back to the piano she had a terrible fright, for standing at the piano was a woman dressed in black with dreadful dead eyes, heavy, pendulous cheeks and a sagging jaw.

Louise was so shocked she felt unable to call out. She just stood there, petrified, as the apparition stared at her. Eventually, composing herself a little and desperately hoping that the figure, despite its grotesque appearance, might be that of her aunt – for who else could it be? – she stammered: "Oh, Auntie! What's the matter? Why are you looking at me like that?"

The apparition didn't answer but continued to glare at Louise for a few more moments before moving across the room, where it slowly dematerialised. Once Louise was sure the awful spectre had really disappeared, she ran upstairs to her aunt. She found her sitting up in bed, combing her hair. Louise asked her if she had been downstairs.

"Of course not. Why do you ask?" replied her aunt.

"Well I thought I heard someone walking about," responded Louise. She didn't dare tell her aunt the truth. In her delicate state, she was in no way ready for such a shock.

Louise prayed to God that she would never see the apparition again, and she didn't, but the disturbances continued. On many a night Louise heard footsteps walking across the bedroom floor upstairs and sometimes there were thumpings on the bedroom doors.

At the time, servants were still very poorly paid, so it was not uncommon for people who weren't particularly rich to have a maid who dealt with the day-to-day household chores. Following upon her illness and not feeling as fit as she had been, the aunt decided to employ a live-in housemaid. The house, like many other houses at the turn of the century, was equipped with wall-fitted bells which were used to summon servants. When, on several occasions, these bells began to ring without apparent cause, the new maid was suspected of playing tricks.

Louise spoke about the matter to her cousin, who suggested that the maid be sent away for a few days. The aunt agreed to this, and the girl was sent home to her parents in Portslade for a week. But the bells continued to ring. As a consequence, Mr Williams, the local ironmonger, was called in to disconnect the bells. However, the mystery footsteps and door bangings continued.

Soon after the housemaid had returned to work, she went into hysterics after hearing the unaccountable footsteps and door thumpings at close hand. After she had recovered, she insisted she could no longer stay at the house.

The aunt seems not to have been as affected as Louise by the inexplicable noises – perhaps she was a little deaf? – so when the three-year lease on the house expired, she expressed her wish to renew it. Louise pleaded with her not do so, but the aunt had found the house to her liking. She explained the noises away as being due to natural causes and renewed the lease for a further three years.

Shortly afterwards, the aunt became ill and died. Louise at once contacted the agent and managed to obtain a cancellation of the lease, after which she moved out of the house as quickly as she could to another house a few streets away.

The new tenant was a Mrs Gibson, a woman who had spent much of her earlier life in India. Louise knew Mrs Gibson slightly, but hadn't dared to tell her about the baffling happenings at the house. However, only a few days after Mrs Gibson had moved in, greatly agitated, she called on

Louise. Apparently, while in the kitchen stoning raisins, she had became conscious of an awful presence close by. She turned to see an old woman glaring at her. She was dressed in black and had a face like that of someone dead.

"I screamed out and flung the dish of raisins at the woman," said Mrs Gibson, "but the dish seemed to pass right through her. I dashed out of the house straight away. You lived there. What is it? I just can't go back."

Louise had to confess her story. After hearing it, Mrs Gibson quickly arranged to have her furniture moved out and took up residence elsewhere. The property was then unoccupied for a considerable time.

Another witness interviewed by Mr Aitchison was William Oldham Dawson, a Brighton barrister. Learning of the house's macabre history, Mr Dawson suggested to two of his friends, a doctor and a clergyman, the Rev Ouseley, who was connected with the Church of the Annunciation in Washington Street, that they stay overnight at the still unoccupied house to discover for themselves if it really was haunted. The friends agreed.

The first night nothing happened. The second night, as on the first, Mr Dawson took a revolver and also his Irish terrier, a fierce little creature who, he avowed, would have bravely faced devil or man. At around midnight, Mr Dawson left the sitting room to go upstairs, his dog running just ahead of him. Before the dog reached the top of the stairs it suddenly stopped, then it retreated down the stairs until it was between Mr Dawson's legs. He told the dog to go on, but then perceived it was quivering with terror.

At that moment Mr Dawson heard the doctor, who was still downstairs, call out for him. He rejoined the doctor, who he saw was now very agitated, in the sitting room. The Rev Ouseley was already present, having come from another downstairs room.

The doctor told the two men that he had just seen the figure of a woman dressed in a dark grey or black dress enter the room and walk across it before disappearing. He insisted that what he had seen was clearly defined and that there was 'something most awful about it'. The three men thoroughly searched the house, but found nothing.

Some time later the Rev Ouseley told Mr Dawson that he had visited the house alone. On that occasion, the spirit had appeared and he had called on it to make a full confession of any evil it had done. It had, apparently, made such a confession. But the Rev Ouseley claimed that in addition to the hapless earthbound spirit whom he had sent to eternal rest, the house was still possessed by a real influence of evil. The Rev Ouseley suggested to Mr Dawson that he could, if he wished, take part in an exorcism to rid the house of the evil spirit. Mr Dawson agreed, and two nights later the men arrived at the still empty house.

Under the Rev Ouseley's instructions Mr Dawson drew a circle, in chalk, on the floor of the front room. The circumference was then marked with certain signs, as instructed by the priest. Mr Dawson was then called upon to swing a lighted, incense-filled censer, which had previously been blessed by the priest, around the circle, stopping more particularly to cense the specially marked spots. This ceremony was carried out so as to create a wall of influence which could not be penetrated by the evil power.

"If you so much as let any part of your clothing fall outside of the circle once the incantation has begun," said the priest, "the consequences to you may be most terrible."

The Rev Ouseley, dressed in cassock and biretta, then began to read the invocations in Latin as decreed by the Roman Church for the exorcism of evil spirits. The immediate result was a disturbance of air which increased to become more and more violent.

Mr Dawson said afterwards: "It seemed as if we were in the centre of a mighty, rushing whirlwind. It was whirling with tremendous velocity around the circle where we were standing. It was the fury of something hideously evil. I felt that some horrible, unclean thing was raging around us, but I could see nothing. Only hear and feel. It went on for about 20 minutes, reached a climax, then gradually died away. Presently, it was gone altogether. Then there was peace."

The Rev Ouseley closed his book, saying that the evil spirit had been sent back to where it came from and that it was now safe to step out of the circle.

Author's note: The credibility of this story, which has more than a whiff of a Dennis Wheatley novel about it, might seem to fall down with its description of a Protestant minister using a Roman Catholic ritual, but it should be pointed out that the Church of the Annunciation (described as Anglo-Catholic), was at the time involved with Ritualism, a movement which aroused considerable passion in the mid- to late 1800s for its adherence to certain Roman Catholic practices. Indeed, anger among local Protestants gathered so much momentum that the Rev Arthur Wagner, one of the movement's leaders, had a pistol fired at him.

The story didn't end at this point. After the house had stayed empty for a few more months, a Mr and Mrs Robinson moved in. By then Mr Aitcheson had completed his report of the hauntings up to the time of the exorcism and had turned to writing about other matters, but when he found out that the house had new occupants, he decided to contact them.

Told about the exorcism, Mrs Robinson said: "When we were looking over the house, I saw the chalk ring on the floor of the sitting room and thought someone had been playing marbles."

However, when he first spoke to the Robinsons, Mr Aitchison, not wishing to alarm the couple, didn't mention the exorcism, preferring to broach the subject gradually. The Robinsons did volunteer that after moving in, they had heard peculiar sounds in the house, but hadn't attached too much importance to them.

When Mr Aitchison told them there had been an exorcism at the house, the new tenants became more forthcoming. Mr Robinson said that, one night, it was getting close to bedtime and his wife had been kneeling in front of the fireplace, making sure that the dying embers in the grate presented no fire hazard, while he had been seated in an armchair in a corner of the room.

All of a sudden, a guitar hanging on the wall played an arpeggio of three notes: A, C, E. Astonished, they both jumped up and looked at the guitar. As they looked, the guitar sounded the identical arpeggio a second, and then a third time, before finally remaining silent. They examined the instrument, but found nothing unusual.

The Robinsons had taken on a servant girl and she slept in a room on the first floor. Two nights after the guitar incident, the Robinsons were awoken by the girl's screams. They tried to calm the girl and asked what was the matter. She said she had been awakened by the crash of crockery outside her door, adding that this was followed by a sound that seemed like snakes hissing. The Robinsons laughed and told the girl to go back to bed, saying that she must have had a nightmare.

A few days later, Mrs Robinson's sister, a lady who in her younger days had played principal boy in provincial pantomimes, came to reside briefly at the house. The servant girl was accommodated elsewhere for the duration of the sister's stay so that the latter could sleep in her room.

The sister, on the day of her arrival, had been told about the antics of the supposed ghost. At breakfast the next morning she derided the Robinsons for following up the story by trying to frighten her through banging on her door three times with what sounded like a heavy stick. The Robinsons were perplexed, for they had taken part in no such prank.

Subsequently, two clergymen were invited to the house to see if they could rid the building of its continuing hauntings. They offered up appropriate prayers and seem to have succeeded, for this time the house remained peaceful.

Mrs Robinson later researched the history of the house and discovered that, in early Victorian times, a mentally deranged woman had hanged herself in the doorway of the bedroom where her sister (and the servant girl) had slept.

That part of Preston Road facing Preston Park was once notable for its large, detached houses, but most have long since been demolished to make way for modern office blocks. One of these grand properties, Whitchurch House, was the scene of a peculiar haunting at the beginning of the 1900s. The story is told by a Mrs M E Holland, who was then employed as a housemaid.

The dining room at Whitchurch House had a small room next to it called the den, and Mrs Holland's duties included cleaning this room, which she did at about 6.30 every morning. At this precise time each day, peculiarly, the room's French windows slowly opened, and then slowly closed again.

Initially, Mrs Holland thought that the wind was responsible, or that another member of staff was playing a trick on her, but both of these possibilities were ruled out when the phenomenon continued on successive mornings, even though she knew that the windows had been securely locked and bolted. Another oddity was that when the windows opened, only cold air came into the room, even on the hottest days.

Once, she tried to stop the windows opening with her hands, but she pushed in vain. It was as if some irresistible force was at work. On another occasion, she deliberately opened the doors before half-past-six, but they at once closed, only to re-open again at exactly 6.30am.

Unsure as to whether he would believe her, the unnerved maid decided to tell her employer about the phenomenon. At first he laughed, but she persisted, so he arose early one morning to see for himself. He was flabbergasted to find that Mrs Holland had been telling the truth. He sold the house soon afterwards, but it is not known if this action was a consequence of the haunting.

Port Hall, a listed building standing at the corner of Dyke Road and Port Hall Road, once excited much comment as to its origins. Its castellated roof, ecclesiastical-style window with a statuette of a monk and a further statuette of a knight above the doorway seem to indicate great age and possibly a religious connection.

However, more recent research appears to put its construction date at about 1800 when it was, apart from Port Hall Mill Cottage and other mill cottages, the only residential building in Ditchling Road. Sir Charles Page Dick lived there from 1820. Sir Charles was honorary curator of a museum situated on the first floor of the Royal Pavilion from 1862 to 1873, after which the museum's collections were transferred to the newly opened Brighton Museum and Art Gallery.

There have been suggestions in the past that the house was haunted by a Red Crusader. It is possible that the statuette of the knight combined with the house's initial isolation in what were more superstitious times gave rise to the legend of a ghostly knight. Certainly the current occupier, who has resided in the house for about 50 years, has stated that nothing of a supernatural nature has been experienced by anyone in the house during that time.

In 1915, when aged seven, Joy Channon lived in a large house in Beaconsfield Villas. When her parents went out for the evening, the housekeeper was given the responsibility of looking after her. But once Joy had settled down in bed, the housekeeper was apt to creep out of the house to find solace in a local pub.

Joy wasn't immediately aware of the housekeeper's night-time excursions in search of a tipple. She was, anyway, quite used to being alone and content to be left with her thoughts as she drifted off to sleep. But before sleep took over, she often had a visitor; a nun dressed in a black habit. Sometimes the nun would be standing. At other times she was seated in a chair.

The nun, with a gentle face and always silent, only appeared for seconds. Joy Channon doesn't recall being frightened by the apparition's arrival. Initially, she thinks, the idea that the nun could be a ghost had not occurred to her. At that time she only had a vague notion of what ghosts might be, and this particular apparition looked quite solid and three-dimensional.

Inevitably the indiscretions of the housekeeper came to light and she was sacked. The new housekeeper, a woman who took her duties seriously, always sat by her charge until she was fast asleep. Joy never again saw the nun.

Some two or three years after the Second World War, when he was about 11 years old, Steve Wandsworth (not his real name) lived with his family in Clyde Road. One night, when he was in bed but still awake, the door of his wardrobe swung open with a thump. As far as he knew, it had been locked, but he got out of bed to close and re-lock it. He had only just climbed back into bed, when it swung open again. There were two other evenings when the phenomenon took place, except that on these occasions the locked wardrobe door opened only once.

One day he was in his bedroom when, from his sister's bedroom above, came the sound of a woman singing softly. Steve knew his sister was out, but the voice was that of someone much older. He listened for a few moments. He knew the song, though doesn't now recall the tune.

Puzzled rather than nervous, because at that point he hadn't associated the singing with anything ghostly, he crept up the stairs. Standing outside of the door to his sister's bedroom, he continued to hear the singing. Though the voice was still soft, now that he was close, he could hear the words clearly. He reached out his hand to grasp the doorknob. At the precise moment that he opened the door, the voice stopped. He found the room empty.

At a later date, Steve once more heard the sound of a woman singing in his sister's room. He was alone in the house at the time, but on this occasion, being now fearful, he decided to remain where he was. He listened to the crooning voice for several minutes until it ceased.

One day he was on the ground floor when there was an enormous crash. It was as if some very heavy piece of furniture had been dropped from a height. It was so loud and so close that he cried out with the shock of it. His father, who was upstairs at the time, heard both the crash and his son's cry. He responded by dashing downstairs to investigate, but no reason for the noise was found.

In 1950, when aged 12, Cyril Simmons lived with his family in Shanklin Road. One Sunday morning as his mother was washing up, she told him to go upstairs to get the cups and saucers that she and her husband had used for their early morning tea. Cyril made his way to the first floor bedroom used by his parents, picked up the cups and saucers, and walked back along the corridor leading to the top of the stairs. Towards the end of the corridor were three steps, then a small landing where one turned into the main flight of stairs.

Reaching the landing, Cyril moved towards the stairs, at the same time looking back along the corridor. As his hands were full, he had left his parents' bedroom door open. Now he was horrified to see a strange human face looking out from the doorway. Incongruously, the face was only about two feet up from floor level.

Cyril screamed and hurtled down the flight of stairs in two or three leaps to land in the passage below, fortunately without sustaining anything worse than a jarring. The cups and saucers flew out of his hands to tumble down the staircase with him. With only a brief glimpse of the face, he had been unable to tell whether it was that of a man or of a woman.

Alerted by his scream his father, mother, and elder brother raced to the bottom of the staircase. After listening to his brief, gabbled story, they hurried upstairs, but a thorough search revealed no intruder and nothing that could have been mistaken for a face. The matter might have been entirely put down to imagination, except that it was not the only curious incident to take place.

On another occasion Cyril was in the kitchen at the rear of the ground floor with his parents when he was asked to fetch the evening newspaper which, shortly before, had been pushed through the front door letterbox. The passage leading from the kitchen to the front of the house had an internal door about half-way along it.

As it was a cold day, Cyril closed this behind him as he made his way to the front door – houses at the time were often kept warm by a single coal fire, and there had been a parental admonition that doors should always be kept closed to retain the heat. Picking up the newspaper, he made his way back along the passage. As he went through the internal door once more, he felt something invisible grab his ankle and he sprawled forward on his face.

His sister, Margaret, had a small bedroom on the first floor. One year she was quite ill and had a high temperature. As she lay in her bed, she saw a spectral woman drift out of the wall and then, only seconds later, fade away. She was told that, as she had a fever, she had probably hallucinated. But had she?

The family cat used to wander freely around the house, but one day it careered down from the first floor, its fur standing on end and obviously very disturbed. It never again ventured upstairs.

At times, usually when he was awake in his bed, Cyril would hear a parent calling out: 'Who's there?' or something similar, in response to unaccountable sounds in the house. His father or elder brother sometimes went to investigate, but no reason for the noises was ever found. In retrospect, Cyril thinks it possible that his parents might have been keeping something back so as not to frighten him.

A former Mayoress of Brighton once had a mild skirmish with the supernatural. This was Anne Johnson, the wife of Major Alan Johnson, who was Mayor of Brighton in 1960-61.

Shortly after the Second World War, she moved into a flat in Prestonville Road. Every night at bedtime she had the curious sensation that someone was sitting at the end of her bed. After a while, she became used to the presence of this unseen visitor until the day arrived when, for some reason, the visitor came no more.

Not long afterwards, she vacated the flat. Later, on speaking to a retired police officer, she learned that years before, the flat had been the scene of a murder. A man had killed his wife in the very bedroom where she had slept.

Some time in 1951, the Counihan family moved from their flat by Preston Park to a Victorian house in College Terrace. The house, comprising four storeys and a basement, was to be their home for nine months, the brief duration of their tenancy being due to a combination of financial considerations and the family's harassment by a somewhat sinister entity.

On the first night of their stay, as the beds hadn't yet been assembled, the family slept on mattresses laid out on the ground floor. Mr and Mrs Counihan occupied the front room for the night, while the four children – Liz, aged ten, Deirdre, aged eight, John, aged six, and Michael, aged two – slept in a back room.

That night, Deirdre felt a compulsion to reach up inside the chimney of the room she was sleeping in. Her fingers alighted on something rectangular, and when she brought her hand down, she saw that she was holding a large, walnut cigarette box. Lifting the lid, she found it was empty. She wondered who had placed it there, and why. But this was a minor mystery compared to what was to take place, for over the following months there were a series of chilling and inexplicable events which were to especially affect the children.

After the initial flurry of activity associated with moving into a new home, the family settled down. The parents had a bedroom on the third floor. Mr Counihan, a radio broadcaster and journalist, also had his study on this floor. The four children had bedrooms on the top floor. The family were soon joined by a friend, an elderly lady, who occupied the second floor.

It wasn't long before the children, if still awake in their beds at night, began to hear a curious sound. It was as if a ping pong ball had gone tap-tapping down the uncarpeted stairs from the landing outside of their bedrooms to the floor below. It was an occasional occurrence for which there seemed to be no explanation. But incidents far more disturbing were to follow.

Some time later Mr Counihan gathered the three older children in his study and demanded to know who had been hitting Michael. Apparently, bruises had been found on his body. At his tender age his vocabulary was limited, but from what he did say, his father felt that the bruises were no accident. Each of the older children denied any responsibility. A few weeks later, new bruises appeared on Michael. Once more, no cause could be established.

One day, Michael cried out and was found sprawled at the bottom of the stairs. Now past his third birthday he had added to his vocabulary so, on being questioned by his father, he was able to make the astonishing claim that he had been pushed down the stairs by a girl aged about eight. She had, he said, brown hair in ringlets, and was wearing a green, 'furry' (velvet?) dress with a white collar, black-buttoned shoes and white socks.

He also stated that his earlier bruising had resulted from her attacks though, bizarrely, she always appeared before him bearing a silver tray in her hand on which there was a green jelly! Because Michael's experiences took place so many years ago and when he was very young, there is no recall of whether these attacks were made with the girl's free hand, or whether the tray and jelly were dispensed with before the attacks.

On another occasion, John made the startling assertion that while taking Michael upstairs from the basement, a hand had shot out of the wall as if to grab his younger brother. Mr and Mrs Counihan wondered if this claim was due to a too vivid imagination fired by a knowledge of the strange events that had already taken place in the house.

The basement was mainly given over as a play area for the children. They were acutely conscious of its spooky atmosphere. One day, some additional toys were found among the others in the basement room. These comprised three or four small metal vehicles. Deirdre particularly recalled that one of these was a green-coloured lorry. Where they had come from, no one knew. Inexplicably, they just appeared.

In August 1951 Mrs Counihan gave birth to her fifth child, Sally. Soon afterwards, she moved to the third bedroom on the fourth floor, partly to give a sense of comfort to her other children.

Truth is sometimes stranger than fiction, and there were two unlikely coincidences which took place years later. Deirdre, by this time a teacher, was additionally involved in the editing of a private press magazine. An artist providing illustrations for the magazine happened to mention he was moving to College Terrace. Amazingly, it transpired that he was moving into the same house that had been occupied by Deirdre's family, except that the house had since been converted into flats.

Later, Deirdre had occasion to visit him – his flat took in the two top floors of the house – when she noticed that the atmosphere was quite different to that which she remembered. The house now seemed tranquil rather than troubled. Because the artist had to live there, Deirdre chose not to mention the disturbing events once experienced by her family.

Some months after this, when Deirdre was taking a class, the subject of ghosts came up, and she took the opportunity to mention the eerie happenings that had plagued her former College Terrace home. Later that day, one of her pupils asked if he could have a word with her. He revealed that his father had, when still a boy, lived in the College Terrace house.

Apparently, his father's parents had been so troubled by the malevolent atmosphere of the house and by a variety of eerie incidents (which they had not divulged to their son for fear of frightening him), that they had asked a priest to exorcise the building. It seems the exorcism was successful; a fact which could explain the pacific atmosphere experienced years later by Deirdre on visiting the house.

There is one question regarding the above story that might be pondered on. Was there any significance to the colour green – a green dress, a green jelly, a green lorry – in these events?

In 1951 Banjo Banham lived with his parents in a terraced house in Foundry Street. He was aged six at the time. One night he awoke to the horrifying sensation of being strangled. He felt cold fingers tightening around his neck and though his bedroom was dark at the time, he had the distinct feeling that it was a man who was leaning over his bed. Threshing and struggling in the darkness, the young Banjo wanted to yell out, but he could only gurgle through his constricted throat as the persistent fingers pressed down. A few moments later, the fingers released their grip and the boy sensed that the hovering presence had gone. He'd had bad dreams and nightmares before, but this harrowing experience was so real that even now, some 50 years after the event, it still remains vividly in his memory.

Interestingly, when Mr Banham was well into adulthood, he came across a bound volume of local newspapers dated 1868 and looking through these, he came across the story of a murder. It concerned a baby that had been killed by strangulation before being dismembered. The body's parts were later discovered in a bucket. The murder had taken place in the house that had been Mr Banham's boyhood home!

From 1945 until 1953, by which time she was 13 years old, Lesley Webster lived with her mother and her brothers, Ian and John, in a flat in Alexandra Villas. The flat was haunted by the ghost of a man wearing a trilby hat and a light-coloured overcoat of the type worn in the 1920s or 1930s. All four members of the family saw the ghost at various times during the eight years they lived at the address. The phantom was usually seen walking up the stairs to a bathroom on the next floor.

On another occasion, about a year before the family vacated the flat, Miss Webster was alarmed to see the ghost of a nun materialise in a chair standing close by her bed. The spectre faded away moments later.

Once, during the family's stay at the flat, Miss Webster's mother had a particularly uncanny experience. The mother awoke early one morning to see a glowing golden cross on the wall to the right of her bed. The cross, about two to three feet high, continued to glow eerily for three or four minutes before fading. The following morning the mother learned that the woman living in the flat below, with whom she was very friendly, had died overnight. Her death had taken place at about the time the glowing cross had appeared.

Towards the end of 1953, the Websters moved from Alexandra Villas to a house in Montpelier Road. Unknowingly, they had left behind one haunted building to live in another. Their new home was rented from a doctor who lived elsewhere, but who had purchased the property with the intention of using the ground floor as a surgery while letting the rest of the house.

The first indication that something was not as it should be came when the doctor complained about the Websters' cat. A black cat, he said. Could they ensure that the animal was kept to their part of the building so that it didn't wander into his surgery? But the Websters had no cat. They suggested that it might be a cat that had strayed into the house.

In the days that followed, Miss Webster and her mother both saw the cat the doctor had described, and on more than one occasion. It was mostly seen lolling on the staircase, a few feet away from the surgery. But they also became aware of its spectral quality, for they noted that it was only visible for seconds. The doctor also came across the cat again, strolling around his surgery, but he had to recognise its ephemeral nature when the animal faded away before his eyes.

One day, when she was in her early twenties, Lesley Webster was passing the foot of the staircase leading to the family bedrooms when she looked up to see a man running up the last few stairs before entering her bedroom. Puzzled, she ran up after him, thinking the man was one of the doctor's patients who had accidentally strayed upstairs – perhaps looking for a toilet?

Reaching the bedroom, she had a momentary glimpse of the rear of the man and was just about to speak to him when she saw him walk through the closed door of the room's built-in wardrobe. She never again saw the apparition after this, but her mother did.

The mother was in her sons' bedroom, making their beds, when she saw a man in the doorway. She, like her daughter, had presumed the man to be a patient who had strayed from the doctor's surgery – it had happened a number of times in the past.

She said: "He was a pleasant-looking, middle-aged man with rosy cheeks and wore a waistcoat over a check shirt. For some reason, he wasn't wearing a jacket. He looked quite real, but as soon as I opened my mouth to tell him that he was in the wrong place, he vanished."

Alfred Mason died in 1957. Up until that time he had held the tenancy of the Old Forge Nurseries, in Falmer, living in the adjacent cottage (today known as Old Forge Cottage – the land itself now forms part of the playing fields of the University of Sussex). On the day of the funeral, family and friends gathered at the cottage following the funeral service. Later, after the rest of the mourners had left for home, Mr Mason's married daughter, Doris Williams, and her husband Owen, put on their coats to leave.

As they stood at the back door of the cottage before leaving, they paused for a moment and looked out over the rain-swept lawn. In that instant Owen Williams saw the figure of Mr Mason. He was standing quite still upon the lawn, but was visible for only a second or two. His wife, whose attention at that moment was elsewhere, saw nothing.

Mr Williams, sceptical about the concept of ghosts, put his experience down to the high emotion of the day, believing that what he had seen was some projection from his mind. However, what he saw on that day was almost certainly what psychic researchers refer to as a crisis apparition, where it is not essential to be aware of a death to be able to see the form of the deceased (see Chapter 1).

In the early 1960s, Horace and Olive Wenham occupied a house in Heath Hill Avenue. Mr Wenham's widowed father, who had lived alone in his house in Yorkshire for many years, was becoming very old and frail, so Mr Wenham decided to use part of his annual holiday to journey north to be with him for a few days.

During the time her husband was away, Mrs Wenham woke up with a start one night to find the mirror of her dressing table glowing with the picture of a woman. Horrified, she stared at it for a few moments, after which the vision disappeared. The following morning, she wondered if she should phone her husband to tell him of her experience, but finally decided not to worry him, especially as he was due to return home two days later.

When he arrived home, she was quick to relate her story. On hearing the description of the woman on the mirror, Mr Wenham opened the suitcase he had brought back and produced a large photograph which he had collected from his father's house. It was of Dolly Wenham, his mother, who had died in the mid-1930s while she was still quite young.

Olive Wenham instantly recognised the photograph. It was in every way identical to the picture she'd seen glowing eerily on her dressing table mirror. It was the same face, the same expression, the same hairstyle, even the same dress! Prior to that moment, Olive Wenham had little idea of what her husband's mother had looked like, for she had still been a little girl at the time of the woman's death, while the only photographs she had ever seen of her had been a few small, fuzzy snapshots.

Hanover Crescent, immediately to the east of The Level, is an attractive row of listed houses built around 1822. Among former distinguished residents were Sir Rowland Hill, the initiator of the penny post, who lived at number 11, and novelist Horace Smith, who lived at number 10.

During the 1960s, Susan Hudson lived with her husband and four children in one of these elegant houses, while six doors away in another lived a friend, Lesley Afzali, and her husband and three children. Mrs Hudson's house was haunted and the first indication of this took place one evening after the two friends had returned to Mrs Hudson's house for coffee after seeing a play at the Theatre Royal.

Mrs Afzali's car had been used as transport and once inside her friend's house, Mrs Afzali placed her car keys on the large pine table standing in the centre of the dining room. At around one o'clock, Mrs Afzali arose from her chair to leave, but when she came to pick up her car keys, they were missing. There had been nothing else on the pine table and both women had seen the keys placed there. No one else could have removed the keys, for Mrs Hudson's husband was away on business and her children, sound asleep, would have been noticed had they woken and ventured downstairs. So where were the keys?

Starting with the dining room, the friends scoured through the house in an effort to find them. After a long but fruitless search, Mrs Afzali decided, realising nothing more could be done, to return home, but as the two women were walking through the dining room on their way to the front door, there were the missing keys, back on the pine table!

At a later date, Mrs Afzali was washing up some crockery in Mrs Hudson's kitchen after the two had had tea together. The kitchen sink was situated just below a window, and as she was washing up, Mrs Afzali became aware of a reflection on the glass which was additional to her own. It was the face of a woman, clear and distinct, but when Mrs Afzali turned around, she found no one there. When she looked again at the window, the image had gone.

One of the most disturbing incidents took place about two years later. Mrs Hudson was redecorating the ground floor rooms and Mrs Afzali offered to assist. One of the first jobs was to strip off the wallpaper. While Mrs Afzali was at the top of a stepladder in the dining room beginning this task, she became aware of voices behind her.

Mrs Hudson's four children were at home at the time, so Mrs Afzali presumed they were coming along the corridor towards the room and that it was their voices she was hearing. But as the voices came closer, they no longer sounded like those of children. The childlike chatter was now rising in volume and becoming a discordant babble.

As Mrs Afzali turned to see who was making this awful noise, the voices took on an evil quality. It was as if some terrible hobgoblins were squabbling among themselves. But looking around her, Mrs Afzali found she was alone in the room. Scared and shaking, and feeling very unsafe at the top of the ladder, she stepped down two or three rungs. At that moment, the unholy jabbering ceased. Mrs Afzali forced her trembling legs down to the floor and fled from the room to look for Mrs Hudson. As she stopped for a moment to listen, she could hear her voice. It was coming from the first floor and she was talking to the children.

In her own house in Hanover Crescent, Lesley Afzali had just the one brush with the paranormal. It was late in the evening and her childen were in bed. Otherwise, she was alone in the house. As she went about a few domestic tasks, she heard an unexpected sound. It was the clip-clop of horses' hooves coming closer, together with the heavy rumble of coach-wheels. The sound stopped immediately outside of her house and then there was a scraping, metallic noise, which she couldn't positively identify, but thought it might be the sound of a gate closing. When she looked out of her front window, the road was deserted.

Over the two years prior to his marriage, Ben Gosden shared a basement flat in College Road with his mother and grandmother. In 1967 he married his girlfriend Val. The newly-weds thought themselves fortunate when they found they were able to rent a first-floor flat in the same house, but after only ten months, they were glad to move away. Indeed, they would have moved out earlier if circumstances had allowed.

At first, they were quite happy in the flat. When, soon after their arrival, the indoor aerial of their TV set was found on the floor and snapped in half, they presumed it was due to some weakness of manufacture, but when the oven door on their cooker swung open and all the shelves and a baking tray shot out onto the floor, they recognised that something uncanny was taking place.

By this time, the whistling had started. This was the main and continuing phenomenon. Every night without exception, there would be a low-key whistling. It started at around 10pm and carried on for at least two hours, but sometimes it lasted for five or six hours. Both Mr and Mrs Gosden heard the whistling. It seemed to rise up from the floor, though they were never able to establish the exact point of origin. Initially, because of their disquiet, they would often remain awake for hours, but familiarity with the phenomenon finally led to fewer disturbed nights.

"It was as if someone was whistling for their dog," said Mr Gosden. "It was a warbling, slightly discordant sound, and it continued until we were able to leave the flat."

There were other incidents. The largest room in the flat was used as a bed-sitting room. Here, sometimes, the ceiling lamp and a table lamp would dim before returning to normal. An electrical fault? Possibly, but on one occasion the Gosdens watched TV for about four hours before switching the set off. Mr Gosden then, as a safety measure, went to pull the plug out of the wall socket, but mystifyingly, when he bent down to do so, he found the plug already out and several inches away from the socket.

On one occasion, all the groceries and other items standing on the top of a kitchen cabinet shot onto the floor and twice, while the Gosdens were in bed, some invisible force pulled the bedclothes from them.

Following their marriage in 1968, Terry and Lyn Mockford rented a ground floor maisonette in Sandown Road. In May 1969, Mrs Mockford gave birth to their first son, Colin. Their landlady lived in the maisonette above, and from the beginning she took a great interest in the new arrival, buying the occasional gift and sometimes playing with him as he grew older.

When the weather was fine, Colin was sometimes placed in his pram and wheeled into the back garden for a while. When this happened, the landlady would often lean out of the kitchen window of her maisonette and call Colin, clapping her hands to gain his attention. He would react with a smile or a movement of his arms. Around the time the boy was about seven months old, the landlady died in her sleep.

As the months passed, Colin grew old enough to play on his own in the garden. One day, his mother looked out of the window and saw him waving to someone upstairs and then holding up his toys for that person to see. The maisonette had been left empty by the landlady's next-of-kin, so puzzled, Mrs Mockford went out into the garden and looked up. She could see no one at any of the windows so she asked her son who he had been waving at.

"Lady was waving at window," he responded.

It was a scenario that was to be repeated frequently. Colin was seemingly reacting to someone by looking up, waving, laughing, and showing off his toys. Mrs Mockford was able to establish that it was the kitchen window that was the focus of his attention, but though she often went into the garden and looked up, she never saw the mysterious 'lady', nor did any other member of the family. Soon after Colin's third birthday, the family moved to another part of Brighton.

The 7 February 1972 edition of the *Evening Argus* reported a haunting at St Martin's Vicarage, in Upper Wellington Road. In addition to unexplained door slammings and the sound of footsteps moving across squeaky floorboards, there was the more unusual phenomenon of food smells.

The vicar's wife, Lesley Baden, said at the time: "I have woken up in the middle of the night and smelled lovely meals cooking and bread baking. At first I thought it must be just the smells of my own cooking.

"Last week our daily char was alone in the house when a door opened behind her. Later, the children's door suddenly slammed, yet it was a calm day. Our char also heard footsteps upstairs. When we returned she was terrified. I thought I would have to advertise for a child-loving, dog-loving, vicar-tolerating, ghost-loving char!"

Mrs Baden and her husband, the Rev Peter Baden, said they were not worried about the ghost, while the char, Celia Knight, got over her fear and said she would remain. The children, James, aged two, and Caroline, aged three, were thought too young to be at all concerned.

"It seems a very friendly ghost and my husband thinks it's a bit of a joke," said Mrs Baden. "We first noticed something strange soon after we moved in four years ago. My husband suddenly sat up and said: 'There's somebody upstairs.'

"We put it down to the fact that it's an old house with creaking joists, but since I wrote about it in the church magazine, a number of people have told us the place is haunted."

St Martin's Vicarage was demolished in 1975 after a new vicarage had been built alongside.

In the 1970s, married couple John and Sylvia Henty lived in a house in Charles Street. On one occasion, tea-making equipment that was on top – but well away from the edge – of a chest of drawers in their bedroom, shot through the air to crash onto the floor. The couple, while resident at the house, found that an area at the foot of the stairs leading up from the hallway would sometimes become unnaturally cold with a temperature significantly lower than that in other parts of the house. No cause could be found for this phenomenon.

At a later date Mr Henty, a journalist and broadcaster, was relating these experiences to someone he came into contact with during his work. This person, on learning that Mr Henty lived in Charles Street, said that he thought he knew the number of the house, for he had already heard that the place was haunted. The street number he suggested was, indeed, that of the house where Mr and Mrs Henty were living.

One of John Rawson's interests was old clocks. He'd buy clocks that were no longer working, take them to pieces, repair any evident damage, then put the parts together again in the hope that they would once more mark the passing hours with accuracy. A favourite piece was an old chiming carriage clock, but although he stripped it and re-assembled it on two or three occasions, he could not get it to work.

At 4.10am on 24 November 1977, John Rawson died while in a local hospice. His son, also called John, and his daughter, June, were with him at the time. His wife Joan was at home in Cuckmere Way where she, knowing that her husband was probably in the last hours of his life, remained awake and busying herself while anticipating that news of him might come at any moment.

At 5am, Joan Rawson was startled to hear the carriage clock, which her husband had never been able to get working, chime five times. She went over to the living room mantelpiece where it was standing and saw that its hands were registering the correct time and that it was ticking. From that time on, the clock continued to function properly.

Wykeham Terrace, by the south end of Dyke Road, is comprised of a row of architecturally interesting terraced houses built between 1827 and 1830 in the Regency Gothic style. Originally intended for the use of retired clergy, by the 1850s some of the houses (number 1-5 and 8-11) had been taken over by St Mary's Home for Female Penitents, which was concerned with the rehabilitation of prostitutes.

Some were child prostitutes and these were sent to classes at the nearby Swan Downer School, a charitable institution for the education of poor girls founded in 1816. The school had moved to the Gothic-styled building at 11 Dyke Road on its completion in 1867. It closed in 1939, and the building has since been used for a variety of purposes, including spells as a chapel and as a night club.

In the 1930s, 6 Wykeham Terrace was occupied by the Rev Montague Summers, who wrote numerous books and articles about ghosts, werewolves, vampires and witches. He helped author Dennis Wheatley with his research on Satanism for *The Devil Rides Out,* a best-selling book first published in 1934. Wheatley thought Summers a sinister individual and later used him as a model for a black magician in another book, *To the Devil a Daughter.* Despite his interest in the supernatural, the Rev Summers never claimed that his Wykeham Terrace property was haunted, although he did report hauntings in some of his other homes.

Wykeham Terrace was substantially restored in 1970 following its occupation by squatters. Later, number 7 became the home of actress Dame Flora Robson, who remained there until her death in 1984.

A married couple, John and Diana Barrymore (not their real names), moved to Wykeham Terrace in 1973. From that time on they were plagued by the frequent and unexplained disappearance of objects left around the house. Pens, tools, chequebooks and other items vanished, only to reappear later, usually in a different place, and often where least expected. In most instances the missing objects returned within 24 hours, though it could be up to two days.

One night in the 1970s, Mrs Barrymore, who had been in poor health for some months, found sleep difficult and left her bed to relax on a settee in the lounge. She had only been there a few moments when she saw the apparition of a mummy, encased in discoloured bandages, materialise a few feet away from her. She was horrified to see that the eyes of the mummy were not only visible, but moving from side to side.

The mobility of the eyes, and their seemingly startled look, gave Mrs Barrymore the impression that the spectre was as surprised to see her as she was to see it, but despite the intimidating appearance of the mummy-like vision, she felt a comforting feeling of tranquility descend upon her. It was as if the figure were projecting an enveloping aura of calm.

In the next few moments there was a voice from the entity. It appeared to be aware of her health problems and assured her that there was no need for concern, for her condition would rapidly improve. A few more seconds passed, then the apparition was gone.

Immediately following the departure of the weird, mummy-like phantom, Mrs Barrymore noted an immediate sense of well-being, while only days saw a marked improvement in her health. She eventually made a full recovery from her illness.

Helen-May Harding lived in Wykeham Terrace for four years. One evening at the beginning of the 1980s, she left her house to go for a stroll. While she was walking past a house just a few doors from her own, she noticed a woman standing by a first floor window. The woman was looking downwards, as if reading a book, though no book was actually visible. Oddly, she was wearing what seemed to be a green velvet dress with a bustle.

The woman was seen in profile and Mrs Harding noted that she was slightly stout and short in stature. She seemed to be about 50 years of age. Mrs Harding knew the occupants of the house and was sure that the woman she was looking at was not one of them. Puzzled, she hesitated for a moment to take a harder look, but as she did so the woman faded away. Uncertain as to how her neighbours would react to a description of what she had seen, Mrs Harding decided to remain silent, though she did relate her experience to some friends.

When, in the late 1970s, Alan Burrell rented a room in Argyle Road, he didn't anticipate he'd be sharing it with a woman 'companion', but he'd only been there a few weeks when he awoke early one morning to find an old lady sitting at the end of his bed. He noted that she was small of stature and dressed in rather old-fashioned, dark clothing. As she slowly turned her head towards Mr Burrell, he saw that there was a smile on her face. She then faded away.

Later that day he told the story of what he had seen to his landlord and landlady, who showed some amused interest. They apparently knew all about the ghost, for it had been seen in various parts of the house on a number of occasions.

"Don't worry!" the landlord insisted, adding: "The old lady is quite harmless."

Mr Burrell wasn't so sure, but over the following year the little old lady 'visited' him several times. At first, these materialisations mildly shocked him, but as the spectral old lady had a gentle face and was always smiling, he soon ceased to be perturbed. Sometimes she would appear seated on the bed; at other times she would be standing.

Around 1980, the family Mr Burrell was staying with moved to Rugby Road, but he elected not to join them in their new home. However, he remained friendly and later learned that the ghost seemed to have moved with the family. Generally, ghosts do not move away from their usual environment, but in some instances the focus for a ghost is not a building or place but instead, a person, an item of furniture or some other object that has been transferred.

Some months later, a local priest was called in and a prayer service held to rid the house of the phantom. This action followed an incident involving a man and a woman who lodged at the house. The couple were together in the sitting room at the time. He was stretched out on the settee, while she was seated in an armchair facing him. As they were conversing, the woman, who had heard about the ghost but never seen it, jumped up and became hysterical.

The reason for her hysteria was that the ghost of the old lady had appeared on the settee with much of the bottom half of her body seemingly passing through the recumbent figure of the man. Strangely, the man neither saw nor felt anything. As the woman's trauma prevailed for a few days and as she was nervous about continuing to stay in the house, the family felt it wise to ask their priest for help.

Late one afternoon in the summer of 1982, Clare Radford, aged 17, entered the house of a friend living in Dorset Gardens. As the friend was unsure about the time he would be finishing work that day, he had given Miss Radford a spare key so that she wouldn't have to wait in the street.

She hadn't been inside the house before, but she quickly found the living room and was glad to sit down on the settee, for it had been an oppressive day and she had walked quite a distance. The settee faced a tiled fireplace and among the items on the mantelpiece were four wineglasses, still unwashed from some previous tipple.

As Miss Radford sank back into the settee and looked around her, the warmth of the room seemed to ebb away. A moment later, one of the glasses shot off the mantelpiece and landed upside down and almost at her feet. Then another glass flew into the air to land on its side close to the first. A second or so later, and a third glass shot off the mantelpiece. The first two glasses had remained intact, but this third glass shattered as it struck the floor.

At this, Miss Radford jumped up in horror and fled from the room. It transpired later that the fourth glass had been unaffected. Her friend, on arriving home and learning of Miss Radford's frightening experience, assured her that during his residence at the house he had never seen or heard anything of a paranormal nature, but he did add that a former resident had hanged himself. It seems probable in this instance that Miss Radford herself was the focus for a modest poltergeist effect.

In 1984 Lorna Jenkins, then aged 17, moved into a ground floor flat in Buckingham Road. It was her initial venture into independence from her parents. Financially, circumstances were difficult, and for the first of the four years she lived there her furniture consisted of little more than the most basic items, together with a few boxes in which she kept her personal belongings. With no money for carpeting, the floorboards stayed bare.

Only days after she had taken up occupancy of the flat, she returned from work one evening to find that some of the boxes had been moved from their normal positions. She thought there might have been an intruder, but a search through her limited belongings revealed nothing had been taken. It was the first of a series of baffling events that were to take place over the following months.

The mysterious movement of boxes, and additionally of items of furniture, now began to take place every few weeks. Then the lights in the flat began to switch on and off of their own accord. Frightened and worried, she called in an electrician, even though she could ill afford it. A thorough examination revealed nothing faulty in the wiring. She contemplated moving out of the flat, but because of her financial circumstances, felt unable to do so.

The occasional movement of furniture and the switching on and off of lights continued, but Miss Jenkins gained some sense of security through the acquisition of a dog, a half-labrador. Further companionship was provided by a Persian cat; a gift from a friend. Though there was no respite from the scary disruptions blighting her life, familiarity with their pattern helped to ease her fears and, comforted by her pets and with her financial position improving, life became more tolerable. But the passing months were bringing her closer to a bizarre and devastating ordeal which was to rekindle her fears and terminate in tragedy.

The beginning of the ordeal took place about two years after Miss Jenkins had moved into the flat. It was a pleasant summer afternoon and she was enjoying a drink and a chat with a male friend. Later, the friend wandered out from the kitchen and into the garden at the rear of the flat.

Returning, he stumbled on a step and fell against the kitchen's French windows, though without injury to himself.

However, both of the windows' large, single panes of glass were shattered. Miss Jenkins and her friend carefully knocked out the broken pieces of glass that remained in the doors and placed them in a box, along with the glass that had fallen on the floor, and carried the box to a point just inside the front door of the flat. Two days later, the box of broken glass was taken by car to a rubbish tip.

A fortnight passed and Miss Jenkins had more or less put the incident to the back of her mind, even though reminded of it each time she saw the still boarded-up windows. When a couple of friends called one day, she made some coffee and sat down with them for a while, but eventually she excused herself so that she could feed the cat. As she prepared the bowl of meat, the cat nudged appreciatively against her legs. The kitchen's boarded-up French windows had been left open so as to let in the light and, the bowl of food now ready, she went out onto the patio and placed the bowl down. The cat eagerly followed her.

As the cat started to eat, Miss Jenkins began walking back into the kitchen, but after taking only two or three steps, she turned to look at the cat. The sight that confronted her was horrific. The cat was crouched over the bowl of food, almost as if it were still eating, but one eye now hung out of its socket. The other eye was bulging unnaturally, while a trickle of blood oozed out from the neck to form a growing, scarlet pool. Only two or three seconds has passed since she had put down the bowl, so what had happened seemed impossible.

Miss Jenkins' cries of horror quickly brought her friends into the kitchen. The cat was found to be almost lifeless, but the friends volunteered to take it to a veterinary surgeon in their car. Miss Jenkins carefully gathered up the cat in some old clothing and they quickly drove off.

The vet examined the cat and declared that it was close to death. In fact, it died while in the surgery. The vet suggested that the cat must have been attacked by another animal, which had taken it by the neck. Had there been a dog around?

Miss Jenkins hadn't considered that her own dog might have been the culprit. After all, it was gentle by nature and had been sprawled out in the garden, some ten feet away from the flat, at the time she had fed the cat. And as she and her friend had left with the injured cat, it was still snoozing peacefully in the place where she had last seen it. Anyway, the dog and cat had always been on friendly terms.

Miss Jenkins pointed out that she had only had her eyes off the cat for two or three seconds, that there had been no noise of a struggle and that, in fact, the cat was still positioned as if it were eating, which would be unlikely if it had been savaged by another animal. However, the vet did comment on the wound, which he said looked more like a straight cut rather than something caused by the teeth of another animal.

Distraught, Miss Jenkins returned to the flat with her friends. It was late afternoon before she felt able to go into the kitchen again, where she knew one of her tasks would be to wash down the patio, still stained with the congealed blood of the cat.

As she walked through the kitchen door, a new fear threaded through her, for as she approached the boarded up French windows, she saw on the floor by their base five or six pieces of broken glass, each about the size of a human hand. She was shocked to see that each piece of glass was embellished with the slightly frosted pattern of the windows that had been shattered a fortnight before. But she knew that every sliver of this broken glass had been removed from the house!

Following the tragedy with the cat, the occasional movement of furniture continued, but there was still one more curious event to take place before Miss Jenkins was finally able to say goodbye to the flat and the fears that went with it.

One afternoon she was in the front room, enjoying a chat with an old friend. Suddenly, the two were startled by a loud bang. It sounded like a shot from a gun and seemed close enough to have originated from within the room. The nearness of it caused both to throw themselves to the floor. After a few moments, as nothing untoward followed, they rose to their feet and looked around them, wondering what had caused the bang.

Looking towards the window, they noticed that a small hole had appeared in the top centre pane. On examining it, they found the hole completely round, which appeared to confirm the impression that a bullet had caused the hole, except that they wondered why the window had not shattered. Looking more closely at the hole, they had the irrational notion that it had been caused by a bullet leaving the room, rather than by entering it.

Despite this conjecture, the logical explanation had to be that someone outside the flat had fired a bullet, or had thrown or catapulted some other missile, so Miss Jenkins decided to phone the police. They quickly arrived, examined the hole and thoroughly searched the room. No spent bullet or other missile was found, either on the floor or in any wall or item of furniture.

John and Amanda Girling moved into their flat in Mitre House, Western Road, in 1984. After the couple had taken up residence, Mr Girling went to bed each night only to be woken in the early hours by something pressing down on his chest, sometimes fairly lightly, but at other times with such force that he broke into a sweat.

Mr Girling did not understand what was happening and wondered if there was something physically wrong with him, especially as his wife seemed unaffected by the phenomenon. His only relief was to struggle against the pressure and get out of bed for awhile.

The previous tenant of the flat had left behind some unwanted furniture. One of these items was a tatty old wardrobe made of plywood. The Girlings thought the wardrobe to be quite awful. Nor did they like the slightly disquieting 'feel' of it.

Some ten days after the couple had moved in, Mr Girling got a hammer and broke up most of the abandoned items of furniture, including the wardrobe, before transporting the remains to a refuse tip. From that time on the nightly pressures on Mr Girling's chest ceased. The couple also noticed a discernible lightening of the atmosphere in the flat.

In 1985, shortly after he had moved into a first floor flat in Upper Rock Gardens, Len Nott began learning to play the tenor saxophone. One evening while practising in the lounge, he turned his head to see a middle-aged woman standing in the doorway to his kitchen. Grey-haired and wearing a greyish Victorian-style dress, he noted that there was a slight element of transparency about her. She was only visible for two or three seconds. Baffled, Mr Nott searched the rooms of his flat, but found no one.

Two years later, a girl friend who stayed at the flat refused to sleep alone without a light after she had been troubled by an awareness of some unseen presence in her room.

In 1991, Ralph Joy called on a friend living in Rugby Place. A trip into Brighton town centre had been planned, but when Mr Joy arrived, his friend wasn't ready, so he was left on his own in a downstairs room of the house while his friend dressed.

But Mr Joy wasn't alone for more than two or three minutes, for he was joined by the ghosts of a woman and a boy. The woman, he noted, was wearing a Victorian-style dress with sleeves that were puffed at the shoulders, a white pinafore and a white bonnet.

The boy, he thought, was about ten years old, but because Mr Joy's gaze was focused mostly on the woman during the brief two or three seconds the spectres were visible, he was uncertain as to the details of the boy's clothing. Told of the experience, Mr Joy's friend said that only one supernatural incident had taken place in the house in the past, when he had witnessed a table move of its own volition. This had taken place in the same room as that in which the ghostly woman and boy had appeared.

In 1990, student Nichola Gover moved into a house in Montpelier Road. There she occupied a bedroom where, during her two year stay at the house, she was disturbed on several occasions by knocks on her door when no one was outside the room. She also heard the sound of footsteps pacing across the floor of the attic room above her when she knew that the occupant of this room was out, with the door locked.

But the attic room's occupant, student Justine McNicholas, had a more vexatious problem. She was being disturbed by a disembodied voice that called her by her first name. She wasn't sure whether it was a male or a female voice, for it had an odd, asexual timbre. She discovered later that the previous occupant had also been troubled by the phantom voice.

Investigation established that no one was was taking part in a hoax. Miss McNicholas, after enduring the discarnate voice on several occasions, agitatedly snapped back at the unseen entity when it next intruded upon her.

"I don't want you here," she cried. "Do please go away!" It seems that her phantom tormentor did just that, for she was never again troubled by the mystery voice!

A much friendlier ghost, at least to women, exists in another part of Montpelier Road. The site of this haunting is Sillwood House, which was built in 1827-8 for Sir David Scott, who named it after his family's estate at Sillwood Park, Berkshire. A listed building, the elegant interior includes a magnificent cast-iron staircase. In 1880, the building was converted into the Sillwood Hall Hotel. In about 1961, it was taken over by Debenhams, whose store was then in Western Road, primarily for storage purposes. In 1989, work commenced on converting the building into luxury apartments.

The spectre is believed to be that of a servant girl, aged about 16, who is said to have been seduced by the master of the house – or his son – when the building was still a private residence. Later, finding herself pregnant, the girl committed suicide.

She has not been seen for some years, but several residents have had strong 'impressions' of her in more recent times, even to feeling their skin prickle. Following the conversion of the building, the ghostly girl confined herself initially to the ground floor at a point beneath the staircase, but in the years since, her unseen spirit has ventured into other parts of the building, though it seems she never makes her presence felt when there is a man in the vicinity. Might this be due to her unfortunate experience at the hands of a man?

Wendy Grantley-Oxberry, a resident at Sillwood House from 1993, said she experienced the presence of the servant girl on a number of occasions.

She added: "It's difficult to explain how you know the girl is close by, but it's quite an intense sensation. But she doesn't seem to be present as often as she used to in the two or three years that followed my arrival at this house."

In the early 1990s, Simon Sheppard moved into a bedsitter in Ship Street. He lived there for about two years, during which time he was involved in a perplexing incident which, in retrospect, he presumed must have had a supernatural basis.

An instructor in karate and oriental kick-boxing, he was due to take an afternoon class and was almost ready to set off. Putting on his jacket, he went over to his dressing table to put on the gold signet ring his mother had given him a few years before on his eighteenth birthday.

He was surprised to see no sign of the ring. He felt sure he had left it on the dressing table. Perhaps it had fallen on the floor? He made a rapid search then, failing to find it, elected to search more thoroughly on his return. Later in the day, on arriving back at the bedsitter, he carried out a more thorough search, but the missing ring was nowhere to be found.

Three days later, after he had spent a few hours in town with some friends, he returned to the bedsitter. On unlocking and opening the door, his eye was instantly attracted by the sight of a square sheet of white paper in the middle of the room. Its whiteness stood out against the worn, dark-patterned carpet on which it lay. In the centre of the square of paper was the missing ring!

While the disappearance and reappearance of the ring was mysterious enough, the presence of the sheet of paper was at least as baffling, for Mr Sheppard possessed no paper of this kind.

In the summer of 1992, a young Swiss girl arrived in Brighton to continue her English studies. She had enrolled with a local language school and had been found accommodation with a family in Freshfield Road. Some weeks later, during an interval in her classwork, she related a curious tale to her teacher.

She had found the family she was staying with pleasant and the room she was occupying quite comfortable, but now she was fearful because of an experience she had just had. The previous night she had gone to bed fairly late, but had woken an hour or so earlier than usual to find a woman sitting at the bottom of her bed. The student, dismayed at finding a stranger in her room, was further alarmed by the uncanny sensation the woman seemed to project.

The student stared, mesmerised, as the woman slowly turned her head. When her face became fully visible, the student could see that it was the face of an old woman. She looked kind and motherly, but at this point, despite the benign appearance of the apparition, the terrified student elected to hide herself under the blankets where she remained, cowering and awake, until her normal time for getting up.

Immediately following her ordeal, the student didn't attempt to wake her hosts, for what would they have made of her story? At breakfast time, however, she could contain herself no longer and blurted out the account of her dawn experience. She was astonished to find her hosts showing little surprise. The old woman's spirit, it transpired, had caused consternation by appearing before to other people who had stayed at the house.

Smilingly, the landlady explained: "We don't tell students about the ghost, otherwise they'd refuse to stay here!"

Vera Haywood is skilled in the art of flower arrangement, as was her mother before her. When, on a summer evening in 1992, Mrs Haywood held a flower arrangement party at her home in St Luke's Terrace, she was pleased to welcome the eight or nine people who had been invited.

Prior to the arrival of her visitors, Mrs Haywood moved the table in the centre of her dining room to a position where she would be able to use it to demonstrate her flower arrangement expertise. She then positioned some chairs in front of it. She also rolled up a small rug and stood it up in a corner of the room.

After their arrival, the visitors chatted among themselves for awhile before settling down to watch Mrs Haywood's nimble fingers set to work, moving flowers and foliage around to produce a succession of floral decorations and displays, while at the same time commenting on what she was doing and answering questions.

Some minutes after the demonstration had begun, there was an unexpected interruption as a radio in the room suddenly blurted into sound and then went silent again. No one had been near it. There was a murmur of amusement from one or two of the visitors before Mrs Haywood, slightly perplexed, carried on with what she was doing.

Just minutes later, everyone in the room was startled as the radio again sprung into life. Music burbled forth from its speaker for a few moments, but before anyone could attempt to turn it off, there was silence once more. As the evening advanced, the radio started playing music two or three times more of its own accord, before once more falling silent. Mrs Haywood presumed there must be some fault with it.

With the addition of an interval for tea and snacks, it was after midnight when the visitors eventually left. One of the visitors was a close friend and hadn't any transport, so Mrs Haywood offered to drive her home, but before leaving, the two women returned all the chairs that had been in use to their normal place. Mrs Haywood resolved to attend to the rest of the tidying up on her return.

She arrived back at her house some 30 minutes later. By this time the responsibilities of the evening had caught up with her and she felt completely drained and in no mood to continue with the clearing up of the dining room.

Taking out her key, she let herself through the front door and switched on the hall light before carrying on to the dining room. Her hand reached for the electric switch and she flicked it on. As the room filled with light, her eyes widened in disbelief. What she was seeing was surely impossible?

No one had been in the house while Mrs Haywood had been taking her friend home, but the table that had been left to the side of the room was now back in its central position, while the small rug that had been rolled up was again on the floor in its usual place.

But considerably more puzzling was the fact that all the flower petals, stalk cuttings, stripped leaves and the other debris of the evening that had been scattered over the table and on the floor around it had all disappeared. Furthermore, they had disappeared without trace. They weren't in the waste bin. Indeed, they were nowhere in the house. Neither were they to be found in the dustbin outside. Nor were they seen again.

Disturbed and needing someone to talk to about the incident, someone who might give her a few words of comfort, Mrs Haywood phoned two friends – one being the friend she had driven home. She then went to bed.

Mrs Haywood had only been in bed a few moments when she felt the end of the bed sag. It felt just as if someone was sitting there. Raising her head from the pillow, she saw that it was a woman. The woman was looking towards her, her face illuminated by the street lighting that filtered through the window. Mrs Haywood saw at once that it was her mother, who had died almost two years earlier.

But there was one significant difference. At the time of her death, her mother had shortish hair, but this apparition had long, thick hair that tumbled across her shoulders and down her back. Once, many years before, the mother had had long hair just like this and had been very proud of it, but the hair had eventually been cropped in the cause of fashion.

The 24 December 1992 edition of the *Brighton & Hove Leader* reported that some mysterious force was turning on the central heating radiators in a house occupied by Jane Druce, this at exactly the same time each morning. In addition, the electric lights throughout the house sometimes noticably dimmed before returning to normal.

The house, just off the busy Lewes Road, dates back to 1870. At first, the six radiators turned themselves on for just the first two days of each month, but this rapidly escalated to become a daily event, with the heating switching itself on at 5am each morning. Plumbers were called in, but eventually left after failing to find any cause for the phenomenon.

Married couple Terry and Elaine Wheatley, together with two of their children, Tony and Jessie, moved into a house in Rose Hill in the late summer of 1992. The house was rented from an acquaintance. Six months later they had left, driven away by supernatural forces.

All was well until about two months after the family had moved in, when Mrs Wheatley had an experience that she didn't immediately associate with the paranormal. The couple had gone to bed in their first floor bedroom. There was a television set in the room and Mrs Wheatley was sitting in bed watching it. Engrossed in the programme, she was only slightly startled when she felt fingers prodding into her side.

Her first thought was that her husband was trying to tickle her, but as the intrusion on her TV watching quickly became painful, she moved to push her husband's hand away. When her hand failed to find his, she turned and was surprised to find that her husband was sound asleep and facing away from her. The next morning she found three small bruises near her waist.

Two weeks later, Mrs Wheatley was again watching TV while in bed – a light sleeper, she often relaxes in this way before seeking sleep, unlike her husband, who quickly falls into a heavy sleep. As she watched on this particular night, she heard her name being called. Puzzled, she turned off the TV and listened more intently. There was certainly someone softly calling her, and it was a man's voice.

The voice seemed to come from the direction of the bedroom window, which looked out onto a small balcony. The discarnate voice was calling 'Elaine', which was unusual, for all of Mrs Wheatley's family and friends call her Laine or Lainey, never Elaine. Frightened, she tried to rouse her husband, who was sound asleep beside her, but finding him difficult to wake, she had to wait until the following morning to relate what had happened.

It was a phenomenon that was to be repeated on about 15 occasions over the months leading to the time when the family finally moved out. However, the first three of these chilling experiences were but a prelude to other inexplicable phenomena. When the unearthly voice next came to disturb Mrs Wheatley, it was accompanied by an apparition.

On this occasion as she lay in bed listening once more to the eerie repetition of her name, her eyes swivelled around the room. When they reached the bedroom window, Mrs Wheatley was dismayed to see a shadowy figure standing there. It was that of a man wearing a black cloak which had a collar made up of three overlapping drapes. He was pressing his body against the wall of the small alcove by the window in a posture which, possibly, suggested that he was trying to avoid being seen by someone in the street below.

The cloaked figure appeared on five subsequent occasions, but Mrs Wheatley confessed that he might have been present at other times when she was too scared to look towards the window after her name had been called. The spectral man always appeared in the same spot, but only at the same time as the ethereal voice was calling her name. Usually, the man barely moved, though on two or three occasions his head half turned, as if to look at her. She never saw his face, for it was always shadowed.

On relating her experience to a friend, the friend suggested that when she had her next experience she should call on the tormenting spirit to go away, but when Mrs Wheatley endeavoured to carry out this suggestion, the voice, which up to then had not seemed aggressive, now took on a gruff and menacing tone, so much so that the frightened Mrs Wheatley hid her head under the duvet. This action failed to placate the entity which, for another few minutes, continued its chilling repetition of the word 'Elaine'. The voice reverted to this threatening manner on several more occasions. Once, son Tony, then aged 17, also heard the voice. He was staying up late and was by the ground floor staircase at the time. No word other than 'Elaine' was ever uttered.

One night, there was a quite different experience for Mrs Wheatley. Her wardrobe, three feet away from the bed, had two very stiff doors which, once properly closed, could only be opened by pressing down on the handle and pulling forcefully. On this particular night one of the doors, for no obvious reason, opened slowly to its full extent, while the other opened slightly. Puzzled, Mrs Wheatley got out of bed and closed the doors. She had only just returned to bed when the one door again opened wide.

This time, Mrs Wheatley gingerly reached out with her foot to shove the door back, but once more it creaked open to its full extent. This time, she remained petrified in bed! But this was not the end of the matter. As she watched, almost mesmerised, the door closed again of its own volition and then began to open and close with successive clicks for about 20 minutes before it finally came to rest. Understandably, Mrs Wheatley was terrified. On yet another occasion, the duvet brushed past her face as it rose several inches from the bed before falling back again.

What of Mr Wheatley during all of these incidents? As already mentioned, he is a heavy sleeper, but some other force seemed to be at work when his wife was being plagued by these alarming events. Mrs

Wheatley, when subjected to the actions of whatever was haunting the house, usually resorted to repeatedly shaking and tugging at her husband in an endeavour to wake him, but it was all to no avail. Once, especially distraught, she resorted to punching him, yet still he remained asleep. Both Mr and Mrs Wheatley felt sure that normally he would have responded to these determined efforts to bring him out of his sleep.

Other people in the house also had to deal with events that defied explanation. Son Tony slept in an attic bedroom just above his parents' bedroom. Several times, while in this room, he heard the sound of a baby crying. While the sound seemed to come from the direction of the window, the exact spot, when investigated, remained elusive. Tony's girlfriend, Tina – they were later to marry – also heard the cry of the baby on three occasions. There were no babies living in the adjacent houses.

Both Tony and Tina once saw dark shadows pass across the top of the stairs when no one else was present. At another time, Tony heard low voices mumbling in the empty passage outside of his bedroom when no one was there.

When the Wheatleys learned that their landlord had a vacant property in the Sussex village of Steyning, they asked if they could move there. Their wish was granted, but within five days their new home was burgled. The family felt so insecure after this misfortune that they felt unable to remain. While their landlord was sympathetic to their situation, he was only able to offer them their old home in Rose Hill. The Wheatley family's stay in Steyning lasted just three weeks.

Reluctantly, they moved back to Rose Hill, but just for as long as it took them to find alternative accommodation. During the two months they were there, they slept only on the ground floor, an area that had previously been unaffected by the supernatural. Nothing unusual took place during the family's brief, second stay at the house.

In 1993 the same road was the location for another eerie story. During that year, Tim Meredith and his partner, Janet Walters, were living in a flat in Rose Hill. Sharing the flat with them was Miss Walters' friend, Amanda Purdy (not their real names).

One night in the autumn, Miss Purdy went to a Brighton night club with a Geordie friend, Kevin Reynolds. After an enjoyable few hours together, they left the club and returned to Miss Purdy's flat at about 2.30am for coffee and a chat. Despite the time, Miss Purdy and Mr Reynolds continued to converse for more than an hour.

Eventually, Mr Reynolds exclaimed that as it was so late and as he was feeling very tired, could he stay; sleeping on the settee, perhaps? Miss Purdy told him he could remain, but as the settee wasn't very large, which would mean he would feel cramped, she suggested that he could, if he wished, sleep with her in her double-sized bed. Although Mr Reynolds was not her regular boyfriend, she felt she had known him long enough to trust him and she also indicated that she would use a rolled-up duvet to separate them in bed.

At around 6.30am, Mr Reynolds awoke. He heard Miss Purdy breathing in a rather strange way, and in the dim dawn light that filtered through the closed curtains, he turned over and stretched up on his elbows to see if she was all right. He was amazed to see a man lying on the other side of her (the bed was quite a large one). He then lifted himself higher in the bed so that he could get a better view of the 'intruder'. This more agitated movement disturbed Miss Purdy.

For a moment or two, as she slowly awoke, she became aware that her Geordie friend was sitting up in bed. Almost in the same moment, she noticed the stranger, who by now was sitting close to her, on the edge of the bed. Later, when describing the incident to other people, she said that she hadn't been conscious of any strange figure lying alongside her. As for Mr Reynolds, he had not, it seems, noticed an observable movement of the ghostly intruder. One moment, he had seen the man lying on the bed, while in the next moment, he observed that he was now sitting on the edge of the bed. It was like two single frames from a strip of film, with the frames in between taken away.

The subdued light was sufficient for Miss Purdy to observe that the stranger was middle-aged with dark, wavy hair. He was wearing a multi-coloured, lumberjacket-style shirt and black trousers. As she looked at him, he stared steadily back at her. At this point, Miss Purdy began to get agitated, more with unease than with real fear. Whether the apparition was aware or not of her discomfiture, it chose that moment to vanish.

Miss Purdy and Mr Reynolds then leapt out of bed. Mr Reynolds immediately went to the flat's front door to check if it was still locked, while she went to Tim Meredith's room to wake him and his partner and to tell them what had happened. All searched the flat, but nothing was found to explain what had taken place.

Two weeks later at about 4am, Tim Meredith arose from his bed to go to the toilet. Switching on the corridor light, he proceeded to the bathroom. His steps took him past Miss Purdy's bedroom. He noted that she had left her door almost fully open, but following the eerie experience of a fortnight earlier, he knew she felt less trapped by doing so.

But glancing in the room as he passed, he was surprised to see, by the light from the corridor, that she wasn't alone in her bed. He hadn't been aware that she'd had a visitor that night. The next morning he teased: "I didn't know you had your boyfriend staying with you last night".

"Boyfriend?" responded Miss Purdy. "I had no one staying with me last night." She immediately came to the conclusion that it must have been a return visitation of the ghost.

Whose ghost might it have been? A possibility is that it was that of Miss Purdy's father. He died when she was only three years old, so she has little memory of him. However, the face of the spectre was similar in appearance, she said, to that depicted in photographs of her father.

Stuart Bowers lives in Eaton Place. In the spring of 1994 he was relaxing in his sitting room when a metal candlestick and candle shot off the TV set on which it stood and landed on the floor. Somewhat shocked, Mr Bowers placed it back on the TV.

The same thing happened several times more, but with slight variations, over the following six months. There appeared to be no explanation for the phenomenon. Once the candlestick struck Mr Bowers on the back of his head during its trajectory, but its impact was so slight that he felt no pain and suffered no injury. Remarkably, the candlestick always finished the right way up after its flight from TV set to floor. On one occasion the candle had been lit and it remained alight at the end of its journey.

Early on during this time, Mr Bowers experienced another odd happening. He was relaxing in his sitting room one evening when he sensed he was not alone. Looking up, he saw an old woman standing by the far wall. Strangely, the wall itself appeared different, with a different wallpaper and strange pictures. Perhaps it was the wall as it might have looked in some bygone age? Unfortunately, the vision lasted but a second or two before fading, so Mr Bowers didn't have time to take in the finer details.

Troubled by the continuing candlestick incidents, Mr Bowers eventually agreed to have a Spiritualist – not actually a practising medium – call at the house to conduct an appropriate prayer session. This action apparently proved successful, for there were no further incidents.

In 1994, Kim Yallop moved into a house in College Gardens. Over the following months, she learned to live with the unexplained noises she heard there. So did her children, Daniel and Laura. While no ghost was ever seen, doors clicked open and then closed again of their own volition, while ghostly footsteps were sometimes heard on the staircase. Twice, pictures fell off the wall for no apparent reason and without the glass breaking. While the Yallop family came to accept their invisible entity, a visitor to the house who had not been told of the haunting had a nasty fright on a summer day in 1996.

Clare, a 19-year-old student and friend of the Yallops, needed somewhere quiet to continue her studies, so Mrs Yallop suggested that, as her house would be unoccupied for most of the day, she might like to study there. The offer was accepted. Clare duly arrived with her books and settled down to her task. Time ticked by and she was progressing well when she heard unexpected noises coming from upstairs. It was as if someone was moving around. There was the click of a door handle and the slight creak of a door opening. This was followed by the pacing of footsteps and the sound of another door opening or closing. Terrified, Clare fled from the house.

In the autumn of 1996, Ben Solomon and Frederique Niot moved into a ground floor flat in Buckingham Road (though situated in the same road, not the same building as that mentioned earlier in this chapter). They had only been there for a few days when the first of a number of odd incidents took place. Initially, various objects fell over or tumbled to the floor for no obvious reason and both, separately, heard mysterious knockings on one of the windows. A door swung fully open of its own accord, while an eerie, unseen presence seemed sometimes to invade the bedroom.

One evening, a friend called round. While he was there, the radio was switched on to what should have been BBC Radio 4. Only it wasn't! Puzzled, Mr Solomon turned the dial in search of the station and was bewildered to discover that no station was where it should have been. It was as if all the stations had been jumbled up.

After a few minutes, Mr Solomon found what he believed was Radio 4, even though the station was well away from where it should have been on the dial, and the friends sat down to listen. Suddenly, all three were almost shocked out of their seats when the volume of the radio inexplicably surged to its maximum power. After the departure of the friend, the radio was found to be functioning normally.

Mr Solomon mentioned the weird happenings to the woman living in the flat above. She revealed that she had been bothered for many months by what she thought must be something ghostly, with various objects – keys, pens, and so on – disappearing, only to reappear within a day or two, usually in a different place to where they had last been seen.

Eventually, Mr Solomon called on the services of a medium, who said that the the spirit of an old man was occupying the bedroom, while that of an elderly woman was present in the lounge. There were no further problems following the medium's visit.

Mr Solomon said: "The flat had been empty for quite a while before we moved in, so we didn't know in advance that it was haunted. The previous tenant, whoever it was, could have been trying to tell us something, for left on top of the heater in the bedroom was a tattered book entitled *Great Irish Ghost Stories*!"

A house in Varndean Road, built about 1850, has been home to the Routh family since 1962. Thelma Routh, except for several months during 1968 when the family lived in Africa, resided in the house for 34 years until her death in 1996. During this time she often experienced the sensation that she was being watched by someone unseen. This feeling was usually accompanied by a noticable drop in room temperature. Over the years, other family members reported similar experiences.

While the Rouths were in Africa, the house was rented to another family. The incoming tenants had no knowledge of the house's spooky reputation, but the Rouths learned on their return to Brighton that the temporary occupants had been sufficiently affected by the atmosphere to call in a psychic investigator for an opinion.

Adam Routh, Thelma Routh's son, spent some of his childhood in the house. In the mid-1980s, circumstances brought him back to the family home for a few weeks. One night, while sleeping alone in one of the bedrooms, something caused him to wake up. Opening his eyes, he immediately became aware of a small white light. It was about two inches across and it seemed to emerge from the empty fireplace before bobbing around the room. Its trajectory was erratic, and it even disappeared under his bed for a moment. When it reappeared it was only for another second or two, then it was gone.

Mr Routh said: "I tend to be sceptical about ghosts and the supernatural, but I'm positive the light was no dream. I just can't explain it."

Towards the end of 1996, Adam Routh returned to live in the house with his wife, Clare, whom he had married earlier that year. Mr Routh, not wishing to alarm her, said little about the odd reputation of the house, but soon after moving in and while sitting alone on a sofa positioned in the centre of the living room, she became aware of some discarnate presence behind her.

The Rouths have never had any cause for unease while living in the house, believing that the entity, whatever it may be, is quite friendly. However, just in case, the sofa was moved back against the wall!

On 30 October 1998, BBC Southern Counties Radio broadcast a pre-Halloween programme which featured listeners' experiences of the paranormal. These included the story of a Brighton woman who had once occupied a flat in Marine Parade. Apparently, both she and her daughter heard what sounded like chamber music coming from the rear bedroom while living there. It had an odd, ethereal quality. No explanation was found for the phenomenon, though on occasions the room's temperature turned almost icy compared to the rest of the flat.

Some months after the woman had sold the flat, she was in town when she happened to meet the two men who had bought the leasehold. They complained that she had omitted, at the time of the sale, to tell them that the place was haunted. They said that while they had not themselves experienced anything unusual in the flat, their female partners had been disturbed by the sound of ghostly music.

20 *Council house visitations*

WHILE GHOSTLY HAPPENINGS are more usually associated with old buildings, newer properties aren't immune. Almost all of the houses on Brighton's council estates were built within the last 100 years, yet a number of residents have reported eerie activities. Natural causes were found to be responsible for some of these, but others defied a rational explanation.

In 1977, a family living in a council house in Truleigh Close, Woodingdean, was terrorised by an unseen entity. Mr and Mrs Dubeau reported that the unpleasant smell of sulphur kept invading the house, making their 14-month-old daughter Joanne cry out in distress.

Mrs Dubeau said: "Whatever it is comes and goes like a cloud. I believe something terrible must have happened here. We have moved the baby into our room to be with us all the time. Susan Kirby, one of our friends, has also noticed the awful smell."

So had previous occupants Isobel Roper and her small daughter Vicky. Mrs Roper had called in a priest to bless the house, and for a while the smell had ceased, but after a few days the pungent odour returned. She also reported hearing sounds like heavy breathing.

A senior housing department spokesman said: "We are taking the matter seriously because we get complaints of this nature from time to time, and Mrs Dubeau is genuinely convinced that something is wrong."

In the early months of 1978 a family occupying a first-floor council flat in Swanborough Drive, Whitehawk, was so troubled by the presence of a ghost that they fled in the middle of the night, preferring the discomfort of sleeping in the family car for four successive nights to the weird events taking place in their home. The series of unexplained happenings began when Frederick Cronin and his wife, Florence, went out one evening, leaving their 18-year-old daughter, Christine, at home watching TV. When Mr and Mrs Cronin returned, they found their daughter in hysterics.

"We have an old hunting horn on the wall and Christine said something had told her to look at it," said Mr Cronin. "The horn then seemed to come away from the wall and drop slowly to the ground."

One night Mr Cronin was in his bedroom when, looking down through a window, he saw a slim, young woman walk along the passage outside. She was wearing a long, hippy-style coat and a light-coloured head-scarf over fair hair. Mr Cronin didn't recognise the woman and thought there was something strange about her.

Only days later, Mrs Cronin spotted the same young woman in the bathroom. She appeared to be crying. The shocked Mrs Cronin made her way to the bedroom, where her husband was already in bed. Mrs Cronin had only just finished telling her husband about her experience when the apparition of the young woman appeared briefly in the bedroom doorway. As Mrs Cronin was very upset by these happenings, her husband suggested she go to the kitchen and make a cup of tea. But the ordeal of the Cronin family was about to move on a further notch.

Mr Cronin said later: "As my wife went into the kitchen she screamed and fainted. Christine rushed in and screamed as well. They found that all the glasses that had been lining the shelves were now lined up on the draining board. It was very creepy."

It was then that the family decided that they'd had enough. They vacated the flat immediately, and the whole story was told in the *Evening Argus* of 30 March 1978. Brighton's housing department helped to arrange an exorcism, calling in a church minister, and also re-housed the family.

Ray Spratling, deputy housing manager at the time, said: "We were satisfied that the couple concerned, who were good tenants, were convinced in their own minds that the flat was haunted and that it would have been intolerable for them to have continued living there."

On 19 November 1982, the *Evening Argus* reported that Harold and Bessie Baker, of Halland Road, were being terrorised by a ghost. Shadows flitted eerily around the house, doors opened and closed, and lights switched on and off for no obvious reason, while phantom footsteps paced the rooms upstairs, which was a part of the house where the family's alsatian dog refused to venture. Mr and Mrs Baker's 17-year-old son Stephen kept his bedroom light on all night, while their 14-year-old daughter Lisa was so scared she moved out of the house.

It was because of reports like these that, early in the 1980s, Brighton decided to enlist its own investigator. Andrew Green, of Robertsbridge, a parapsychologist and author of numerous books on ghosts and hauntings, was engaged by Brighton Council to investigate and offer advice and assistance in respect of a number of bewildering incidents affecting council houses.

At the time, both Mr Green and Brighton Council stressed that his services did not cover ghost hunting, but were more correctly 'parapsychological investigations'. Parapsychology is described as being 'the field of study concerned with the investigation of the evidence for psychic phenomena which cannot be explained by the theories of orthodox psychology'.

"We use Mr Green's services very infrequently," said a Brighton Council spokesman, "but these cases do crop up. We are very concerned about the welfare of our tenants. We assess the situation and try to find the best solution. This is usually done in consultation with a doctor, and he is kept informed of what's going on.

"Mr Green investigates things that are not quite normal or which appear strange, and by using his services we save a lot of time and money. This is because he is often able to offer an explanation without having to refer to doctors or housing officers."

Mr Green has spent more than 40 years studying aspects of the paranormal. A member of the Society for Psychical Research, in 1949 he founded the Ealing Society for the Investigation of Psychic Phenomena and in 1951 was co-founder of the National Federation of Psychic Research Societies. He was approached by Brighton Council after an executive, concerned about the welfare of a number of council house tenants who believed their houses to be haunted, had attended a course on the paranormal conducted by Mr Green.

Mr Green said: "Some people, very few, are irrationally upset by seeing what they believe to be a ghost when, in fact, they may be the victims of hallucinations. These incidents, to the witness, can seem very real and because they are unable to find an immediate cause, they can become very distressed. While my counselling was seen to save the Council time and money, of greater importance was the need to rationalise the situation and enable affected tenants to resume a normal life style."

John Ash, who followed Mr Spratling as deputy borough housing manager, reported around a dozen instances of alleged hauntings during his six years with Brighton Council, but he stated that virtually all of these, on investigation, turned out to have a more conventional origin than that associated with the supernatural.

Emotional, marital or medical problems, or a combination of more than one of these, were frequently factors involved in reports alleging the presence of psychic phenomena in council properties. In other instances the cause of the problem turned out to be prosaic. One investigation revealed that strange thumps and rattling noises were the result of draughts coming up from under linoleum which had been laid on a paper base.

Another investigation led to the discovery that the peculiar 'humming and roaring' noises heard were due to the fact that the tenant, unknowingly, suffered from tinnitus, a medical condition connected with the inner ear which can generate such noises. The rocking in the wind of a TV aerial mounted on a chimney-stack was found to be the source of 'ghostly' thumpings and rattlings on the ground floor, the sound travelling eerily downwards through the walls so that its origin was masked.

In another instance, single mothers occupying a small block of furnished flats had been frightened by a shadowy figure 'haunting' the building. A council officer investigated the matter and recognised that the environment of limited lighting, shadowed corners, dull paint and dark curtains might contribute to a sense of unease in women living on their own (except for their children). It also seemed that there had been a mutual build-up of tension after one young mother had broadcast her own fears. After the ambient lighting had been improved, dark areas repainted in lighter tones and brighter curtains fitted, there were no further reports of a shadowy form.

Council officers found that in most instances where a tenant moved from an allegedly 'haunted' property, the reported 'happenings' did not follow them into their new home. Neither did subsequent tenants of the 'haunted' properties report any strange manifestations. Local housing authorities are aware of the fact that some tenants, desirous of moving from one council house to another in the shortest possible time, may 'invent' a troublesome ghost to aid their application for a transfer.

However, no restive tenants were involved in the peculiar circumstances which affected a council house in the Whitehawk district of Brighton in the late 1970s. The incident took place in one of Whitehawk's shortest streets (to save distress to present-day residents, for the story is particularly gruesome, the street is not identified here).

It was a warm summer evening and seven or eight children were chasing up and down the pavement alongside a row of houses. One of the houses was unoccupied and had been boarded up by workmen to prevent vandalism. As the children played, they heard a baby start to cry, which they thought odd, for the sound seemed to be coming from the empty house. As the baby's cries rose to an agitated crescendo and then to screams, the children became increasingly concerned and stopped their play to listen.

"I was only eight at the time," recalled Eric Levington (not his real name). "I was the youngest kid there, the others being aged between ten and 14. The baby's screaming went on for about 15 minutes, by which time a few neighbours, distressed by the constant crying and screaming, had come out onto the pavement.

"Immediately after the baby's screaming stopped, there was a repetitious banging sound coming from within the house. It was as if someone was hitting a floor with a heavy object of some kind. This banging went on for several minutes before one of the neighbours decided to break into the house to see what was going on.

"He first went into his own house. He was a collector of militaria, and he came out a moment later with an old sword in his hand. He then kicked open the door of the house where the baby had been crying and rushed in. The instant he did so, the banging stopped. He found the house completely empty.

"I later heard it said that a few years before, a baby living in the house had been killed by its father. Driven to distraction by the continuous screaming of the child, the father had struck it with a hammer."

21 *Smugglers and spectres*

IN 1927 THE EXISTING County Borough of Brighton was extended to include some adjoining villages. Among these was Rottingdean, which stands in a fold of the Downs and adjacent to the sea on Brighton's eastern perimeter. The name Rottingdean is said to derive from Rotyngs, the name of a Saxon family which long ago lived there, and 'dene', the Saxon word for a hollow.

The chipped flint arrowheads and axeheads of Stone Age people have been unearthed in and around the village and an ancient burial ground close to Rottingdean Windmill has yielded the 3,000-year-old bones of four adults and a child. But another discovery, connected with Rottingdean Windmill, had a less fortunate outcome.

The *Sussex Weekly Advertiser* of 7 June 1802 contained a report which stated that workmen excavating the foundations of the windmill had discovered the skeleton of an ancient warrior, together with his sword. The workmen had left the skeleton and sword while they went to dinner. On returning to the site, they were dismayed to find that both had been stolen. They were never recovered.

The Parish Church of St Margaret is the village's oldest building, although the original construction forms but a small part of the church as it exists today. The tiny stone church built by the Saxons was altered and added to by William de Warenne after he had founded the Priory of Lewes in 1077. The Norman alterations and extensions were followed by those of the Plantagenets and the Victorians.

In 1377 French pirates went ashore at Rottingdean, their aim being to reach the prosperous town of Lewes. Sweeping through the village, they killed, plundered and set fire to the houses. Some of the villagers, including a number of children, sought safety in the tower of the church.

The French marauders, frustrated at not being able to seize these villagers, who had pulled up behind them the ladder they had used, started a fire inside the church beneath the tower. The terrified villagers were roasted alive. A red tint, which can still be seen on some of the church's central pillars and on the western arch of the tower, is a grim reminder of the event.

Smuggling was rife in the village during the 17th and 18th centuries. With its isolated position and a providential gap leading to the sea, Rottingdean was ideally situated to receive illicit shipments. Smugglers even used the sails of Rottingdean Windmill to let the captains of offshore ships know that all was clear to deliver the contraband held in their holds.

The illicit cargoes were stored in caves set in the cliffs before being carried through the honeycomb of secret tunnels which threaded underneath the village. It is possible that the muffled underground sounds of voices murmuring, sacks being dragged and barrels being rolled could have made some of those people wandering above ground fearful that the strange night noises were those of ghosts or demons.

The Elms, an attractive 18th century building standing close by the village pond, was occupied by Rudyard Kipling from 1897 to 1903. The ghost of a smuggler is said to haunt the house and there was a period in its past history when the occupants found it almost impossible to keep servants because of the eerie noises emanating from below stairs.

One ghost that hasn't appeared at The Elms is that of Rudyard Kipling himself, though his spectre has allegedly been sighted at Bateman's, in the Sussex village of Burwash. He moved there to escape the sightseers who had plagued him during his time in Rottingdean.

Nearby is The Grange, a listed Georgian building dating back to around 1740, which includes modifications by Sir Edwin Lutyens. It was a vicarage until 1908, one of its former residents being Dr Thomas Hooker who, in addition to his duties as a vicar and schoolmaster, acted as a lookout for a local gang of smugglers. The artist Sir William Nicholson, who lived at The Grange from 1909 to 1914, gave the building its present name. The house was purchased by Brighton Corporation in 1953 and is now a museum, art gallery and library administered by the Rottingdean Preservation Society.

A large house occupied the site for several centuries before The Grange was built, and in 1355 the Black Prince, eldest son of Edward III, is said to have stayed there. Legend has it that despite the destruction of the original house, the ghost of the Black Prince remains to haunt the present building. For some inexplicable reason, he is to be seen on dark and stormy nights clambering across the roof of The Grange.

While the phantom rooftop royal was undoubtedly the product of some fertile imagination in the past, a more recent incident has a sounder basis. In the spring of 1996, a waitress working in the tea-room at The Grange had reason to go to a storeroom at the back of the building. As the waitress unlocked the door, she felt the air around her become unnaturally chilly and at the same time she became aware of a ghostly presence. The experience upset the waitress sufficiently for her to leave her job. The priest in charge of St Margaret's Church was called in to conduct prayers so as to expel any lingering ghost.

Down House is just to the north of the village pond. With its Georgian facade of squared flints, it is notable for its secret passages and priest holes. A stone slab let into the east wall carries the date 1619, which is believed to indicate when the house was built. In 1909, the house passed out of the hands of the Beard family, who had occupied it for centuries, to become a school for boys, after which it reverted back to its initial use as a private residence.

After 1945, a part of the house became a separate dwelling, taking the name Old Farm House. Sheila Doughty lived there for ten years until 1982, though her parents were occupants for about 30 years. While there, the family often heard the sound of ghostly footsteps. Mrs Doughty recalled that there was a narrow, winding staircase leading to the attic. During the years the Doughtys lived at Old Farm House, and at least once a week, one or another of the family would hear the phantom footsteps ascending the staircase. The phenomenon always took place at about 11.30pm. Sometimes, visiting friends heard the footsteps. Mrs Doughty said that the family always regarded the ghost as friendly.

Vic Masters, who followed the Doughtys as occupier of Old Farm House, carried out constructional alterations to the interior. These activities uncovered a secret priest-hole. Two building workers engaged on the refurbishment told Mr Masters they had seen the ghost of a woman in a grey dress.

Another haunted property is the Rottingdean Club, situated at 89 High Street. Dating from the 16th century, it was once part of the former Olde Place Hotel. An indication that the building was haunted came in 1988 when a barmaid went down to the cellar to get some stock. While there, she saw a grey-haired man who appeared to be sorting bottles. She only had a rear view of him and presumed it to be Don Goodchild, who was then running the club with his wife, Diane (the couple have since retired).

The barmaid, who had just come on duty, called out a greeting and was surprised when there was no response. On returning to the bar, her surprise turned to astonishment when she learned that Don Goodchild was upstairs and that no one else could have been in the cellar.

That some supernatural entity was present at the club was confirmed over the following months when the Goodchilds' son, Jeremy (the chef at the time, though he later took control of the club) saw a ghostly figure disappear through the cellar door. Jeremy Goodchild only had a back view of the spectre, which was wearing a raincoat. Later, the Goodchilds learned that earlier occupants of the premises had reported seeing the apparition of a man sitting in an armchair by the fireplace.

In 1996, Jeremy Goodchild had an encounter with a ghost that was completely different in appearance to the one he had seen before. He was sitting in the middle bar of the club, making a phone call, when he felt someone brush past his shoulder. It was shortly after midnight and believing that he was alone in the bar, he wondered who it could be. Turning his head he saw, walking away from him, a man dressed in a frock coat. The man, who had black hair falling over the collar of the coat, was visible for only a second or two before vanishing.

Local resident Margaret Ward, recalling her life and times in Rottingdean in her book, *One Camp Chair in the Living Room,* wrote about a ghost seen by her father when he was a young man and living in a cottage called The Mascot, which has long since been demolished, but which stood opposite the old, flint-faced village school.

The father was sitting alone in the front room when he heard a thumping sound. On looking around, he saw an old-fashioned wicker invalid chair bumping down the stairs with a man in it. When the chair reached the bottom of the stairs, chair and occupant passed straight through the wall. Mrs Ward stated that her father, a devout Christian, never told a lie.

The Black Horse Inn, in the High Street, dates back to 1513, which makes it one of the oldest buildings in the Brighton area. Some of the inside walls are built of a mixture of cow dung and chalk and remain as strong today as they once were. A blacksmith's forge used to stand where the lounge bar is now.

One custom that used to take place at the Black Horse around 1900 was the celebration of Tater Beer Night. At that time, farm employees usually worked a six-day week, but a Mr Brown, who owned the local potato farm, allowed his workers to stop at 1pm on a Saturday in April. This enabled them to plant their own potatoes on land provided by the farmer for their private use. In the evening, all the farm workers gathered in the Black Horse where the landlord, known as Old Uncle Tommy, would put a pot of new clay pipes on the counter and also an enamel bowl in which all would drop their coins to provide beer for the evening.

There have been references in print to the Black Horse being haunted, but if any ghostly tales are attached to the pub, they must belong to a long past age. One landlord who spent ten years at the pub reported nothing at all ghostly during that time. Certainly, more than a century ago, the pub was used by smugglers, and it possible that, as with other meeting places for those involved in the supply of contraband goods, the suggestion that spectres might be hovering around the pub would have been sufficient to keep the curious at bay.

In 1970, Len Nott was an 18-year-old electronics student at the former Brighton Technical College. Three student friends, who lived in rented accommodation in Rottingdean, invited him to join them for an evening drink at the local Plough Inn. Later, all four returned to the rented house, which was located near the top of Nevill Road.

Soon after their arrival, Mr Nott found he had run out of cigarettes. Leaving the house, he hurried downhill to The Chocolate Box, a shop in the High Street, where his friends had told him there was an exterior cigarette vending machine which had managed to survive growing vandalism. Having obtained his packet of cigarettes, Mr Nott began his return journey.

As he neared the top of Nevill Road he spotted a middle-aged couple crossing the road. He was perplexed to see that the bodies of the couple, who were wearing overcoats, didn't appear to be fully solid. In addition, although he wasn't absolutely certain, the couple seemed to glide along rather than walk. His discomfiture increased when he saw the couple drift through the closed gate of a front garden and continue through the closed door of the house. He noted there were no lights on in the house.

More than a little shocked, he carried on to the house of his friends, which he now realised was only three doors above the house entered by the ethereal couple. On seeing him, Mr Nott's friends commented on his ashen face. On relating his story, he was told that the house in question had been unoccupied for a considerable time.

Some buildings have a history of regular hauntings, while others attract only a rare visitation. Yet other buildings are notable for the fact that just the one strange event has taken place (though there may have been other, unrecorded incidents). The Plough Inn, situated at the south end of the village pond, falls into the latter category.

Paul Woodhall was the landlord of the Plough from 1977 to 1991. When Mr Woodhall moved to the Plough, he took with him a barman and a waiter who had worked at his previous pub, the Beachy Head Hotel. One night, a year or so later and about an hour after the pub had closed, Mr and Mrs Woodhall went to bed. As they settled down to sleep, they heard footsteps pacing the floor of the room above, which was occupied by Graham Barham, the waiter they had brought to the pub.

The sound of footsteps continued; backwards and forwards, backwards and forwards. Mr and Mrs Woodhall concluded that Mr Barham was unable to sleep because of some personal worry, but eventually, as they found the heavy footsteps were preventing them from getting to sleep, Mr Woodhall went out onto the landing and shouted up the stairs for Mr Barham to go to bed and be quiet. The pacing footsteps stopped.

About two hours later, just after 2am, the Woodhalls were woken up by a loud knocking on their bedroom door. Mr Woodhall hurriedly jumped out of bed to find an agitated Mr Barham on the other side of the door.

Mr Barham claimed that he had only just got back to the pub after visiting some friends (he was still wearing his street clothes). He had let himself in with his key, had gone upstairs to his bedroom and had opened his bedroom door and switched on the light. But as soon as he had done so, he had become aware of some invisible but frightening presence in the room. Too fearful to remain, he had immediately rushed downstairs to wake the Woodhalls. Calmed by Mr Woodhall, Mr Barham was later able to go back to his room, where he found that the atmosphere had returned to normal. Mr and Mrs Woodhall wondered whose footsteps they had heard two hours before.

Early in 1985 the then proprietor of the Olde Cottage Tea Rooms in the High Street discovered an old, dust-covered box hidden beneath the stairs leading up from the ground floor. The box had, it seems, been left there undisturbed for many years, and was found to contain letters and childhood mementoes. These, apparently, had belonged to a Martha Mockford who, with her husband, had looked after the shop about a hundred years before at the time it was a greengrocer's.

Shortly after this discovery, the ghost of an oldish woman, presumed to be Martha, appeared several times in the vicinity of the staircase. She was seen by the proprietor and also by two waitresses, the sisters Caroline and Lisa Fischer. The ghostly visitations spanned only a short period of time and there have been no further manifestations since. It is thought that the discovery and movement of the box may have briefly disturbed the spirit of Martha Mockford, though she appears not to have been unhappy about the find, for her face was seen to be kindly and smiling.

On 20 June 1819, Colonel John Harvey, who was enjoying a long sojourn in Rottingdean to benefit his health, sat astride his horse and cantered out towards the downland north of Saltdean. It was to be his last ride, for his lifeless body was found some time later. A local newspaper reported that he had fallen from his horse in a fit, but the exact cause of death remains an enigma. Shortly afterwards, an inscribed stone was placed at the side of the bridleway where he had fallen. Sometime between 1873 and 1898, a more fitting memorial was erected at the spot; a marble cross on a stepped, stone plinth.

Initially referred to as Harvey's Stone, but later known as Harvey's Cross, the memorial and the fence around it were badly damaged during the Second World War when the area was used for target practice by Canadian soldiers. In this state, it became overgrown with weeds and bramble. In June 1999, in part to celebrate the Millennium, a replacement cross was erected.

Following Colonel Harvey's death, there were stories of a ghostly horse and rider in the vicinity. Local historian and author Bob Copper wrote that his father knew of the ghost, which he related had been seen several times. The father said that at the sight of the spectre, 'strong men blanched, dogs rolled their eyes and howled, and horses shuddered from nose to croup and refused to budge'.

In 1969, a mention of Harvey's Cross in the *Sussex Express* brought a response from a Mr E Stubbs, of Lewes, who wrote that some 40 years before he had been riding on the Downs with two children. The time was about midday and he and the children were galloping towards a gate when, in the bright sunshine, he saw a man apparently sitting in the air above the gate. The man was dressed in a waisted coat and a billycock hat.

Mr Stubbs' mare snorted and stopped dead in her tracks, and he felt a shiver pass over her loins and under the saddle. She, he thought, would have seen the horse, which he could not see as her head and mane blocked it from his view (seemingly, the children must have been riding a little way behind him, so did not see the vision). Mr Stubbs was forced to dismount and drag all three horses through the gate.

He reported: "I did not tell the children what I had seen, but they were puzzled as to why the ponies were suddenly so scared."

Mr Stubbs had no knowledge of Harvey's Cross up until that point, and it wasn't until he returned the borrowed mare to her owner and related his experience that he was told the story. He later re-visited the scene of his encounter to find that the memorial to Colonel Harvey was about a 100 yards away.

Two years later, Mr Stubbs continued, he was waiting for the bus to Brighton when a couple in a car drew up and offered him a lift. When the car reached the crossroads at Falmer, the wife, looking towards Rottingdean, said to her husband: "It was along there that you met your ghost on horseback, wasn't it?"

Naturally, Mr Stubbs was eager to learn more. The husband said that on the night his daughter was born, he was returning home after visiting the nursing home where his wife had given birth. During his journey from Rottingdean, he had seen a ghostly horseman high up on a verge. He had presumed it to be the spectre of a highwayman, but when he went on to describe the rider's clothing, it became apparent to Mr Stubbs that they must both have seen the same ghost.

Top woman jockey Jayne Moore, of Ingleside Racing Stables, Woodingdean, believes that she saw the ghost of Colonel Harvey in 1974 when out riding – she was aged 15 at the time. Dusk was already spreading its mantle as she and her twin sister, Karen, turned their ponies homewards. As they ambled along a bridleway just to the north of Pickers Hill Farm, Jane had the uneasy feeling they were being followed. Looking behind her, she was horrified to see a greyish man astride a greyish horse coming along behind them. She knew at once that this was no ordinary rider and mount. With the spectral duo but a few yards away, Jayne called out to Karen, who instantly sensed her sister's fear. The two girls urged their ponies forward into a gallop.

Mrs Moore cannot recall what the ghostly rider was wearing. "It's a long way back to remember," she said, "and at the time I was so frightened that all I wanted to do was get away from the spot as quickly as possible.

"I'd heard of Harvey's Cross, but had thought it was the name given to a place where some bridleways crossed. It wasn't until two years afterwards that I found out about the memorial and learned of its association with a ghost. Later, I went to look for the memorial and found that my sighting had taken place about a 100 yards away from it."

Another strange phenomenon has been reported in the vicinity of Pickers Hill Farm. A bridlepath wends its way south-east from the direction of Balsdean, and at the point where it nears the farm there is a gate close to where the branches of trees form a natural 'tunnel'. Over the years, there have been numerous reports of horses reacting to something they become aware of close by this gate. Their eyes bulge, their ears prick forward, and they snort and show a reluctance to continue along the path.

A number of riders have mentioned this phenomenon to Jenny Pope, the owner of Rottingdean Riding School. Indeed, riders using this bridlepath popularly refer to the unseen presence as 'The Ghost on the Post'!

There are other stories of the supernatural associated with Saltdean. A local woman claimed she had seen spectral Roman soldiers in Tumulus Road (certainly, Roman coins, pottery and other items have been unearthed in the area), while there have also been reports of a headless horseman spied in Saltdean, though one elderly resident recalled that tales of this spectre were circulated many years ago by anxious parents wanting to deter their children from wandering onto the Downs.

There are stories, too, of people seeing what they at first thought were ordinary flesh and blood individuals but who, on later reflection, wondered if they had actually had a brush with a discarnate entity.

Gary McCarthy was faced with this dilemma in December 1994. He remembers the time well, for his son was born in the following January, and it was because his wife was pregnant that he found himself walking the family's three dogs along Westmeston Avenue and into Whiteway Lane, a road linking Saltdean to Rottingdean, early on a cold winter's morning.

He had walked the dogs along this route on numerous occasions before, but this had usually been an early evening exercise. For their morning walks, the dogs looked to Mrs McCarthy, but as her pregnancy advanced, it became necessary for Mr McCarthy to take over the morning outings. As his work required an early departure from home, there was nothing for it but to take the dogs out at 5am or earlier.

By mid-December he had accompanied the three dogs through the silent, empty streets of Saltdean on about a dozen occasions at this pre-dawn hour. Certainly, he had never before seen anyone in Whiteway Lane at 5am, for it is an isolated road close to the downland and it quickly peters out into a rutted chalk track, but on this particular morning he was surprised to see, in the halo of yellow light provided by distant street lamps, a man walking some 50 yards ahead of him. He was even more surprised to observe the incomprehensible behaviour of the man, for he was progressing along the road in a peculiar serpentine fashion, though not as a drunken man would walk.

With the built-up area of Saltdean behind him, Mr McCarthy had let his dogs off their leads only a few moments before. Normally when released, they would bound forward excitedly, but on this occasion they kept close to his heels. Mr McCarthy then saw the man, who was wearing light-coloured clothing, turn down a track leading towards Dean Court Road, where he disappeared from sight.

It wasn't until later that Mr McCarthy began to wonder if he had seen a ghost. There was the subdued behaviour of the dogs, the unusual hour for seeing someone in a dark and isolated road, the erratic walk of the man, and the slight luminosity of his clothing.

In his book *A Song for Every Season,* Bob Copper describes a boyhood experience which has remained forever vivid in his mind. His father sometimes took him out at a very early hour to go rabbiting or to pick mushrooms, but one midsummer morning young Bob was roused from his bed at 3am for a quite different purpose. He was to be taken on a three-mile journey over the South Downs to Kingston Ridge, where the sole object would be to witness the glory of the sun rising between Mount Caburn and Firle Beacon.

So it was that father and son set out from their Rottingdean home at an hour when the stars were still scattered across a blue-black sky. Reaching a suitable vantage point, they settled down with a flask of tea and some sandwiches to wait, and then to wonder, as the emerging sun slowly chased the shadows away, and to watch as the swells and dips of the downland gradually changed hue.

In 1973, about two years after the book had been published, some of Bob Copper's friends suggested that they should join together in an early morning walk across the Downs so as to experience the same sense of exultation as that described in the book. As they were approaching Kingston Ridge during the subsequent trek, two of the small number of friends taking part had a remarkable encounter.

Tony Payne and Bob Copper's son, John, had walked some way ahead of the others when they saw, coming along a downland path towards them, a man wearing an old-fashioned light grey topcoat and a dark-coloured homburg hat. Although it was about 3.30am at the time, he was reasonably plain to see, for though there were small pockets of mist clinging to the earth, the night was otherwise clear, while in the far distance the feathery luminescence of dawn was beginning to unfold from the east.

As the man came close, the two friends greeted him with a 'Good morning', but there was no flicker of response from the shadowed face. In the following seconds the figure came right up to them... and vanished. To Tony Payne, it seemed as if the man had disappeared in the instant of reaching them, though John Copper had the impression that the man had walked past before disappearing.

Their friends, some 100 yards behind, saw no one, and it seemed unlikely that anyone would choose to deviate from the security of the downland track at that darkened hour.

One night in 1990, Paul Mantell and his girlfriend, Tracy, were motoring through the Sussex countryside. With romance in mind, they turned into a quiet road. A couple of miles further on, they found themselves in a small village. Here, Mr Mantell switched off the engine and lights, and the couple left their front seats to take a more comfortable place in the back of the car.

Mr Mantell had been paying little attention to road signs, so was not aware that he had stopped in Telscombe, which is a rather isolated village tucked away in the downland, nor had he realised that he had parked close by the old Norman Church of St Lawrence, which stands at the southern end of the village, for it was a very dark place at that late hour.

Only minutes after the couple had moved to the rear seats, there was a loud bang on the bonnet of the car, followed by another on the roof. Mr Mantell got out of the car at once, but saw nothing to account for the noise. At first he thought that a leaping cat might have been responsible, but on further consideration, he felt sure the noise had been too loud for an animal of that size. It was only then that, peering through the gloom, he saw that he had parked by the 12th century church which, unbeknown to him, had been the site of other unusual happenings. It wasn't until a later date, on making enquiries, that he discovered the name of the church.

There might well be a rational explanation for the experience of Mr Mantell and his girlfriend, but it would be harder to find a logical reason to account for what happened to Darrell Cook and a friend while in the same village, and by the same church, about a year after the above incident.

It was well after midnight when Mr Cook and his friend, having enjoyed a pleasant evening out, decided to round things off with a drive through the country. They had no particular destination in mind, but given the hour, they at least knew that the roads would be quiet. Some time later, they found themselves in Telscombe. Driving on through the village, they eventually drew level with St Lawrence's Church. At which point the car came to an abrupt halt.

Mr Cook, who was at the wheel of the car, swore under his breath. It was far from being an ideal place to break down, for the village was dark, silent, and asleep, with not a glimmer of hospitable light coming from the small scattering of houses. It was then that a surprising thing happened. The church bell began to ring, slowly and insistently. The friends found the sound of the bell especially surprising, for the time at that moment was about 1.30am.

The cause of the car's breakdown seemed to be due to some problem with the electrics, for the headlights and dashboard lighting had also packed up, but Mr Cook, a garage employee, knew the car had just been serviced, so didn't immediately elect to look under the bonnet. Instead, after flicking the ignition key backwards and forwards a few times without success, he paused for a few moments. Bizarrely, he noted, the church bell was continuing to peal. When he again tried to start the car, he was unsuccessful at the first few attempts. Then suddenly, as he twisted the ignition key for the umpteenth time, the engine sprang into life and the headlights came on. At that instant, the church bell stopped pealing!

What happened that night? A few years later, while looking through a book about Sussex, Mr Cook came upon a reference to the hanging, in 1821, of a Telscombe man who had been found guilty of sheep stealing. He was the last man to be hanged in Sussex. The man met his death on the village gibbet, which at one time stood a short distance from the church. Later evidence indicated that he was probably innocent.

As there appeared to be no logical explanation for what had taken place on that night in 1991, Mr Cook wondered if some ghostly entity connected with the man's death might have been responsible. However, as the following stories might suggest, if there are any ghosts lurking near the church, they are those of a man and his dog, with the man wearing clothing of a later time than 1821.

Author's note: Villagers questioned about the above incident, including a married couple living close by the church, had no recollection of being woken by the church bell at such an unlikely hour in any past time (though it is relevant that they were being asked to think back eight years). Yet both Mr Cook and his friend insist that they heard the bell ring for about five minutes. Over the years, there have been many reports of someone seeing a ghost, while others standing next to them at the same time have not. It may be that a similar phenomenon can take place with sound. In this instance the sound of the bell, while seemingly real, was truly 'ghostly'. There may be a more rational interpretation, of course.

Just a stone's throw from Telscombe's village church is a short terrace of ancient dwellings known as Bank Cottages. In 1979 these were gutted and transformed into a youth hostel. Margaret Botting became the hostel's first manager, holding the post for 11 years.

One day, early in the 1980s, she was sitting in the ground floor sitting/dining room, attending to some paperwork, when she became aware of a bright light shining down the staircase from the first floor. It was as if some curtains had suddenly been opened on a sunny day. She was amazed to see, surrounded by this bright light, the shadowy forms of a man and a dog. Moments later the bright light, and the man and dog, had gone. There was no obvious explanation for the phenomenon.

About two years later, a male youth hosteller came down from his room to enquire about a light-coloured dog which had woken him from his sleep during the night. It had, he said, pattered around his bed and then was no longer there. There was no dog in the hostel at the time.

Some months after this, a female youth hosteller said she had seen a strange man and his dog appear briefly in the dormitory. Again, there was no explanation to account for the sighting. On another occasion, a child living in the village spied, from a bedroom window, a ghostly man and dog standing by St Lawrence's Church.

Michael and Patricia Andrews moved to Telscombe in 1976, where they occupy a three-bedroomed house that is almost opposite the church. The oldest part of the house dates back to the 15th century, while an extension was added about 100 years ago. On moving in, they allotted the oldest bedroom in the house to their two daughters, who were then aged five and seven.

On the family's first night in the house, Mrs Andrews had not long gone to bed with her husband when she heard a baby crying. The sound seemed to be coming from the direction of their daughters' bedroom. Mrs Andrews asked her husband if he could hear the crying. He could, so Mrs Andrews climbed out of bed and crept over to the girls' room. She was still able to hear the baby-like crying as she did so, but at the moment she placed her hand on the handle of the girls' bedroom door, the crying stopped. Looking into the room, she found her daughters sound asleep.

The two girls continued to sleep in the same bedroom for about a year. During that time, Mrs and Mrs Andrews regularly heard the sound of a crying baby coming from within this room, but were never able to establish the cause of the sound (the house is detached and there were no young children in nearby houses). Strangely, the two girls heard nothing unusual during their occupancy of the room. After a year, the girls were given their own separate bedrooms, with Mr and Mrs Andrews taking over the bedroom the girls had vacated. From that time on, the sound of the crying baby was never heard again.

However, there was another odd happening during that first year. It was the occasion of an evening social function in the village, and some other children were to sleep overnight in the house. This arrangement meant that only one child-minder would be needed, thus enabling other parents to attend the social function. As the two children of Margaret Botting (referred to in previous story), a boy and a girl, were among those sleeping overnight, she offered to lend a hand with making the beds. When she came to the bedroom in the older part of the house where the Andrews' girls slept, she found she was unable to enter the room. Aware of some unnatural presence on the other side of the door, the hair at the nape of her neck stood on end and she felt a distinct coldness. Indeed, Mr Andrews, who was standing close by, actually saw her hair rise!

About two years after the Andrews family had arrived in Telscombe, there was a woman visitor to the village. She was a former resident who was calling on old friends. Introducing herself to Mr and Mrs Andrews, she went on to enquire about the well in their garden. The enquiry came as a surprise, for Mr and Mrs Andrews knew of no well, but the visitor insisted that there had been a well there. She added that, many years ago, a little girl had tumbled into it and drowned. Could this tragedy be linked to the ghostly sound of crying heard in the house?

Remarkably, only two days after this conversation, while looking out of the window onto the garden, Mrs Andrews was astonished to observe a roundel of subsidence close by the edge of the lawn. The old well, it transpired, had revealed its whereabouts! After this, Mr Andrews topped up the depression on the lawn with earth and stones on several occasions, but a hollow in that part of the garden still persists.

While the baby's cries are now in the past, one phenomenon continues in the house. This is the disappearance of various objects for hours, but more usually for days. This phenomenon began soon after the family had moved in and has continued over the years. Several weeks will pass without incident, and then there might be two or three disappearances in a matter of days, although recent years have seen a lessening of the phenomenon.

Commonplace objects, such as brushes and combs, vanished without trace, only to reappear later, almost always in the same place. Even an electricity bill disappeared for a couple of days before returning to the same spot. On one occasion, Mrs Andrews noticed that her watch was no longer around her wrist. Four days later, while cleaning, she found it under a settee cushion. Peculiarly, the strap had been wound tightly around the watch.

There have been no sightings in recent years of the headless horseman who used to appear on a hill known as The Gallops, which overlooks Telscombe. There were once racing stables in the village – indeed, Shannon Lass, the winner of the Grand National in 1902, came from the stables – and the story is that during the 1920s one of the stable lads spent a roisterous evening in a pub in a nearby village. Returning to Telscombe full of bravado, he 'borrowed' a racehorse and took it up to the hill. Galloping at a fast pace across the ridge with only moonlight to guide him, he was thrown violently from his horse.

Unfortunately, he was close by a fence at the time, and his body was catapulted at speed in such a way that his neck hit the taut wire that ran from post to post. The following morning his body was found, together with its decapitated head. The reports of a phantom headless horseman, seen on the Gallops, persisted over the years following this tragedy.

A map will show that the residential area of Telscombe Cliffs is but a short distance from Telscombe village. However, at present, there is no easy access between the two places, for they are connected only by rutted tracks across the downland or by a circuitous route of several miles via Southease.

Telscombe Cliffs is a comparatively new development, though a small number of buildings, primarily the coastguards' cottages, belong to earlier times. One older building, The Warren, along with its stables and accompanying cottage, was demolished in 1968. Built in the 1870s on the site of an earlier grand house having the same name, it was originally surrounded by farmland which, in the early 1900s, was sold to a development company.

For most of its existence, The Warren was occupied by the MacKay family. Captain MacKay, a former cavalry officer and the head of the household during the family's final years at the house, used the stables to establish a riding school. After his death, the building was converted into a social club, but this role lasted only a few years prior to its demolition.

The Warren was well-known for being haunted. Indeed, it was not unknown for people to visit the place at night in the hopes of seeing the woman in a red crinolene dress who was said to haunt the place. While the lady in crinoline has been seen by a number of people over the years, a quite different experience came the way of Barbara Bunce. In the mid-1950s, when in her late teens, she was employed as a groom at The Warren. By that time the riding school had closed as a commercial enterprise, but four horses had been retained by the family for sentimental reasons.

Living in the house was a Mrs Chantler. The sister of Captain MacKay, she was into her 80s, in declining health, and needing constant care. The woman who looked after her at night chose to leave and Barbara volunteered to attend to the night care until a replacement was found. Shortly after taking up her duties, Barbara was with Mrs Chantler in the latter's bedroom when she heard horses' hooves clip-clopping around in the drive outside.

"The horses must be loose," she exclaimed. "I'd better go down and put them back in the stables."

"No! No!" responded Mrs Chantler, "Stay here. It's quite all right."

Mrs Chantler went on to explain that the sounds were of a purely ghostly nature and that she had heard similar noises in the drive on many occasions, though no phantom horses had ever been seen. Despite the reassurances of Mrs Chantler, Barbara was so convinced that the horses had escaped from the stables that she went outside to investigate. She found the horses quite safe in their stalls.

One Christmas Day at a time when The Warren was already in the early stages of demolition, Barbara and her sister Jean, together with their mother, Phyllis Bunce, went for a walk, partly to offset the effect of a substantial Christmas dinner. Their walk took them past The Warren. As both girls had worked as grooms at the house (Jean had been employed there for two years from 1955), they were curious about what the place was now like inside.

Managing to find a rear door unlocked, with their mother they began looking around the building. On the first floor was a large room which in earlier times had been the music room. The three women, as they ascended the wide, sweeping staircase, were astonished to hear the soft babble of voices coming from beyond this door. It was as if a well-attended party was being held within. Curious, though apprehensive, they approached the door, but at the moment they began to open it, the sounds they were hearing ceased. Fortunately, they didn't move any further forward, for on the other side of the door was a sheer drop. The floor of the room had already been demolished!

Many years ago, it is said, a maid was found murdered at the foot of this staircase. Jean recalls that there was a door at the bottom of the staircase which led into the butler's pantry. For some reason, this door was not only locked but also crudely boarded up – this on the pantry side – so that a different door had to be used to gain access to the pantry. There seemed to be no logical reason for this, and she never took the liberty of enquiring, but in retrospect, she has wondered if there was a connection with the murder. A cottage at the rear of The Warren was rented out. The tenants claimed that, on occasions, objects were thrown around one or another of the rooms by something unseen.

Sightings of the ghostly woman in crinoline were not confined to The Warren itself, for she was more often seen outside of the house, in one instance by a slightly inebriated reveller who was passing by and who was quickly sobered up by a sighting of her. The woman's spirit also wandered into Telscombe Cliffs Way, the road in which The Warren was situated. Indeed, sightings of the spectre have been reported in this road since the demolition of the building.

One such encounter took place early one winter evening in 1977 as Michael Andrews was driving past where The Warren had stood. With him in the car was his niece, Carina. Suddenly, she covered her face with her hands and shrieked: 'Look out!' She had become aware that the car was bearing down on a woman who had just appeared on the road in front of them – a woman in a crinolene dress! Mr Andrews could see nothing, and the car apparently drove right through the apparition his niece had observed.

The fact that many of the ghostly happenings have taken place outside of The Warren, and that the spectre is that of a woman wearing crinoline, a form of apparel worn early in the 19th century, might indicate that the haunting has an association with the original house on the site (which was possibly more extensive), rather than the later building.

22 *It's haunted Hove, actually!*

HOVE IS NOTABLE today for its elegant Regency squares and broad avenues, but until the early 1800s it was just a small fishing village comprised of a cluster of houses around a single street (where Hove Street is today). In 1800, the population was only about 100. By 1820 it had climbed to 300 or so, but from this point on, expansion was rapid.

Brunswick Square was built in 1825-8 to provide grand houses for the rich and influential. Other fine buildings were erected in the surrounding area to create Brunswick Town, as this part of Hove became known. It was a superb example of town planning. Cliftonville, another part of Hove, is more renowned for its attractive examples of Victorian housing. This development began in the 1850s.

As the population expanded, to more than 33,000 by 1897, some of the town planning and architecture was less worthy. As Hove continued its growth, the villages of Aldrington, Blatchington, Hangleton and Portslade were incorporated. The population of Hove today is about 85,000.

An entity known as Wick Woman (named after the locality) is probably Hove's first recorded ghost, though nothing is known about this phantom female beyond the fact that in the 1800s she haunted the gap which in earlier times ran down the beach from Lansdowne Place. Her unexpected arrival on the scene provided a scary reception for some of the local lads using the pathway when running down to the sea for a swim.

You wouldn't expect to find a building erected as recently as 1973 to be haunted, but Hove Town Hall is. The current building is Hove's third Town Hall. The original Town Hall, completed in 1856, still stands in Brunswick Street West – the premises are today used as a snooker club (even this building is said to have been haunted at one time). In 1882, a new and larger Town Hall was opened in Church Road, but this burnt down in somewhat mysterious circumstances in January 1966.

Unusual occurrences have taken place ever since the present building opened. Patrolling security staff have heard the sound of footsteps in the ground floor committee rooms when these have been empty, and sometimes the lift has gone up and down of its own accord (though this could have been due to a mechanical fault), but the more fascinating incidents have taken place in the basement of the building, which is used as a computer room. That this area remains structurally much as it was when it formed part of the previous building could be a factor contributing to the odd events which have taken place.

Most of the computer staff once employed in the Town Hall's basement had experiences that defied rational explanation. Early in 1988, senior computer operators Greg Austin and Wendy Masters observed a bunch of keys shoot from their place at the top of a notice board to land on the floor a few yards away.

Computer operator Alan Ralph was present on several occasions when, without warning, computer tapes and computer tape collars shot onto the floor from their normal resting places. At other times, cases containing computer tapes inexplicably moved around. Mr Ralph once observed this phenomenon while it was taking place. In addition, mainframe printer doors slammed shut of their own accord. He claimed that such incidents took place, on average, about once every two or three months.

In 1991, computer operator Peter Taylor, while on night duty, saw a misty figure just inside the closed entrance door of the computer room. The figure, about ten feet away from him at the time, moved forward two or three paces before vanishing. The apparition was too amorphous for its gender to be established.

In 1993, Mr Taylor saw a white face staring through a window into the computer room, which was odd, because whoever the face belonged to must have been standing in a small patio area which can only be entered through an easily observed barred door from the computer room itself. In October 1994, Mr Taylor once more witnessed a misty figure close to the computer room entrance.

That autumn saw other incidents, for only days later a woman visiting the computer room was disturbed when she felt a sudden chill envelop her. In the next instant, she was astounded to find a shadowy male figure standing next to her, though the image presented itself for only a second or two before fading.

A few minutes later, Mr Austin, while standing in the same area, felt a brief but significant drop in temperature and at the same time was conscious of a prickling sensation all over his head. While on duty a week or so after this, Mr Austin reached out to pick up his phone, but before he could do so, the handset jumped off its base, as if lifted by a hidden hand and then dropped.

There have been no reports of strange happenings in more recent years. There are now fewer computer staff on duty during the day, while night-time activities have been reduced to a minimum.

The former Hove General Hospital, in Sackville Road, has a ghostly tale or two associated with it. The hospital, which closed at the end of 1997 prior to being converted into flats, began its life in Farm Road as a branch of the Brighton and Hove Dispensary. In 1888, after the dispensary began to accept in-patients, it moved to Sackville Road. It became Hove Cottage Hospital in 1902 and, eventually, Hove General Hospital.

Late one night, Geoffrey Roberts, the hospital's night porter from 1983 to 1986, was about to make a pot of tea. As he made his way to the porter's lodge to put on the kettle, he happened to pass a window overlooking the street. In that moment, he saw someone on the pavement outside. Peering a little harder, he observed it was a policeman. It was a cold night and drizzling with rain and the man was wearing his cape to keep the elements at bay.

Thinking the policeman might appreciate a cup of tea and some shelter from the rain, Mr Roberts tapped on the window and went through the motions of drinking from an imaginary cup before gesticulating for the constable to make his way to the front entrance. As the policeman seemed to be responding to this suggestion, Mr Roberts hurried on to the porter's lodge to fill the kettle and light the gas. It suddenly came to him that he hadn't unlocked the front door which, being a small hospital, was usually kept locked at night. The policeman would still be waiting in the rain.

Taking some keys from his pocket, Mr Roberts hurried back to the front entrance, hoping that the constable hadn't moved on. He was pleased to see the man already standing in the reception area. Someone, obviously, had accidentally left the front door unlocked. Greeting the policeman and calling on him to follow, Mr Roberts turned to walk back to the porter's lodge, but after a couple of paces he hesitated, realising that for security reasons he ought to lock the front door.

Turning again, Mr Roberts was surprised to see no sign of the policeman. Hurrying to the front door, he was further surprised to find the door locked. As he stepped back in puzzlement, he became aware of a peculiar smell. It was that of hot metal and carbon.

When thinking about the matter further, Mr Roberts recalled that policemen, in Victorian times, had carried oil-burning lanterns while on the beat, though in his brief glance at the ghostly policeman, Mr Roberts hadn't noticed such a lantern (they were known as bulls-eye lamps).

A more established presence was the hospital's Grey Lady. This apparition confined its activities to the catering and physiotherapy departments, which were located in the basement and linked by a narrow corridor. The Grey Lady was seen on a number of occasions over the years. One sighting involved Janet Rogers, a cook who worked at the hospital in the mid-1980s.

At the time, Mrs Rogers was washing up in the kitchen at the end of her evening duty of cooking suppers for the patients. Her colleagues had already left for home. As she worked, she had the feeling she was being watched. On turning, she was startled to see an old lady wearing a long grey dress standing in the doorway, some six feet away. There was something uncanny about the visitor, and the cook felt her skin prickle.

In the next moment, the old lady turned to walk towards the physiotherapy department. Although apprehensive, Mrs Rogers hurried over to the door and looked down the corridor to see where she had gone. There was no one in sight. Warily, Mrs Rogers went on to search all of the basement area, but the old lady was nowhere to be found.

In 1990, catering worker Sylvia Hughes was alone in the staff changing room, close by the kitchen. She had just changed into her uniform and secured her locker. As she opened the door to leave the room, she felt someone unseen brush past her.

One of the most bizarre incidents involved two young male students who were employed as cleaners for the duration of their holidays. One evening they stepped into the lift by the physiotherapy department. Pressing the button to take them up, they lowered their buckets and mops onto the floor. Almost at once, the startled students saw the buckets and mops leap a couple of feet into the air and crash against the now closed lift door.

While dramatic incidents such as the above were separated by months or years, some catering and physiotherapy workers were frequently conscious of a vague presence in the basement. Even new employees, unaware of the ghostly reputation of this area, would mention this curious sensation.

Hove Museum, in Church Road, was built in 1877 as a family residence by John Olliver Vallance, who named it Brooker Hall after his father, John Brooker Vallance. The Vallance family played a prominent role in Hove's history, owning a substantial amount of land and being very involved in the town's commercial life. John Brooker Vallance became Lord of the Manor of Hove in 1867.

During the First World War, Brooker Hall was used for the detention of German prisoners-of-war. In 1924, the Vallance family offered the house to Hove Council. It was purchased two years later for £4,000. Following refurbishment, the building opened in February 1927 as Hove Museum and Art Gallery. After Hove Town Hall burned down in 1966, the museum building was used as a town hall for seven years before being converted back into a museum, reopening in March 1974.

In 1985, some ghost researchers visited the museum, taking with them a variety of equipment. Though no ghostly noises were recorded, a temperature reading close to a large ecclesiastical embroidery dating from about 1550 showed a small area to be two degrees warmer than the rest of the room, while an ozone-sniffer started to bleep whenever it reached that part of the embroidery featuring a crucified Jesus on the cross. This area also registered a temperature rise of two degrees.

One of the ghosts haunting the building is believed to be that of Sarah Vallance, the wife of John Brooker Vallance. Witnesses of the ghost have remarked upon its similarity to a painting of Sarah Vallance.

There was once a caretaker's flat at the top of the building and one caretaker, Dennis Parkinson, encountered this ghost on several occasions during his employment at the museum. The flat has since been converted into additional museum space, but in 1988 it was still being used as a residence by caretaker Les Whitehead, his wife and his stepdaughter. In that year, one of Mr Whitehead's friends stayed overnight. Before falling asleep, the friend was surprised to see a woman come into the room and move around several times before leaving again. The light was very dim, but he presumed that it must be Mrs Whitehead who had, perhaps, needed some objects from the room.

The total silence of her movements, he thought, must be due to her respecting the fact that he might already be asleep. However, when he made a light-hearted reference to the matter at breakfast time, the Whiteheads seemed puzzled and went on to assure him that none of the family had entered his room.

On another occasion, a 10-year-old girl, a friend of the stepdaughter, who was staying briefly at the flat, was woken from her sleep by someone tucking her in. In the darkness, she presumed it to be the caretaker's wife, but it transpired that no such nocturnal visit had taken place.

Two years earlier, Mr Whitehead was in conversation with Terry Sharp, who was then supervisor at the museum. Their conversation stopped short when they distinctly heard someone walking along the staff passage towards the rear of the museum. At the time, believing they were alone in the building, they thought it must be an intruder, but a search failed to find anyone.

In 1989, just before the museum was due to close for the day, senior attendant Joan Carey looked into the room by the Church Road entrance. There she saw a woman in a long, grey dress. The woman was showing no interest in the exhibits, but instead was looking through the front window of the museum, except that the window had long been bricked up. Slightly puzzled, Mrs Carey returned to the reception counter.

"Are you locking up now?" enquired a colleague who had just arrived on the scene. "Everyone seems to have left."

"No, not yet," responded Mrs Carey. "There's still someone in there." She waved her hand towards the room where she had seen the woman in grey.

A minute or two later, Mrs Carey looked into the room again. There was no sign of the museum's last visitor. Nor was she to be found elsewhere. And she could not have left by the museum's only open exit without having been observed.

Cardinal Newman School, in Upper Drive, is haunted by a nun, though sightings of her have been infrequent. The original school building dates from 1877. A year later the Sacred Heart Convent, incorporating a private girls' school, was founded on the site.

Shortly after the closure of the convent in 1966, the buildings were reopened as the De La Salle College, providing education for boys under the tutelage of monks. Another change came in 1972 with the establishment of the present Cardinal Newman School.

Over the years, the spectral nun has been seen in various parts of the school buildings and grounds and also in Upper Drive, which fronts the school. Joan Edwards, who taught at the school for 25 years until her retirement in 1995, was left quite shaken following a weird experience she had in the late 1970s. At the time, some pupils and teachers were preparing for a presentation of *HMS Pinafore,* the Gilbert and Sullivan operetta. Miss Edwards was one of the teachers involved.

One evening, her duties as producer of the operetta took her to an office situated in what was then a PE changing area, but which is now used for home economics' activities. She was alone at the time, though expecting a colleague to join her. While she was looking through some papers she noticed the office door swing open a little. Thinking someone was on the other side, Miss Edwards rose from her chair and opened the door wider to see who it might be.

There was no one by the door, but she noticed a distinct chilliness, while peering along the darkened corridor outside she was astounded to see a white form drifting towards the far end. While its shape was ill-defined, its size was that of a human. Moments later, the figure dissolved into the gloom. Miss Edwards, by now feeling very uneasy, quickly left the area.

In 1994, a group of girls were playing football on the school playing field. A hefty kick by one of them propelled the ball beyond the edge of the field and into a small patch of land which had been the burial ground of the former convent. One of the girls, 16-year-old Sara Crunden, ran to retrieve the ball. As she picked it up, she saw a nun appear a few feet away from her. The nun, dressed in a black habit, was running – almost skipping. There was laughter on her face, but no sound could be heard, and as she ran her head swivelled, as if she was looking at someone. Except that no one could be seen at the end of her gaze. A few more steps took the frolicsome nun into a cluster of trees, where she vanished.

A few months later, Sara Crunden had another rendezvous with the paranormal. She was strolling through Dyke Road Park with a friend, when they came across a group of girls. The friend recognised one of them and stopped to talk to her. Miss Crunden decided to walk on a few yards and wait for her friend by the nearby children's playground.

Here, among the children at play, she noted a boy and a girl sitting on the swings. There was nothing particularly odd about these children except that their clothing seemed a little old-fashioned. The boy, who Miss Crunden thought was aged about seven, was wearing a white, short-sleeved shirt with a grey waistcoat on top and a bow tie of an indeterminate colour. His shorts were grey and they almost covered his knees. On his feet were brown shoes.

The girl, who was aged about four, had straight blonde hair with short pigtails. She was wearing a short, pale blue dress which seemed almost transparent. On her feet were black, patent leather shoes and white ankle socks.

What happened next gave Miss Crunden quite a jolt. The swings on which the two children sat were actually in motion when a mother carrying a young child advanced towards the swing on which the girl was sitting. Miss Crunden thought the moving swing must hit the mother and her child, but at the point where this would have happened, the occupants of the swings vanished and the swings themselves now appeared to be quite still.

As she placed her child on the swing, the mother was clearly unaware that anything unusual had taken place. At this point, the bewildered Miss Crunden ran to relate her experience to her friend. Both hurried back to the playground to see if the ghostly children had returned, but nothing out of the ordinary was seen.

Businessman Rudolph Egeler had a remarkable experience in the mid-1970s when living in a terraced house in Goldstone Road. He shared the house with his business partner, Alastair Campbell. Each weekday, the two men commuted to and from their London office.

On this particular morning, Mr Egeler opened the front door to take in the milk. As he did so, a cat in the vicinity ran towards the house, trotted up to the front door and nudged against Mr Egeler's legs. It then bounded through the front door and raced upstairs. There it encountered Mr Campbell, who had just emerged from the bathroom.

At the sight of Mr Campbell, the cat screeched and fled down the stairs, as if panic-striken, before hurtling through the still open front door and into the street. But was it the unexpected appearance of Mr Campbell that had unnerved the cat or, in the light of subsequent events, was it something else unseen that had sparked the cat's terror?

Following breakfast, Mr Egeler and Mr Campbell set off for London as usual. Their day's work over, they arrived back in Brighton fairly late in the evening, by which time the episode with the cat had virtually been forgotten. Both retired to bed soon after their return. Mr Egeler, whose first floor bedroom overlooked Goldstone Road, is unsure as to how long he slept, but he remembers being awoken by the sound of a banging door and the pounding of footsteps on the stairs.

Mr Egeler's initial reaction was that some individuals – the noise seemed to indicate that more than one person was racing upstairs – had broken into the house and were intent on harming him or Mr Campbell, who was sleeping in a room at the back of the house.

Mr Egeler immediately leapt out of bed and moved over to his dressing table, feverishly wondering if, in the dim light, he could find anything there which might be used as a protective weapon. As he reached the dressing table, the sound of pounding feet stopped abruptly. In the next instant, to his amazement, the apparition of an elderly woman appeared. She stood just a few feet away from him.

"I could see the woman quite clearly by the light coming through the window from Goldstone Road," Mr Egeler recalled. "Her face was quite friendly and tranquil and I didn't feel fearful in any way. She was fairly short, rather stocky and wore a pinafore over a light blue dress; the sort of dress you might have seen in the 1950s. I suppose she would have been about 65.

"After staring at her for a moment or two, I decided to try talking to her, but it was most strange, for when I opened my mouth, no sound came. I found I was totally unable to speak. I then attempted to get nearer to her. She was about eight or nine feet away, but after I'd taken two or three steps, it was as if I'd come up against an invisible barrier. I just couldn't get any closer.

"She eventually faded away. It's hard to say how long she was present in the room, but I would have thought it was a minute or so at the most. During this time I wondered if I was just having a dream and I pinched myself to make sure I really was awake. Anyway, what happened was more vivid than any dream. I can clearly recall every detail.

"I waited until the morning before telling Alastair. He had, apparently, slept right through the crashing up the stairs – hadn't heard a thing. He knew that I didn't believe in ghosts or anything like that. In fact, I'm an atheist and have always rejected any suggestions of a spirit world, so when I told him what had happened, he accepted it without question. I hoped that at some future time the apparition would reappear, but it never did."

Most ghosts seem benign, but there are the exceptions. The creepy spirit that afflicted the Stopford family in 1985 had all the hallmarks of a malign entity, but there were others who believed that the frightening manifestations were entirely due to poltergeist activities centering on a young member of the family.

A year after Bryan and Linda Stopford and their children had moved into a terraced house in Elm Drive, they had to call for outside help after they had endured a string of unsettling events. The house had been empty for four years and they had been surprised at how cheap it was.

Strange things began to happen on the day they moved in. Mr Stopford put some pictures on a wall. Later, two of these fell to the floor, though at the time the Stopfords didn't consider the incident too unusual. The Stopford's four children, Mark, aged 13; Jayne, 11; Rebecca, three, and one-year-old Daniel, were also affected. Rebecca told her parents that she had seen a lady in the house who had frightened her by waving her arms.

Mr Stopford said: "A three-year-old does not go romancing about things like that."

On another occasion, Mrs Stopford encountered the apparition. She said: "I saw someone standing above Rebecca's head. I just put both children in the pram and got out."

Mark was in the room when a cup of hot coffee rose from a table to fly across the room and tip its contents over baby Daniel. Mrs Stopford rushed the baby to hospital where it was treated for scalds.

Following minor building work at the house, the inexplicable events increased in number. Ornaments fell off shelves and there were strange noises in empty rooms. Once the upstairs lights spontaneously switched off and refused to work for a time, though no fault could be found. On another occasion, a birdcage shot across the room.

Mrs Stopford claimed to have seen a black cat which kept appearing then disappearing. Sometimes, only the eyes and ears were visible and it had a miaow that sounded electronic. By the autumn, Mr and Mrs Stopford were too terrified to spend the night in their bedroom and spent six weeks sleeping in armchairs in a downstairs room, together with baby Daniel.

Jayne said at the time: "None of us will go into mum and dad's room now. It is so cold, and you either see something or feel it."

Eventually, Mrs Stopford, convinced that there was something evil in the house, bought a silver crucifix in the belief that it would offer some protection for her family. But within a few hours of presenting it to her husband, the chain broke twice for no apparent reason. Later, on his way home, Mr Stopford called at Flickers video shop which was, until its closure, also situated in Elm Drive.

While talking to the assistant about the bizarre events that had affected his family, Mr Stopford took the crucifix from his pocket and placed it on the counter. What happened next had Mr Stopford and the other people in the shop doubting their eyesight, for with no one near it, the end of the crucifix curled up. Dumbfounded, Mr Stopford picked it up to look at it more closely, whereupon it broke in half. Tina Hunt, co-owner of the shop, confirmed the story.

When religious services held in the house had no effect, Father Dominic Walker, the Vicar of Brighton, was called in (he went on to become Bishop of Reading). Father Dominic, a leading Church of England adviser on the paranormal, dismissed the idea of the house being taken over by an evil spirit. He suggested, instead, that poltergeist-related phenomena were responsible for the series of events, adding that poltergeist activity was fairly common among families with teenage children.

The *Evening Argus* quoted him as saying: "We know it is caused by an energy carried by a human being in distress. In a way, it is the opposite of prayer."

Finally, Ken Limage, a medium from Seaford, volunteered his help. He arrived with his mother – also a psychic. Mr Limage claimed that an evil spirit in the house was in conflict with another resident spirit, a kindly, elderly woman named Hannah. The evil spirit, Mr Limage said, was lodged in the painting of a crying boy and several dolls owned by the children, and he went on to advise that these items should be burned. The picture and the dolls were placed in a plastic bag and burned on a garden bonfire. Mr Stopford stated that the picture was difficult to ignite; he had to use lots of paraffin to make it burn.

Mr Limage said he had left Hannah with the family to provide spiritual protection. Following the burning 'ceremony', there were further paranormal incidents of a minor nature, such as pictures falling off walls and items falling over, but nothing frightening. At least, not until Margaret, a friend of the family, came to stay.

Mrs Stopford said that Hannah didn't seem to like their guest, for the spirit appeared on a wall in front of Margaret and subsequently disturbed the whole household with repeated bangings at night and an increase of items falling off walls. When Margaret left, things returned to normal.

In 1975, Nicky Rice and her two children, Jonathan and Amanda, moved to a house in Fonthill Road. Built in the late 1960s, it is not the type of building that one normally associates with a haunting, but by the time the family moved out some six years later they were considerably relieved to have left the house and its spine-chilling memories behind them.

Soon after Mrs Rice agreed to purchase the house, the vendor made it plain, almost to the point of aggressiveness, that she needed to vacate the property as quickly as possible. Later, Mrs Rice was to learn from a neighbour that the vendor had once told her, with some agitation, that 'something was there in the house'. Mrs Rice also discovered that the house had changed hands five times in as many years.

The first indication that something was amiss came a few weeks after the family's arrival, with the sound of whistling within the house. There would be just one, two, or three notes, as if at the start of a song. More usually, it would be just two notes; one high and one low. Mrs Rice was the first to hear the whistling. It seemed to originate from the landing outside her second floor bedroom. A few days later, Amanda, at the time aged 11 and occupying a bedroom across the landing, also heard the curious whistling noises. It was a phenomenon which was to take place at intervals over the following years.

While the whistling sounds more usually emanated from the direction of the landing, on occasions they seemed to come, as if generated from the air itself, from within one or another of the two bedrooms. Soon there were other unexplained noises. The doors of both bedrooms were left open at night with the landing light on, but sometimes, from the deep shadows of the rooms, came the sound of ornaments and other items 'being fiddled with'. While the illumination provided by the landing light was comforting, from time to time this too was affected by whatever entity was at work, for it would go on and off, though no flick of a light switch was heard.

Worse still, there was occasionally the rasp of sudden, sharp exhalations of breath which were often uncomfortably close to the ears of Mrs Rice or her daughter. Then there were slight hissing noises and at other times the beginning of what seemed like laughter, except that it stopped almost as soon as it had started. There were noticeable temperature changes as well and, more disturbingly, changes in the air pressure. On occasions, these changes were substantial enough to cause a 'popping' of the ears.

Jonathan, aged 14 at the time the family moved in, had a bedroom on the ground floor (the first floor was comprised of a lounge, kitchen and WC). While the upper part of the house seemed to bear the brunt of the paranormal activity, Jonathan did meet with some unusual happenings on the ground floor. Certainly, from time to time, he was aware of the baffling changes in air pressure, while on one occasion a marble-sized ball-bearing suddenly shot across his bedroom of its own accord.

The incident which especially scared him took place at about 6am one morning. Normally he woke up an hour or so later, but on this particular morning his sleep was interrupted by a loud buzzing noise. It was as if a large insect was flying around the room, but no insect was visible. The intensity of the buzzing quickly escalated to a very loud pitch, all of the time moving around the room as if generated by an actual insect. After a few moments the sound, now much louder than that made by any insect, moved close to Jonathan's head before it struck his left ear with an intensity that was almost physical. His head filled with a crescendo of noise, which then faded quickly away. The bedroom window was closed at the time.

Amanda appears to have been the most sensitive to whatever was haunting the house. She was the only member of the family to see the entities, though they were always ephemeral, ill-defined manifestations.

One entity was a small child of uncertain sex; a white, wispy form that brought with it a playful energy. The second was a girl, or possibly, a young woman. She was the most frequent visitor, a blue-ish, slight, hazy figure that exhuded a sense of melancholia. On occasions, the arrival of this entity seemed to initiate the changes in air pressure. At other times, Amanda discovered, its presence seemed to be linked to the 'pressing-down' sensation which she sometimes experienced while in bed.

The third entity, more insubstantial than the other two but seemingly male, had a slightly menacing aspect. Fortunately its presence seemed to be confined to the bathroom, situated on the second floor, where there would be a palpable atmosphere of disquiet.

The supernatural activity almost always took place at night. There was the occasional daytime incident, but generally the family were able to enjoy a normal life during the hours of daylight. Eventually, even the night-time experiences lost some of their edge through familiarity. However, after three years or so, Mrs Rice decided to call in a priest to bless the house. Although it was hoped that this action would bring a cessation of the haunting, in fact there was an upsurge of supernatural happenings following the priest's visit.

This increased activity continued over several weeks with the Rice family becoming increasingly troubled and fearful. Made aware of the situation, the church authorities sent a priest who was more experienced in the matter. He arrived at the house with incense and holy water to conduct a full exorcism. This action didn't immediately bring an end to the disturbances, but over subsequent months the family were less and less troubled by the various manifestations. In time, they ceased altogether.

Interestingly, the Rice family discovered, a year or so after moving into the house, that it had been built on land where the Goldstone had been buried (the Goldstone, which now stands in Hove Park, is a sarsen stone associated with the legend of Devil's Dyke, but which in fact is thought to have had a use in pagan rituals in about 2000 BC – see Chapter 25). Indeed, the house may actually stand on, or be very close to, where the stone was once located.

The Bow Street Runner public house, in Brunswick Street West, is so named because it stands where Hove's first police station once stood. The pub is haunted by the ghost of a woman who is said to have died in the cells of the former police station.

This early police station wasn't a very impressive structure, being little more than a large shed which had previously been used as a fire station (it housed just one fire engine and two water carts). The walls of the police station were decorated with staves, handcuffs, lanterns and short swords – the latter were carried by constables patrolling the coast roads while on the lookout for smugglers.

Hove's first policemen commenced their duties in 1830. There were just three of them and they were employed by the Brunswick Square Commissioners. Each wore a black tail-coat with a red collar, white trousers and a black top hat. The conversion of the fire brigade's shed took place to accommodate this modest force.

As Hove grew, so did its police force. The uniform eventually changed to fall in line with that of other police forces, but there were early oddities. For example, police issue boots were identical in shape so that they could be swapped over to cut down on uneven wear. Policemen were told not to wash their feet in soap and water, but instead to keep them in good condition by rubbing in sweet oil each evening.

When Hove's first Town Hall, next door, was completed in 1856, a new police station, with cells, was incorporated and the old police building demolished. History is a little vague as to when a pub was built on the site of the old building, but the Station Inn, the pub's original name, was listed in street directories of the mid-1860s.

Offenders were locked up in rudimentary cells situated at the rear of the police station. Late one night, a couple, believed to be a prostitute and her pimp, were arrested for being drunk and disorderly and thrown into the cells. The woman died. It is believed she choked from her own vomit. Ever since, from time to time, her ghost has drifted through the rear wall of the pub from where the cells once stood and into the bar.

One former landlady, nicknamed 'Dodo', saw the spectre on several occasions during her years at the pub until leaving in the 1970s. The ghost was also seen by author Michael Harrison, who lived in Palmeira Square until his death in 1991. His numerous books include several about Sir Arthur Conan Doyle and his fictional detective, Sherlock Holmes. While enjoying a quiet drink in the pub shortly after morning opening time, Mr Harrison was intrigued to see the woman emerge from the wall and walk part of the way through the bar before fading away.

There were, from time to time, unexplained knocking noises emanating from the pub's rear wall. In addition, numbers of bottles toppled to the floor overnight, while on one occasion, a former tenant came downstairs in the morning to find that all the metal caps on a quantity of beer bottles had been prised off, the beer in each bottle remaining intact. Sometimes, too, measures of gin mysteriously vanished from the optics (could that be because gin was the phantom woman's favourite tipple while she was still of this earth?).

Once, a former landlord arrived downstairs to find the bar dartboard on the floor. He was certain that it had been very securely screwed to the wall. In the late 1980s a landlady at the pub, having washed her hair, switched off the electric hairdryer she had been using. In the next moment she felt waves of heat running up and down her back. It was just as if some invisible hairdryer was being used for the task!

Long-time customers at the pub claim that odd things happened to an old, framed picture of a thin-faced man, which once hung in a corner close to the bar's rear wall. They affirm that the expression on the man's face seemed sometimes to alter.

"It was quite creepy to look at," said one customer, adding: "It was taken down around 1985 I think. I've no idea what happened to it."

In 1995, joint tenants 'Robbie' Roberts and David Harrop were amazed to see glasses shoot off the shelf above their heads and smash on the bar floor. This phenomenon was witnessed twice by Mr Roberts during the first half of the year. On one occasion, bottles also flew off a shelf behind the counter. Mr Harrop's 'flying glasses' experience took place in the early summer. In both instances, customers were also present.

In the autumn of 1995, Mr Roberts was working behind the bar when he heard a loud crash. Turning, he saw that the curtain across the front window of the pub, together with its brass rail, had fallen to the ground. It was especially perplexing for this to happen, for the rail was so securely fixed that it could not have fallen under normal circumstances. In the spring of 1996, there was a period of several days when the air conditioning system automatically switched itself on and off at intervals. No fault was found.

Tim Calmore and Hazel Dunne (not their real names) met for the first time at the beginning of the 1980s. Their fondness for each other rapidly escalated into a stronger emotion and they decided to live together. They soon found an affordable first-floor flat in Cambridge Road.

Early one evening, a few months after they had moved in, Mr Calmore arranged to meet his mother in the Robin Hood pub, in Norfolk Place. Miss Dunne was to have accompanied him, but she had some business telephone calls to make and also wanted to change her clothes, so Mr Calmore said he'd carry on to the pub so that his mother wouldn't be left alone, but as it was dark, would return in half-an-hour to pick up Miss Dunne.

When almost an hour had passed without a sign of Mr Calmore, a fuming Miss Dunne decided to set off for the pub on her own. Arriving, she swivelled her eyes around and quickly spotted Mr Calmore and his mother. Confronting her partner, she demanded to know why he hadn't returned to pick her up.

"But I did return for you," he responded, "but when I opened the door and saw you had visitors, I didn't want to intrude. I thought it best to leave quietly and perhaps call back later."

"But I've had no visitors," protested Miss Dunne. "There's been just me, waiting for you to turn up!"

It appeared that Mr Calmore, on opening the front door and seeing a number of men and women whom he hadn't recognised standing around, had believed them to be business people who had called at the flat in connection with Miss Dunne's freelance work, possibly as a result of her telephone calls. Though Mr Calmore hadn't seen her among the visitors, he had presumed she was in the kitchen. The visitors had not seemed to notice his presence in the doorway, so he had thought it best not to intrude and go silently away.

Might this have been a time slip experience? Possibly, but there was one other odd happening. This occured shortly after the above incident and during the time Miss Dunne's brother was spending a few days at the flat. As there was only one bedroom, the brother had slept on a settee in the living room. Each night he placed a packet of cigarettes and an ashtray on the floor by the settee. He'd light a cigarette before going to sleep, then another before getting up in the morning. Only this particular morning, something prevented him from doing so.

Awaking, he tried to turn his body so that he could reach for his cigarettes, but something invisible and of considerable weight pressed down on his chest. Panic stricken, he twisted and struggled to free himself from the uncanny pressure, but to no avail. He wondered how long the crushing sensation would last, but after a minute or two the pressure subsided.

The ghost of an elderly man haunts an off-licence in Victoria Terrace. In 1990, Frank and Pat Donnelly became managers of the off-licence. Soon after moving into the flat above the shop, the couple had the odd feeling that someone unseen was watching them, while there was sometimes a mystifying chill in the air. There had been no contact with the previous managers, so the couple had no reason to believe that anything supernatural was at work.

Soon after the couple had settled in, they collected their dog, a bearded collie, which had, temporarily, been left with a relation. The Donnellys were distressed to discover that the dog seemed most unhappy in its new surroundings. Indeed, it frequently seemed consumed with fright and at nights, cowering, it often jumped on the Donnellys' bed for comfort; this, almost always, and for no obvious reason, at about 2am.

A few months later, an acquaintance, on learning of the dog's distress, suggested that they use the protection of a crucifix, just in case some supernatural force was involved. This suggestion was duly taken up, the crucifix being fixed to the door of the living room. Remarkably, from that time on, the dog ceased to have its bouts of shaking and was clearly much happier.

However, while the crucifix seemed to bring with it a benign influence as far as the dog was concerned, it had no obvious effect on other paranormal events. Mr Donnelly had his first sighting of the spectral old man before the arrival of the crucifix, but he had a further meeting with the spectre some two years later. Also, in subsequent years, there were two occasions when his pyjamas were tugged by some unseen entity when he was on his way to the bathroom.

Another perplexing phenomenon was the unexplained ringing of the off-licence's entrance door bell. Normally activated by the opening of the door, it began to ring outside business hours when the door was locked and the Donnelleys upstairs in their flat. Their daughter Lesley, when visiting outside of business hours, also heard the sound of the bell.

Frank and Ethel Waren moved from Croydon to Hove in the early 1960s. Their new home was a first floor flat in Kingsway, which they rented from the owner of the house, an old and, as they soon discovered, rather cantankerous woman who lived on the ground floor.

Soon after Mr and Mrs Waren had moved in, they learned from their neighbours that they had been preceded by a succession of other tenants who had moved out after becoming disenchanted with the woman's hectoring manner. All, apparently – like the Warens – had been required to sign a three-year lease. None had stayed to complete the period of their lease. Possibly the woman's manner was deliberate, for departures prior to the end of a lease meant more money in her pocket!

Some time after the Warens had moved into their new home, they noticed that a strong smell of scent sometimes permeated their rooms. Then there was the occasional sound of footsteps on the landing, but when they looked outside their rooms, they found no one there. On mentioning this matter to a neighbour, they were intrigued to learn that a previous tenant, a woman who had lived alone in the flat, was sufficiently worried by the strange footsteps to move out.

Then other odd things began to happen. The toilet roll in the bathroom was often reversed. But something much stranger took place one night after Frank and Ethel Waren had each had a bath. After her bath, Mrs Waren went straight to bed and was soon asleep. Mr Waren then had his bath. Afterwards, he briefly pottered around in the living room before making a final visit to the bathroom.

On doing so, he was dumbfounded to find that the bath, which he had left quite clean, was now covered on its inner sides and on top with a thin coating of a brown, gelatinous substance. He ran his finger along the bath to gather some of the substance on his finger and held it to his nose. There was no perceptible odour.

Entirely unable to explain the phenomenon, but too tired at that late hour to bother with cleaning the bath, he decided to leave the matter to the next day, especially as his wife was already asleep. But in the morning, on entering the bathroom, he found that the brown substance had vanished.

"Not only had the jelly-like substance entirely disappeared, but the bath was cleaner and brighter than we had ever seen it before," he said. "Like all old white enamelled baths, it had become a little stained with usage, but amazingly, it looked as good as new."

The Warens occasionally went away for the weekend. Returning to their flat after one of these weekend breaks, they were dismayed to be falsely accused by the owner of sub-letting the flat to someone else in their absence. The owner insisted that while standing outside the house one morning, she had glanced upwards and seen, through the first floor windows, a young man cross from the kitchenette to the living room. The Warens at first thought they might have been the victims of a burglary, but they found nothing had been disturbed.

The mystery deepened a few weeks later when Mrs Waren looked down the stairs and saw a young man in a long, belted raincoat standing in the hall. As she peered to see who it might be, the man vanished into thin air.

"I've seen that man before," she thought. Rummaging through some framed photographs which the owner had given her (being no longer wanted), she came across the two or three photographs she sought. They showed, she felt sure, the young man she had seen in the hall.

Mrs Waren, without mentioning that she'd seen an apparition of the man, showed the photographs to the house's owner, and asked who it might be. The owner replied that the photos were of her dead son-in-law. In the next few moments, the woman made it clear why she no longer wanted these particular photographs. Making her antipathy to the man ever more evident as she talked, she went on to relate how unpleasant, in every respect, her daughter's husband had been, and how his early death had given her little sorrow.

The biggest shock for the Warens was still to come. After the owner had died, her solicitor rang to ask the Warens what they were going to do about her funeral.

Mr Waren responded: "She's nothing to do with us. We're only tenants in the house."

The solicitor replied: "Well, I'm afraid she is something to do with you now, for she's not only left you the house, but all its contents!"

The Warens were totally flabbergasted, especially as they believed the woman's daughter to be still alive, while their own relationship with the owner had never been close – indeed, sometimes positively icy. On Mr Waren's retirement a few years later, this windfall property was sold and the couple moved to a bungalow in Bodmin, Cornwall. Intriguingly, they discovered that the bungalow also has a ghost: a woman in a white raincoat who walks up the garden path, but who only appears when it is raining. This ghost has also been seen by the Warens' daughter and granddaughter.

The strong smell of lavender once drifted through the basement of a cake-making and cake decoration enterprise known as Woodnutt's, which was situated in Church Road. The business consisted of a retail shop and a school where cake decoration was taught, with offices on the upper floor and a storage area and mail order operation in the basement. The business closed in 1990.

Whether the perfumed smell had a supernatural origin is not known, but no other reason for the phenomenon was apparent. Manager Vicky Mann often noticed the lavender smell during the ten years she was there. Another employee, Collette Santer, who was with Woodnutt's for three years, only came across the strongly perfumed atmosphere once, but she said that she had been told by other employees of occasions when they had been aware of sudden and inexplicable drops of temperature while working in the basement area.

Eventually, the vacated building was taken over to become an extension of the already established Ashoka Tandoori Restaurant next door. If there have been any lingering floral fragrances present since that time, they have been lost within the exotic aromas associated with Eastern cooking, for the restaurant staff have noticed nothing unusual.

In February 1996, art student Alexandra Pinon (not her real name), moved into a rented, furnished flat in Brunswick Square. In the following May, she lent her bicycle to a friend. Before doing so she removed the front lamp and placed it in a plastic carrier bag which already had other items in it. The carrier bag was left under a small table in her bedroom.

A week or so later, she went to bed and slept soundly until waking at around 6am. This was about an hour before her alarm clock was due to ring. She doesn't know what caused her to wake at that time, but when she opened her eyes, she was horrified to see a strange man standing at the foot of her bed, though she was immediately aware that she was seeing an apparition.

"He looked as if he might be around 50, but his face was very thin and worn," she said. "He had fair hair which seemed to be turning grey. When he turned his head, I could see a short plait of hair. I can't describe what he was wearing, except that it was a rough, black material of some sort, for I was mainly looking at his face and he was only visible for about three seconds.

"Immediately he had vanished, I was aware of a light in the room. I could see it out of the corner of my eyes. Turning my head, I saw there was a glow coming from the carrier bag I had put under the table. I knew the lamp was in it. I also knew the battery was dead, but I was too scared to get out of bed and investigate. I just pulled the blankets up over my head and remained still, staying there for quite a while until I felt it was safe to get up. When I did, I saw that there was no longer any light coming from the bag and on looking inside, I found the switch on the torch was in the 'off' position. I switched the torch on to check if the battery might be working. It was not."

When Miss Pinon first moved into the flat, she found a number of books. She concluded that they had been left behind by the former tenant. One day she decided to use three of the books – they were in the German language – for a still life painting, and arranged them on a coffee table. But before she started painting, she decided to make a cup of tea.

She sat drinking her tea in a chair close to the coffee table. Glancing at the books, she noticed that there were two spots of what appeared to be water on the top edge of the hardback cover of one of the books, which was standing up. One of the spots of water stayed where it was, transparent and glistening, but the other rolled down the side of the book, but so very slowly it could have been treacle. As the globule descended, it turned red.

Miss Pignon got up from her chair and touched the two spots of water. The one seemed what it was; a spot of water. The other, though red, certainly wasn't blood. But it did appear to be red-coloured water (the book cover itself was grey). Miss Pinon checked the ceiling above. There was no evidence of any leak; no sign of any water.

There were other disturbing incidents. The bathroom light was operated by a cord-pull switch. Miss Pinon had earlier removed the plastic 'acorn' at the end of the cord-pull and replaced it with a small, attractive seashell, which had been securely fixed. But while she was having a bath some days later, the seashell shot off the end of the pull and sideways into a porcelain dish.

After a few weeks, she sub-let one of the rooms in the flat to another woman. Later, the woman gave Miss Pinon a gift of a small, metal owl. Miss Pinon placed the owl on her mantelpiece, but it had disappeared by the time she next looked there. Three days later, Miss Pinon, on taking some laundered clothes into the woman's room, was surprised to see the missing owl lying on its side on a table. She mentioned the matter to the woman on her return to the flat. The woman seemed as puzzled as Miss Pinon as to how the owl had got there.

In 1971, Colin and Eileen Saunders, together with their four-year-old son Mark, moved to a house in Margery Road. They had only been there a few days when they heard a baby crying. The sound seemed to come from the top of the house. Puzzled, Mrs Saunders went to investigate. Reaching the top of the stairs, she was disconcerted to find that the crying sound was coming from the loft, which was used only for storage purposes.

The sound of a crying baby was to repeat itself many times in the following months, but when either Mr or Mrs Saunders went into the loft, they found nothing to explain the phenomenon. Indeed, always at the precise moment the loft door was opened, the sound ceased. Later, Mrs Saunders learned from a neighbour that a single mother and her baby had once occupied the house.

Mrs Saunders had always rejected the idea that ghosts might exist, but one day, wearying of yet more infant cries, she made her way into the loft and called on whoever or whatever might be there to stop bothering the family. She was surprised when her initiative brought a result, for there were no more crying sounds.

Early in 1982, Shahin and Sarah Vaziri became managers of the Brunswick public house. Soon after their arrival at the Holland Road pub, Mrs Vaziri ventured into its cellar and was intrigued to find a quantity of dust-covered bric-a-brac. Little seemed of much use or value, so she resolved to tidy it up as soon as possible, throwing out those items which were obviously junk.

Beginning the task, she came across what she at first thought was a framed picture, but on cleaning the glass she saw that the frame contained not a picture, but what appeared to be a certificate that had been presented in connection with some poetry competition. It was inscribed with the name 'George Bennett'.

As she endeavoured to read the faded document, she noticed that the temperature around her seemed to drop a few degrees. At the same time she had the feeling that someone else had joined her in the cellar. Looking up, she saw the shadow of a man move across the barrels and floor before melting into the gloom.

She mentioned the scary incident to her husband, then, when she had got to know her regular customers better, she related the story to some of them. An older customer told her that the pub was supposed to be haunted and that the ghost was said to be in some way linked to the framed certificate.

"Move the frame and, apparently, you disturb the soul of the dead poet," said the customer, adding: "At least, that's what I've been told."

Mr and Mrs Vaziri wished that, on their arrival at the pub, someone had told them about the ghost. From time to time over the months that followed, the Vaziris often had the feeling that someone unseen was watching them when their duties took them to the cellar.

In 1994, Ron Crossley and his wife took over as managers of the Brunswick. They arrived to find a clean and tidy cellar. Of the framed certificate there was no sign – they didn't know of its former existence until told at the beginning of 1995. But that didn't mean that all remained normal at the pub.

"It's odd," said Mr Crossley, "but the light switches turn off of their own accord on occasions. This can happen anywhere – in the bar itself, or upstairs. There's no evidence of an electrical fault. From time to time there are also unexplained bumps and knockings upstairs," he added.

Mr Crossley previously managed the Palmeira public house, in Cromwell Road (in past years, because of the road name, the pub was for a time known as the Oliver Cromwell). One night in 1993, soon after closing time, he was counting the cash in the bar till when he became aware of someone walking behind him. Turning, he was mystified to see a grey-haired man walking away from him and to the end of the bar before fading away. The man was wearing blue trousers and a grey pullover.

Some weeks later when assistant manager Paul Judd was washing his hands in the gents' toilet, an identically-dressed phantom appeared briefly just a few steps away from him.

Some ten or more years previous to this incident, the then managers of the pub found that their dog refused to venture onto the first floor. If forcibly taken there, it would howl until released, when it would hurtle downstairs.

One pub in Hove has what could be a patriotic ghost! The spirit is said to be that of a former landlord whose tenure included the years of the Second World War. This ghost tends to become more active in the May of each year. Why this should be so is not certain, but there may be a clue in the fact that around the 50th commemoration of VE Day (8 May 1995), there was even more activity than usual.

The ghost, on its rare visual appearances, materialises as a wispy, greyish figure. These manifestations always take place near the bottom of the stairs leading to the first floor. Spooky activities at the pub include sudden temperature drops, rappings, the movement of objects and the occasional touch on the shoulder of bar staff.

The ghost seems to dislike some of the brasher American TV programmes – it has been known to turn down the volume on the television set in the bar to demonstrate its disapproval. But it possibly likes one thing American, for it once increased the volume when Nat King Cole was singing! The present tenants are not desirous of any publicity in the matter, so the pub must remain anonymous.

The landlady said: "We've got used to him over the years. He's quite harmless and sometimes, if he's making his presence felt in some way, I talk to him. I hope he can hear me. The staff are sometimes a bit nervous, especially if they're new to the pub, but my husband and I wouldn't want him to go away."

Legend has it that a spectral dog roams the beach at Aldrington, Hove. But is it just a legend? A former Mayor of Hove, when in his early twenties – it was before the First World War – took a night-time stroll along the beach. Moonlight illuminated the barren stretch of shingle, but he was so familiar with the terrain that he needed little light to guide him on his way.

As his footsteps crunched along close to the water's edge, he found he had been joined by a dog. The dog had appeared from nowhere and he found its presence quite disturbing. There was something unearthly about the animal, and he felt a sliver of fear ripple down his spine. Deciding that the best policy might be to pause for a moment and talk to the dog, he turned and mumbled a few friendly words.

The dog had now stopped and was glaring at him. And then, as suddenly as it had appeared, it vanished. The future Mayor looked around him, but though the moonlight enabled him to see a short distance, there was no sign of the dog. Mystified, he made a little mound of pebbles as a landmark and resolved to return to the beach the next morning. He then observed there was no place where the dog could have hidden.

From the late 1970s until the end of the 1980s, Elizabeth Rushton lived in a flat which formed part of a house in Lower Market Street. Because she lived on her own, she preferred to leave her bedroom light on while she slept, but after spending only a few nights in her new home, she found that some unseen spirit had a different idea.

Besides leaving her light on, Mrs Rushton habitually left her bedroom door closed. But this particular night, before she had even gone to sleep, the door swung open and, almost at the same time, the light went out. Puzzled, she stayed where she was for a few moments and listened. Hearing nothing, she apprehensively ventured out of her bed and looked around the flat. Nothing was out of place. Checking the front door, she found it securely locked.

As the next two or three weeks passed by without incident, the memory of the disconcerting experience slipped to the back of her mind. Then, one night, the invisible entity struck again. Once more the bedroom door swung open, and again the light inexplicably switched off.

From then on and throughout the 12 years Mrs Rushton remained at the flat, the phenonemon repeated itself many times. While initially nervous, she became so used to the uncanny ritual of the door and the light that it ceased to trouble her. While at first she got out of bed to investigate, she eventually never bothered, having reached the conclusion that whatever was at work must be quite harmless.

A short distance away from this haunted flat is a building which has been the site of some quite extraordinary events. The Old Market Centre in Upper Market Street opened in 1828 as an indoor market to serve the newly built Brunswick Town district of Hove, but it failed to maintain its early commercial promise and in 1840 the building was converted into a riding academy. In 1888 it was acquired by Alfred Du Pont, when it became known as Du Pont's West Brighton Riding Academy.

A relic of those days, a large steel wheel, some 10ft across, is still suspended in its original position on the first floor. Formerly used for the lifting and lowering of carriages (when in need of repairs), fodder, coal (from the basement) for the on-site blacksmith's forge, and other materials, a man was once dragged to a grisly death against the wheel after becoming entangled in the upward snaking chain.

The emergence of the motor car led to a decline in the riding academy's fortunes and in 1929 the building was adapted for use as a provisions warehouse. In more recent years, the building has been used by music and drama groups for the presentation of plays, concerts and other artistic activities. In 1996 a new charitable organisation, the Old Market Trust, was formed to oversee the administration of the building, the aim being to convert it into a performance and recording venue for the Hanover Band and an arts and community centre serving the local populace.

In the early 1980s, when the small theatre/cinema within the building was still in use, Gabbus Denney, a director of the Brighton & Hove Arts Centre, was alone in the control box when he was tapped quite firmly on the shoulder. Thinking someone had crept in to attract his attention, he turned, only to find that he was still alone. Around the same time, Tony Shoesmith, the centre's technician from 1978 to 1985, had a similar experience while in the control box.

On another occasion, some people involved in the making of a video film were standing around in the theatre. They were expecting the imminent arrival of Mr Shoesmith, who was to assist them with their project. On hearing footsteps coming towards them, they turned to greet him, only to discover no one there. Mr Shoesmith was in another part of the building at the time and there was no one else on the premises.

In the summer of 1984, Mr Shoesmith was coming up the steps from the basement. At the top of the steps he looked behind him and was surprised to see a glow coming from the basement he had just left, for he felt sure he had switched off all the lights. Descending the steps to investigate, he was even more surprised to see the glow fade away as he approached it. On one occasion a visitor to the centre who had brought his Yorkshire terrier with him found that the dog cringed back, apparently terrified, when he tried to coax it into the basement

During the late 1970s and early 1980s, several visitors complained about being pushed or nudged by someone unseen while ascending or descending a flight of stairs leading from another part of the ground floor. Indeed, one such encounter resulted in a woman spraining her ankle.

At this time, the Brighton & Hove Arts Centre was responsible for the administration of the many activities taking place at the Old Market. Hilary Wishart was involved with the Brighton & Hove Arts Centre for a number of years prior to becoming its chairman in the early 1980s.

During the day, Mrs Wishart usually worked on her own in a ground floor office. In 1984, not long after taking up her duties, she was alone in the office when she had the feeling that she was being watched. Turning her head, she was surprised to see the face of a man staring at her from behind the single pane of glass at the top of the office door. He was a little distance away from the glass and was only visible for two or three seconds, but in that time she observed that he was wearing army clothing. She rushed to investigate, but found no one. It was an incident that was to repeat itself on several occasions over the following months.

During this time Mrs Wishart was able to make out, even though the area outside of the office was a little gloomy, that the man was either a private or an NCO, for he was wearing a collarless khaki shirt (but no jacket), and a basic peaked cap on which there was a regimental badge. Because of the poor light, she was unable to identify the badge. There was a later, seemingly unimportant incident, which in its peculiar way might have had a connection with the supernatural soldier.

At the time, the Old Market Centre's licensed bar was equipped with a counter which had become surplus following the modernisation of a pub bar at London's Victoria Station. The counter was installed in its new home in 1980. Some years later, when the counter was being dismantled prior to its removal, an army cap badge fell out. It was the badge of the West Yorkshire Regiment.

Mrs Wishart believed the spectral soldier to be benign and never felt any fear, but she eventually became a little irritated as the visitations continued.

"After all," she said, "it's uncomfortable to feel you are being watched while you're working, so one day when the soldier appeared, I went outside of the office. I found no one actually there, of course, but I still called out for whoever it was to come in to be identified. I don't know why it should be, but after that, the face never appeared again."

While the soldier might have retreated from the Old Market, the echo of horses long since dead have sometimes been heard in the basement of the building. Stephen Neiman, chief executive of the Old Market Trust and executive director of the Hanover Band, heard the sound of horses snorting, neighing and pawing the ground on three separate occasions during 1996. He also heard a scuffing noise and the rattle of an invisible stable door. It was as if a horse was bumping against it.

"I used to muck out horses as a boy," he said, "so found all the sounds very familiar."

Martyn Barrett, who became building manager of the Old Market Centre at the beginning of 1996, heard similar equine sounds on six occasions over a period of 18 months. Until the matter came up in conversation one day, Mr Barrett and Mr Neiman weren't aware that each had had similar experiences. They also found that they had only heard the ghostly sounds while in one small part of the basement.

In March 1997 it was announced that the Old Market Trust had received a grant of nearly £3.9 million from the Arts Council Lottery Fund. The grant represented three-quarters of the cost of restoring the

Old Market building to enable it to become one of the leading arts centres in Britain. At the time of the grant, the building was little more than a shell. Have all the disturbances associated with reconstruction put a stop to the intrusions from another dimension? Time will tell.

The building of Hove's Cliftonville Estate began in the 1850s, but it took more than 20 years to complete, with a number of the developers working on it going out of business. Forming a constituent part of the Hove of today, it is not surprising to find that three local public houses are associated with the name.

The Red Lion, in Hove Place, was previously known as Mary Pack's, this name being that of the rather flamboyant landlady who once looked after the pub, but when it was built in 1856 it was called the Cliftonville Inn (for a time, it was also known as the Sea Horse).

In 1898, Alfred Daniel Taylor became the landlord. During his stay he built up the largest cricket library in existence. By the time he died in 1923 he had accumulated 1,700 separate publications relating to the sport, this library being kept on the pub's first floor.

The ghost of a woman is said to haunt this floor and a former landlord, in about 1980, claimed to have seen the apparition on the landing. Ernest and Sandra Wright were managers of the pub from 1985 to 1997. While they saw no spectre during their stay, they had other experiences which caused them to wonder. Though the couple were dubious about the existence of ghosts, they were at a loss to explain how glasses spontaneously shot off the shelf above the bar counter on five or six occasions during their time at the pub. In 1993 not only Mr Wright, but two of his bar staff and some customers, were witnesses to one such happening.

In the same year, Mr and Mrs Wright were disturbed in their sleep by a loud bang, followed by the crash of broken glass. It sounded as if someone had thrown a brick through one of the pub's windows, so Mr Wright immediately leapt out of bed and rushed downstairs. Arriving in the bar, he found that all was quiet and undisturbed.

Peculiar knockings were fairly regularly heard from various parts of the pub, but the Wrights believed these to be quite natural sounds associated with the age of the building.

Close by Hove railway station stands a pub having what is said to be the longest pub name in the country – Bertie Belcher's Brighton Brewing Company At The Hedgehog And Hogshead, It's Really In Hove, Actually. If the reader thinks the length of this name might have something to do with the *Guinness Book of Records,* the thought won't be disputed! But it was originally known as the Cliftonville Hotel.

During the Second World War the pub became a rendezvous for individuals involved in the black market, for its proximity to Hove railway station offered a quick link with London. But the hostelry has also known shady activities of a different type!

A shadowy apparition seen in the cellar by a barman was too ill-defined to be classified by gender, though there have been no reports of a sighting for some time. But a very odd incident took place early in the 1990s. A bracelet worn by one of the barmaids unaccountably broke and fell to the floor in several pieces.

As the pub was fairly quiet at the time, it being prior to the lunchtime rush, the landlord suggested to the barmaid that as long as she returned straight away, she might like to take the broken bracelet to a local jeweller. The landlord produced an envelope into which the barmaid placed the broken bracelet. Sealing the envelope so as not to lose any of the pieces, she put it in her handbag and made her way to the jeweller. On her arrival, she took the sealed envelope out of her handbag, when she was astonished to find the envelope empty. The bracelet was never seen again.

It stretches credulity to the utmost to suggest that all three Hove pubs having a link with the name 'Cliftonville' might be haunted, but there is evidence to suggest that this could be so. While the two pubs mentioned above once had Cliftonville as a name, one major pub group elected to pay homage to local history by giving the name Cliftonville to its first Hove pub, which opened late in 1995 in George Street.

The haunting is a modest one. Soon after the pub first opened for business, some staff working on the first floor, which is used for storage and other purposes, had the feeling they were being watched by something unseen, while there were reports of lights spontaneously turning on and off. However, all evidence of the paranormal has tailed off since then.

Interestingly, reports of unusual activities were reported by employees of the Tesco supermarket which previously occupied the site. The supermarket opened in the late 1970s and closed in 1992 on the completion of a larger Tesco store in the area. Sue Clevett, who managed the store for its final five years, said that the first floor, used primarily for storage, had a constantly creepy atmosphere and often seemed unnaturally cold. Twice, when alone and working underneath this floor, and when she was certain there was no one there, she heard footsteps pacing the floorboards above her.

Hangleton Manor, now a public house, is the oldest domestic secular building in Hove. Situated in Hangleton Valley Drive, it was built by

Richard Bellingham, a one-time Sheriff of Sussex, sometime between 1540 and 1553. Its features include 16th century panelling and floor tiles, a Jacobean fireplace and a Tudor heraldic ceiling and inscriptions.

In the grounds of the manor is a 17th century dovecote which is said to have been cursed by a monk. It is believed he was furious about the continual droppings of the birds. At one time the dovecote had 526 nesting boxes.

The manor was sold to the Sackville family in 1597 and the freehold remained with them until 1967, though the family itself didn't live there. For around 300 years the Hardwick family were tenants. They farmed the surrounding land, though legend has it that they originally came from Derbyshire to help quell the local smugglers. Seeing the rich pickings, it wasn't too long before they joined the smugglers themselves.

Before leaving Hangleton Manor in 1914, the Hardwick brothers told of strange voices and of hearing the tramping of heavy boots across the floors. Another unexplained sound came from the Long Gallery at the top of the building. They were of the opinion that it must once have been used as a skittles alley, perhaps in Elizabethan times, for the sound of heavy wooden balls being rolled was regularly heard, followed by the sound of scattering skittles.

One of the Hardwicks was sitting in a downstairs room when he had a rare sighting of a male ghost. A door opened and a man, dressed in what seemed to be a white velvet cloak, strode into the room. His silent steps were accompanied by a faint jingling sound – perhaps the sound of spurs?

Two female ghosts are said to haunt the manor. One is more sensed than seen, though if she disapproves of someone, she is said to gently push them. Others have felt this ghost sweeping past to leave a chill in the air. It is said that many years ago, a maid working at the manor tumbled downstairs to her death. Might these ghostly phenomena be connected?

The other female ghost is believed to be that of a servant girl who was seduced by her employer. Though she endured the nightmare months of her pregnancy, soon after the birth of the child her reason snapped and she threw the baby out of her attic bedroom window. Immediately regretting her action, she screamed continuously.

Her ghost is said to search endlessly for the lost baby and there have been strange shrieks in the night and knocking noises coming from the panelling. Sometimes a pair of white hands manifested themselves.

The two Hardwick brothers slept in a bedroom close by the Long Gallery and they claimed they often saw the white hands resting on the door handle to their room. Sometimes there was a knock on the door and one of the brothers would open it to find the pale hands on the outside handle. Occasionally, the spooky hands appeared over the top of the door when it had been left open. If this happened, the brothers found the door would only close when considerable pressure was exerted against it.

Author Robert Thurston Hopkins was particularly interested in Hangleton Manor. The building was unoccupied at this time, but as he was friendly with the owner, he was allowed to come and go as he pleased. One bitterly cold autumn evening he went for a stroll along the edge of the Downs. Accompanying him was his spaniel, Dusty.

The walk took the author close to the manor. As it was empty, all of the window blinds were down, but this didn't prevent Mr Hopkins from noticing a pair of slender white hands fluttering from behind a small window at an end gable of the house. Though the spaniel's barks were normally deep, on this occasion there were just a series of shrill yelps from the animal, which apprehensively crouched low to the ground.

More than one witness reported seeing a brown silk-like skirt sweep through the house to the accompaniment of a rustling sound. Which of the two female ghosts said to haunt Hangleton Manor this skirt belongs to is a matter for conjecture.

By the end of the 1960s Hangleton Manor was boarded up and fast deteriorating following a spell as a residential hotel, but in 1982 publican Frank Saunders came to the rescue, restoring the building to much of its former glory. Though Mr Saunders died in 1992, his wife Jennifer continued as landlady.

The incidence of ghostly phenomena has fallen off sharply in recent years, though in 1994 came a reminder that the spirits have not completely deserted the building. It was shortly after closing time one night and the bar staff were waiting for the arrival of the taxi which was to take them to their respective homes.

As they stood in a group chatting, the toilet door in the saloon bar swung wide open. As the bar staff wondered who might have pushed it, they were amazed to see the outer, latched door of the bar also fly open. It was as if some invisible being had thrown open both doors during its progress across the bar and out through the exit door.

West Blatchington Windmill was built on a tall flint and brick tower erected through a complex of barns in about 1820. The south barn was burnt out in 1936 and the north barn demolished in 1939, leaving just the west barn, which is today used as a reception and museum area. In 1977 the north barn was in part rebuilt by the then owners, Hove Borough Council, as part of continuing restoration work being carried out in conjunction with the Friends of West Blatchington Windmill, a voluntary organisation.

While by 1928 most of West Blatchington had become an urban parish within the borough of Hove, the district continued to retain most of its village characteristics for some years after this. Indeed, the windmill and barns were still situated on farmland in April 1934 when the *Brighton & Hove Herald* reported a haunting at the north barn. The news story told of a shepherd who had been confronted by a spectral woman in white.

At the time of the haunting it was the lambing season, and for a period of a few weeks it was necessary for the shepherd to attend to his sheep and recently born lambs in the barn each night. On one of these nights, carrying his storm lantern, he entered the barn, but soon afterwards his lantern was 'put out by something'. Then there was a rattling of the doors and shutters, followed by the appearance of a bright light at the far end of the barn.

The light quickly materialised into the white-clad form of a woman. This slightly-glowing apparition then floated along the wall on one side of the barn before vanishing through the open door of a small, dark room situated at the opposite end of the building. The shepherd made frantic efforts to re-light his lantern, but to no avail.

During the spectre's appearance, the shepherd's collie dog, which had been left outside the barn, barked furiously, while within the barn, the sheep huddled together and shrunk back in terror as the phantom drifted past. Curiously, after leaving the barn, the shepherd was able to light his lantern with a single match, despite there being a fair wind blowing.

On the following night, apprehensively, the shepherd again entered the barn when the same occurrence took place, even to the inexplicable extinguishing of the lantern. However, the third and fourth nights were without incident. On the fifth night, the whole weird spectacle took place once more. Much shaken, the shepherd refused to venture into the barn again, and from then on the farmer provided him with a different building in which to carry out his duties.

Peter Hill, chairman of the Friends of West Blatchington Windmill, said the shepherd's experience is the only recorded haunting associated with the windmill and its barns. In earlier times, of course, windmills were frequently used by smugglers who would deliberately put about scary stories of ghosts so as to keep the curious away from the activities of their illicit trade. The windmill, situated in Holmes Avenue, is open to the public at specified times.

23 *Phantoms of Portslade*

WHILE PORTSLADE is mentioned in the Domesday Book of 1086, it was a home for Stone Age man long before this, as evidenced by discoveries in the old gravel pits under Vale Road. There were also Roman and Anglo-Saxon settlements. For many centuries it was primarily a farming community, though with some fishermen's cottages at the sea edge. Portslade Old Village evolved in the 16th century. From 1840 onwards, stimulated by the arrival of the railway, the village grew, bringing with it industrial development. Portslade remained an independent local authority until 1974, when it was merged with Hove.

The Blue Anchor public house, in Station Road, Portslade, is said to be haunted by an old lady in a grey dress, though this spectre has not been seen for many years. However, William Kew, a former manager, claimed that on occasions the pub's beer taps turned off of their own accord, while the same fate sometimes affected the gas cylinders controlling the flow of beer to the bar.

Shortly before morning opening time in December 1993, he was working outside at the rear of the pub, moving crates of empty beer bottles prior to their being collected. He had his back to the open door leading into the pub at the time, when behind him he heard a soft voice saying "Door! Door!"

He immediately turned to see who had called, but saw no one. But he did see that the door was swinging shut and was just in time to stop it closing. Had he failed to do so, for it had a self-locking mechanism, he would have been locked out, as there was no one else in the pub at the time.

Another haunted Portslade pub is the Stag's Head, in the High Street, which dates back to 1674. The ghost of a former potman (a person who collects empty 'pots' or glasses from the tables) has been observed on a number of occasions in the past, usually in the cellar. Customers can see what this ghost is supposed to look like for, based upon the descriptions of witnesses, an art student has sculpted its face. This bust stands on the counter of one of the pub bars. The phantom potman has not been seen for many years, though former landlords have reported such odd happenings as the swapping over of beer lines from full to empty barrels.

In the late 1970s, Christopher O'Reilly (not his real name), found lodgings in St Andrew's Road, Portslade. Several times during the early months of his stay there he heard footsteps approaching his bedroom, but when no one actually knocked on his door or entered the room, he would look out onto the corridor, only to find it empty. Investigation ruled out the possibility of a prank.

He mentioned the unexplained footsteps to his landlady, but she denied any knowledge of the matter, though he had the impression that she was evasive and might have known more than she was prepared to admit. But something more disquieting was about to take place.

He awoke one morning to see an elderly woman standing by the window. She was wearing what looked like a white nightdress and was gazing at him with unmoving eyes. She was visible for about five seconds before fading. Mr O'Reilly was petrified by this experience and asked the landlady to put him in a different bedroom, but there were no vacant rooms and he was obliged to share a room on a different floor with another lodger. However, this man was unhappy at having his privacy invaded and he made his hostility evident. It didn't take long for Mr O'Reilly to become throughly disheartened with the ongoing antagonism shown by the man, so he told his landlady that he would like to return to his old room. Hopefully, he thought, there would be no more ghostly happenings?

Several weeks passed, and while Mr O'Reilly was prepared to tolerate the sound of strange footsteps out in the corridor – and he did hear them on a couple of occasions – he was unable to cope with the reappearance of the woman in white, some three months after he had returned to the room. He left the house as soon as he had found new lodgings.

The *Brighton & Hove Leader* reported on 30 June 1988 that an elderly Portslade resident, David Meaden, was experiencing unusual events at his North Lane bungalow, where he had lived since 1956. In the early 1980s he had been puzzled to see the gate at the rear of his home repeatedly opening and closing of its own accord. There were also odd, unexplained noises coming from the loft of the house.

Then in 1985, when he was alone watching television, he felt that someone else was in the room. Turning, he saw an old woman wearing Elizabethan clothing, but she was facing away from him, so he never saw her face. She vanished moments afterwards. Mr Meaden never saw this ghost again, but he sometimes noticed the lingering smell of burning wood in his living room.

The Foredown Tower, in Foredown Road, was at one time a water tower for the Foredown Isolation Hospital. The hospital opened in 1883, originally as the Hangleton Hospital. It closed down in 1988 prior to the site being redeveloped for housing. The water tower was constructed in 1909 to provide a reliable water supply for the hospital. Hove Borough Council purchased the tower from the housing developer as a preliminary to converting it to its current use as a country centre. A main attraction is its camera obscura.

Rumours that the Foredown Tower is haunted have circulated for many years, especially among some of the children living in the area, though this perception may have been influenced to an extent by the face-like appearance of the tower's facade. The fact that the building was once used as a temporary morgue has added to its ghostly reputation. However, the evidence suggests that the rumours have a basis.

Foredown Tower opened to the general public in July 1991, and from the beginning staff were sometimes aware of some eerie but unseen entity when they were in the upper part of the building. Indeed, one former member of staff said that she had actually seen an apparition; a man wearing greeny-brown tweed trousers and a longish jacket, the latter being obscured to some extent, as if by a mist.

That there was something odd about the place gained greater credence in the summer of 1992 when Paula Huntbach, a senior ranger at the tower from the time of its opening, was awoken very early one morning by her remote electronic alarm, which indicated there could be an intruder in the building. She immediately left for the tower, where she was joined by a male friend she had alerted. Before proceeding upstairs, Ms Huntbach switched on the video monitor to check if an intruder was in the building. The system includes an audio function. While nothing showed on the screen, the distinct sound of footsteps could be heard pacing across the floor of an upstairs room, then hesitating before walking again.

As Ms Huntbach and her friend believed the sound to be human in origin, the police were called, but a search of the building revealed no sign of an intruder. Over the next few days, Ms Huntbach made several checks of the video system when alone in the building, but no sound equating with the footsteps was heard again. Whether the incident was a catalyst of some sort is unknown, but over following weeks the incidence of 'unusual' atmospheres on the upper floor dropped to nil. There has been a complete absence of anything out of the ordinary since 1992.

The *Evening Argus* of 21 July 1984 told of ghostly happenings taking place at Southern FM radio station (then known as Radio Southern Sound) in Franklin Road. The station occupies the former Rothbury Cinema. Some presenters and reporters claimed that while working late at night they saw weird lights, heard ghostly footsteps and were aware of a presence, while a cleaner complained about 'being watched'.

Presenter Russ Williams said: "I was alone when I heard footsteps coming from where the projectionist used to be located." Later, on mentioning the matter to regulars in a nearby public house, Mr Williams was told that some children had been scared of walking past the former Rothbury Cinema after dark.

Keith Belcher, the radio station's managing director at the time, said the idea of the place being haunted was bunkum. He put the stories down to the fact that when it was taken over it was an eerie building with fading cinema posters on the walls. But despite Mr Belcher's comments, the ghost refused to lie down!

Presenter Chris Copsey heard phantom footsteps on five or six occasions over several years after joining Southern FM in 1983. The footsteps were heard pacing the floor immediately above the ground floor studio when it was certain no one was up there.

Nicky Keig-Shevlin, presenter of the *Breakfast Show*, also heard the sound of ghostly footsteps on one occasion, but at a subsequent date she had a quite different experience, which was all the more unnerving because she was alone in the building.

Working later than usual one night in preparation for an early morning show and realising that there were only a few hours to go before she would again be on duty presenting the first programme of the day, she elected to sleep in the building overnight. She hadn't been asleep for long before she awoke to a feeling of intense and unnatural cold.

The room had been fairly warm at the time she had closed her eyes, but now the temperature had dropped by several degrees. There was no apparent reason for the drop and she found the temperature outside the room to be quite normal.

Another presenter, working on his own in the building, was astonished to see a heavy door swing open of its own volition, almost to its full extent, then slowly close again. Because of its heavy weight, the door was not affected by draughts.

One of the most amazing incidents took place in 1990. At the time, producer and presenter Peter Quinn was interviewing Betty Shine, the well-known medium, during a regular programme called *The Eleventh Hour*. Mrs Shine was talking about the subject of mind control when, for no apparent reason, the tape recorder behind Mr Quinn started to play of its own volition. As he turned to switch it off, all hell seemed to break loose.

The controls console started flashing, the monitor screen blacked out, the building was plunged into darkness as all the lights went off, electric doors automatically locked and all the burglar and fire alarms went off. The shrilling burglar alarm quickly brought a police car to the scene.

It was also found that two of the station's three emergency generators had packed up. Meanwhile, curiously, the studio where Peter Quinn was interviewing Betty Shine was still able to broadcast, albeit in darkness, and even though other studios in the building were out of action.

As she had another appointment, Mrs Shine left the building as soon as she could, but Mr Quinn continued to broadcast, though he soon found himself working in sweltering conditions because the air conditioning system had also failed. Hours passed before the station was able to provide a normal service.

The station engineer found no fault that could explain the power failure, but Mrs Shine said that bizarre happenings were sometimes an accompaniment to her activities. She refers to the Southern FM incident in her book, *Mind Magic*. Interestingly, nothing of a paranormal nature has been reported at the radio station since that remarkable event of 1990.

The Portslade Community College comprises several buildings. One of these, situated in the High Street, houses the Sixth Form. It is said to be haunted. The premises were once used by pupils of Windlesham House School, but this private school moved out in 1938 prior to the building being purchased by Hove Borough Council. Later, what had been the school's swimming pool was filled almost to the top with hardcore. This was then covered by a thick layer of concrete, after which a library was built on the spot.

Allegedly, a bizarre tragedy accompanied the filling in of the pool. There were three men working there at the time. When lunchtime came, two of the men went to a nearby pub, but the third, a plumber, wanted to complete his particular task of dismantling the water supply system. When the men who had been to the pub returned, they were only mildly surprised to see no sign of their colleague. As he had carried on working, they presumed he was now enjoying a late lunch. Or perhaps he had gone to the company's office?

A little later, the first lot of concrete was poured onto the hardcore which was already in place in the redundant pool. As the afternoon progressed, more concrete was added until it was level with the edge of the pool... And the plumber was never seen again!

Was the missing man buried under all those tons of concrete? Could he have accidentally fallen onto the hardcore in the pool and, injured, remained unconscious and hidden below the edge of the pool as the liquid concrete gushed in? Who can tell? It wasn't until much later that concern about the missing plumber began to mount, by which time the wide expanse of concrete had hardened to the point where it would have taken days to rip up using pneumatic drills. And who was to say there really was a body beneath the concrete, anyway?

Fairly regularly since that time, the water pipes in the vicinity, some of which travel across the ceiling, thump and bang in a disconcerting way. Often the knockings take the form of distinct raps. The library has since been converted into a computer room, but the weird noises continue. Is there a phantom plumber at work?

Sixth Form teacher Martin Watts said: "Many people have heard the noises which, of course, could be attributable to a quite natural cause, such as airlocks in the water system.

"There is an intriguing aspect to the suggestion that the building is haunted, for some years ago there was a photograph in circulation which showed a ghostly figure entering what was the chapel at the time the building was still a private school. I saw the photo myself."

In her book *Haunted Portslade,* author Judy Middleton presents a number of local ghost stories. One concerns Hector Read, who by 1900 had already established a thriving retail business in the High Street. While primarily a draper, his shop also offered a variety of other goods designed to meet the needs of what was then a compact village community.

Conveniently, Mr Read and his family lived next to the shop in a house much larger than its frontage suggests. It is this house which later gained a reputation for being haunted. Old photographs show him with a generous moustache and wearing a long white apron. He retired in 1937, but continued to live in the house until his death. After spending 40 years there it seems that he was reluctant to leave, for signs of his continuing – albeit discarnate – presence, have been reported.

Former residents Fred and Lynn Powell were in the kitchen one day when they heard footsteps tramping along the passage to the back bedroom. Their collie dog also noticed the sound, pricking up its ears. The footsteps were heard on other occasions. After the passage was carpeted, the sound was still as if someone was walking on a wooden floor. Not wishing to alarm their two young children, the subject was never mentioned in their presence. However, after the Powells had moved to another address, it was found that the children had long been aware of the footsteps, but had unconcernedly accepted them as going with the house.

Subsequent occupants Paul and Julia Davies were unaware of the spooky reputation of the house, but it wasn't long before they, too, heard the ghostly footsteps. Interestingly, they noted that the footsteps were heard only during the daytime; never at night. Though they never saw a ghost, a woman friend who stayed at the house did witness the apparition of a man. Shown an old photo of the shop which included Hector Read, she immediately recognised him, and had no doubt that it was his apparition she had seen.

Whatever entity is present is seemingly benign. Indeed, the present occupants derive much pleasure from the tranquillity of their home, though they report that nothing of an unusual nature has taken place in recent years.

Betty Figg spent her childhood at 50 High Street, Portslade, living there with her parents and grandmother. In those days it was a small, flint-faced cottage. An extension was added in the 1960s, and the interior was progressively modernised over following years. During the Second World War, Betty's mother, Daisy Tidy, looked after the cafe next door to the cottage. Several Canadian Army units were billeted in the vicinity and soldiers from these regularly crowded into the cafe.

At around noon on Christmas Day 1992, Victoria Lynch, who was then living in the cottage, awoke to the tantalising smell of Christmas dinner being cooked. Despite it being the festive season, her job involved shift work and she had only got to bed a few hours before. She had invited her family to join her for Christmas and because she had been working late and needed her sleep, they had offered to prepare the Christmas meal.

As Victoria luxuriated in bed for a few extra moments prior to getting up, she was astonished to see a soldier materialise in the bedroom. He wore a Second World War uniform, though his head was bare. He was tall and young-faced, and as she watched, he half-raised his hands. During his brief appearance, the name Robert Levy or Leroy seemed to come into her mind.

Was the apparition that of a wartime Canadian soldier? Though Victoria Lynch only saw the ghost clearly on that one occasion, there had been several earlier instances when she had sat at her dressing table and felt a presence in the room.

Another story from Judy Middleton's book is concerned with the extraordinary sequence of events which took place in an old villa in Portslade, but the narrative first sets the scene with a reference to the long relationship of two women while they were living elsewhere.

Wealthy Hannah Brackenbury, born in 1795, spent her declining years in a house in Adelaide Crescent, Hove, with her 51-year-old companion,

Alice King. There is no doubt that the two women were very fond of each other. In her will Hannah made provision for a villa in Portslade to be purchased for Alice, who named it Sellaby House. Hannah, who died in 1873, also made generous provision for all the King family. Despite Hannah's renowned generosity – in her lifetime she gave large sums to charitable causes – Alice's family had never warmed to her. Indeed, Hannah had only been dead for a month or so when architect John King, Alice's avaricious brother, was pressing for money from the trustees.

Alice King lived in Sellaby House until about 1900. From that time on there were several private owners. The last of these died in 1938, and the house was then purchased by East Sussex County Council. Since that time the house has been used for a variety of purposes; as a health centre, adult education centre, and more recently, to cater for the care and education of children with special needs.

Whether Sellaby House was haunted by the wraith of Alice King or some other former occupant is not known. Descriptions of the spectre's clothing suggested that it more likely belonged to some time after the 1930s, and that it might be the spirit of a servant girl.

Joyce Ball worked in Sellaby House for about 17 years and she sometimes had the feeling she was being followed. When it was a private house the basement was used as the servants' quarters, and it this part of the building that was said to be especially haunted.

Vic Hart, who lived in the flat at the top of the house in 1962, found that his whippet-cross dog would not venture into the basement. It used to hover nervously at the top of the stairs, its fur hackling.

Once, while in the garden during the early evening, Joyce Ball saw a woman wearing a headscarf and a long dark coat. After the woman had ignored her cheerful 'Good evening', Joyce turned to observe where she was heading, but was surprised to see no sign of her.

On a later occasion, and also during the early evening, Vic Hart's wife Dorothy saw an identically-dressed woman walking across the garden. After this seemingly flesh-and-blood woman had looked straight ahead and ignored her greeting, Mrs Hart, on entering the house, immediately peered through a window to take another look at the woman, but she had vanished.

In the house itself a large painting of a sunset, which had been hanging above a mantelpiece, was mysteriously taken from its hook and deposited on the floor nearby. Another painting in the hall was thrown to the ground and smashed, and a heavy lamp overturned.

Once, when the couple were relaxing in front of the TV in their flat, an invisible hand patted Mrs Hart's head. Sometimes the floor creaked and the settee vibrated, while the front door would bang and the cast-iron door-knocker thump. The bedroom door occasionally swung open for no apparent reason, and once, the loft door opened of its own accord, which was particularly surprising because of its great weight. From time to time there were bad smells on the staircase, though no cause was found.

In 1987, a Methodist minister conducted prayers on the premises to assist whatever unquiet spirit might be present to go on its way. This intervention seems to have been successful, for there were no further reports of paranormal incidents at the house.

24 *Shades of Shoreham*

TO THE WEST OF HOVE stands Shoreham-by-Sea. Despite its modest size, the town's place in history has been quite significant. There was a Bronze Age settlement in the vicinity of Stoney Lane around 1100 BC. Some 2,000 years later in 1199, and just six weeks after the death of Richard the Lionheart, King John landed at Shoreham from France, prior to journeying to London to assert his claim to the crown.

In 1346, Shoreham provided 26 ships for Edward III's invasion of France. In 1348, it is believed that Shoreham was the entry point for the Black Death, which was to decimate the population of the country. On 15 October 1671, Shoreham Harbour was the embarkation point for Charles II when he set sail for France in the coal brig *Surprise,* so evading capture by the Parliamentary army of Oliver Cromwell after the defeat of the Cavalier forces at Worcester.

In 1940 a fleet of small ships left Shoreham to help bring back the bloodied survivors of Dunkirk. Later in the war, the harbour played a significant part in the Dieppe raid before, eventually, another cavalcade of ships sailed from its waters to play their part in the D-Day assault on Normandy's hostile beaches.

A minor event at the beginning of the Second World War was the evacuation of pupils from Queen's School, a boarding school for girls located in Windlesham Gardens, Shoreham, to a safer part of Britain because, with its port, power station and industrial facilities, the town was considered to be a prime target for enemy air raids. The vacated school was later taken over to provide wartime accommodation for Army personnel (the building is today the HQ of the National Federation of Sub-Postmasters).

When, shortly before the end of the war, the 6th Regiment, Royal Horse Artillery (equipped with 25-pounder guns mounted on tracked vehicles), moved from its previous base in Suffolk to Shoreham, the former school was used to house most of the men. However, additional living space was needed and a number of unoccupied houses between

Windlesham Gardens and Shoreham railway station were taken over to accommodate the rest of the men.

One of these houses was occupied by soldiers of the Royal Electrical & Mechanical Engineers whose main responsibility was to maintain and repair the artillery regiment's vehicles. From the time they moved in, it was apparent that not all was right in this particular house.

One top floor room seemed damper and colder than the rest, so it was used only for storage. The occupants of the house were intrigued to discover that a pet mongrel dog belonging to one soldier absolutely refused to enter this room. If carried in, it would go berserk and struggle out of its owner's arms to rush for the door.

In the evenings, most of the soldiers went out, either to local pubs or to catch a train from the nearby railway station to Brighton. The few who stayed behind in the ground floor lounge to read, or to write letters home, occasionally heard strange footsteps descending the bare, wooden stairs (army budgets rarely permitted carpeting!). But on the occasions when anyone bothered to investigate, there was no one there.

Nobody took the incidents seriously. Indeed, the footsteps remained just a subject for light-hearted banter. One soldier decided to add his own concept of fun to the situation. One night, when there were just six or seven men relaxing in the lounge, he crept to the top of the stairs. In his hands was a length of chain.

Earlier in the day he had secreted some chains from the vehicle repair garage into the house. Although no sound of rattling chains had ever accompanied the footsteps of the alleged ghost, the prankster thought it would be an amusing accompaniment to his proposed ruse. After all, he conjectured, weren't some ghosts supposed to be encumbered by clanking chains?

Poised at the top of the stairs, he began his slow descent with heavy, deliberate footsteps and an effective rattle of the chains he carried. He hoped the men in the lounge would hear him and become suitably apprehensive. But he'd only taken a few steps when he became aware of someone behind him, which was a nuisance, he thought, for his joke might be spoiled. He paused and turned to look, but could see no one in the gloom. In the next moment, the mystery footsteps had gained on him.

There was an immediate sense of coldness and the swish of invisible cloth brushing his hand as an unseen being passed by. The sound of phantom footsteps continued downwards for a few more stairs, then faded. The terrified soldier dropped the chains he was carrying and raced for the safety of the lounge.

His comrades looked at his ashen face and listened to the blurted-out story of his stairway encounter, but their initial response was to laugh. But remembering the strange footsteps a few of them had heard in the past, was some of the laughter tinged with unease?

A phantom nun haunts Manor Road. The odd thing about the nun is that her legs seem to be cut off at the knees. This phenomenon is attributed to the fact that the original road was lower than the present one, with the ghostly nun proceeding along the old elevation.

On 17 September 1990, the *Evening Argus* reported odd happenings at the Schooner public house in Shoreham High Street. Managers Brian and Gillian Eastoe, who had moved into the pub just a month before with their two children, Christopher and Jennifer, claimed that the pub's cellar was haunted. Mr Eastoe had become aware of a presence in the cellar, while his wife claimed she had witnessed the ghost of a woman.

Two mediums were called in to advise. One of these collapsed on the cellar floor and began speaking like a child. According to the mediums, the cellar was haunted by a young girl and her nanny, a woman of about 26, who had been victims of a sudden flood which has swept along the High Street and into the cellar (the River Adur is close by). Dennis Hobden, a former Brighton Mayor and Labour MP for Brighton's Kemp Town constituency from 1964 to 1970, suggested that the spirit was probably trying to manifest itself through eight-year-old Jennifer.

Mr Hobden, a Spiritualist, said: "If it is the first time there has been an appearance, there is obviously someone providing the power to enable the manifestation to take place, and it is quite often young children. It is a perfectly natural phenomenon. The little girl might have appeared because she wants to convey some message or strike up a friendship with the child."

Joint managers Philip Dodd and Shirley Fraser arrived at the Schooner in February 1995 and left the following October. They were unaware of the pub's spooky past when they took it over, so were shocked and puzzled some five months later when they came downstairs one morning to prepare for opening time, only to find the bar counter area swimming with water.

The cause of the chaos was the electric glass-washing machine at the end of the counter, which was whirring away and which, through its open door, was spraying water in all directions. It was something that, logically, should not have happened, for each night the machine was always switched off, the drain plug taken out and the door closed.

Now, inexplicably, it could be seen that the switch was in the 'on' position while, when switching the machine off, Mr Dodd found that the drain plug was in place. A further puzzle was that the machine's built-in safety device was supposed to prevent it from working if the door was open.

On its own this single incident could have been put down to an electrical fault, but there was to be a far more dramatic event several days later. The bar had been cleared up after evening closing time and Philip Dodd and Shirley Fraser had gone upstairs prior to retiring for the night. It was a hot summer and despite the late hour, it was still quite warm and both were thirsty. Mr Dodd offered to go down to the bar to get a couple of glasses of orange squash.

As he entered the bar, the only illumination to guide him was the shaft of yellow light coming from the electric bulb in the hallway at the bottom of the stairs and, through the windows, the glow of nearby street lamps. It was sufficient to find the squash bottle and to top up the glasses with water, but as Mr Dodd turned to go back upstairs, he was stopped in his tracks.

At the back of the bar a slowly spinning circle of dazzling white light had appeared, its outer circumference tinged slightly blue. Its diameter was about three feet across and it hovered between floor and ceiling. It remained there for a few seconds, continuing to revolve, then it faded away.

In that instant Mr Dodd noticed a young girl just by the front door of the bar. She was huddled up on the floor with her back against the wall. Mr Dodd noticed that she had red hair, but because the ambient light was limited and because she was resting her face against her hands, he had no adequate view of her clothing or of her facial features, though he thought her size indicated she was about six or seven years old. He opened his mouth to speak to the girl, but found that no words came. Some strange force was preventing him from speaking. A few moments later, the vision of the girl faded.

Over the following days, one customer, on being told of the incident, revealed that she had once, when visiting the toilet, seen a little red-headed girl sitting on the floor just inside the hallway by the toilet. It had been some years before, and she remembered being a little puzzled, for she knew that the managers at that time had no children, but presumed it must be the child of visiting relations or friends.

Another customer told Mr Dodd that she had once seen the apparition of a woman dressed in black. There were few people in the pub at the time and she had been standing well away from the bar and the couple of customers who were sitting there. One moment the woman in the black dress was visible; in the next, she was gone.

Ron and Jenny Hamilton managed the Schooner from October 1995 to July 1996. They returned in October 1997 on learning that there was an opportunity to purchase the pub. As was the case with their predecessors, when they initially moved into the Schooner they had no knowledge of its haunted past. Soon after the Hamiltons arrived, they had the first inkling of something being unusual about the place when they heard their son Jordan, then two-and-a-half years old, talking to someone. At the time he was in the hallway area at the bottom of the stairs leading to the first-floor residential part of the pub. Knowing no one else was there, Mrs Hamilton asked him who he was speaking to. He said it was a young girl.

Many children, when young, talk to imaginary people while they are playing, so at first the Hamiltons didn't pay too much attention to the matter, but when Jordan, who had learned to speak at an early age, quite frequently talked to this unseen girl, they showed more concern.

Jordan, apparently, couldn't understand why his parents were unable to see the girl, and would point, saying: "She's there. Can't you see her?" He said that she was taller than him, that her name was Rose and that she had told him she lived 'behind a barrel in the cellar'. After the Hamiltons returned to the Schooner towards the end of 1997, Jordan resumed his conversations with the invisible girl, though less frequently.

Once, Jordan said that he had seen a woman in a black dress who was drinking Guinness (which he knew by its appearance), but the bar was empty at the time. His imagination at work? Perhaps, but first of all the Hamiltons weren't aware (until told by the author of this book) that a customer had also seen the apparition of a woman in black. Second, as with many other haunted pubs, the gas cylinders in the Schooner's cellar sometimes turn off of their own accord, except that in this instance it is almost always the Guinness that ceases to flow!

Late one night after closing time, the Hamiltons' son James, then aged 16, went into the kitchen at the rear of the pub to get something to eat. As he came into the bar with his plate of food, he heard a loud knocking noise behind him.

It was so loud that Mrs Hamilton, who was at the bar clearing up, not only heard the knockings but felt the vibration of the noise beneath her feet. The cause could not be found. Moments later, when James resumed his journey through the public bar and into the lounge bar, something unseen tugged his arm.

There was a even stranger phenomenon one night shortly before closing time. All the customers had left but one. Mrs Hamilton was in the public bar talking to this customer when both heard a peculiar scraping sound coming from the lounge bar. Wondering what was causing this, Mrs Hamilton immediately went through to the lounge and was astonished to see four lumps of unburned coal on the floor. They were scattered a few feet away from the fireplace in the bar – but this fire is a gas fire utilising artificial coals! The latter were undisturbed.

Early in 1998, Mrs Hamilton bought a compilation audio tape to play in the bars. The tape included Kylie Minogue singing *Give Me Just A Little More Time.* When first purchased, this tape was perfect, but later Mrs Hamilton noticed that the Kylie Minogue number stopped suddenly when some way through, after which there was a small but definite pause. This was followed by a second or two of girlish laughter, after which the Minogue song continued (the tape has been heard and examined by the author of this book).

Cross the footbridge from the main part of Shoreham to Shoreham Beach and close by the River Adur you will find the Waterside Inn. Formerly known as the Lady Jane and before that the Tudor House, it was used as a mess for senior officers of all three services during the Second World War.

The Waterside is believed to be built on the site of a former priory associated with the Knights Templars. This seems quite possible, for this military Religious Order, founded in 1118, had by 1159 acquired and built on land to the south of the High Street (the Knights Hospitallers also had a presence in this area). Indeed, the Abbot of St Florent, patron of the parish church of Shoreham, complained that the Knights Templars had built an oratory on Shoreham parish land without his approval.

The exact sites of these early religious buildings are not known, for the land was swallowed up by the sea for many years before, eventually, the present shingle bank was formed and the River Adur forced to take a different course. The ghost of a monk has occasionally been seen in the Waterside, which would appear to confirm the chance building of the pub on the site of a former religious structure.

In the 1970s Dave Pugh was serving in the Merchant Navy, but when on leave, being friendly with the landlord, he quite often helped out in the bar. One night in 1979, soon after the last customers had left, he went down to the cellar and switched off the pumps, but by the time he was ready to leave for home, the regular bar staff had decided to stay on for a drink and chat, with the landlord joining them.

Mr Pugh straight away changed his mind about going home and took upon himself the task of dealing with the 'orders'. As he was filling the glasses with beer, he remembered that he had switched off the pumps only a short while before. So how could the beer now be flowing? After he had supplied his colleagues with their drinks, he went down to the cellar to discover that the pumps were, indeed, unaccountably switched on.

At that point, though slightly puzzled, he didn't think much about the matter and, believing that his colleagues would want to go home after their one drink, he switched the pumps off. When, later on, some of those present decided to have a second drink, Mr Pugh went to the bar to refill the glasses and again, forgetting for a moment that he had switched off the pumps for a second time, started to fill the glasses. He almost instantly realised this could not be possible and, going to the cellar, once more found the pumps switched on.

It was a mystery, and the phenomenon repeated itself when 'tested' a couple of times. There was a final switching off of the pumps before the staff left for home. In the morning, the pumps were found to have been switched on yet again.

Might there have been a fault with the switch mechanism, or was there something deeper to the affair? There was no further trouble with the switch, but in 1982, some months after Mr Pugh had left the Merchant Navy and taken full-time employment at the pub as a bar-cellarman, there was a more significant event.

One day, on opening the cellar door, he saw someone standing a few feet in front of him. The cellar light was off, but the electric light on the stairs behind him illuminated the figure to some extent. Mr Pugh could see that it was clad in a loose-fitting garment of some sort, but because of the limited light and the angle of the face, he couldn't make out if it was male or female. The entity vanished at the instant the cellar light was switched on.

Three years passed before Mr Pugh had another experience of the paranormal. On this occasion he was in the cold cellar – a room off the main cellar which is kept refrigerated. He was bending over, 'tapping' a barrel, when he became aware of someone standing close by.

"What do you want?", he enquired, without disengaging from his task. When he did look up, there was no one there.

In 1986, a married couple were enjoying a drink at a table situated a short distance away from the kitchen and the nearby cellar steps. Looking in that direction, the woman was shocked to see the figure of a monk. The apparition was only visible for seconds. Her husband said he saw nothing.

Vic and Becky Askey became managers of the pub in December 1992, remaining for two years. Mrs Askey said that when alone in the cellar she occasionally felt that someone else was present. On one occasion she was startled to see a human-shaped shadow moving across the cellar.

Steve Thomas, who took over as manager of the Waterside in March 1997, said that on two occasions when alone in the cellar he had had the very tangible impression that some unseen entity was there with him.

In the summer of 1997, three bottles of Pils beer shot off a bar shelf. This was the only instance where an unusual incident took place outside the cellar and the small kitchen area at the top of the cellar steps. One afternoon in May 1998, barmaid Liz Parsons briefly saw a dark, shadowy figure standing by the door into the kitchen.

There is one other mystery associated with the Waterside Inn, though it probably has no connection with the ghostly monk. High on one of the walls in the cold cellar is a hatch door. Behind this is a tunnel which runs towards the River Adur, not many yards away. The tunnel has collapsed upon itself a little way along. The pub has only stood there since 1935, so possibly the tunnel belonged to an earlier building on the site.

It is unlikely to have run underneath the river, for this would have required very costly engineering. The tunnel might have extended just to the river's edge, where it could have been used by smugglers in earlier times, with small boats surreptitiously ferrying contraband to the river end of the tunnel from larger vessels anchored off Shoreham. Once, a cat was heard mewing behind the hatch door, which was prised off the wall to allow it to be released. But how had the cat got there and where had it come from? It is another unsolved mystery.

Former landlords and staff at the Ferry Inn, in East Street, were troubled over many years by unexplained noises coming from the cellar, when it was known that no one was there. The sound of beer barrels being dropped and rolled over the cellar floor was a regular phenomenon. However, this particular spirit has remained quiescent in recent years.

Hospice, workhouse, school, civic centre... St Wilfred's, in Ham Road, Shoreham, was all of these in its long history before being demolished to make way for the Somerfield supermarket which now stands on the site.

The ghosts of young schoolgirls wearing grey dresses with white pinafores were occasionally seen in the old buildings, sometimes accompanied by a man wearing a dark, Victorian-style suit with a black top hat. Just as mystifying was the sound of pianos being played, even though there were no pianos in the building.

When the Adur Civic Centre moved from St Wilfred's, prior to the latter's demolition towards the end of the 1970s, to a new building in the same road, it turned out to be a case of moving from one haunted location to another. The new building is on the site of the former Coliseum Cinema, which had originally been built as a music hall during the First World War, with its first customers being locally-based soldiers.

While the Adur Civic Centre is a modern building, at least one ghost from the past seems to have remained. The evidence for this came early when Rod Hotton, the centre's computer systems manager, transferred from the old St Wilfred's site to the new Ham Road building. His initial task, in 1980, was to establish a computer network.

At about 11pm one night, soon after the move, he was working in the ground floor computer area, along with two colleagues. While standing with his back to the large reception area, he heard a noise behind him.

There was a rustle of clothing and the sound of double swing doors moving – these being a few feet away. He turned to see a woman on the other side of the swing doors. She was walking away from him.

Mr Hotton knew that only he and his colleagues were supposed to be in the building at that late hour, so he turned and raced after the woman, who he noted was dark-haired and wearing what seemed to be a pale blue cardigan with a navy blue skirt. Although he couldn't see the woman's face, her figure and brisk walk suggested she was young. As the woman advanced into the reception area, Mr Hotton was close on her heels, but in the next moment she had vanished. At the time, there was minimal lighting in the reception area, and he thought she had disappeared into the gloom, but he found no trace of her. Checking the building's exit doors, he found them locked.

He had no previous knowledge of a haunting in the building and found it hard to accommodate the idea that he had seen a ghost. "Ghosts are supposed to walk through doors, not push them open," he wryly commented. Some months afterwards, a cleaner working in an upper floor office reported seeing just the spectral ankles and shoes of a walking woman. Later, other cleaners were to report seeing the ghost of a man wearing green overalls. It has been suggested that this apparition is that of the former caretaker of the Coliseum Cinema.

A ship's bell, from the sloop *HMS Shoreham*, has hung in the reception area since the building opened. This is fixed at a height of about 10ft so that, even with the short rope hanging from its clapper, it is out of the reach of even the tallest person. Yet from time to time, the bell rings out. Usually, it is a single peal. When this happens, according to witnesses, there is no observable movement of either the rope or clapper.

There were many people present in 1996 when the bell pealed loudly during the annual Adur Carers' Night. Some chairs had been placed against the wall immediately under the bell and these were occupied by several women engaged in the separation and folding of raffle ticket stubs in readiness for the picking of winners. There were other people milling around, so anyone tampering with the bell would have been seen.

Rod Patterson, assistant security superintendent at the Civic Centre, heard the bell ring on several occasions while on duty. He also experienced sudden drops of temperature in a ground floor corridor of the building.

"You can be walking along the corridor and the temperature will seem normal," he said. "Then you suddenly come up against a wall of unnatural cold."

For several years until transferring to Brighton at the end of 1996, a first floor room of the Adur Civic Centre was used as a broadcasting studio by

Coastway Hospital Radio. Some of the windows and also the balcony in this part of the building overlook the reception area. The radio station was manned by volunteers, who broadcast request music programmes to several local hospitals.

Late one evening in 1994, radio presenter Richard Goodyear was going off duty, having just closed the station down for the night. As he walked along the balcony he heard the sound of the bell – just a single peal. There was no one else in the building at that moment.

In the autumn of 1996 at about 10pm, presenter Ben Charman, having completed his broadcasting duties, was walking along the balcony towards the exit when he heard a succession of distinct taps on the bell, which he described as being not very loud. At the time, he was alone in the building.

Presenter Craig Burchell had a quite different experience. He was in the studio, playing a selection of requested records. He had his back to the entrance door at the time, so when he heard it click open, he presumed a colleague had just arrived. As he was busy, he didn't turn immediately to see who it was, but he did note the reflection of the person on the windows around him and saw that it was moving across the glass towards him. But no one seemed to actually reach him so, puzzled, he turned, only to find he was still alone in the studio. The door, he noted, was closed.

Presenter Graham Geal said that one visitor reported seeing a misty, green-coloured apparition near a drinks vending machine in the reception area. Once, a former presenter looked out of the studio window onto the reception area below one night to see, in the dim light, someone sitting on a seat close by the ship's bell. The presenter, knowing he was supposed to be the only person in the building at that late hour, phoned the police, who in turn contacted the keyholder and drove him to the building, but on their arrival, no intruder was found.

On a later occasion, a visitor had a similar experience. He was making an evening call at the broadcasting studio and not knowing where it was situated, he first went up to the glass entrance doors of the Civic Centre and peered through. Seeing a shadowy figure sitting just under the ship's bell, the visitor rapped on the doors with his knuckles. As this had no effect, he knocked again, but more loudly. Again there was no response.

Frustrated, the visitor went around the back of the building, where, fortuitously, he found the entrance to the broadcasting studio. On referring to his frustration at not being able to gain immediate access to the studio, the presenter on duty told him that the shadowy figure he had seen in the reception area was probably not of this world, for there was no one else in the building!

At about 2am one morning in 1988, Nicky Reynolds was driving over the

Shoreham flyover when her headlights picked out a young man walking from one side of the road to the other. It was an unexpected place to see a pedestrian, especially at that early hour, but before she had time to think about the matter, the man vanished into thin air.

"He was only visible for a moment or two," she said. "I think he was wearing blue jeans, but his appearance was so brief that I wasn't really able to take in what he looked like or what he was wearing."

Later, on relating her experience to an acquaintance, she was told that she had probably seen the ghost of a young man who had committed suicide. He had hanged himself from the flyover during the time of its construction. Her acquaintance told her that other people had also seen the apparition.

At Old Erringham, on the road that runs over the Downs from Shoreham to Beeding, the ghost of a headless lady is said to roam, apparently wringing her hands in anguish. She usually appears at twilight, and for many years the possibility of encountering her made God-fearing locals wary of being in the area at eventide.

North of Shoreham lies the village of Bramber where, by the ruins of Bramber Castle, the ghosts of a young boy and girl are said to roam. Thin and dressed in rags, they beg piteously for food. Known as the Babes of Bramber, the ghostly children, for some reason, appear only during the bleak days of December. The castle was built by William de Braose, who was a close friend of William the Conqueror. His successor, also named William, incurred the displeasure of King John through his support of reforms, though these were eventually incorporated in the Magna Carta.

The king decided to make an example of de Braose. William and his wife and children were arrested and imprisoned in the dungeons of Windsor Castle, where they were starved to death – though one version of the story suggests that William managed to escape to Ireland.

Another version has the father and mother escaping to Ireland with only the children being imprisoned. In this account, the king demanded that the children remain in custody as proof of de Braose's loyalty. Yet another version has de Braose escaping to France, where he spent his final years as a beggar. While it is believed there were four children from the marriage, only two appear in ghostly form.

During the early part of its history, St Mary's, a 15th century timber-framed house situated in Bramber, is said to have been occupied by four monks of the Benedictine Priory of Sele. There may be a connection with this fact and the ghostly thumps that have been heard on a door in the house which, it is believed, at one time provided access to an underground passage leading to St Botolph's Church.

There have been other strange happenings. A child wearing an Elizabethan doublet and hose has been spied playing on the upper landing, while Mimi McConnel, an elderly member of the family which occupied the house during the 1930s, saw a phantom lady in a grey dress on more than one occasion.

Canadian soldiers were billeted at St Mary's during the Second World War and during this time a spectral monk was seen strolling along Monk's Walk. Land-girls also witnessed some 'manifestations' during the war years, but no descriptions have been recorded.

The knockings on the door ceased a long time ago, and there have been no reports of apparitions in recent years. However, one unexplained phenomenon still takes place from time to time. This is the smell of musky perfume which lingers for awhile at the foot of the stairs and outside the Painted Room.

Since purchasing St Mary's in 1985, Peter Thorogood, assisted by curator Roger Linton, has extensively restored the building, which is open to the public for part of the year.

When, in 1989, Paul and Jilly Sewell took over the Merry Monk public house, in North Road, Lancing, the existing managers stayed on for a few days to help out until the Sewells had got to know their way around the place.

Initially, the Sewells had grave doubts about their new location. They wondered if they had made the right decision in agreeing to manage the Merry Monk. The outgoing managers were still occupying some of the residential rooms, so initially the Sewells were obliged to use two of the top floor rooms for sleeping and living purposes. One of these rooms seemed to be permanently chilly, while the other had an atmosphere which Jilly Sewell, especially, found distinctly uncomfortable. When the outgoing managers eventually departed, the Sewells lost no time in moving to more congenial rooms.

One of the early indications that something was amiss came when the postman, handing over the morning mail, commented on the possible cost of lights being left on frequently during daylight hours.

"What lights?" the Sewells enquired.

"The lights on the top floor," responded the postman.

A few months later, the Sewells had become used to the fact that lights switched off on the top floor were quite likely to be switched on again later by some discarnate being.

The Sewells also began to get used to the fact that things would mysteriously disappear, only to turn up hours or days later in a different place. Usually, these would be small objects, like keys or items of jewellery. Mrs Sewell always kept her pairs of earrings together, but sometimes one would go missing, only to reappear somewhere else in the pub a day or two later, often in the most unlikely place.

Sometimes it would be a larger item, such as a handbag. It might eventually turn up on a table known to have been clear but an hour before. The Sewells came to accept the antics of the capricious spirit responsible for these 'tricks', for the missing objects always turned up in the end.

The ghost also had tidy habits. Items of clothing left in disarray would, inexplicably, be found later, neatly folded. One trainee manager based briefly at the pub had an especially discomfiting experience. He was an ex-army man and had heard about the strange goings-on. A tough, no-nonsense type, he expressed his disbelief forcibly. "Ghosts? A load of rubbish," he snorted.

Visiting trainees usually occupied one of the bedrooms on the top floor. One night this particular trainee manager awoke to find all the bedclothes being dragged off him. He switched on the light to discover that the blankets and top sheet from his bed were now arranged in a neatly folded pile on the floor!

When Mr Sewell's sister came to stay at the pub for a few days, she brought her dog with her. The dog, a spaniel, resolutely refused to venture upstairs, even though it normally responded quickly to its name.

During the time they were at the Merry Monk, the Sewells were told that the married daughter of a previous manager had once stayed at the pub. She had a three-year-old son who, while there, became ill. While he was in bed recuperating, he had a visitor.

"Who was that lady?" he enquired of his mother, when she came into the room a little later.

"What lady?" the mother countered, puzzled.

The boy described the middle-aged woman who had stood by his bed and recounted how she had said that he must keep to his bed if he was to get well soon. There had been no flesh-and-blood woman present!

The ghost hasn't been so active in recent times. Deborah Cody took over as manager in 1996. She said that the lights on the upper floor still switched on without human aid, while her cat was most reluctant to go up to this floor. Some think the ghost is that of a former landlady. She had a strong personality and a sharp tongue, and ruled the pub back in the 1930s when it was known as the Railway Hotel.

During the early part of the 1900s, Goring-by-Sea was linked to Worthing by a road that was little more than a narrow lane bordered by hedges and lofty elms. A barn that once stood on the north side of this road at a point well into Goring parish seemed to have a baleful influence on horses. On reaching the barn, horses would either swerve nervously to the opposite side of the road, or refuse to pass it. Oddly, this phenomenon was only evident at night. Riders had no trouble with their mounts during the hours of daylight. The barn was eventually demolished.

25 *Roadside wraiths and a devilish plot*

PRIOR TO THE CONSTRUCTION of the M23 motorway and the new A23 section of road at its southern end, the old, narrower A23 was the main road linking London and Brighton. In the 1930s, despite there being fewer vehicles, it was still a very busy road and there were frequent accidents. The emergency services weren't as sophisticated as they are today and people killed in an accident would often be kept in a nearby morgue until their bodies could be examined by a doctor and an appropriate vehicle commissioned to take them away.

One such morgue was located in the cellar of the Plough Inn, in the village of Pyecombe, just north of Brighton. With such a past, it is not too surprising to learn that the pub has been the scene of some curious episodes. John Cragg, the son of a former landlord of the Plough, lived there with his parents from 1932 until 1956. He recalls that, as a young lad, his lonely walks to and from the village school on bleak, foggy winter days were somewhat clouded by the fact that dead bodies were sometimes laid out in the pub where he lived. While he didn't personally experience any paranormal incidents, he was aware that the Plough was said to be haunted by a nun.

Certainly, 30 years later, Geoff Copeland, who with his wife looked after the Plough from 1988 to 1991, recalled several odd incidents. Bottles sometimes fell off shelves of their own volition. Then there was the breezeless summer day when the bar window's curtains were stripped from their rails by some inexplicable force. And the Copelands were never able to coax their German shepherd dog into the ladies' toilet.

Roy Cragg, a relation of John Cragg, managed the pub for six months from his arrival in August 1993. During his short spell there he found that his two dogs, a collie and an alsatian – as with the Copelands' dog – refused to enter the ladies' toilet, while the collie (only) would not enter the cellar.

A reason for the reluctance of dogs to enter the ladies' toilet was provided by an incident which took place some time after Martin and Lin Moore had become owners of the Plough, in 1997. A regular customer returned from the toilet to exclaim that, while there, she had seen the apparition of a nun. On another occasion, Mrs Moore had just finished serving a woman customer and was handing her the change when the customer, looking shocked, exclaimed that a woman wearing a black dress and a white apron had just very briefly appeared at the back of the bar and behind Mrs Moore. The bar was quiet at the time, and the customer was a stranger.

The Plough stands close by the A23 and this main highway has its own ghosts. A 1972 report referred to the apparition of a limping blonde girl on the A23, just north of Pyecombe. The girl is believed to have been the victim of a motorcycle accident, but the southern stretch of this road is renowned for its spectres. In several instances, their appearances have been so sudden that motorists have driven right through them!

Some of these sightings were reported in the *Evening Argus*. On 2 December 1976 the newspaper told the story of Patrick and June Geary who, after visiting their family in Brighton, were driving back to London when they saw a girl in a white raincoat walking along the central reservation, some ten miles north of Brighton. At the time, which was around 8pm, it was very dark and raining hard.

The couple only saw the girl from the rear and Mr Geary thought it odd that she didn't seem to have any hands or feet. In the next moment and without looking, the girl stepped into the road. It was too late to stop, but Mr Geary instinctively snapped on the main beam of his headlights.

Mr Geary said: "The figure seemed to glide along the top of my bonnet and then disappear. If it had been a person, I know they would have been hit."

This report came to the attention of Michael and Rose Dawes of the Round House, Withdean, and their story was related in a subsequent issue of the *Evening Argus*. They said that eight years earlier, with two friends, they had been driving along the A23 from Crawley to Brighton. As they neared Brighton, Mr and Mrs Dawes and one of the friends saw a figure in a white trenchcoat run across the road to the central reservation and then fade away.

Other motorists claimed to have seen the spectre of a tall, slender woman wearing a cape and hood with a similarly attired child walking beside her. One driver even reported that he had seen the phantom of a man dressed in cricketing clothes!

On 3 January 1977 the *Evening Argus* carried a story about Dave and Joan Wright who, while driving along the A23 on the final few miles of their journey to Brighton, had turned his car around to look for a man he felt sure the car must have struck.

The car's headlights had picked out a man in shirt-sleeves staggering across the road. His appearance immediately in front of the car had been so sudden that Mr Wright felt sure that the man must have been hit, even though he had felt no bump, so he turned the car around and drove back to where he believed the incident had taken place. He found no sign of the mystery man.

On a summer evening in the late 1970s, Joe Harper and his wife Sheila were driving from Shoreham to London. It was just getting dark as they joined the A23, so Mr Harper switched on his headlights. Soon after passing the Happy Eater restaurant on the left of the road, the car took them up a slight incline. As they passed over the brow at the top, the headlights picked out a couple of people crossing the road from right to left.

The car was travelling at about 60 mph at the time and the couple were about 50 to 60 yards in front of the car. Mr Harper decided to switch on his main beam, partly to warn the couple of his approach, and partly to see them more clearly. However, in the instant that he switched on the main beam, the couple, who were wearing light-coloured clothing, just as instantly vanished.

At this part of the A23, pedestrians are rarely seen, for there are no proper pavements. Mr Harper said that as they passed where the couple had been, he and his wife looked around them, but saw no one. He added that the sighting was so brief that neither he nor his wife could tell whether the couple were male or female.

At the beginning of the 1990s, three young men driving along the A23 through Bolney decided to call at the village's Queen's Head public house. As they were about to turn towards the pub's car park, a woman wearing a grey dress appeared suddenly in front of the car. The driver slammed on the brakes, but it was too late. The car seemed to strike the woman, though no bump was felt. It then skidded a few yards before hitting the low wall fronting the pub.

The three men, though shaken, were not injured. They jumped out of the car, but found no sign of the woman. Two people who were outside the pub at the time said that they had seen the woman appear from out of nowhere, before vanishing when hit by the car. The police were called. They could find no trace of the mystery woman. The driver of the car was breathalysed, but was found not to have been drinking.

The woman in grey had been seen on a number of previous occasions. She is said to be the ghost of a woman who, many years before, had been struck and killed on that stretch of road by a passing vehicle. She had been the wife of a man who owned property to the rear of the pub. Interestingly, there appear to have been no further sightings of the spectre since this incident. Might this replay of the death scenario have enabled the spirit to move on? The Queen's Head has since been converted into a residential property.

A more recent spectre, that of an animal, has been seen on the A23. The *Evening Argus* of 26 December 1996 reported that a phantom dog was giving motorists a spooky shock on the road between Brighton and Gatwick. The dog, a fat golden labrador, was seen walking across the A23 close by the exit road to Bolney. Brighton taxi driver Leonard Bish was one witness.

He said: "I was driving along when I suddenly saw this dog just walk slowly out in front of me. I had to swerve hard to avoid it, but luckily I wasn't driving too fast. When I got back home and started telling people about it, they told me I'd seen a ghost. Apparently, a lot of people have seen it. I know one person who says he actually drove right through it."

On 13 February 1997 the *Evening Argus* reported that John Morrison and his girlfriend, Michelle Warner, had seen a similar spectre on the road while travelling on the A23 from their Kent home to Burgess Hill.

"It came from out of nowhere," Mr Morrison said: "It was really strange. I thought I had hit it."

A few days after this report, the *Evening Argus* published a letter from a reader who suggested that the ghost could be that of an old, golden labrador which had belonged to a local farmer some ten years before. The farmer had bought a puppy and the two dogs had become great friends. When the puppy went missing, the older dog seemingly set out to search for it, but was killed while crossing the A23.

The village of Poynings is a short distance from the A23. Close to Holy Trinity Church at the south end of the village stands a small repair garage. To the rear of the garage is a field through which a tiny stream flows. A few yards along, the flow of the stream is interrupted by a pond. In the summer of 1883, this pond was the scene of a terrible tragedy.

It was a Sunday evening and three boys were paddling in the pond. Towards the centre of the pond there must have been a steep drop, for suddenly two of the boys found themselves out of their depth. Unable to swim, they were soon threshing about in terror. The third boy couldn't swim either, but he knew there would be people at nearby Holy Trinity Church, for the evening service was about to begin.

Running barefooted from the pond, he reached the church in little more than seconds, but when he opened his mouth to ask for help, he was so consumed with emotion that he was unable to speak. For a few moments more he struggled to get the words out, but still his voice failed him.

Frustrated and desperate, he turned and raced back to the pond, but he was too late. His friends had already drowned. Filled with sadness and remorse, he drifted into melancholia and a subsequent decline in health which led to his early death. Since then, a number of people have reported seeing the ghost of a boy in the vicinity of the pond. One of the most recent reports was in 1993, when two holidaymakers said they had seen a young boy desperately running along the edge of the pond before inexplicably vanishing.

A former landlord haunts the timbered rooms of the village's Royal Oak public house. An extrovert character, he regularly wore a tartan tunic. His ghost has been seen sitting at a table in the dining area. Kitchen manager Rose Rapely was one witness. She saw the apparition in 1996. He has also been seen walking across the bar before disappearing through the floor at a point where there was once a trapdoor leading to the cellar.

In the past, several bar staff have heard footsteps pacing the creaking floorboards of the pub's upper rooms. One barmaid distinctly heard the sound of a cup of tea being stirred as she approached an upstairs room where the door had been left open, but when she looked into the room, she found it empty. There was no one else on that floor.

Manager and co-owner Keith Davie, who moved into the Royal Oak early in 1999, was twice woken up at about 3am by a noise which sounded as if a party was taking place in the bar. No cause was found for the sounds of revelry.

Further up the A23 are signs pointing to Hurstpierpoint. In this attractive village you will find the New Inn where glasses have shot off shelves and where once a leather strip of horse brasses disengaged from a hook to shoot onto a nearby table. Other objects in the pub have sometimes moved well away from where they have been placed without logical cause. A landlord who was there in the early 1980s reported that, although no reason was apparent, he sometimes smelled cigar smoke in the cellar.

Roger and Sharon Norminton were in charge of the pub for seven years until leaving in 1992. They were baffled when the gas cylinders in the cellar inexplicably turned off from time to time, but the most eerie experience was to come after they had converted a room at the back of the pub into a restaurant. They were preparing for a wedding reception and Mr Norminton was busy in a marquee in the pub's rear garden, while his wife was working in another part of the pub.

Suddenly, there was a very loud bang from the restaurant. Both rushed to the source of the noise. They were astounded to find that a glass ashtray, which had been left on the counter of the restaurant, had shattered into eight triangles of glass, each triangle being virtually identical in size. Just two weeks later, the incident was repeated, with another glass ashtray 'exploding' into eight almost identical triangles.

In 1996 regular customers John and Jeanne Stewart were in the bar quietly enjoying their drinks when they saw an an electric light bulb fall from its ceiling fitment. The peculiar thing was that the bulb still glowed as brightly as it did when alight throughout its downward journey until shattering into a golden shower of glass.

A temporarily employed drayman who called at the pub a year later, and who had no knowledge of the pub's haunted past, said he saw the apparition of a man walking through the cellar door. Unfortunately, the drayman left his employment soon after and was unable to be contacted for further details.

For Peter Harcourt and his girlfriend, Jill Medhurst (not their real names), Walpurgis Night, which falls on 30 April, had no special significance. That is until Walpurgis Night 1979, when a pleasant evening out was transformed into a night of horror.

Mr Harcourt today owns a shop in central Brighton, but at the time he was a 20-year-old sales assistant working in a clothing store. His friend, Ken Smith (not his real name), had suggested that the three of them should drive to the village of Bolney, some 20 miles north of Brighton, wander around the countryside for a while, and then have a pub meal before returning home. Mr Harcourt and his girlfriend agreed and so, early in the evening of 30 April, the trio set off along the A23 with Mr Harcourt at the wheel of his Ford Consul.

Mr Smith, however, was very interested in the occult, and the main reason he wanted to go to Bolney was to take a more than casual look at Wykehurst Park, an impressive 105-room mansion set in 18 acres of parkland. A friend with similar interests to himself had alleged that strange, arcane ceremonies, possibly connected with black magic, sometimes took place at the house.

Walpurgis Night is the night on which, according to Germanic legend, witches ride to a given rendezvous where they indulge in revels with the Devil. Reports have, in the past, indicated that this pagan eve of May Day event is still celebrated by practitioners of the darker rituals.

If the house was to be observed, and more importantly, its visitors, for weren't some prominent people mixed up with the black arts, what better occasion to do so than Walpurgis Night? Certainly Mr Harcourt and his girlfriend, sparked by Mr Smith's enthusiasm, were happy to accord with his suggestion.

It was still light when the friends reached Bolney. They were not long in discovering the whereabouts of Wykehurst Park house which, with its elaborate architecture – it includes pointed towers – might seem more appropriate to Bavaria than Bolney. Strolling past the building, they came across notices which not only warned of the penalties for trespass, but also indicated the presence of guard dogs. Surveying the mansion, they saw nothing of immediate interest, so continued their walk. Later, at about 10 o'clock and after their pub meal, they returned to the house.

They initially parked close by the entrance to the drive leading to the house, believing that this vantage point would enable them to observe the arrival and departure of visitors. After about 20 minutes of watching and waiting in the darkened car without seeing a single person, they became a little bored and decided to move nearer to the house.

Mr Harcourt started the engine and edged the car slowly forward. Remaining in a low gear, he nosed the vehicle into the drive before coaxing it as silently as possible towards the house. As the silhouette of the building loomed nearer, he decided to turn and complete the last few yards in reverse so that the car would face the exit, thus permitting a quick getaway should either humans or guard dogs appear on the scene. For the same reason, he kept the car's engine ticking over.

With the car now parked close by the house, the friends found they were able to observe the main entrance and many of the windows. Most were in darkness, but they were intrigued to note that where there was light – emanating from two ground floor windows – it seemed to be provided by candlelight rather than by electricity. But though the minutes ticked by, there was a disappointing lack of visitors. Nor was there any indication of sound or movement from within the house.

Then, suddenly, the friends became aware of a distinct chill. The evening had been warm, but this coldness filled the car. Almost in the same moment a dark cowled figure, some six feet tall, drifted past the car. There was no face beneath the cowl and no hands at the bottom of the sleeves. It was like a totally black, three-dimensional shadow.

The trio of friends were terrified. Mr Harcourt immediately pressed down on the accelerator to send the car lurching back along the drive and onto the public road. He didn't stop the car until it had travelled about two miles when, in subdued voices, they discussed what they had witnessed.

After they had calmed down a little, they elected to proceed back to Brighton, but when Mr Harcourt turned the ignition key, the car failed to respond. He discovered that the battery was absolutely flat! Eventually, the AA were called to give the car a jump-start. Mr Harcourt, a car enthusiast who regularly spent hours of leisure time ensuring that his Ford Consul remained in tip-top condition, found it hard to believe that his battery, which was fairly new, had so suddenly failed.

In view of the above story, it is interesting to note that Wykehurst Park house, which was built in 1871 by Austrian banker Henry Huth, was the backdrop for such horror films as *Demons of the Mind* and *Hell House*.

Kathleen Doyle lived at Wykehurst Park from 1971 to 1978. During that time, she says she never came across anything that might be described as supernatural, but she did discover that a Miss Esme Tudor Greenyear, who occupied the house during the 1930s, had delved into the history of the building which had previously stood on the site and had been so horrified by an aspect of its history – which she refused to reveal to others – that she immediately moved out, locked up Wykehurst Park house, and never lived there again.

On a summer morning in 1986, Bolney resident Ann Gardiner was in her back garden hanging out the family washing, when she heard the sound of a child's laughter coming from the garden next door. Peering through a small gap in the hedge separating the two gardens, she was able to make out the figure of the four-year-old girl who lived in the house. In the next moment, Mrs Gardiner's eyes caught another movement in the garden. It seemed that the little girl had a playmate on that day.

Mrs Gardiner was friendly with the girl, and often talked to her. To assist such conversations, she kept an upturned milk crate nearby, which she used to stand on so as to look over the hedge. Curious as to who the girl's playmate might be, she placed the milk crate against the hedge and stood on it. A small children's chute had been erected in the next garden and Mrs Gardiner saw that the girl, who was wearing a swimming costume, was walking towards this. A few paces away from her was a small boy dressed in navy blue shorts and sandals. He was bare from the waist up, except that he had an old-fashioned navy blue sailor's cap on his head; the type with a soft brim.

The boy, who had followed on the heels of the girl, watched as she climbed the steps of the chute. He then moved to the front of the chute so as to see her slide down it to land with a splash in an inflated plastic paddling pool. As the girl landed in the water, the boy clapped his hands in glee. Mrs Gardiner, not wanting to interrupt the children's play by calling out, returned to hanging out her washing (she was later to recall that the boy's handclaps had been soundless).

That afternoon, when chatting to the mother of the girl, she mentioned the boy in the sailor's cap. The mother, baffled, asserted that no child other than her daughter had been in the garden that day. She also pointed out that the garden gate was kept locked while, in addition, the family's pet dogs would not have permitted a strange child to enter the garden without at least barking. However, as Mrs Gardiner insisted that she really had seen a boy in the garden, the mother questioned her daughter, but the daughter averred that she had been quite alone while playing that morning.

There was just this one paranormal incident associated with the house next door, but in the mid-1990s there was an odd occurrence involving Mrs Gardiner's own house. One day, while on the first floor landing by a staircase leading down to the back door, she became aware of a strong smell of perfume. The smell seemed to be of freesias and it was so powerful that she called her 26-year-old daughter, Gail, who was in the front room of the house. The daughter hurried to the bottom of the staircase.

"Do you notice that smell?" enquired Mrs Gardiner. Her daughter responded by saying she did, and confirmed that the scent seemed to be that of freesias. The perfume seemed to occupy a specific area around the stairs, for Mrs Gardiner found that just a few paces took her entirely away from the scent. There was nothing to account for the smell, for there were no freesias growing in the garden.

Some days later, while out in the village, Mrs Gardiner mentioned the incident to a man who had resided in Bolney for many years. He informed her that the woman who had previously lived in the house (and who had died), regularly used a perfume smelling of freesias. As with the boy in the sailor's cap, there was just this one inexplicable incident in the house.

Devil's Dyke, a large cleft in the South Downs situated close to Poynings, is a popular beauty spot steeped in folklore. Legend has it that the Devil was infuriated to discover that the people of Sussex, one of the last strongholds of paganism in England, had converted to Christianity. He was especially angry to find that the men of the Weald were building churches in every village, so he decided to dig a channel right through this part of the Downs so that the sea could burst through and drown all these new adherents to the Christian faith.

The Devil's rage was so great that he set about completing the task in one night. His spade thudded into the ground and huge clods of earth shot into the air. As midnight approached, the noise the Devil was making reached the ears of a little old lady. Looking out of her cottage window, she saw what the Devil was up to. Lighting a candle, she placed it on her window-sill and then held a sieve in front of it, allowing the candle's flame to transfer it into a glowing orb.

The Devil turned his head and saw what looked like the rising sun. Although all his thoughts and energy had been directed towards his task so that time had become a blur, he felt sure that it couldn't yet be dawn. In the next moment, however, a cockerel crowed, so he thought it must really be sunrise and sped off, his task unfinished. But the wily woman had caused her cock to crow by knocking it off its perch. The enormous hole excavated by the Evil One became known as Devil's Dyke!

The legend has several versions. In one, four great clods of earth that the Devil sent flying into the sky eventually struck the ground again to become Chanctonbury, Cissbury, Rackham Hill and Mount Caburn, while as he fled across the Channel, a great dollop of earth fell from his cloven hoof to become the Isle of Wight.

The first mention of Devil's Dyke appeared, albeit without any detail, in Lieut. Roy's *Survey and Sketch of the South Coast,* dated 1757, while a 1910 edition of the *Gentleman's Magazine* contains what is believed to be the first printed version of the legend. Set in verse, it was written by William Hampner.

There is an associated legend. The Devil, pausing for a rest while digging the Dyke, was disturbed by a mass of golden stone which rolled down and struck him on the hoof. Enraged, he gave it a mighty kick. A part flew high in the sky to land in Hove, where it became known as the Goldstone (it's actually a sarsen or greywether stone). It still stands in Hove Park, close to the former football ground which took its name.

About 160 years ago, the area where the stone first stood was farmland. The farmer became exasperated with the hordes of people trampling over his corn to view the stone, so in 1834 he had it buried. In 1900, one of the Hove Commissioners heard the story. As a consequence, in 1906 the stone was transferred to Hove Park.

The Devil's Dyke Hotel, situated at one of the highest points in the area, was built in 1955 some ten years after an earlier structure of the same name had been destroyed by fire. This latter hotel, dating from 1871, was reputed to be haunted. This building had itself replaced the hotel which had been built on the site in 1831. Prior to this, from 1818, a refreshment room had stood there.

There is an intriguing story about Devil's Dyke which, one feels, must belong to the 'time slip' category. It concerns a Mrs Stevie Hobbs, who told her story in a letter appearing in the *Evening Argus* on 26 February 1996. Mrs Hobbs was born in 1930. When aged four, she was taken to the Dyke for an outing by her foster mother. As they were walking across the top of the hill overlooking the Dyke, the young Stevie was surprised to see there was no cable railway there. She asked her foster mother what had happened to the 'train on a rope'.

The foster mother was quite upset by this question, and told Stevie not to make up such a story, adding that there had never been such a thing there. But the child had just had a vision of a former time when she was younger and when someone other than her foster mother had been holding her hand. As she had stood there with this other person, she had watched someone she believed to be her real mother getting into the cable car and waving goodbye (in fact, Stevie's mother had disappeared from her life well before her fourth birthday).

Many years later, Mrs Hobbs came across a book which told the story of Devil's Dyke. Looking through it, she discovered that there had indeed been a cable railway just where she had so vividly pictured it. It had been in use between 1894 and 1909, but it eventually become a financial burden and had closed down (a two-car, steep-grade railway also ran down the northern slope of the hill towards Poynings from 1897 to 1908, while a conventional railway linked the Dyke with Brighton and Hove from 1887 until its closure in 1938). So the cable railway had ceased to exist some 20 years before Mrs Hobbs was born! (If this was a time slip experience, the presumption must be that the woman the young Stevie saw was mistakenly identified by her as her mother.)

Mrs Hobbs is fairly certain that her foster mother, who was born in 1873, must have known of the cable railway's existence, for she lived locally and the opening and eventual closure of the railway would have been well reported. She believes that the woman's scolding was probably her way of dealing with a situation she was unable to comprehend.

26 *Ditchling and Wivelsfield*

The attractive village of Ditchling, just north of Brighton, has its origins in Saxon times, although there is also evidence of occupation during the Stone Age, while Ditchling Beacon was the site of a Roman camp. The oldest building in the village is St Margaret's Church, which dates from the 13th century. In its later history, the village became a rendezvous for smugglers with the local church choir, the notorious 'Ditchling Singers', being entirely involved in the illicit trade.

Some of the eerie stories relating to the village have an origin in more credulous times, though as late as the summer of 1935, shepherds tending their sheep close to Ditchling Beacon, one of the highest points in Sussex, claimed to have seen the spectral packs of 'wish-hounds' (from 'whisht', an old term for spooky), or witch-hounds, which raced across the sky and which had been reported over countless years by other shepherds. The sheepdogs are said to have cowered in terror as the awful black creatures swept overhead, their ghastly howls filling the air.

Might there be a connection with another ghostly phenomenon said to take place in the same area, where all the sounds of the hunt are heard – horses' hooves, the cry of the hounds, the tootle of the hunting horn – but nothing is ever seen?

Another eerie animal tale is associated with Black Dog Hill, on the road between Ditchling and Westmeston. This stretch of highway was named after the headless spectral hound which once haunted the area. But let us move away from tenuous legends to more recent tales of ghostly activity.

On a chilly autumn night in 1991, David Moore set out to drive from Peacehaven to Crawley. It was prior to the construction of the new A23 road, so he chose to go via Ditchling. Reaching Ditchling Beacon at about 10.30, he entered the steep, sharply twisting hill that leads down into the village. As he came to the bottom of the hill, the car's headlights picked out the figure of a man attired in what seemed to be a brown cloak, while around his face was what seemed to be a piece of brown cloth.

At first, Mr Moore thought the figure was that of a tramp who had wrapped something around his head to keep himself warm, but in the next instant he realised that the cloth, which hid most of the man's face, was actually a cowl. Mr Moore's foot had already moved to the brake pedal, but as the car slowed to a crawl and while still illuminated by the headlights, the figure in brown dissolved.

In 1312, Edward II granted John de Warenne the right to hold a weekly market at Ditchling. Many years later, the nearby Bull Hotel was built, and it soon developed a close association with the market. While there is no precise record of when the Bull was built, it certainly existed in 1636, when it was listed in *A Catalogue of Taverns in Tenne Shires about London,* by John Taylor, while local historian Muriel Benham believes it dates back even further to 1509. Taking into account this long history, it is not surprising to discover that the Bull has a spectre or two.

A barman who worked there in 1996 claimed to have witnessed a full pint glass slide along the bar counter. The nearest person was some distance away. He also referred to the sudden rattling of the pub's door handles, for which there was no explanation.

Corinne Bailly became manager of the Bull towards the end of 1997. Soon after arriving she heard footsteps on the first floor of the pub when no one else was present, and more than once she had the impression of being followed by an invisible entity.

At around the same time, assistant manager Sarah Searby was cleaning a first floor bedroom when the handle of the half-open door leading into the room began to rattle furiously. She went to see what was causing the rattle, but found no one near the door, nor even on that floor. On another occasion, she was in the first floor manager's office when she heard the sound of light furniture being moved around in the bedroom next door. An investigation offered no explanation for the noises. Staff at the pub also reported that internal doors opened and closed of their own volition.

Donal O'Doherty became manager of the Bull in April 1998. The Bull offers bed and breakfast, and one overnight resident told Mr O'Doherty that he had woken up to find that the curtains in his room had fallen to the floor while the curtain rings to which they had been attached were still on the curtain rail.

While pictures on the walls of the pub's upper floor have sometimes been switched around by a mysterious force, there is a more intriguing phenomenon at work on this floor. Normally responsible for making the beds in the residents' rooms, Mr Doherty's wife Linda, and his sister Norma, have occasionally been startled to find that a bed that had already been made would later acquire a mysterious 'bump' about the size of a small animal, such as a cat, under some part of the duvet. On pulling the duvet back, no reason would be found for the bump, though the area where it had appeared would, curiously, be warm to the touch.

Another Ditchling hostelry associated with the supernatural is the White Horse. Bert Maybury was the pub's landlord for 11 years until leaving in 1991. During that time he experienced several baffling incidents. Doors opened and closed without human aid, while in the cellar, from where gloomy passages lead towards the parish church, the gas cylinders that are used to pump beer to the bars periodically turned off without reason.

Barman Bob McLaren was once locked in the cellar while moving some crates, after the door at the top of the cellar stairs had unexpectedly thudded shut behind him. It was a happening which, because of the way the door hangs and the type of catches fitted, should have been impossible.

Ian and Mary Turner took over as managers of the White Horse in 1992. It wasn't long before the couple found that keys left in the bar and other parts of the pub sometimes disappeared for hours. Almost inevitably, regardless of where the keys had been left, they would turn up later in the cellar. On one occasion, a bunch of keys left in the bar took two days to re-appear.

There is a sump in the pub's cellar. This has a capacity of eight gallons and the pump used to empty the water accumulating in the sump can only be operated by manually using a pulley to lift the float. In addition, the equipment will only function when the sump is full, or very nearly so.

One day in 1997, Mrs Turner was working alone in the cellar when she was shocked to hear the pump start up of its own volition, especially as it had only been emptied that morning. After a few moments, and just as inexplicably, the equipment stopped again.

Whatever invisible entity haunts the White Horse, its gender appears to be male, for it seems to like to stroke the heads of women. Two barmaids and Mrs Turner have experienced this odd phenomenon.

It has been suggested that the haunting has a connection with an incident which took place at the pub in October 1806, when it was known as the White Hart. Mr Harnott, the landlord, awoke to the sound of someone breaking in. Leaping from his bed, he silently made his way to the bar where he found two men; Robert Bignall, a known murderer and smuggler, and John Tingley, his accomplice.

On seeing Mr Harnott, Bignall tried to pull out a pistol, but the landlord overpowered him. Tingley chose to make his escape, but was later apprehended by the landlord of the Swan Inn at Chailey. Following his catalogue of crimes, Bignall was hanged in front of 3,000 people at

Horsham. It has been suggested that the pub's ghostly reputation is due to the return of Bignall's spirit. As Bignall didn't meet his end at the pub, and as the resident ghost appears benign, this seems unlikely.

Wings Place, in West Street, is Ditchling's oldest house. The earliest part of this picturesque building dates back to approximately 1450, though most of the Tudor construction around it belongs to about 1520, with the court being added in 1560. It is probable that there was once a wing to the east, where the White Horse now stands.

The house is haunted by a young, pleasant-looking girl with long dark hair and wearing a white blouse with a criss-cross pattern at the front, together with a dark skirt. While the present owner of the house has not seen the apparition, some visitors have, usually in the bedroom normally used by guests, which is the oldest bedroom in the house. The phantom girl has also appeared in the kitchen.

The *Evening Argus* of 29 December 1982 carried a story about the sale of Pardons, a 17th century house in East End Lane, Ditchling. The report mentioned the spectre of a frail old woman which haunts the house. Each time she appears, the eerie notes of harpsichord music may be heard.

Although the house was owned by the Furzfield family for some 200 years, the family let the house to various tenants towards the end of this period. A representative of estate agents Clifford Dann and Partners, who handled the sale, said that the little old lady had been seen a number of times by people renting the house. Each time, the sound of harpsichord music accompanied the vision.

"One of the tenants told us the ghost's presence gave the house a tremendous sense of well-being," he added.

Travelling north from Ditchling takes you past the wide expanse of Ditchling Common, an area that has a slightly sinister atmosphere after sunset. At the north-east edge of the common lies the village of Wivelsfield. Despite its modest size, for only 1,200 people live there, the village has been described as being the most haunted in Sussex. It is thought that Wifelesfelde, to give the village one of its more ancient titles, has its origin in the name of a Saxon chief, and legend has it that this chief was a vampire.

Vida Herbison, writing in *Sussex Life,* catalogued a number of ghosts. She once lived at Antye, a large Tudor farmhouse in the parish. The building was haunted by a small girl dressed in a frilly white night-dress who glided down the stairs, while outside by the well, the ghost of a carter sometimes appeared. Wearing a Regency-style hat he would sit on a low wall, binding the stock of his whip. Dogs normally shy away with fear in the presence of the supernatural but, unusually in this instance, the family dogs when in the vicinity would run over to sit by the spectre.

Near to Antye stands Theobalds, another large farmhouse. It is built on the site of a larger building which is believed to have had a moat. Miss Herbison stayed there as a child when convalescing after measles and recalled that her elder brother and her nanny, who were also staying at the house, sometimes heard a spinet being played in the middle of the night. Their hostess informed them that she had herself heard the instrument on numerous occasions. The lane leading to Theobalds was said to be haunted by a great ghost hound which bounded towards the house before disappearing in the garden.

Miss Herbison reported that two different people had told her they had seen a spectral man attired in a monk's robe walking along the path outside the little Norman Church of St Peter and St John the Baptist. A visitor once took a photograph in the south chapel, which was built around 1300, and was surprised to find what looked like a shadowy, gowned figure on the print.

Miss Herbison also reported that a former vicar had told her that while he and his wife had lived at the vicarage, the figure of a young woman was several times seen in one of the bedrooms. The former occupiers of another old Wivelsfield property, Lunces Hall, reported hearing ghostly footsteps on the landing while living there, though nothing was ever seen.

The ancient manor house known as Great Ote Hall is hundreds of years old. In the 18th century it was the home of Selina, Countess of Huntingdon. Leaning out of a window, this gentle Christian woman preached to enthusiastic gatherings assembled on the lawn below. In 1778 the countess built Ote Hall Chapel. A benevolent ghost has been seen in Great Ote Hall from time to time and it is thought that this could be the shade of the good countess.

A spectral collie dog sometimes sits under a walnut tree by a house called The Botches. It has been seen by Vida Herbison and her father, who once lived there, and also by a number of other people. At Clevewater, a part-medieval farmhouse, there is an upstairs room into which no dog will venture.

Other Wivelsfield ghosts include a phantom lady, advanced in years and dressed in white, who is sometimes seen standing near a bus stop on the road from Newick, and ghostly footsteps which can be heard in what was once the chauffeur's quarters in a large Victorian house known as Coldharbour.

No review of haunted Wivelsfield would be complete without some reference to the three pubs in the area, for each offers a fascinating story. The Royal Oak is said to be haunted by at least two ghosts. The inn, built about 1700, is associated with a trio of frenzied killings which led to the perpetrator becoming one of the last men in Sussex to be hanged before a public audience.

The murders took place on 26 May 1734 after Jacob Harris (also known as Jacob Hirsch), a travelling pedlar whose stock-in-trade included smuggled goods, had led his pack pony into the yard of the inn and booked a room. That evening, Harris overheard the landlord, Richard Miles, mention that he had taken around £20; a considerable amount of money for the times. The weather had been unusually hot, and thirsty farmworkers had flocked into the pub. Harris decided to get his hands on the money.

The following morning, Harris seized his chance. Creeping quietly up behind the landlord, who had gone to the stables to feed the pack pony, he slashed him twice across the neck and left him for dead. He then made his way to the bar and to the oak box that was used as a till, but the money he was seeking had been removed. At that moment, he became aware that someone was coming downstairs. It was the inn's young serving girl, so he rushed from the bar to twice plunge his knife into her.

The landlord's wife, Dorothy, who had been ill and in bed for several days, was disturbed by the girl's cries and called out. At this, Harris went upstairs and stabbed the horrified woman before carrying on his search. He failed to find any money. By now, concerned that someone might at any moment call at the inn and discover the carnage, he decided to flee, stealing only a riding coat, valued at ten shillings.

The landlord, though greviously wounded, managed to drag himself to the road and call for help. He was later able to identify his assailant, but his death was not far away and he finally succumbed on 30 May. His wife and the serving maid had died almost instantly.

Harris quickly made his way to the Cat Inn, at West Hoathly. He knew the inn well. Built as an alehouse in about 1450, its strategic position halfway between London and the coast made it a haunt of smugglers and those who traded with them, which included Harris.

Thinking he was safe, Harris went into the bar parlour, but was dismayed to find a group of smugglers excitedly talking about the militiamen who were searching for a knife-wielding murderer. Then he became aware that widow Mary Brooks, the inn's landlady, was staring at him. For the first time, Harris noticed that he had streaks of blood on his sleeve.

Fleeing once more and aware that the militiamen were closing in on him, he decided to seek refuge in nearby Selsfield House, a manor-type building. Gaining entry, he hid on a ledge in the parlour chimney. Unfortunately for him, some mounted militia officers who had been given permission to search the house were allowed to light a fire with which to dry their rain-soaked topcoats. Overcome by the smoke curling up the chimney, Harris collapsed onto the flames. He was immediately arrested and transported to Horsham Gaol.

In August, Harris was indicted for murder and sentenced to death. His execution followed on 31 August when he was led to the gallows at Horsham. Then, as a warning to other possible transgressors, his body was cut down and transferred to Wivelsfield where it was strung up on a gibbet erected just 250 yards south of the Royal Oak, the scene of his infamous deed.

The gibbet was left where it was as a reminder of the crime. It became known as Jacob's Post and, for some unknown reason, credited with curative powers. As a result, chips of wood were regularly cut from the post, some people travelling many miles to do so.

The much depleted original post was eventually dug up and a replacement post erected. But even this had to be renewed from time to time as people continued to cut away pieces of wood. A replacement post erected at the end of the 19th century was topped with an iron rooster bearing the fateful date. This original rooster is now under the guardianship of Ditchling Parish Council. A replacement copy has been made by Uckfield schoolchildren. A part of the original post hangs on a wall at the Royal Oak. Legend has it that a ghost, said to be that of Jacob Harris, haunts the vicinity of the post and in earlier times local people avoided the area after dark. The gruesome story spawned a jingle:

Child: have you seen the ghost,
Which comes to Jacob's Post?
I nearly did – almost!
Nurse: Hush! Do not talk so wild.
There are no ghosts, my child.

While the haunting of Jacob's Post may be based more on fear than fact, the Royal Oak itself endures a continuing history of paranormal phenomena. In the 1960s, Wivelsfield resident Hilda Banks and her married daughter, Joyce Fairburn, were enjoying a quiet drink in the bar when there was a sudden swell of excited chatter coming from another part of the pub. The focus of the excitement was a large wall mirror. Mrs Banks and her daughter joined those customers who were staring at the mirror and they were astonished to see that a large cross had appeared on its face.

Mrs Banks said: "It was a misty, grey colour, but quite clearly a cross. We were still looking at it when it finally faded away."

Steve Carey, manager of the Royal Oak from 1984 to 1989, recalled two outstanding paranormal happenings during his time there. One night after the pub had closed for business, he sat down in the saloon bar to enjoy a game of dominoes with his girlfriend June – they were later to marry – and four friends.

At around 2am, one of the friends, having lost all his small money in the game, held up a £20 note and asked if anyone could provide change. One of the other players jestingly tried to snatch the banknote from him, whereupon a third player joined in the fun by attempting to grab the note. During the horseplay, the half-crumpled note fell to the floor. At that moment, the doors of a locked, glass-fronted cupboard mounted on the wall of the bar shot open and around 15 sports' trophies tumbled onto the floor.

"Even if vibration had caused the cupboard in some way to fly open and the front row of trophies to fall out," said Mr Carey, "I can't see how the back row could possibly have followed them. Anyway, at that early hour and in a fairly isolated area, there was no passing traffic to cause vibration.

"It's interesting to consider that there might be a link between the fact that Jacob Harris was seeking to steal £20 and that it was a £20 banknote that was dropped during our game of dominoes. Might that fact have triggered something?" he added. The trophy cupboard has since been taken down.

On another occasion, Mr Carey was asleep in a first floor bedroom. At around 4am, possibly later, he awoke to find he was no longer alone in the room, for in the emerging light of early dawn he could see a woman in a long, white dress with a grey shawl around her shoulders. A white, snood-type cap hung down onto her neck, partly covering what he thought was fair hair.

The bedroom used to have two doors, but one of these was bricked up many years ago. The spectral woman appeared to be pushing against where this door had been. Holding out her outstretched hands she pushed hard for a moment, hesitated, stepped back a pace, then moved forward to push once more. Then she vanished. As a discarnate being could easily have passed through the bricked-up doorway, it is possible that the ghostly woman was re-enacting a traumatic time during her earthly life when she was imprisoned in the room and was seeking to escape.

Eddie Dupoy became landlord of the Royal Oak in 1992. From that time on he became aware of a number of weird incidents. Staff working in the kitchen were sometimes touched on the shoulder by an invisible presence, while from time to time the door leading to the kitchen seemed to take on a life of its own.

The door is of the free-swinging type, which enables staff to move to and from the kitchen with ease, even with both hands full. But from time to time an unseen force pushed the door to initiate a series of swings. Stranger still, the door sometimes stopped at an acute point during its swing, remaining in that half-open position for a few moments, before being released again. Experiment has shown that the mechanism of the door should not let this happen.

Mr Dupoy has an interest in antiques. In 1994 he bought an Edwardian chiming clock, but it wasn't in working order, for its pendulum was completely wedged against its case, so preventing all movement. Nevertheless, from time to time, the clock was heard ticking for a few minutes. At other occasions, on looking at its face, Mr Dupoy would discover that the hands had moved quite a distance around the clock. This movement was not random, for the hands almost always stopped precisely on the hour or half-hour!

In 1997, Tony Harman became the Royal Oak's landlord. He had only been at the pub for a few months when kitchen staff told him that they had come on duty that day to find that cooking pans had mysteriously transferred themselves from a kitchen shelf to the floor. Subsequently, and on several occasions, he found that some unknown agency had turned off the gas cylinders in the pub's cellar.

In nearby Wivelsfield Green stands the 200-year-old Cock Inn. Originally known as the Fighting Cock, the inn was once used by smugglers as a half-way house. In the 1970s it was tenanted by Charles Cary, a wartime bomber pilot, and his wife Joyce. They discovered that one of the bedrooms had a cold spot, while from time to time various objects moved eerily around, propelled by some paranormal force. In addition, the first-floor curtains were sometimes snatched down without apparent cause.

Landlord Terry Parrott and his wife Chris took over the Cock in 1987. They had no knowledge of the earlier incidents, but in 1989 they also had the scary experience of finding that curtains on the first floor landing had been torn down by some supernatural force and left in a crumpled heap on the floor. In 1991, the incident was repeated.

In the same year, Mr and Mrs Parrott had not long gone to bed when they were startled to hear the window in the next room – their lounge – squeal open. Thinking it was an intruder, Mr Parrott immediately jumped out of bed and rushed into the room. Switching on the light, he found the sash window wide open and the curtains billowing in the night breeze.

Moving swiftly over to the window he looked out, but there was sign of an intruder or of a ladder.

Mr Parrott was puzzled, for in addition to the window being very tight-fitting and therefore difficult to open, it also had a security fitting designed to prevent it from being opened on the outside. A minute or two later, when Mr Parrott attempted to close the window, he found that it had been forced open so violently that it had become wedged.

There was yet another incident in 1991. Mr and Mrs Parrott had departed to Lanzarote on holiday, so bar manager Matthew Simmonds was left to look after the pub. One night he was woken by the banging of a door. As it was a cold winter's night, he had closed every window, so no doors should have been affected by a draught. As he sat up in bed, he was alarmed to see the shadowy figure of a woman cross the room.

One night in 1994, a couple of hours after they had gone to bed, Mr and Mrs Parrott were woken by a loud screeching noise. It seemed to come from the direction of the landing, some ten yards away. Mr Parrott said it sounded a bit like the screech of an owl except that it continued for about a minute. He added that no owl outside of the building could possibly have sounded as loud.

In January 1995, two customers sitting in one of the bars during a quiet time of the evening were astonished to see some bottles shoot off a bar shelf to land on the floor a few feet away from them. On a separate occasion, another customer who had been sitting alone in the bar claimed he had seen the ghost of a woman walk across the room before fading away.

Once, a table-lamp situated by a bar window repeatedly flicked on and off of its own accord. It had been left switched off, and a close check of the lamp revealed nothing untoward. The lamp's power plug was situated behind fixed furniture, so a panel of this was unscrewed to check the plug. Inexplicably, the switch next to the plug was found to be off. As it was permanently left on behind the panel, who could have switched it off? And with both the lamp and plug switches in the off position, how could the lamp have repeatedly lit up?

Just beyond Wivelsfield and alongside the old turnpike road leading to Haywards Heath stands the Fox and Hounds. This ancient hostelry, part of which dates back to the 18th century, was originally an alehouse called the Anchor. Chris and Anne Worrall were in charge of the pub for 20 years until leaving at the end of the 1980s.

Mrs Worrall said that a ghost nicknamed 'Fred' occasionally threw bottles and other objects around in the oldest part of the building, while one friend who stayed on at the pub after closing time insisted he saw an spectral old man sitting in a corner. In addition, some customers who had called at the pub in earlier years claimed they had seen the apparition of a woman wearing a grey dress in the area of the ladies' toilet. A major modernisation of the premises in 1995 could well have chased away any lingering spirits.

27 *Weird tales*

IN HIS BOOK *Ghosts Over Britain,* author Peter Moss tells the story of a modest, 16th century manor house located in a hamlet not far from Brighton which was the scene of some particularly disturbing manifestations. The exact site of the house is not revealed, for the owner was an international airline pilot whose capacity to fly might have been questioned had he been associated with the claims of the story.

The initial evidence of something unusual came in 1961 when the pilot's wife, referred to in the book as Mrs Forster, was sitting down to breakfast with her four children – her husband was away at the time. They were surprised to hear piano music coming from the room immediately above them, for there was no piano in the house.

Mrs Forster described the tune as unidentifiable – more like an improvisation. The least surprised member of the household was Mrs Forster's youngest son, then aged six, who chose that moment to reveal that he had heard the mystery piano playing on several earlier occasions. The ghostly music episode was to repeat itself several months later.

All was then normal until 1963 when a particularly unnerving incident took place. Mrs Forster was in the kitchen, ironing her daughter's white school blouse, when a spurt of red liquid, apparently blood, dropped onto one of the sleeves. Mrs Forster thought that her nose must have started to bleed, but when she found this was not the case, and seeing no other reason for the red stain, she attempted to wash it out in cold water, but the stain refused to go away.

Returning to the ironing board, Mrs Forster was astonished to see a fresh globule of red liquid on the cover. Looking up, she noted that the ceiling was unmarked, nor was there any crack in the plaster that might have allowed something to seep through. As with the piano music, the blood-like substance was to make a reappearance. This came 13 years later in 1976 when Mrs Forster went into the kitchen to find a still wet pool of the scarlet liquid on a melamine-surfaced table. The table was situated in a quite different position to that of the ironing board.

Earlier, on an autumn evening in 1973, Mrs Forster had supper with the children in her daughter's bedroom prior to retiring early to her own bedroom to read before going to sleep. Shortly after she had climbed into the four-poster bed (her husband was away on duty at the time), she heard the door of the room swing open with the usual click of the latch and creak of hinges. She looked up from her book, assuming that one of the children had entered the room. Instead, she was astonished to see the figure of an elderly lady who was unknown to her.

The woman seemed to be quite solid and real. She peered through a pair of metal-rimmed spectacles and had slightly wavy grey hair which was drawn back into a bun. Her long, grey, classically-styled dress featured a lace jabot at the neckline. After pausing for a moment, the woman clasped her hands in front of her and with light, short steps began to walk towards the bed. Bewildered rather than frightened, Mrs Forster called out to ask the woman who she was, but at the moment that the words left her lips, the unexpected visitor faded away.

Subsequently, Mrs Forster discovered, her description of the ghostly woman tallied with that of a Miss Thynne who had lived in the house 15 years earlier and who had tragically perished in a fire. The bedroom in which Mrs Forster slept was the one Miss Thynne had used during her residence in the house.

Some 12 months later, in the summer of 1974, a young man from the Argentine who was a guest of the Forsters slept in the same room. He was unaware of the supernatural aspect of the house, but at breakfast one morning he asked who had been calling under the window at night. The Forsters were shaken when he revealed the words the caller had used. They were: "Miss Thynne! Miss Thynne!"

The most frightening happening at the house had already taken place two years earlier when a friend of the family, a hospital nurse, stayed overnight in the bedroom next to the one in which the elderly lady was to appear. The nurse awoke to a sensation of suffocating heat which was quickly followed by a prickling of the scalp. Her alarm greatly increased when she saw a pair of disembodied hands and arms at the far side of the room. They hovered at normal body height before moving slowly towards the bed. The hands began to make menacing movements and a palpable sense of evil filled the room.

At this point, the nurse opened her mouth to scream, but with fear paralysing her throat, no sound emerged. By this time the hands, with fingers extended and slightly curved, had reached the bedposts. In desperation and hurrying her words, the nurse began reciting the Lord's Prayer. Such was her terror at the time she can't recall whether she did so silently or aloud, but whichever it was, on reaching the line 'Deliver us from evil', the threatening hands went away and the atmosphere of the room returned to normal. Although continuing to visit the house, the nurse could not be persuaded to sleep there again.

Duncton Down, by the village of Clayton, is the site of two windmills known as Jack and Jill. Jack is a black tower mill built in 1866 to replace the old Duncton post mill, which in 1808 had dragged a young man named Penfold to a terrible death when his smock became caught in the cogs. Jack ceased working in 1908 and is today a private residence. Jill, a white post mill, was originally built in 1821 on the site of the previous Old Hove Mill in Dyke Road, but in about 1852 a team of oxen was used to pull it over the Downs by trolley sledge to its present site. This mill was kept in use until 1909. Restored by enthusiasts, it is now open to the public on specified days.

After the mills had ceased to operate, geologist and naturalist Henry Martin used Jack as a holiday home. The two cottages situated by the mills had for many years been occupied by the miller and a shepherd. This situation continued for a while, though with a carter replacing the miller. In 1911, biographer Captain Walter Anson and his wife took over the mills and associated cottages.

The couple lived mainly in the cottages while using Jack as a workroom and for storage purposes. Captain Anson died not long after the First World War, but Mrs Anson remained to spend a total of 40 years at the mills. An elderly lady companion, Miss Jones, and an ex-naval stoker who dealt with the heavier chores around the place, stayed on after Captain Anson's death. Mrs Anson died eventually of a chest infection.

In 1953 Henry Longhurst, golf correspondent of the *Sunday Times*, acquired the mills and cottages. He and his wife soon discovered that the spirit of Mrs Anson was reluctant to leave the home which she had grown to love.

Captain Anson had installed six bells in the kitchen of one of the cottages. These were connected to various rooms, and up into Jack, and were of the type used to summon servants. Prior to the furniture being moved in, Mrs Longhurst and the builder were alone in the kitchen when all six bells rang at once. They not only heard the bells, but could actually see them ringing. They checked to ensure that no one else was in the cottages. Soon afterwards, the builder opened a kitchen cupboard and an old broom shot out at him.

On their very first night in the house, the Longhursts had their sleep interrupted by the ringing of a bell. Mr Longhurst jumped out of bed, grabbed a torch, and went into the nearby kitchen. He saw that the third bell from the left was swinging. He began to follow the wire, but his nerve failed him. When morning came, he traced the wire to the other cottage and a small room where it terminated with a meagre length of wire hanging from the ceiling.

On a later occasion Mrs Longhurst and her mother were sitting by the fireplace in the granary when a pair of tongs leapt into the air and shot across the fireplace. Sometimes, objects in the house were found to have been moved. Little happened during the Longhursts' residence beyond these few eerie incidents but for one persistent happening. This was the sound of Mrs Anson's characteristic cough, which came from the bedroom she had once used. The dry cough was heard both when the room was empty and when someone was sleeping there. In 1963 the cottages, not very comfortable and difficult to maintain, were knocked down and a modern dwelling was erected on the site. In 1973, the location was used in a spy film, *The Black Windmill.*

For almost 40 years, Muriel Attmere lived in one of the most unusual homes in Sussex, for Tunnel Cottage is not only perched directly above the busy London to Brighton railway line, but it also looks in part like a medieval castle, for a castellated Gothic tower stands at each end of the cottage. To add to its curiosity, the place is also haunted!

The cottage, above the north end of the mile-long Clayton Tunnel, near Hassocks, was built in 1836. Initially it was used as a pay office for the navvies digging the new cutting and also by railway police, but in 1841 a railwayman called Russell began living there with his wife and nine children.

Mrs Attmere and her former railway guard husband moved into Tunnel Cottage in 1956 when the rent was just 20 old pence (9p) a week. When she moved out, in 1994, the rent had climbed to £22.50 a week! Mrs Attmere brought up her six children and three grandchildren in the cottage and was very happy there, though she did say the place was haunted.

There were, she claimed, two ghosts; 'Old Charlie' and a White Lady. Old Charlie was quite friendly, but Mrs Attmere did brick up a small tunnel behind her shower tiles to deaden his ghostly footsteps. And she occasionally heard what sounded like a man's groans. Though Mrs Attmere never saw the White Lady, she was sometimes aware of her presence. Once, however, two of her grandchildren called from their bedroom to ask her to take away 'a white-looking woman' who had appeared in the room.

There was also a mysterious white light which sometimes appeared on top of one of the towers. In addition, Mrs Attmere heard groans and what seemed like conversations coming from the tunnel itself. There were also, she said, clammy feelings which came without warning and stenchy smells which followed her around. Other people, when close by the entrance of the tunnel itself, claim to have heard faint, agonised cries coming out of the blackness.

The ghosts are believed to be victims of one or more of the several tragedies which have taken place in the tunnel. In August 1861, 21 people died and almost 200 were injured when trains collided in the tunnel. In 1897, a man who entered the tunnel late at night was horribly mangled by a train. In 1926 there was another train disaster with 26 deaths. The victims of both disasters were laid out in the orchard which slopes away from the cottage. In the early 1970s, four soldiers from the Territorial Army were killed by an oncoming train after they had lost their way and ventured into the tunnel.

When Roger Lewendon became landlord of the Ringmer Inn, in the Sussex village of Ringmer, in 1976, he wasn't aware that it had a ghostly past, but over the following months he experienced a number of weird incidents; the till ringing up when no one was nearby, bottles shooting off shelves, gas cylinders in the cellar turning off, locked doors swinging open, cellar lights switching on and off, and the shuffle of ghostly footsteps on the landing.

In 1977, he reported a regular late night banging which he likened to a sledgehammer hitting the walls. Exasperated, he called in some local ghost hunters, who spent a night at the pub with their cameras and recording equipment. Unexpectedly, following upon their vigil, all anomalous incidents ceased, seemingly for good. In the early 1990s the pub was refurbished prior to reopening under a new name, the Classic. It finally closed at the end of 1997 prior to demolition.

After dark one night in 1981, Rod Patterson was driving the five miles from Lewes to visit a friend in the village of Laughton. Turning into a side road on reaching the village, he was slightly surprised when his headlights picked out a white column of what he thought was mist, for it was otherwise a clear night. At the exact point where the car reached the mist, perplexingly, the engine stopped and the headlights went out. The immediate interpretation was that the car's electrical system had failed.

As Mr Patterson peered out of his car, he saw that the column of mist had dispersed. He also found that the car's electrics were once again working. Later, on thinking about the incident, he recalled that the column of mist was about human size.

It used to be said that a man could be living dangerously in more ways than one if he took his mistress away for a naughty weekend at the King's Head Hotel, in South Street, Cuckfield, for he might suffer the disapproval of the delightfully named Geranium Jane, a resident ghost that strongly objected to men who engaged in extramarital activities. Regrettably, the hotel closed in 1996 prior to being converted into flats.

The building dates from about 1840 and was a replacement for a hotel of the same name which had been built in the 1790s at the corner of Ockenden Lane. This earlier building was used by the Prince Regent (later to become George IV) as a rest stage during his coach journeys between London and Brighton. The new King's Head took over the business of its predecessor when that establishment closed, both hotels having the same proprietor.

The ghost known as Geranium Jane is that of a maid who worked at the King's Head for a period during the latter half of the 1800s. The landlord at the time took a liking to her and an illicit affair began. The girl eventually became pregnant. An argument between the two took place one day in one of the bedrooms and the landlord, in a fit of fury, smashed a pot of geraniums on the poor girl's head. She died almost immediately.

The ghost of Geranium Jane is said to bring with it the smell of the flower associated with her nickname. She has no quarrel with women, reserving her appearances for men alone. While men faithful to their marriage vows might catch a fleeting glimpse of her, those straying from the path of fidelity might find themselves subjected to tangible signs of disapproval.

On one occasion, a married male employee living-in at the hotel woke up to find his bed being pushed around the room by some unseen force. He had been enjoying an affair with another woman, but his terrified nocturnal cries indicated that his clandestine activities were no secret to Geranium Jane. On numerous occasions, ornaments and other objects around the hotel mysteriously vanished, only to reappear hours or days later, while lights switched on and off of their own accord.

Ted and Christine Murphy were 'mine hosts' at the King's Head in the 1970s. Number 2 bedroom was the room in which Geranium Jane met her death and in 1972, Mr Murphy, a former Mayor of Cuckfield, briefly came face to face with the misty apparition of a woman close to this room.

One breakfast time two or three years later, Mr Murphy was confronted by a very agitated building trade executive who had stayed overnight in Number 2 bedroom. He had woken up to find his bed vibrating wildly and the window curtains billowing and flapping in an unnatural way. Only a few nights earlier the man had stayed at the hotel with a woman who, it transpired, was not his wife.

Geranium Jane is not the only spooky resident reported, for the ghost of a small boy haunted the bar. Although not seen in more recent years, he made his presence felt from time to time by causing a small area of the bar to become unnaturally cold. On these occasions, any dogs brought into the bar by customers would apprehensively circumvent the area, sometimes with their fur hackling.

While the King's Head was almost certainly haunted, it has been suggested by some that the story of Geranium Jane is an addition invented by a landlord of many years ago to provide extra colour to an existing haunting.

Writer Virginia Woolf, who lived at Asham House, Beddingham, near Lewes, from 1912 to 1919, is said to have based her short story, *The Haunted House,* on the ghosts that inhabited her 19th century cottage, which was demolished in 1993.

'Whatever hour you woke, there was a door shutting. From room to room they went, hand in hand, lifting here, opening there, making sure – a ghostly couple.'

The spectre of a veiled woman in a white dress haunts Isfield Station, the main station on the private railway line operated by the Lavender Line Preservation Society. The story of this ghost dates back to the 1914-18 War, when the line was part of the old London, Brighton & South Coast Railway.

A local woman married to a private soldier bade him farewell at the station prior to his departure for the battlefields of France. He never returned. Soon after the War Office telegram reporting his death reached the woman, she walked to the station and threw herself in front of the Lewes-bound train.

Reports of the spectral woman in white date back to the 1920s, but since the line, which had been derelict for some years, was acquired by the Lavender Line Preservation Society in 1983 and brought back to functional use, the wife of one of the directors and at least two volunteer staff have witnessed the apparition.

The woman in white is seen to emerge from the staff entrance of the station buffet, which used to be the ladies' waiting room, before walking along Platform 1 until she reaches the level crossing gates. She then crosses the line to the signal box, where she disappears.

A sidelight to the story is that a bowl of water, regularly placed by the main buffet entrance for the use of thirsty dogs, was once temporarily moved to the staff door, from where the ghost is said to emerge. It was noticed that dogs became most reluctant to use the bowl when it was in this position.

But the woman in white is not the only ghost haunting the station, for a man wearing an old-fashioned railway uniform has been seen in the vicinity of the railway shed. One old engine shed, said to have a spooky atmosphere, was bulldozed in the 1980s. Now, though the building no longer stands, some say that the area still exhudes a forbidding aura.

There is also a railway ghost story connected with the Bluebell Line at Sheffield Park. This relates to a ghastly presence said to have been seen as a consequence of a murder which took place in a gangers' hut known as Pope's Cottage. Research has established that no such murder took place, though of course there may be some other ghostly visitation associated with the railway line.

28 *Shadowlands*

IN SEPTEMBER 1933, Mr and Mrs King moved into the manor house at Denton, Newhaven. Settling in with them was their 12-year-old daughter; also Mrs Heasman, Mrs King's elderly mother. The house, comprised of 14 rooms and a gloomy cellar, was built in 1724, close by the local church. The house became a rectory in 1973.

All was peaceful until the November of 1933, when there was a mighty crash from an upstairs room. It was as if a heavy piece of furniture had toppled over. The Kings found no reason for the noise. On the following Sunday, Mrs King was walking along an upstairs corridor when she was faced by a phantom figure. Its gender was uncertain, for its appearance was indistinct, but it was terrifying enough to bring screams to the lips of the woman. The screams brought her husband from a bedroom.

Wondering if his wife had come across an intruder, Mr King grabbed a walking stick before racing into the corridor. In the corridor he also saw the apparition, and rushed at it with the stick raised. When he brought it down, the stick went straight through the spectre before making a groove in the plaster of the wall. At the moment the stick struck the wall, the shadowy figure faded from sight.

As the figure departed, four thunderous crashes reverberated throughout the house. Over the next four days, these crashes were repeated with frightening regularity at about five-hourly intervals. They were loud enough to be heard in the nearby lane and seemed to originate from the centre of the building, being usually heard at twenty to, or twenty past the hour.

Mrs King, especially, was very distressed by these events. As a consequence, on the third day, the local rector was called in. The Rev Pinnix arrived in time to hear the crashes for himself. Although he said prayers in an attempt to stop further manifestations, the noises were heard again that day, and the Kings sought sanctuary in a house a quarter of a mile away.

The haunting was beginning to attract some attention and that night a group of local people gathered outside the house. A police constable, provided with a house key by the Kings, was posted at the front door of the property. The vigil was not in vain. At 10.20 that evening, there was a series of bangs. The constable decided to investigate. No doubt more than a little apprehensive, he allowed some of the onlookers to join him as he searched the house. Nothing was found, though one of the searchers claimed to have felt some invisible being brush past him in the darkness.

The *Evening Argus* despatched a reporter. Arriving, he found that the Kings were already packing their belongings. With Mrs King close to collapse, the family felt they could no longer remain in such a frightening environment.

The journalist reported: 'I heard the noises myself. I was standing in one of the rooms talking to the rector when suddenly, from the direction of the scullery, there came the sound of four distinct knockings, followed by a shriek from Mrs King.' The reporter also commented on a cellar door which he observed was wide open, even though he knew it had been bolted moments earlier and that no one had been near it.

After the Kings had left the house for good, hundreds of people arrived by foot and car, and even by coach, to gather in the lane in the hope that something might happen. For two successive evenings the crowds waited, shivering in the damp cold of November, but all in vain.

On the third night, a Saturday, as nothing had taken place over the previous two evenings, the number of onlookers had dwindled. But this time those who remained until well after darkness were rewarded with the chilling sound of four loud crashes coming from inside the empty house. Though there were further vigils over the following evenings, it was the end of the manifestations. There were no further incidents and the following occupants commented that the house radiated quite a peaceful atmosphere.

Later, there were suggestions that the ghost was that of a Miss Catt, a former owner of the house, who resented the fact that Mr King had felled two trees in the garden which she had personally planted. It was reasoned that as the manifestations took place only while the Kings were in residence – except for the Saturday incident – the matter was self-evident. Others suggested that the whole affair was a poltergeist phenomenon centered on the Kings' 12-year-old daughter.

Though small, the Sussex village of Hellingly, near Hailsham, has several haunted sites. One is Horselunges Manor where, in 1547, John Busbrig died while fighting off a gang of poachers. His ghost is said to haunt this 15th century timber building.

While ghosts are not too uncommon in old hotels, to find such spectral 'guests' haunting a newer hotel is rare, but it does happen. The Forte Travelodge in Hellingly is such a hotel, for it was only completed in 1991. Here, a spectral woman has been seen by both staff and guests.

Sally David stayed at the hotel over two nights during March 1995, she and a lady friend occupying Room 15. Miss David slept soundly on the first night of her stay, but sometime during the second night she awoke to see a woman standing by the window of her room. At first she thought it was her friend, but in the next moment she realised her friend was still fast asleep in the bed next to her own.

In view of this, the perplexed Miss David took a harder look at the figure by the window. Dawn was filtering through the drawn curtains and it had become light enough for Miss David to establish that the woman was wearing a cream-coloured cloak that seemed to entirely hide her arms and hands.

The woman appeared to be fairly tall, and despite the rather voluminous garment, Miss David had the impression that she was quite thin. The woman's hair was short with large curls, as if rollers had been used, then removed, with the hair being left uncombed. She seemed to be staring out of the window, even though the curtains were drawn.

After just moments, the spectral figure slowly faded. Miss David said she felt no alarm, but what she found unusual about the episode – and this may be of especial interest to readers engaged in paranormal research – was that the woman appeared to her in sharp detail. Normally, being short-sighted, Miss David would have had to be wearing spectacles to achieve such visual precision.

Approximately a month after her initial visit, Miss David again stayed at the hotel, this time being allotted Room 2. She didn't know whether to be relieved or disappointed to find that on this occasion her sleep remained undisturbed by any ethereal entity.

Miss David, on enquiry, learned that an apparition clothed in the same voluminous robe as she had described had, in the past, been seen at various times by both chambermaids and guests, though usually in a different room. Some chambermaids, aware of 'a peculiar atmosphere' in a certain part of the hotel, have preferred to work in pairs while carrying out their duties. It has been suggested that the ghost is that of a pig farmer's wife who lived in the cottage which once stood where the hotel now stands, and who ended her life by suicide.

Not much more than a stone's throw from the Travelodge is the Boship Farm Hotel. As the name suggests, the building was once a farmhouse. It dates back to 1652 and is allegedly haunted. The fascinating thing about this hotel's ghost is that it tucks people up in bed and kisses them! Over the years, a number of hotel employees and guests have reported the bedtime attentions of the spectre, which seems to be quite gentle in its approach.

One hotel employee, describing her experience, which took place just after she had switched off the light and gone to bed, said that the bedclothes, which had been over the lower part of her head, were pulled down so that they were just below her chin. What followed she described as being not so much a kiss as a momentary feeling of warmth on her face, after which there was another slight adjustment of the bedclothes by the unseen visitor!

No one is recorded as having actually seen the ghost, but some hotel employees, while going about their duties, have referred to a feeling of being watched by an unseen presence. It is not certain how long the kissing ghost has haunted the building, but it was certainly around in the 1940s. It was still a farmhouse at the time, but the farmer rented rooms to holidaymakers and an elderly lady and her friend, staying at the farmhouse, both reported being tucked in and kissed by the ghost.

Might there be a connection with the ghost at the Boship Farm Hotel and a ghost seen in an adjoining field? In 1989 the field was being used as a caravan park and in the summer of that year Hilda Banks and her three married daughters – Joyce Fairburn, Valerie Price and Jennifer Pearce – spent a weekend in one of the caravans.

They had been playing cards and during an interval one of the daughters peered out of a window. The light was just beginning to fade at the end of the day, but at the bottom of the field she could distinctly see a woman dressed in a long white gown. It seemed an odd thing to be wearing in such a place, but there was also something about the woman that seemed unearthly.

She called on the others to take a look and all four women huddled around the caravan windows. As they watched, the figure in white seemingly rose from a depression in the ground before vanishing. It later transpired that the occupants of the caravan next to them had also seen the mysterious woman in white and had also thought she was a ghost.

In 1985, Robert Saunders was relaxing in a deckchair in the garden of his in-laws' house, The Fair Place, in the village of Lower Dicker, near Hailsham. He and his wife Caroline were spending the weekend there. As he turned the pages of his newspaper, he became aware that he wasn't alone in the garden. Looking up, he saw a young woman walking past some shrubbery just a few yards in front of him.

His wife and her parents had not long left the house to go shopping in

Hailsham, so presuming the woman had come to see his in-laws, he rose from his deckchair to apologise for their absence. At the sound of his voice, the woman faded away. Mr Saunders recalled the disorientating experience.

"She was passing some bushes, so I couldn't see the bottom half of her. She had short, dark hair and was wearing what seemed to be a darkish blouse. She looked as if she was in her late twenties and was only in view for about three seconds.

A lady in blue and a man in a white coat are reputed to haunt Deans Place Hotel, in the ancient village of Alfriston. Staff have also reported lights and radios switching on and off without human aid. The hotel was initially a manor house. The earliest reference to private occupation links it with John de Dene and early records describe the property as Dene's Place. In time, common usage led to it being known as Deans Place. There was an earlier building on the site which belonged to Wilmington Priory.

Towards the end of the 19th century a woman was washing up in the back kitchen when she heard a rap on the door. Calling on the visitor to enter, the woman was surprised to be confronted by a beautiful lady in a bright blue dress. A moment later, the lady in blue had vanished as abruptly as she had appeared.

Over the years, the phantom lady was sighted by a number of guests and staff, as well as in the 1960s by the five-year-old daughter of a Mrs Saddler, of Hastings. One of the most recent sightings took place in the early 1990s when the phantom lady materialised in front of an astonished resident as he was walking along one of the hotel's corridors.

The ghost of a thin man in a tall hat and wearing a white coat has also been seen at Deans Place. Which of the two ghosts was responsible for resoundingly ringing the dinner gong some years ago is a matter for conjecture, but it gave the duty receptionist quite a shock, for the gong was sited close by the reception desk and there wasn't any human to be seen striking it.

Andrew Hillier, the hotel's general manager, reported an even stranger incident. In 1993, an elderly couple staying at the hotel decided to spend the evening in their room watching TV. The man, who was disabled and needed two sticks to help him walk, had settled in an armchair. Eventually, he drifted off to sleep. Some minutes later his wife, who had remained awake, was horrified to see some invisible force lift her husband out of his chair and lower him gently onto the floor some two or three feet in front of the chair.

On another occasion, in the early 1990s, an American visitor to the hotel approached Mr Hillier to tell him that he had seen a ghostly dog running around the hotel car park – a small white dog that faded into thin air as he watched. Might this spectral animal have a connection with another Alfriston ghost, that of a former heir to the Chowne Estate who, in the 18th century, lived at Place House, Frog Firle?

One evening, this young man decided to go out for a stroll along the White Way, a stretch of road that runs between Deans Place Hotel and Frog Firle. With him was his faithful white dog. This particular evening a gang of rogues waylaid young Chowne and clubbed him to death. To cover up their crime, the men hurriedly buried their victim in a field by the road, but when they found that the victim's whimpering dog was determined to remain by its dead master's grave, they decided that it must die too.

Seven years later, a young couple were out for a walk along the White Way when they were surprised to see a white dog running alongside them. They were wondering who it might belong to, when it vanished. Legend has it that every seven years since then, the ghost of the young heir, sometimes with his dog and sometimes not, returns to haunt the White Way.

Early in the 19th century workmen discovered the crouching skeleton of a man during excavations to widen the road, and it was concluded that this was the murdered heir. The affair was commemorated in a song, one verse of which goes:

When evening closes in with shadows grey,
And the ghostly vapours overhang White Way,
And the crescent moon hangs gloomy in the west,
'Tis then the spirit of young Chowne can't rest,
But walks abroad with melancholy stride,
A-down the path that skirts the chalk hillside.

There is a footnote to this story. According to author Ronald Boyd, some years after the murder of the heir, an old tramp confessed his involvement as he lay dying in a London lodging house. As the tramp's final hours ticked by, he revealed that he had taken part in the robbery of the young heir, but not in the actual murder. The murderers, he said, were some harvesters who were with him. All they were after was some money to enable them to go drinking, but the situation got badly out of hand.

Alfriston's ancient Star Inn, a residential hotel, is another haunted property. Originally built in the 13th century, it is one of the country's oldest inns. Major rebuilding work took place in 1450. There was further rebuilding in 1520, when the inn was known as the Star of Bethlehem.

Looked after by the monks of Battle Abbey, it was a resting place for pilgrims making the journey to Canterbury and also to Chichester to visit the shrine of Richard de Lawych, who became St Richard of Chichester. A red lion figurehead positioned on a corner of the inn is said to be from a Dutch naval vessel sunk at Sole Bay in 1672 by the warship *Duke of York*.

Two ghosts have been reported as haunting the hotel. One is that of a man wearing medieval dress; the other is described as looking like an old farmer. The farmer is the most active of the two spectres – the man in medieval dress has not been seen for some years, though he may be responsible for the ghostly footsteps sometimes heard walking the corridors of the hotel.

In 1996 several residents witnessed the spectral farmer at the same time when he appeared for a few moments in the lounge, sitting underneath the clock. The farmer also materialised twice in the attic bedroom of maintenance man Don MacDougall. The bedroom is situated next to a storeroom and a door connects the two rooms.

In 1995 Mr MacDougall was in bed awake when he saw the farmer walk across the room as if emerging from the storeroom. The farmer then stood still for a moment and seemed to stare at something before turning on his heels and retracing his steps. Mr MacDougall always left his bathroom light on at night with the door ajar, so was able to see the farmer quite clearly.

Two months later, Mr MacDougall witnessed the apparition again. This time he was in bed watching television and had just got out of bed to switch the TV off. The farmer's movements, he observed, seemed exactly to replicate those of the previous visitation. Oddly, Mr MacDougall never actually saw the farmer enter or return through the door leading to the storeroom. The farmer just materialised and dematerialised a couple of paces away from it.

Mr MacDougall described the man as being about 60 years of age and of medium build. He was wearing a floppy, trilby-like hat, a smock, and tied-on leggings – the latter looked as if they were made of hessian. All of the man's clothing was grey in colour.

On the next floor down and immediately underneath this attic bedroom are two adjoining bedrooms which seem especially to attract paranormal activities. The lock on the door of one of these rooms self-locks from time to time and both residents and staff have found themselves locked in and have had to use the internal telephone to gain their release. The fitting of a new lock made no difference.

In March 1996, a married couple stayed in one of the rooms. When the woman went into the bathroom to take a shower, the recessed light in the shower area repeatedly switched on and off. The woman, unaware of the room's spooky reputation, reported the 'fault', but an electrician failed to find anything wrong. When the couple went to bed, the woman, who liked plenty of fresh air, opened the window wide. When she awoke, she was puzzled to find it closed. Other residents have reported that the room's shower unit mysteriously turns off while in use.

Late one evening in April 1996, catering manager David Piper and barmaid Toni Houghton left the hotel's kitchen, each with a cup of freshly made coffee in their hands. Having locked the door behind them, they began to make their way to the reception office, but had only taken a few steps when they heard a mighty crash from the kitchen. On unlocking the kitchen door, they were amazed to find that a kitchen unit carrying a variety of pots and pans had toppled over. Logically, there was no way that this free-standing unit could have fallen without being forcibly pushed.

Many years ago, some Star Inn employees were accommodated at a nearby cottage, but they didn't remain long because of the frightening ghostly activities they had to endure. Later, they heard that there had been a murder on the premises.

Another Alfriston hostelry, the 600-year-old Smugglers Inn, also known as the Market Cross Inn, is haunted by a woman wearing a long white gown. She has been seen walking across a bar at the rear of the pub before drifting through a wall. A builder, who was also a customer, was once carrying out some repair work at the pub. When in the area of the men's toilet, he experienced a disturbing atmosphere and was touched on the shoulder by something unseen.

Ronald Boyd, in his book about Alfriston, tells of a motorist and his wife who, many years ago, stopped at the inn. The wife claimed she had seen three men enter the inn carrying a heavy load. They were dressed in the style of the early 19th century and appeared to be quarreling, though no actual sound came from their lips. The inn was originally a private residence known as Market Cross House. It was at one time the home of Stanton Collins, the notorious leader of a band of smugglers known as the Alfriston Gang.

Tuckvar, a fine 200-year-old house in Alfriston's West Street, might have three ghosts. One is that of an old man, possibly a groom, who wears a long apron and who has been observed peering through the windows of the house. Another phantom is that of an elderly, grey-haired woman, said to be a former housekeeper. On one occasion she materialised in one of the bedrooms prior to tucking in and kissing a child.

The third ghost is of a cat, though the animal is never seen. Sometimes the sound of purring can be heard on the top of a writing desk, but only if someone is actually seated there. It is said that the desk was purchased from a woman who bred cats.

In 1976, Gary Buckland was an 18-year-old civil engineering apprentice living in Sussex whose daily journey to work by motorcycle took him into the adjoining county of Kent. One evening after work, while travelling homewards along the stretch of road between Alfriston and Drusilla's Zoo Park, he was disturbed by a clattering noise. Thinking something was wrong with his motorbike, he immediately braked. He then realised the noise had nothing to do with his bike, for the sound he now heard was the measured clip-clop of horses' hooves and the rattle of steel-rimmed wheels.

Mr Buckland quickly flicked off his ignition to hear the unfamiliar sound as it drew away from him before fading into the distance. It was as if some invisible horse-drawn waggon had trundled past. He waited and listened for a while, but no further noises broke the silence. He stirred his motorcycle into life once more and continued his journey.

Might there be a connection between this incident and Drusilla's? Up until 1923, the mill which once stood on the site of the zoo was used for grinding animal bones to produce glue and fertiliser. It is said that the horses pulling the waggon-loads of bones and end products to and from the mill could sense the aura of animal death that pervaded the place and often displayed a nervousness when approaching it.

29 *Michelham Priory*

MICHELHAM PRIORY, in Upper Dicker, near Hailsham, seems a tranquil place, yet it has had a troubled history. Possibly this turbulent past has contributed to it being considered one of the most haunted buildings in Sussex. The priory was founded in 1229 for a group of Augustinian canons by Gilbert de l'Aigle or d'Aquila, whose family came from the town of L'Aigle in Normandy, but work on the building proceeded at an exceedingly slow pace.

Six years after building had begun, de Aquila returned to his Normandy home, leaving the priory only half-completed. This enraged Henry III, who had granted the Licence for the foundation, causing him to demand the return of substantial tracts of land surrounding the priory.

Over the following years, priors arrived and departed with disturbing frequency, while a number of irregularities took place to discredit the Order. Meanwhile, the completion of the priory seemed to remain frustratingly fixed on the horizon. In 1348 the Black Death scoured through the local community. It reduced the resident number of canons from 13 to a mere five.

In 1374 the appointment of John Leem as prior heralded a more productive period for the priory. A generous and warm-hearted man, he brought energy and enthusiasm to his work, but it was a time fraught with danger, for an angry peasantry was rising up against the vicious poll tax and French raiders were regularly attacking along the coast. In the circumstances, one of Prior Leem's initial tasks was to enlarge the small gatehouse so as to provide greater protection for the priory. He also organised the help of villagers in forming a defence force to combat the intermittent and devastating incursions of the French.

John Leem's dedication to his duties and his friendly nature gained him a loyal and responsive following, which helped significantly to increase the funds of the priory. However, the 43 years of devoted service he contributed to his community was soon negated by his less worthy successors. Their apathy and incompetence meant that priory buildings were allowed to decay and food stocks diminish. The continuing mismanagement led to a curtailment of the financial support that came from a number of sources. As a consequence of all this, it became not uncommon to find demoralised friars drunkenly disporting themselves in nearby hostelries.

The reign of Henry VIII eventually led to the closure of the priory. The king required the wealth of the monastries to boost his coffers and to provide for the defence of the realm. By his decree, the religious houses of England were closed between 1536 and 1540 and their property confiscated. Michelham Priory was dissolved in 1537. The jewels, silver vessels and church ornaments were sold, as were the priory's five magnificent bells, and the church and the eastern range were demolished for their salvage value.

In 1556 the Crown sold the priory to John Foote of Arlington, who had been the tenant since 1542. He remained until 1574 and during this time he modified the western range and erected an extension to live in. After two changes of ownership, during which time the priory was allowed to deteriorate, it was purchased in 1587 by the influential Herbert Pelham, whose forefathers had arrived in England with William the Conqueror.

Although Herbert Pelham had an income from a foundry owned by the Pelham family in addition to the income he gained from the farmland surrounding the priory, his lavish building programme at Michelham and his purchases of land elsewhere led, in 1599, to his bankruptcy. As a result, all of Mr Pelham's property was placed in the hands of trustees so that it could be used to clear his debts.

In 1601 the trustees sold the priory to Thomas Sackville and for almost 300 years the property remained as part of the Sackville family's extensive estates, the buildings and surrounding land being occupied by a succession of tenants. In the 1890s the Sackvilles decided to sell the priory outright. One potential purchaser, a rich farmer, was greatly enraged to discover that while negotiations were still taking place, the Sackville family had, without telling him, sold the property to James Gwynne, a prosperous Midlands industrialist known as 'The Iron Master'.

When, in the autumn of 1896, an arrogant Mr Gwynne arrived on the scene astride a white stallion like some conquering warrior to claim his property, the furious farmer quickly made the Midlander aware of his feelings. Mr Gwynne's horse was soon galloping riderless into the distance with its bruised and humiliated owner left fuming on the ground.

To his credit, even though he continued to reside at his own home, Folkington Manor, James Gwynne dutifully continued with the restoration of the priory. He and his family restored the prior's chamber and added a top floor and roof to the west wing. Possibly the financial commitment became too burdensome in the long run, for in 1925 the Gwynne family sold the priory to Richard Beresford-Wright, who continued the restoration work, paying especial attention to the near-derelict refectory.

In December 1927 a disastrous fire swept through the priory, gutting the Tudor Wing. Only days after the fire, Mr Beresford-Wright was dismayed to find that the horses in his stables were covered in sweat and shaking with uncontrollable terror. There was no evident reason for their distress. Some weeks later, the horses again showed signs of terror, contorting their bodies and violently kicking the walls of the stables. Arriving on the scene, Mr Beresford-Wright questioned the stable boy, who suggested that their fear could have been precipitated by a huge white stallion which had appeared on the scene on several occasions without warning.

No explanation was ever found to account for the sudden and startling appearances of the white horse, but another mystery followed. Several times, friends visiting the Beresford-Wrights reported that they had been met at the gatehouse by 'a charming gentleman who smiled, and pointed to where the house lay, as if directing us'.

Descriptions of the man, who always stayed silent, indicated that he was wearing the apparel of an Augustinian prior. This comprised a dark cloak, a white underskirt and open sandals, while his hair was cut to resemble Christ's crown of thorns. If, after leaving him, the visitors turned around, their eyes would search in vain for a sight of the man. The owners were puzzled by these reports, for they had no knowledge of any prior-like figure, though the height and friendly nature of the individual described suggested that these visitors might have been witnessing the apparition of Prior John Leem.

Another ghost was soon to make its appearance. This time it was an unhappy-looking lady dressed in a grey gown. She was first seen by a couple of friends of the Beresford-Wrights who, as it was a mellow summer evening, had decided to take a stroll through the priory grounds. They saw the woman in grey standing on the bridge in front of the gatehouse. She was despondently staring into the moat.

Returning to the house, the friends enquired about the identity of the woman. Puzzled, their host informed them that they were the only visitors that weekend. The incident was more or less forgotten until, over subsequent months, other visitors reported seeing the mystery woman. Mr Beresford-Wright made his own enquiries, but failed to arrive at any logical conclusion. It was later thought possible that the visitors might have encountered the phantom figure of a member of the Sackville family whose young daughter had accidentally fallen into the moat and drowned.

Possibly, Mr Beresford-Wright, in his enquiries, didn't have the advantage of knowing that a certain Martha Bates, born in Rye in 1870, had already compiled a private journal of ghostly phenomena which referred to a phantom woman in grey seen at Michelham.

Miss Bates had become fascinated with the supernatural after her enthusiasm had been fired by her grandfather, who delighted in relating tales of ghostly goings-on to his eager young listener. While still young, she decided to compile a private journal listing the various ghost stories that came her way, adding new stories over most of her adult life.

She reported that a phantom lady, dressed in grey and looking quite stately, was known to haunt Michelham Priory. The ghostly figure had been seen to walk through a closed door and into one of the bedchambers. It then moved to a window by the bed and acted as though drawing curtains before looking down on the bed as if watching someone asleep. The apparition was then observed to shrink back, as if disappointed, before leaving the room.

During the early part of the Second World War, the priory was occupied by evacuees from Rotherhithe, but as Sussex moved into the front line with a German invasion expected at any moment, the children moved out and Canadian troops moved in. A memento of this time is the plan of the Dieppe Raid of 1942, drawn on a wall in the gatehouse. After the Canadians left, in 1943, the priory became the East Sussex HQ of the Auxiliary Territorial Service.

In 1951, the ownership of Michelham Priory was transferred to Mrs Joyce Storey. In 1958, Mrs R H (Stella) Hotblack purchased the priory with the aim of preserving it for posterity. With an endowment from Kenneth, Earl of Inchcape, Mrs Hotblack gave Michelham Priory in trust to the Sussex Archaeological Society in 1959.

Ensuing years have seen the Society continue with repairs to the priory. These have included a restoration of the gatehouse, a return of the mill to working order, and the re-roofing of the barn. In 1970, excavation work revealed the foundations of a large hall which had been built in the 13th century.

In 1972, workmen were digging a trench prior to new drainage being installed when one of them came across the top of an old stone jar, which was sticking out of the ground. On being dug up, it was found to be a perfect specimen of a Bellarmine jar. Inside the jar was a round, blackened lump of unidentifiable material into which metal pins had been stuck, although these were badly corroded.

Bellarmine jars, often used to store wine, are named after Bishop Bellarmine, who in medieval times gained prominence for his strong denunciations of witches and magical practices. One side of these jars features a derogatory image of the bishop and they were frequently used as containers for witches' brews and magic spells, so much so that they became known as witches' jars. Some researchers believe that the jars were used in some form of 'sympathetic magic' against the bishop at a time when witchcraft was widespread. Possibly the jar and its contents were buried in the grounds by a disgruntled witch determined to harm the prior – or even all those resident at the priory – by casting an evil spell. The jar is now on display at the priory.

Shortly after lunchtime on a summer day in 1972, a woman in a grey dress approached the ticket kiosk in the gatehouse. The attendant thought she looked thin and ill. He then noticed that she had a small dog and told her that dogs were not permitted in the priory, but the woman ignored his words and continued past a couple of other visitors waiting to buy tickets.

Later, the attendant said: "I was unable to stop her, but I wasn't at all worried, for I knew she would be asked to leave as soon as she was seen by one of the guides. But there was certainly something peculiar about her".

The other visitors, a middle-aged couple, took their tickets and went through the gateway. The woman turned to her husband and remarked on the strangeness of the dress the woman with the dog was wearing. The husband responded by asking what woman she was talking about. He had seen no such woman. The wife, a little irritated, went to point out the oddly-dressed woman, but at that moment, in the sight of the attendant and herself, the woman and her dog 'just faded away'.

Between 1969 and 1972 the woman in the grey dress was seen by other visitors on at least two more occasions. The phantom is believed to be that of the same grief-stricken member of the Sackville family, mourning her drowned daughter, who had been seen in earlier years by guests of the Beresford-Wrights. In the 1980s, a phantom woman in a grey dress was seen chasing a small dog across the lawn at the rear of the priory before fading away as she reached a door of the building.

An even more intriguing paranormal event took place in the main hall of the Tudor Wing, which has been completely rebuilt since the disastrous fire of 1927. A young overseas couple were studying an explanatory notice fixed to one of the walls. On turning around to relate the contents of the room to the notice they had just read, they were astounded to see the apparition of a handsomely-dressed, middle-aged man descending from the ceiling as if walking down a staircase. But there was no staircase there!

As the man neared the floor by the inglenook fireplace, he jumped silently, as if from an invisible step, before gliding away through the end doorway. Before the young couple had time to do anything but stare, another apparition, a middle-aged woman wearing a Tudor-style dress, rushed out of a doorway at the western end of the hall and hurried past them as if in pursuit of the now vanished man. To their amazement, the couple discovered that although other visitors were present, no one else had seen the visions.

The identity of the ghosts remains a mystery and so does the question of whether, prior to the 1927 fire, a staircase had existed at the point of the sighting. Unfortunately, the hall had to be rebuilt without the benefit of a proper record of the previous architecture, while there have been many alterations to the structure since.

There was a new mystery in 1974 when the resident caretakers, Mr and Mrs Lett, distinctly heard the sound of bells ringing while they were walking up a staircase together.

A puzzled Mr Lett said: "There are only two bells and neither was ringing at the time. One of them couldn't, anyway, as it was tied up. The evening was rather sultry with not a breath of wind; just quiet and peaceful".

Another mystery surrounded the occasion when a small group of visitors and their guide, who were standing close to the foot of the priory's main staircase, witnessed two ladies wearing Edwardian dresses descending the stairs. The women proceeded on down the staircase before walking towards a garden exit, at which point they vanished. As this staircase was built soon after the fire of 1927 and slightly away from the room where the original staircase was thought to be located, it seems odd that spectres from an earlier age should follow this route.

Andrew Gottlieb, the director of Michelham Priory from 1980 to 1992 and a member of the priory's Management Committee from 1969, had two remarkable experiences during his term of office. He had always been dismissive about the concept of ghosts, but admitted that he can offer no satisfactory explanation for the events that took place.

The first happened late one afternoon in November 1980. The priory was closed to the public for the winter and the staff, who had been engaged in maintenance work and other activities in preparation for the spring re-opening, had already left.

The weather was blustery, and in the absence of the resident caretaker, who was on holiday, Mr Gottlieb decided to check the Great Barn doors to see if they were properly secured. As he walked past the front of the priory on his way to the barn, he heard a dull thud above his head. Looking up, he was startled to see a window open, though he saw no sign of a hand pushing it.

While this was puzzling, more perplexing was the fact that while the priory was locked and unoccupied to the best of his knowledge, he also knew that the window belonged to a storeroom containing the priory's reserve collection items, with a door that was also locked. Indeed, this room hadn't been entered for two months or more, and there were a further two locked doors leading to the storeroom door, the keys for all three doors being kept in a safe.

Mr Gottlieb didn't immediately investigate, but carried on to check the security of the barn. As it was almost dark at the time of his return, he shone his torch at the storeroom window. It was still open. Just after Mr Gottlieb had re-entered the priory, the chairman of the Management Committee and his family arrived – they were soon to move out of a residential flat they occupied at the priory.

On being informed about the window incident, the chairman offered to accompany Mr Gottlieb to the storeroom. On arrival, they found no sign of a forced entry – all the doors were found to be still locked. On checking the open window, Mr Gottlieb found it to be extremely stiff and requiring some strength to move it at all. The dusty floor, it was observed, showed no evidence of footprints.

In 1992, about 80 executives, actors and technicians were present at Michelham Priory to film an episode in the 13-part TV drama series *All The World's A Stage*. While some of the film crew were in attendance at the priory for three weeks, the actors were only required for ten days; for rehearsals, and for the actual filming.

A part of the priory's undercroft was utilised as a dressing room for males, the rest being used as a make-up and wig room. Each day, shortly before the film crew left at about 7pm, the seven or eight wigs used by the actors were washed and placed on small pedestals to dry overnight. The pedestals were left on chairs in the undercroft.

At 6.45 each morning, a small number of film personnel would arrive to comb out the wigs and make up the actors. On the morning of the third day, the woman in charge of the wigs complained angrily to Mr Gottleib that on each of the three mornings, some of the wigs left to dry overnight had been found scattered across the floor. Being winter, the priory was closed to the public but, she enquired, were there any children living at the priory who could have tampered with the wigs?

Mr Gottlieb assured the woman that there were no resident children and that, anyway, the undercroft was locked up each night and the alarm system switched on, but he promised to look into the matter. In fact, that evening, he personally saw that the wigs were in place and ensured that the undercroft was locked and alarmed, while the following morning he arrived at the undercroft ahead of the film crew to unlock the doors and check on the wigs. He was amazed to find that four wigs lay crumpled on the floor. The disturbance of the wigs continued for the remaining days of filming.

In more recent years, cleaners arriving early at the priory were astounded to find that the bedclothes and mattresses in the two cots on display in the children's nursery had overnight been tossed onto the floor, this on several occasions.

At the end of October 1993, four members of the Surrey-based Ghost Research Foundation visited the priory for an all-night Halloween vigil. Equipped with tape recorders, video cameras, and other equipment, they hoped to discover some evidence of paranormal activity. They were not disappointed.

Furniture in the undercroft was lightly dusted with flour and all doors to the room were locked with the added precaution of being sealed by wire. On the following morning, the skeletal handprint of a woman was found in the dusting of flour on the sideboard. The remarkable thing about this handprint was the fact that it was ten inches long. The four researchers were the only people on the premises at the time. The following day, two of the researchers were leaving the priory to return home. As they passed the area of the cloister, they clearly heard the chanting of monks. The chanting continued for about five seconds.

Fred Overty, the priory's property manager, commented at the time: "I've been living here for five years and there have been many crashes and bangs in the night without any explanation. I have never seen any of the ghosts, but I've no doubt they're here."

Mr Overty had something new to report in 1995, for a variety of tools that had temporarily been left in various parts of the grounds by gardeners and other priory staff were mysteriously disappearing. Among the gardeners there was initially talk of 'unauthorised borrowing' and even of 'theft', but the culprit eventually turned out to be someone or something supernatural, with the tools always reappearing, though usually a day or two later and in a different location.

Some visitors, sensing a disturbing presence, have felt unable to enter the prior's room while others, contrarily, have claimed it has a most peaceful atmosphere. Certainly, during the cooler months, the visitor will detect a distinct drop in temperature as they enter the room, but this can be attributed to the fact that it isn't warmed by central heating, while most of the rest of the priory is!

One woman, while visiting the priory during the summer of 1995, complained to her companions that she found no detectable atmosphere to the place. That was until she entered the prior's room. Proceeding to a far corner of the room, she then claimed that she could sense 'a very angry presence'. It was a claim that normally might not have been taken very seriously, except that the spot she pointed to was the exact spot where a shadowy presence had been reported on several occasions.

The priory gatehouse is not without its eerie tale. Early in the 1990s, so as to provide an added attraction for visitors, the priory mill was used in conjunction with a small on-site bakery to make bread, which was offered for sale. One day, the woman responsible for the baking took her young granddaughter with her. As they were about to leave for home, the granddaughter asked if she could go inside the gatehouse and it was agreed that she could. As they neared the building the granddaughter, excited, ran ahead and up the staircase, but in a moment she was down again, white-faced and distressed.

As the grandmother placed a comforting arm around her, the girl blurted out that she had seen a part of a woman's dress – but nothing else – moving down the staircase. As they hurried away from the gatehouse, the grandmother looked back. She was astonished to see an eerie blue glow filling the first floor window.

30 *Perils of the Ouija board*

BOOKS THAT FEATURE true ghost stories rarely refer to Ouija board experiences. Indeed, when compared with other areas of research into the paranormal, the subject is quite poorly documented. Why this should be so is uncertain, though some researchers acquainted with Ouija practices may not wish to generate curiosity in an area of psychic activity which has very real dangers.

Are the entities contacted by those who use Ouija boards really the spirits of the dead, or are they mischievous – perhaps even malevolent – elemental spirits, pretending to be what they are not? Again, might those present at Ouija board sessions be themselves generating the messages spelled out, with their brains in some subtle fashion initiating involuntary movements of the hands and fingers?

If the several cases of Ouija board usage detailed in this chapter are examples of what might happen where experimentation leads to more than a fairly innocuous message, then it must be assumed that something other than subconscious stimulation is at work. However, regardless of whether a spirit or human agency is responsible, it is well attested that Ouija-related experiences can have an alarming and sinister aspect.

A person may be present on a hundred or more occasions when a Ouija board is used and suffer no harm, yet the moment can come when events take a dramatic and frightening turn. Certainly there have been countless instances of misfortune and tangible evil resulting from the employment of Ouija to obtain messages from 'the other side'. Hopefully, the following stories will be sufficient to dissuade readers from ever involving themselves in the use of Ouija boards, planchettes, or similar devices (it will be noted that the participants in each story appear, in almost every instance, to have approached the use of Ouija in a frivolous fashion. Might this factor have contributed to the dire consequences?).

Bill Streetfield is a young, streetwise builder's labourer with close-cropped hair and tattoos on his arms and chest. He enjoys an earthy lifestyle, regularly going 'out on the town' and drinking with the lads. He had never been interested in psychic matters and would have laughed at the suggestion that he would one day be frightened by a misty, *doppelganger* presence.

Mr Streetfield's home town is Halifax, but he wanted to get away from the restrictions of family life and moved to Brighton in 1992. In the Spring of 1993 he returned home for a week's holiday. While there, he rekindled a friendship with a local girl. Towards the end of the holiday, one of the girl's friends invited them to a party at her house. A part of the evening's 'entertainment' involved the use of a Ouija board.

Mr Streetfield had only a vague notion of what a Ouija board was, but he readily joined in, looking upon the experience as being 'a bit of fun'. The messages received with the help of the board didn't seem particularly relevant to him. He also had more than a suspicion that there was nothing at all unearthly about the messages being received. Obviously, someone at the table was deliberately manipulating things.

Prior to the Ouija board session there had been a buffet meal and drinks. Now Mr Streetfield returned to the buffet table where he poured a glass of wine for his girlfriend and a lager for himself. Shortly afterwards, he began to feel slightly unwell, and began to wonder if the buffet food might be to blame. Until catching his train back to Brighton, a couple of days later, his feeling of being 'one degree under' persisted. On his return south, the sense of not being fully fit continued and he finished each day's work in an exhausted state.

But something else was happening; something more alarming. A day or two after he had returned to Brighton, he became aware of a grey, misty form standing just a couple of feet away from him. It was too shadowy, too amorphous to recognise any features. Usually the shape appeared to the left or right of him, but not always. Describing the entity as looking like a man seen emerging from a thick fog, Mr Streetfield said that when he walked, the wraith-like being moved too, though it seemed to glide rather than walk. By this time, he had become convinced that his troubles had resulted from his participation in the Ouija activities.

The entity appeared but briefly; sometimes for a few seconds, sometimes for minutes and never at any particular time. One day might pass without it being present at all. On another, the strange, grey figure would materialise three or four times. There was no indication that other people could see the ghostly figure. In the circumstances, Mr Streetfield felt it wise to keep secret the existence of his *doppelganger*-type companion. He didn't want his mates or anyone else to laugh at him.

Some six weeks passed and the sense of debility continued. So, also, did the visitations of the weird, other-world entity, although in some ways Mr Streetfield was beginning to get used to his odd, transitory partner.

It was around this time that he revealed his story to one of his friends. He hadn't intended to, but feeling less inhibited after a few lagers, he blurted it out. Mr Streetfield expected his friend to ridicule him, but he didn't. Instead, he appeared to take the seemingly absurd story seriously and suggested his friend get in touch with a medium. Mr Streetfield did so. The medium, it seems, was able to help, for from that time on the feeling of ill-health melted away and there was no return of the misty entity.

A most frightening consequence attended a Ouija session which took place in the Sussex village of Alfriston in 1990. Two Brighton men, Terry Blandon and his friend Joe Adland (not their real names), were invited to a party in the village. Following drinks and snacks, it was announced that someone had brought along a Ouija board, and it was suggested that anyone wanting to contact 'the spirits' should move to the next room.

Almost all the people present at the party were without previous experience of using a Ouija board. As everyone, drinks in hand, moved to the adjoining room, there was a great deal of laughter and banter. The small number of those actually able to participate – because of the limiting size of the table – sat down, with the remainder of the guests, including Mr Blandon and Mr Adland, looking on.

The two friends were intrigued to see the glass moving around the Ouija board, erratically moving from letter to letter to spell out answers to the various questions volunteered by those at the table. After a while, Mr Blandon and his friend returned to the room where the food and drink was and poured themselves another lager.

Their glasses replenished, they remained where they were for a few minutes to discuss what they had witnessed. Suddenly, they heard screams from the adjoining room, and a moment later its door flew open and everyone there rushed out. The friends wondered what on earth had happened to cause such an exodus and went to investigate.

As they walked through the open door of the room where the Ouija activities had been taking place, they were horrified to find absolute chaos. Most of the books and ornaments which had been on the shelves around the walls were now on the floor, and some of the chairs had been toppled over, the latter probably by their fleeing occupants. An oval mirror above the fireplace had, apparently, been sucked out by the invisible force which had scoured through the room but, secured by its chain, had twisted and returned so that its obverse side now faced the wall.

As Mr Blandon and his friend surveyed the disorder, the owner of the house, having recovered a little from his initial shock at the turn of events, returned to the room to see what damage had been done. Pushing past the friends, he looked around the scattered books and ornaments and then went over to the mirror. Lifting it away from the wall, he turned it around so that the mirror side was once more facing the centre of the room.

In that instant, Mr Blandon and Mr Adland, looking towards the mirror, saw in it the image of a cowled, shadowed face. It was difficult to discern any features, but the face seemed to project an impression of intense evil. In the next terrifying instant, a long black tongue shot out from the face on the mirror. Several inches in length, it flicked over a shoulder of the house's owner. Questioned later, the owner claimed he had not been aware of the tongue but had seen a dark, blurred face on the surface of the mirror.

On 7 June 1995, an experimental group of Brighton-based musicians and artists known as Testcard were featured in two programmes on Adur Radio, using the broadcasting facilities available at Festival Radio, in Kensington Street, Brighton.

The overall event had been billed as *An Electronic Exorcism*, the music being interspersed with snippets of audio tape, with some of these taken from a recording of a service held at the local St Bartholomew's Church, and others taken from the more alarming parts of an American film about exorcism.

But there was a further, quite innovative element introduced for the occasion. In a room adjoining the broadcasting studio, some members of the group sat around a table, brought out a Ouija board, and began to address messages to the spirit world. A microphone placed on the table was used to broadcast live extracts from the proceedings. These were mixed with the music.

The Ouija board sessions were conducted by 'Christel', a group member who had organised similar activities in the past. Sitting around the table with her were Ian Helliwell and Amanda Price. Only this time events didn't work out as smoothly as they had on previous occasions. Perhaps an incident which took place just hours before the broadcast began had some bearing on the matter? It was odd enough to be reported in the *Brighton & Hove Leader*.

Because of the large amount of electronic equipment that had to be set up, two taxis carrying some members of Testcard, together with their instruments, arrived at the studio more than three hours before the first programme was due to be broadcast.

One of the musicians, Darius Juste, paying the fare for the taxi he had travelled in, gave the taxi-driver a £20 note. As it was dark, Mr Juste didn't properly examine his change until he had entered the studio. He was shocked, in view of the theme of the evening, to find a battered 20p coin among his change which had the number 666, said to be the Mark of the Beast, deeply stamped into it.

Concerned, he later tossed the coin through an open window into Kensington Street, before immediately regretting that he had done so, for he wondered if any finder of the coin might be subject to malign influences after pocketing it. A search in the darkness, and again when it was light, failed to locate the coin. Adrian Shephard, responsible for the electronic treatment of the group's musical output, tried to lighten the situation by suggesting that it all depended on which way up the coin was held. The number could be 999, rather than 666!

As Testcard commenced their first broadcast at 2.30am, the sitters around the table in the room next to the studio began to direct questions to whatever entity might be called up. But the spirits were, it seems, not in a cooperative mood. The sitters became aware of an unsettling atmosphere and meaningful responses were difficult to obtain, but one very clear but ominous statement that did come through was, "We do not want to take part in your games".

Testcard's first broadcast lasted half-an-hour. The second, a 45-minute session, began at 4am, but the associated Ouija board activities were no more productive than those which had taken place earlier. As the music was faded out at the end of the broadcast, those around the table in the next room prepared to leave. But the occasion was to have a harrowing aftermath.

Prior to that night's activities, Adrian Shephard would have found it hard to remember when he last had a nightmare, but now he began to have regular nightmares, sometimes three or four in a week. Weird alien creatures, dead bodies and an overwhelming sense of decay haunted his dreams and he would frequently wake up feeling vulnerable and stressed. On waking, he was aware of an electric, spine-tingling atmosphere filling the room. These nightmares continued for about five months.

But Mr Shephard wasn't alone in having frightening dreams. Simon Wade, another member of Testcard, was also experiencing nightmarish visions at night. In some of these dreams, his bedroom seemed to be filled with bright light and with strange, human forms which descended through the ceiling. Fortunately for Mr Wade, his nightmares lasted only a few weeks.

Caroline Pountney (not her real name) was housekeeper to a businessman who lived in a large house in Hove and who commuted to London each working day. The man's wife had been killed in an accident during her early thirties and their only child, a boy, was at boarding school.

Mrs Pountney, with a brief marriage and divorce behind her, had been delighted to accept when the businessman, who knew her and had an inkling of her straitened circumstances, suggested that she might like to become his housekeeper. The post, which was live-in, would considerably ease her financial problems, for she had found living in a rented flat both inhibiting and expensive. Her living accommodation was to be in the basement of the house.

At the time she took up her new job, Mrs Pountney had a close male friend, an army captain, but as he was based in Northern Ireland, she saw him only when he was on leave. As a result, she frequently felt lonely. When, at a barbecue party, she was introduced to an affable and quite good-looking man, she enthusiastically took up his offer of an evening out together. Her interest in the man escalated when she discovered that he owned a number of boutiques so was therefore, she presumed, quite well off.

Over the following weeks, the friendship grew until a point was reached where Caroline Pountney recognised that she had to make a decision. She was now very fond of the new man in her life, but she still had a special place in her heart for the army captain. However, she felt sure that eventually one would find out about the other, with the consequence that she might lose both men.

While her army friend was now some distance away in Northern Ireland, soon he would be home on leave and would expect to be with her constantly. What then? What excuses, what subterfuge, would be required to keep each man from finding out about the other?

Marginally, Mrs Pountney felt that she was fonder of the army captain. Indeed, she had presumed that she would one day marry him, even though she wasn't too enamoured with the idea of being a soldier's wife. On the other hand, her friend with the boutiques had a fine house and, quite probably, enough money to provide her with a very comfortable lifestyle.

When some female friends suggested that Mrs Pountney might join them one evening for drinks and a few snacks, she agreed. The friend whose flat was being used for the occasion mentioned that she had borrowed a Ouija board. She added that they could 'lark around with it, and see if we get any messages'.

Mrs Pountney, other than being mildly curious about what took place when a Ouija board is used, gave little thought to the matter. She was interested in the more familiar possibilities presented by the evening... food, drink and some convivial conversation. She arrived on the evening clutching the obligatory bottle of wine.

When an hour or so had passed and the conversation had ebbed, the friends sat down at a table with the Ouija board. The woman who had borrowed the board, being the only person present with any experience of using it, asked the first questions. The glass on the board, touched lightly by each woman's forefinger, slid erratically towards a succession of letters around its outer edge, sometimes spelling out jumbled nonsense; at other times offering replies that generated emotions of amusement, amazement or shock.

As everyone warmed to the 'game', Mrs Pountney knew that she had to ask one cardinal question. When her opportunity came, she nervously outlined her dilemma. Identifying the two men in her love life with a few words, she went on to ask: "Which man should I choose?"

Caroline Pountney felt hardly able to breath as the glass scraped around the Ouija board. Slowly but unremittingly, a five-letter word was spelled out, its individual letters tumbling into their dreadful finality.

D... E... A... T... H.

Mrs Pountney felt a brief stutter of tension in her chest as her thoughts attempted to come to terms with the frightfulness of the word. One of those present broke the shocked silence by suggesting that it might be wise to ask the question again. But once more the awful response was spelled out.

D... E... A... T...H.

A few mornings later, the businessman, following his usual routine, washed, shaved, and dressed, and then went downstairs for breakfast. Finding no sign of Mrs Pountney in the kitchen, he called her name, but there was no answer. Puzzled, he made his way down to the basement and knocked on the door leading to his housekeeper's rooms. There was no reply. He knocked again, but still there was no response. The businessman then tried the door. It opened, and he walked in.

Inside it was ominously still and the curtains were still drawn. He flicked down a light switch. It seemed obvious to move first to the bedroom. Standing in the doorway and with the corridor light behind him, he immediately saw that the bed was occupied. He switched on the bedroom light.

The duvet that lay across the body of Mrs Pountney had only fallen away a little from her shoulders. As the businessman moved closer, he noticed the unpleasant, slightly acrid smell. He then saw the tan-coloured substance that flecked his housekeeper's face and formed a congealed, irregular patch by her head.

A doctor later confirmed his suspicions. Mrs Pountney had been sick during the night and had died through inhaling her vomit. She was found to have a high content of alcohol in her body. Had she been drinking heavily because she had become depressed as a reaction to the Ouija board's baleful message, so that the prophecy was, in a way, self-fulfilling? Or would she have died anyway?

The TV series *Chiller,* screened in the mid-1990s, featured five separate psychological adventures, the first being *Prophecy,* taken from a novel of that name by best-selling thriller writer Peter James. It follows the bizarre fate of some people who take part in a Ouija board session and was based on an actual experience of the author.

In 1966 Peter James was a student at Charterhouse. In that year, on returning to his then Brighton home for the holidays, he quickly joined up with his usual group of friends.

He said: "We used to hang around together and sometimes we would experiment with a Ouija board. One evening, things got a little more serious than usual and one of the group told us her mother was a witch, so we thought we'd invite the mother to mastermind a session.

"For some reason I was unable to go and from what I've heard, I'm glad. One girl asked the board when she would next see her boyfriend and was told she'd see him the next morning. One of the boys asked when he would die and was told it would happen within 24 hours, while another boy asking the same question was told it would happen within five days.

"Apparently, the session broke up then, but the girl told everyone not to take it seriously as her boyfriend couldn't possibly be home the next morning because, just days before, he'd set sail for Cyprus on his Royal Navy ship. But when she got home, her father was waiting up to tell her that her boyfriend would be round the next day because his father had died of a heart attack and he was being flown home.

"The boy who was told he would die within 24 hours was killed in a car crash on the way home from the session, and the other boy was killed in a car crash five days later. That stopped us mucking around with the supernatural."

In 1961 housewife Viv Nicholson achieved brief fame when, after winning £150,000 (the equivalent of almost £2 million today) on the football pools, she disposed of her newly acquired wealth in double-quick time with an orgy of spending which was pounced on by the tabloids, and which later spawned a TV documentary, *Spend, Spend, Spend* (and, eventually, a musical of the same name). In more recent times she told a story of herself which is relevant to this chapter and, although she is not a local woman, the story is recorded here because it has an unusual aspect.

After Mrs Nicholson had lost her second husband, Keith, in a car crash, she turned to using the Ouija board in the hope of contacting him (she had five husbands, but Keith was the real love of her life). One message she received told her that her mother would die at Christmas. Her response to the message was one of bemusement, for she knew her mother was then enjoying good health. But that Christmas, her mother died.

On another occasion while involved in a Ouija session, she saw two strangers walking up her garden path. She asked the board who they might be. The glass at her fingertip shattered instantly. When she went to the door, she discovered that the visitors were Jehovah's Witnesses. Rightly or wrongly, she took the breaking of the glass to be a positive sign, for she later joined the sect (though it is presumed that Jehovah's Witnesses would look with horror upon the use of Ouija!).

Bibliography

Adland, David, *Brighton's Music Halls* (Baron Birch/Quotes 1994)
Aitchison, George, *Unknown Brighton* (Bodley Head 1926)
Beevers, David, *Preston Manor* (Brighton Arts & Leisure Services)
Boyd, Ronald, *Alfriston* (Photo-Life 1970/Goldleaf 1989)
Canning, L, (edited by), *50 Great Ghost Stories* (Odhams 1966)
Carder, Timothy, *The Encyclopedia of Brighton* (East Sussex County Libraries 1990)
Cheal, Henry, *The Story of Shoreham* (G E & P P Bysh 1921)
Copper, Bob, *Early to Rise* (Heinemann 1971)
d'Enno, Douglas C, *The Saltdean Story* (Phillimore 1985)
Erredge, J A, *History of Brighthelmston* (1862)
Funnell, Pamela, *The Story of Bevan Funnell Limited* (1988)
Green, Andrew, *Ghosts of the South East* (David & Charles 1976)
Green, Andrew, *Haunted Sussex Today* (SB Publications 1997)
Forman, Joan, *The Haunted South* (Robert Hale 1978)
Hallam, Jack, *The Ghosts' Who's Who* (David & Charles 1976)
Harrison, J, & North, J, *Old Brighton, Old Hove, Old Preston* (1937)
Hopkins, R Thurston, *Cavalcade of Ghosts* (World's Work 1956)
Longhurst, Henry, *My Life and Soft Times* (Cassell 1971)
Middleton, Judy, *Ghosts of Sussex* (Countryside Books 1988)
Middleton, Judy, *Haunted Portslade* (1995)
Middleton, Judy, *History of Hove* (Phillimore 1979)
Montford, Selma, with Jacqueline Pollard and Robert Sanderson, *The Vanishing Villas of Preston & Withdean*, (Brighton Books 1996)
Moss, Peter, *Ghosts Over Britain* (Elm Tree 1977)
O'Donnell, Elliott, *Haunted Britain* (Rider 1975)
Robinson, L J, *The Lanes of Brighton* (1966)
Spencer, John and Anne, *Encyclopedia of Ghosts and Spirits* (Headline 1992)
Underwood, Peter, *Gazetteer of British Ghosts* (Souvenir 1971)
Thorogood, Peter, *St Mary's, Bramber* (Bramber Press/English Life 1998)

Wales, Tony, *Sussex Customs, Curiosities & Country Lore* (Ensign 1990)
Ward, Margaret, *One Camp Chair in the Living Room* (QueenSpark Books 1988)
Woodford, Cecile, *Portrait of Sussex* (Robert Hale 1972)

Newspapers/magazines

Various copies of Brighton *Evening Argus, Brighton & Hove Leader, Brighton & Hove Gazette, Brighton & Hove Herald, Sussex Express, Sussex Life.*
Peacehaven Post (1.12.1921 and 2.4.1923), *Sussex Genealogist & Local Historian* (March 1986), *The Publican* (13.12.1979).

Index of haunted sites

So as to maintain the privacy of the current occupiers, except where buildings are already on record as being haunted or where they have a past history of some note, the locations of haunted residential properties are indicated by a street name only.

Brighton locations

Hove locations

Other locations